T0190509

Lecture Notes of the Institute for Computer Sciences, Social Informatics and Telecommunications Engineering 584

Editors
Yinjun Zhang
Guangxi Science and Technology Normal
University
Guangxi, China

Nazir Shah
University of Swabi
Khyber Pakhtunkhwa, Pakistan

ISSN 1867-8211 ISSN 1867-822X (electronic)
Lecture Notes of the Institute for Computer Sciences, Social Informatics
and Telecommunications Engineering
ISBN 978-3-031-63141-2 ISBN 978-3-031-63142-9 (eBook)
https://doi.org/10.1007/978-3-031-63142-9

This Springer imprint is published by the registered company Springer Nature Switzerland AG
The registered company address is: Gewerbestrasse 11, 6330 Cham, Switzerland

If disposing of this product, please recycle the paper.

Preface

We are delighted to introduce the proceedings of the third edition of the European Alliance for Innovation (EAI) International Conference on Application of Big Data, Blockchain, and Internet of Things for Education Informatization (BigIoT-EDU 2023). BigIoT-EDU aims to provide a platform for international cooperation and exchange, enabling big data and information education experts, scholars, and enterprise developers to share research results, discuss existing problems and challenges, and explore cutting-edge science and technology. The conference focuses on research fields such as digitization of education, smart classrooms, and Massive Online Open Courses (MOOCs). The use of big data analytics, artificial intelligence (AI), machine learning, and deep learning lies at the heart of this conference as we focus on these emerging technologies to further the role of IT in education.

BigIoT-EDU 2023 had three tracks: the Main Track, the Late Track, and a Workshop Track. BigIoT-EDU 2023 attracted over 700 submissions, and each submission was reviewed by at least 3 Program Committee members in a double-blind process, resulting in the acceptance of only 272 papers across all three tracks. The workshop was titled "Application of Advanced Integrated Technologies in Education Informatics" and co-chaired by Yar Muhammad and Muhammad Al-Ambusaidi from Beihang University, China and University of Technology & Applied Sciences of Oman, respectively. The workshop aimed to focus on the application of the latest cutting-edge integrated technologies for the development and digitalization of education in the modern era.

Coordination with the steering chair, Imrich Chlamtac, was essential for the success of the conference. We sincerely appreciate his constant support and guidance. It was also a great pleasure to work with such an excellent organizing committee team for their hard work in organizing and supporting the conference. In particular, we are grateful to the Technical Program Committee, who completed the peer-review process for the technical papers and helped to put together a high-quality technical program. We are also grateful to Conference Manager Ivana Bujdakova for her constant support along with the whole of the EAI team involved in the conference. We must say that they have been wonderful and it is always a pleasant experience to work with them. Also, we would like to thank all the authors who submitted their papers to the BigIoT-EDU 2023 conference.

We strongly believe that the BigIoT-EDU conference provides a good forum for all researchers, developers, and practitioners to discuss all science and technology aspects that are relevant to emerging trends for digitalization of education. We also expect that the future BigIoT-EDU conferences will be as successful and stimulating as this year's, as indicated by the contributions presented in this volume.

Yinjun Zhang
Nazir Shah

Conference Organization

Steering Committee

Imrich Chlamtac   University of Trento, Italy
Fazlullah Khan   Business Technology Management Group, USA
Mian Ahmad Jan   Abdul Wali Khan University Mardan, Pakistan

Organizing Committee

General Chair

Yinjun Zhang   Guangxi Science & Technology Normal
      University, China

General Co-chairs

Shah Nazir   University of Swabi, Pakistan
Walayat Hussain   Australian Catholic University, Australia

TPC Chair

Yinjun Zhang   Guangxi Science & Technology Normal
      University, China

Sponsorship and Exhibit Chairs

Lan Zimian   Harbin Institute of Technology, China
Izaz Ur Rehman   Abdul Wali Khan University Mardan, Pakistan

Local Chairs

Huang Yufei   Hechi Normal University, China
Wan Haoran   Shanghai University, China

Workshops Chairs

Rahim Khan   Abdul Wali Khan University Mardan, Pakistan
Abid Yahya   Botswana International University of Science and
                              Technology, Botswana

Publicity and Social Media Chair

Aamir Akbar   *Abdul Wali Khan University Mardan, Pakistan*

Publications Chair

Yinjun Zhang   Guangxi Science & Technology Normal
                              University, China

Web Chairs

Mian Yasir Jan   CECOS University, Pakistan
Syed Rooh Ullah Jan   Abdul Wali Khan University Mardan, Pakistan

Posters and PhD Track Chairs

Mengji Chen   Guangxi Science &Technology Normal
                              University, China
Ateeq ur Rehman   University of Haripur, Pakistan

Panels Chairs

Kong Linxiang   Hefei University of Technology, China
Muhammad Usman   Federation University, Australia

Demos Chairs

Ryan Alturki   Umm-ul-Qura University, Saudi Arabia
Rahim Khan   Abdul Wali Khan University Mardan, Pakistan

Tutorials Chairs

Wei Rongchang   Guangxi Science & Technology Normal
                              University, China
Hashim Ali   Abdul Wali Khan University Mardan Pakistan

Technical Program Committee

Shahnawaz Khan	Abdul Wali Khan University Mardan, Pakistan
Mengji Chen	Hechi University, China
Yar Muhammad	Beihang University, China
Mian Abdullah Jan	Ton Duc Thang University, Vietnam
Roman Khan	City University of Information Science and Technology, Pakistan
Muneeb Ullah	Peshawar University, Pakistan
Siyar Khan	Bacha Khan University, Pakistan
Muhammad Bilal	Virtual University of Pakistan, Pakistan
Haroon Khan	Bacha Khan University, Pakistan
Shaher Slehat	University of Technology Sydney, Australia
Xiangjian He	University of Technology Sydney, Australia
Shaheer Jan	University of Engineering and Technology Peshawar, Pakistan
Akbar Khan	University of Peshawar, Pakistan
Malik Ahmad	University of Peshawar, Pakistan
Muzammil Shah	COMSATS University Lahore, Pakistan
Aaiza Khan	Guangju University of Technology, China
Farman Khan	Bacha Khan University, Pakistan
Zia Ur Rehman	Bacha Khan University, Pakistan
Abid Yahya	Botswana International University of Science and Technology, Botswana
Ravi Keemo	Botswana International University of Science and Technology, Botswana
Aaiza Gul	Sirindhorn International Institute of Technology, Thailand
Shahid Ali	Women University Swabi, Pakistan
Muhammad Sohail	Abdul Wali Khan University Mardan, Pakistan
Saad Khan	University of Peshawar, Pakistan
Momin Ali	University of Peshawar, Pakistan
Bilawal Khan	COMSATS University Islamabad, Pakistan
Jamal Shah	University of Leeds, UK
Basit Kazmi	University of Peshawar, Pakistan
Jalal Turk	Staffordshire University, UK
Umer Hussain	Indian Institute of Technology Kharagpur, India
Omer Naveed	Uppsala University, Sweden
Muhammad Ali	Uppsala University, Sweden
Hamza Khan	Hankuk University of Foreign Studies, South Korea
Tariq Khan	Abdul Wali Khan University Mardan, Pakistan

Ehsan Ullah	Abdul Wali Khan University Mardan, Pakistan
Noman Ali	Abdul Wali Khan University Mardan, Pakistan
Ayaan Adeel	Abdul Wali Khan University Mardan, Pakistan
Behroz Khan	Abdul Wali Khan University Mardan, Pakistan
Tariq Khokar	Abdul Wali Khan University Mardan, Pakistan
Awais Marwat	Abdul Wali Khan University Mardan, Pakistan
Naeem Jan	Abdul Wali Khan University Mardan, Pakistan
Anas Akbar	Abdul Wali Khan University Mardan, Pakistan
Mian Ahmad Jan	Duy Tan University, Vietnam
Faisal Ayub Khan	Indian Institute of Technology Kharagpur, India
Faisal Khan	University of Leeds, UK
Yasir Jan	University of California Davies, USA
Ryan Alturki	Umm al-Qura University, Saudi Arabia
Alayat Hussain	University of Technology Sydney, Australia
Muhammad Usman	Federation University, Australia
Naveed Khan	Abdul Wali Khan University Mardan, Pakistan
Azam Khalil	Abdul Wali Khan University Mardan, Pakistan
Hamid Naseer	Abdul Wali Khan University Mardan, Pakistan
Arsalan Jan	Abdul Wali Khan University Mardan, Pakistan
Abdul Samad	University of Nebraska Omaha, USA
Asif Khan	University of Nebraska Omaha, USA
Imtiaz Ali	Quaid-e-Azam University Islamabad, Pakistan
Khadim Khan	Quaid-e-Azam University Islamabad, Pakistan
Usman Nasir	Quaid-e-Azam University Islamabad, Pakistan
Ishfaq Ahmad	Quaid-e-Azam University Islamabad, Pakistan
Jamal Baig	National University of Sciences and Technology, Pakistan
Naseer Baig	National University of Sciences and Technology, Pakistan
Sohail Agha	National University of Sciences and Technology, Pakistan
Raza Hussain	Indian Institute of Technology Kharagpur, India
Ibrar Atta	University of Haripur, Pakistan
Majid Ali	University of Haripur, Pakistan
Afzal Durrani	University of Haripur, Pakistan
Faysal Azam	Indian Institute of Technology Kharagpur, India
Asif Wazir	University of Engineering and Technology Mardan, Pakistan
Talal Agha	University of Engineering and Technology Mardan, Pakistan
Salman Shah	University of Engineering and Technology Mardan, Pakistan

Ibrahim Khan	Iqra University, Islamabad, Pakistan
Raayan Jan	Iqra University, Islamabad, Pakistan
Shameer Shah	Iqra University, Islamabad, Pakistan
Zeeshan Khan	Iqra University, Islamabad, Pakistan

Contents – Part V

**Application of Clustering Algorithm in Intelligent Education Resource
Library**

Application of Association Rule Algorithm in Intelligent Education System

The Application and Practice of New Media in Smart Teaching

Application of Multimedia Simulation Headform System in Experimental Teaching of Stomatology Based on Digital Simulation

Yulin Cao[(✉)] and Lei He

Yiyang Medical College, Yiyang 413000, Hunan, China
omarykaheneko@cumt.edu.cn

Abstract. The diagnosis and treatment of diseases in internal medicine should be done independently by doctors, and the related laboratory teaching, pre-clinical probation and the guidance of internship teachers all play a vital role in the internship effect of medical students. Stomatology is a scientific, skillful and practical clinical discipline. The simulation design of the oral cavity simulation head significantly narrows the gap between laboratory and clinical practice, and enables students to master some basic clinical operation skills before clinical practice, so as to realize the smooth transition from theoretical study to clinical practice. In recent years, with the rapid development of digital technology, virtual simulation technology has made great progress in medical simulation education. We use digital guidance system combined with clinical simulation teaching method to reform the experimental teaching of prosthodontics. The teaching quality is remarkable and good teaching effect is achieved. This paper expounds the multimedia simulation head mold by means of digital simulation and experimental teaching method of Stomatology, analyzes its advantages, and provides a certain experience basis for the formulation of new training scheme and training objectives in experimental teaching of prosthodontics.

Keywords: Digital simulation · Stomatology · experimental teaching · multimedia simulation head model

1 Introduction

Stomatology is a highly practical clinical discipline. Only through a large number of basic skills training can students turn theory into clinical operation ability [1]. Therefore, "in the teaching process of stomatology", besides strengthening the teaching of theoretical knowledge, "the experimental teaching of cultivating students" practical ability should also be placed in a very important position [2]. The diagnosis and treatment of diseases in internal medicine should be done independently by doctors, and the related laboratory teaching, pre-clinical probation and the guidance of internship teachers all play a vital role in the internship effect of medical students [3, 4]. Stomatology is a scientific, skillful and practical clinical discipline. It not only requires students to master

Y. Zhang and N. Shah (Eds.): BigIoT-EDU 2023, LNICST 584, pp. 3–14, 2024.
https://doi.org/10.1007/978-3-031-63142-9_1

solid basic theoretical knowledge [5]. Students are also required to have higher clinical operation skills and clinical analysis ability. With the development of oral experiment technology, at present, the simulation headform experiment courses in many domestic colleges and universities gradually give up the onlookers teaching method and adopt multimedia technology [6]. The simulation design of oral simulation headform significantly reduces the gap between laboratory and clinic, and enables students to master some basic clinical operation skills before clinical practice, so as to realize the smooth transition from theoretical learning to clinical practice [7, 8]. Pre clinical experimental teaching is an important part of oral science teaching. It is a classroom for students to receive practical exercise and improve their practical ability. It is an important process to improve students' learning consciousness and enthusiasm and cultivate students' comprehensive quality and innovative consciousness. It is also a necessary means for students to organically combine basic knowledge with clinical practice [9–11]. How to cultivate and improve the practical ability of medical students through experimental teaching and better open up a shortcut for medical students to enter clinical practice has become a major issue facing the reform of higher medical education [12].

In recent years, with the rapid development of digital technology, virtual simulation technology has made great progress in medical simulation education. We use the digital guidance system combined with clinical simulation teaching method to reform the experimental teaching of prosthodontics, and the teaching quality is remarkable and the teaching effect is good [13, 14]. Digital virtual dental training system has been gradually applied to oral experiment teaching, especially in oral preclinical skills training. Because it can be repeatedly trained, the teeth used are "virtual teeth" without real consumption of consumables, and it is helpful for students to get familiar with relevant operation processes, and at the same time it can record the shortcomings of students' operation, which has been recognized by students and teachers and has become an important supplement to traditional oral experiment teaching [15].

2   Advantages of Simulation Head Mold

2.1   Highlight the Professional Characteristics of Oral Medicine

The simulation head mold system includes a mask made of polymer plastic and a dental model "to simulate the shape of human skull, which is vivid and enhances students" perceptual knowledge and understanding. The skill and operability of internal medicine specialty are very strong, and clinical operation is the main part in daily medical service. Moreover, clinical operation requires specialized treatment equipment, close cooperation between doctors and nurses and cooperation between doctors and patients. Therefore, it is particularly important to do a good job in practical teaching and strengthen the training and cultivation of clinical skills and practical working ability. In view of the different depth and breadth of Stomatology related knowledge mastered by stomatological students at different stages, combined with the different levels of training modules of digital simulation dental training system, a phased and progressive oral preclinical skill training plan is formulated, and the training effect of students is evaluated by a combination of subjective and objective evaluation method, as shown in Fig. 1.

Fig. 1. Construction of training mode of digital simulation dental training system

The buccal mucosa made of silicone rubber simulates the shape of human cheek and oral cavity, so that there is a human like and variable size oral cavity on the head mold. In addition to realistic modeling, this structure is more important for students to master basic skills. At present, the research level of virtual surgery at home and abroad is still in the second generation stage. As shown in Fig. 2.

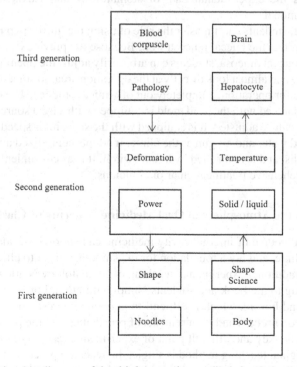

Fig. 2. The relationship diagram of the third generation medical simulation head mold system

Let Zc be the experimental data of Stomatology, and Zin and Z1 be the degree of change of experimental data of Stomatology respectively. Taking the experimental data of Stomatology with multimedia simulation head model experiment, we can get:

$$\begin{cases} Z_1 = Z_c \frac{Z_{it} \cosh(\gamma L_1) + Z_n \sinh(\gamma L_1)}{Z_{it} \sinh(\gamma L_1) + Z_n \cosh(\gamma L_1)} \\ Z_1 = Z_n \frac{\cosh(\gamma L_2)}{\sinh(\gamma L_2)} \end{cases} \tag{1}$$

The head model of the multimedia simulation based on the experimental data of internal medicine is as follows:

$$Z_n = \frac{Z_1 Z_2}{Z_1 + Z_2} = \frac{Z_n \cosh(\gamma L_2)(Z_{it} \cosh(\gamma L_1) + Z_c \sinh(\gamma L_1))}{Z_{it} \sinh(\gamma L) + Z_n \cosh(\gamma L)} \tag{2}$$

Among

$$\gamma = \sqrt{Z_0 Y_0} \tag{3}$$

$$Z_c = \sqrt{\frac{Z_0}{Y_0}} \tag{4}$$

Where Yo is the experimental data of stomatology and Zo is the multimedia simulation head model.

As in the past, students can't master the role of using the mirror to pull the corner of the mouth and protect the buccal mucosa well. Because the previous simple headframe did not simulate buccal mucosa, students can arbitrarily adjust the opening degree of the simple headframe and almost look directly at the operation area, so students always leave the goggles aside for operation, completely out of clinical practice. The comprehensive treatment table matched with the head mold is equipped with a light source, and the front and rear distance can be adjusted. It is equipped with the same high-speed and low-speed mobile phone and water and air gun as the clinic. It adopts centralized air supply, preset water and air paths, and is controlled by a foot switch. It is as convenient for students to use as the comprehensive treatment chair of clinicians.

2.2 It Enlivens the Atmosphere of Oral Medicine Experiment Class

The experimental course of internal cavity medicine can shorten the adaptation period from theory to clinic, and lay a foundation for the smooth entry into clinical practice in the future. The traditional experimental teaching of Stomatology is often carried out by teachers according to the book and students' simple imitation. For beginners, the form is monotonous and boring, which is difficult to generate interest. Vividly showing the clinical preparation process and requirements of prosthetics and the production process of technicians is the key and difficult point of experimental teaching of prosthodontics. However, the original teaching method is single, the teaching process of teachers is difficult to be clearly reflected and recorded, and there is no knowledge data for students to review after class, which hinders students from quickly mastering operation skills and quickly entering the process of clinical practice. Under the original teaching mode, most students unconsciously imitate the operation steps of the teacher, and do not know where their mistakes are. As a result, it is difficult to achieve ideal experimental teaching effect.

By using its perfect teaching equipment and unique advantages in audio-visual aspects, the teaching courseware, picture animation, video materials and real-time teaching operation are displayed on the full screen, with pictures and pictures, combining dynamic and static, and transmitting visual and auditory information to students, which makes the abstract theory intuitive and three-dimensional, knowledgeable and interesting, greatly enlivens the classroom atmosphere of stomatology experiment, and improves students" learning interest and initiative. It is helpful to cultivate students" thinking flexibility and comprehensive quality.

2.3 It Improves the Effect of Experimental Teaching in Stomatology

The operation of internal medicine is delicate and tedious, while the isolated teeth are small in specimen, small in operating field of vision and relatively large in number of students, so it is difficult to see every operation detail clearly and achieve satisfactory teaching effect. The hardness of simulated teeth is "close to that of human teeth, and it can be divided into two types: unmyelinated teeth and pulped teeth". Each tooth has a realistic tooth shape, while pulped teeth simulate the pulp chamber "root canal shape" according to their respective anatomical shapes, and have simulated pulp tissue.

The application of multimedia headform greatly improved the experimental teaching environment of stomatology. According to the purpose requirements of the experimental project, the experimental content is divided into three levels: basic, improved and innovative ". In recent years, corresponding teaching methods have been adopted for different experimental projects in combination with the characteristics and objectives of experimental courses, as shown in Table 1.

Table 1. Application of teaching methods of different simulation head mold experiment courses

	Onlooker teaching	Built-in multimedia teaching	External multimedia teaching
Basic type experiment	Basic operation method, fulcrum and hard object cutting training for dentists	Preparation of tooth cavity in vitro	/
Improved experiment	Keep up with the scaling technique, brew the scaling technique, and smooth the root surface	Rubber barrier, pulp capping, inactivation, filling, pulp opening and pulp cavity preparation, root canal therapy, apical induction, pit and fissure sealing, etc.	Preparation of metal full crown of posterior teeth and porcelain full crown abutment of anterior teeth, preparation of fixed bridge abutment of anterior and posterior teeth, preparation of post crown abutment of anterior teeth, tooth extraction
Innovative experiment	/	Application of surgical microscope	Record and transfer of all-mouth-collar relationship

Virtual simulation dental training is helpful to increase their understanding, interest and sense of professional belonging to stomatology. The training is helpful to master basic operation skills, shorten the adaptation period of professional experimental courses and increase practice self-confidence. As shown in Table 2.

Table 2. Questionnaire feedback results

Problem	Very much agree/ %	Agreed/ %	General/ %	Disagree/ %	Strongly disagree/ %
1. The anatomical models, modules and instrument images provided by the virtual simulation system look very realistic	69.56	30.42	0.00	0.00	0.00
2. The tactile feedback provided by the virtual simulation system feels realistic	52.16	34.77	13.03	0.00	0.00
3. The virtual simulation system has clear instructions and simple format	60.86	39.12	0.00	0.00	0.00
4. I feel comfortable using virtual simulation system	52.16	47.82	0.00	0.00	0.00
5. Virtual simulation system training can help me learn	65.21	34.77	0.00	0.00	0.00
6. The feedback information provided by the virtual simulation system can guide my training	65.21	30.42	4.34	0.00	0.00

(*continued*)

Table 2. (*continued*)

Problem	Very much agree/ %	Agreed/ %	General/ %	Disagree/ %	Strongly disagree/ %
7. The force feedback provided by the virtual simulation system can assist me in training	56.51	43.47	8.71	0.00	0.00
8. Using virtual simulation system can improve visual motor skills	56.51	39.12	0.00	0.00	0.00
9. Using virtual simulation system can expand my knowledge	60.86	39.12	0.00	0.00	0.00
10. I feel more confident in my skills after training in post-use virtual simulation system	47.82	30.42	21.73	0.00	0.00
11. Virtual simulation system will help to improve my pre-clinical/clinical skills in the study of professional experiments in the head mold laboratory	69.56	43.7	4.34	0.00	0.00
12. These skills should be provided to all dental students before operating on real patients	65.21	30.42	0.00	0.00	0.00

(*continued*)

Table 2. (*continued*)

Problem	Very much agree/ %	Agreed/ %	General/ %	Disagree/ %	Strongly disagree/ %
13. I prefer to get more feedback from virtual simulation system than supplementary feedback from tutor or lecturer	43.47	34.77	30.43	0.00	0.00
14. Virtual simulation system is a real pre-clinical experience for me	56.51	34.77	4.34	4.34	0.00
15. Do you agree that virtual simulation system is a useful educational tool in dental training programs?	60.86	39.12	0.00	0.00	0.00
16. Do you agree that the virtual simulation system will completely replace the simulation headgear in preclinical training?	26.08	13.03	30.42	26.08	4.34

The multimedia system ensures that all image data can be transmitted from the teacher's computer to the student's position in real time. The teachers give lectures through courseware to make the abstract knowledge explanation vivid and intuitive. It not only reviews and consolidates the theoretical knowledge, but also makes the students have a preliminary impression of the operation steps before watching the teaching. The root canal of simulated pulped teeth is relatively thick and straight, and the hardness is also large. Students do not have a very accurate feeling of expansion and frustration, and can not experience the hand feeling when expanding and frustrating the root canal of real teeth. Moreover, the pulp tissue in the pulp cavity is easy to stick to the root canal wall and difficult to pull out. Every accurate and subtle demonstration action of the teacher in the experimental teaching process can be carefully observed and carefully imitated by students, forming a concrete impression on the clinical operation of stomatology in limited time and space, and improving the efficiency and effect of experimental teaching of stomatology.

3 The Advanced Nature of the Digital Analog Multimedia Simulation Module

3.1 Accuracy and Intuition of Digital Simulation

The digital simulation system is mainly composed of spatial positioning system, interactive simulation reality system, teaching scoring system and 3D virtual reality technology. The main equipment includes scanners for teachers, cameras, computers, multifunctional experimental head imitation operation chairs, as well as multiple head imitation test benches and displays for students. The system can play the operation points, experimental standards and typical cases on the student machine through the network, which eliminates the disadvantages of students watching and teaching. The teacher's teaching process can also be photographed, stored and reproduced. The enlarged close-up and three-dimensional image reproduction of the local operation of the model can be seen on each student's display, and the real-time monitoring and self-evaluation of the student's operation process can be realized. In 2015–2020, a total of 802 students received the training of digital virtual dental training system, as shown in the table. All the students have completed the related operations within the specified time, and the system scores are all qualified. As shown in Table 3.

The setting of teacher terminal is generally composed of server, teaching software, image acquisition and other systems. The host computer adopts ibm700 server, which is required to have powerful data processing function, so that the collected images can be quickly transmitted to the sub computer, and the image delay should be within is, so as to ensure the synchronization between the teacher's explanation and the student's image; Lingbo multimedia teaching software can send teachers' electronic courseware, image materials, operation images and typical image explanations to students' desk computers in real time, and has the functions of teacher roll call, remote control and so on. For example, in the theory of prosthodontics, it is difficult to understand that the preparation of the common approach and root canal of fixed bridge will be fed back to the display screen in the operation of teachers and classmates, and the accuracy of operation will get accurate results through comparison. This teaching mode keeps the accuracy and continuity of teaching, enables students to have a clear perceptual knowledge before and during the operation by themselves, avoids misoperation and improves the learning efficiency.

Table 3. Training details of students receiving digital analog dental training system

Year	Grade	Number of trainees	Theoretical course	Training mode	Every operation time
2015	Senior	19	Dental pulp course	Open laboratory	1 h
2016	Senior	34	Dental pulp course	Open laboratory	1 h × 4
	Freshman	10	Oral Introduction Course	Introduction, primary experience	30 min
2017	Freshman	104	Oral Introduction Course	Introduction, primary experience	1 h × 4
	Freshman	109	Oral Introduction Course	Introduction, primary experience	30min
2018	Freshman	97	Oral Introduction Course	Introduction, primary experience	30 min
2019	Freshman	94	Dental pulp course	Introduction, primary experience	30 min
	Senior	34	Dental pulp course	Open laboratory	1 h × 2
2020	Sophomore	97	Pre-clinical training course	Primary training	1 h × 3
	Junior	84	Intermediate training interest class	Intermediate training	1 h × 3

3.2 Construction of Digital Simulation Multimedia Simulation Head Mold

In view of the different depth and breadth of stomatology-related knowledge mastered by stomatological students at different stages, combined with the training module of digital simulation multimedia simulation headform, a phased and progressive dental preclinical skills training plan was formulated, and the training effect of students was evaluated by the evaluation method of combining subjective and objective. Students were beginners who first came into contact with prosthodontics experiments, and they were unfamiliar with the operation posture and technique. The biggest problem for students in the operation practice is that they don't have their own understanding and ideas, but they just imitate "drawing a gourd ladle" blindly and imitate step by step with 3D software demonstration, but they can only complete a rough form, which can't meet the teaching requirements. This requires that when we use the digital guidance system, we can't continuously show students 3D operation animation, and we must combine the visual demonstration and explanation of real-time video in key operations. Because of the multi-media teaching in the imitation model laboratory, not only can every student clearly see the teaching operation in the mouth or even in the teeth on the computer in front of him, but also he can watch it repeatedly until he has mastered it completely. It overcomes the shortcoming that only some students can see the process clearly due to the narrow vision of oral cavity when teachers teach. With a large number of self-made experimental models and teaching aids, students can smoothly carry out clinical simulation operation environment after a rapid adaptation period, which greatly improves the problems of single teaching means and low teaching efficiency of oral restoration experiment. Because the imitation headform in the laboratory can imitate a variety of complex movements of the jaw, it is very close to the actual situation of clinical patients. Coupled with adjustable lights and high-speed mobile phones set according to the clinical environment, students begin to gradually adapt to and even operate in full accordance with the clinical requirements in laboratory learning.

4 Conclusions

To sum up, the multimedia teaching system has certain advantages in the experimental teaching of oral simulation head mold. Combining multimedia technology with different oral experiment projects, we can create a backbone teaching team with advanced teaching ideas and strong teaching consciousness, so as to continuously improve the teaching quality of the simulation head mold experiment course. Through the digital simulation system, students' self-analysis ability and self-knowledge ability are cultivated. In the experimental teaching of prosthodontics, the application of this teaching model has reformed the traditional teaching methods, which can stimulate students' active learning interest and improve the accuracy of experimental operation, and make students' experimental learning easier to understand and master. It has been well received by students and teaching supervisors, and laid a solid foundation for further improving the experimental teaching reform. With the establishment of multimedia head model laboratory, the teaching efficiency of Stomatology has been improved, which can better mobilize the enthusiasm of students and improve the quality of students and teachers. The introduction of advanced teaching equipment "is conducive to improving teaching quality. But more importantly, teachers should use their brains more. When using advanced equipment, they should be good at summing up experience, discovering and solving problems.

Acknowledgements. Exploration on Promoting Innovation and Entrepreneurship Education Reform of College Students in Higher Vocational Colleges (Take stomatology as an example) 2020JJ7009.

References

1. Zuo, Y., Tang, C., Cui, X.: The application of Simodont digital virtual simulation dentist training system in the experimental teaching of stomatology. Asia Pac. Educ. (03), 8–9 (2019)
2. Zhong, Y., Zheng, Y., Song, X., et al.: Application effect and evaluation of oral histopathology digital slice based on oral virtual simulation experiment teaching platform. China High. Med. Educ. **000**(006), 3–4 (2019)
3. Jia, Y., Yang, C., Huang, D., et al.: Application of simodont virtual teaching system and dental simulation head model in clinical skills training. Electron. J. Gen. Stomatol. **006**(027), 144–146 (2019)
4. Wang, G., Zhang, J., Zhang, W.: Application of simodont virtual simulation system in the teaching of dental caries experimental course. Chin. Med. Educ. Technol. **31**(001), 33–37 (2017)
5. Niu, Y., Liu, J., Liu, W.: The application of digital guidance system combined with clinical simulation teaching method in the experimental teaching of prosthetics, pp. 125–127 (2021)
6. Liu, Y., Feng, J., Fu, Y.: Application of student-based scenario simulation and role playing in oral medicine training and teaching. Chin. Inf. **000**(010), 136,84 (2019)
7. Tan, H., Guo, Q., Han, J.: Epistemological thinking on the construction of virtual simulation experiment teaching. Chin. J. Multimed. Netw. Educ. (first issue) (12), 22–24 (2020)
8. Li, H., He, D., Han, C., et al.: Application effect of multimedia simulation technology combined with case teaching method in clinical ECG teaching. Chinese Health Industry, v.16; vol. 407, no. 36, pp. 99–101 (2019)
9. Yin, Q., Song, J.: Preliminary exploration and practice of constructing a digital teaching management platform for stomatology. Chin. J. Med. Educ. Res. **15**(001), 89–92 (2016)
10. Gong, Q., Mai, S., Quan, J., et al.: Application analysis of "doctor-patient communication teaching" based on Simodent digital consultation system in oral experiment teaching. Chin. J. Stomatol. Res. (Electron. Ed.) **12**(04), 53–57 (2018)
11. Wang, F., Zhang, Y., Liu, C., et al.: Application of multimedia simulation head model in caries skills training. J. Inn. Mong. Med. Univ. **40**(S1), 220–223 (2018)
12. Li, J.: The construction of virtual simulation experiment teaching system for e-commerce specialty. Chin. J. Multimed. Netw. Educ. (1st Issue) (06), 31–32 (2020)
13. Zhang, L., Chen, R., Wang, L: The application of scene simulation teaching in oral medicine teaching. Sci. Educ. Lit. (Mid-Sate J.) **497**(06), 106–107 (2020)
14. Zhang, G., Song, Y., Liu, Q., et al.: Development of a virtual simulation experiment teaching platform for electrical and electronic courses. Chin. J. Multimed. Netw. Educ. (1st Issue) **2**, 24–25 (2020)
15. Zhang, J.: On the scientific application of multimedia technology in oral medicine teaching. J. Gen. Stomatol. (Electron. Ed.) **006**(017), 147–148 (2019)

Assisted Painting Teaching Based on Multimedia Technology

Jingyu Sun[✉]

Yunnan College of Business Management, Kunming 650106, Yunnan, China
sjy1231202@163.com

Abstract. In the 21st century, mankind has entered the information age. The development of information technology with computer and network as the core has not only affected many aspects of human life, but also brought great development opportunities to painting art education. Information technology has greatly expanded the capacity of painting teaching, enriched teaching means and teaching resources, and opened up new prospects for painting art education. At the same time, painting art education also provides spiritual comfort to people with empty feelings in high technology. It is a means to improve personal quality of life and promote social and economic development. It satisfies people's spiritual life and refined life interest; It can also cultivate people's creativity, which can promote the development of science and technology in the field of science and improve the aesthetic style of goods in the field of design, so as to promote the development of social productivity and social economy. This paper investigates and analyzes the teaching situation and application feasibility of multimedia assisted painting, and expounds the practical significance of multimedia painting education and the future development trend of multimedia painting education.

Keywords: Multimedia technology · Auxiliary painting · Art Education

1 Introduction

With the progress of society and the rapid development of economy, more and more parents begin to pay attention to their children's art quality education. They do not meet the art curriculum in the existing school education. Today, with the continuous popularization of multimedia and network technology, the traditional concept of art education needs to be improved and enriched, because the use of multimedia tools tends to be popular and younger. Students in the lower grades of primary school can operate computers very skillfully [1]. If they can compile some teaching materials and courseware for learning painting skills through multimedia assistance, use multimedia means to optimize art teaching and promote it, they can get twice the result with half the effort, so that primary school students can get twice the result with half the effort without the guidance of professional teachers after class, anytime and anywhere (as long as there is computer equipment), Through the use of this set of multimedia assisted teaching courseware, we can learn painting skills and techniques step by step, systematically and comprehensively, and improve painting ability and artistic quality.

© ICST Institute for Computer Sciences, Social Informatics and Telecommunications Engineering 2024
Published by Springer Nature Switzerland AG 2024. All Rights Reserved
Y. Zhang and N. Shah (Eds.): BigIoT-EDU 2023, LNICST 584, pp. 15–25, 2024.
https://doi.org/10.1007/978-3-031-63142-9_2

In a technology oriented society, the subjectivity of painting has been re mentioned. The technical relationship has been discussed as a subject and object in the long process of development, but it is obviously outdated at present. The relationship between painting and technology is clearly no longer a purely theoretical knowledge and applied technology issue. The philosophy of technology tends to believe that technology is a practice, a system, a medium, and a catalyst, including organization, procedures, symbols, and so on. Technology affects the relationships between social groups, and it has become a way of doing things or a state of mind. The common practice represented by a certain technology not only leads to cultural and gender identity construction, but also brings unique rights for practitioners to practice a certain technology. The profession was born from this. Many professions we are familiar with, such as doctors, lawyers, engineers, and scientists, claim exclusive rights to certain tools and technologies. However, will artists talk about technology dividends like people in other professions? Will sculptors and painters make a splash by mastering certain techniques? It seems that in the field of art, technology has long been seen as an auxiliary means.

The discussion of the relationship between technology and art needs to trace back to the concept of craftsmanship in ancient Greece, which includes emphasizing the ethical relationships of media, materials, and virtues, aesthetics, and aesthetic education in artistic production from the perspective of handicrafts. In today's vision of technological philosophy, technology has given new knowledge the possibility of production, and even rewritten human understanding of their own form. German philosopher Martin Heidegger once warned that human beings in the technological era were pushed into obscuration in a particularly conspicuous way. Heinz used abstract discourse to illustrate that the "framework" of technological manufacturing imprisons people's thinking and cognition, and the impact of technology on people is more like silent taming. People are facing an unprecedented technology (media) oriented or dependent society. The work "How We Become Post Humans" by Katherine Hayes, a philosopher of technology, while praising human-computer interaction, deeply discusses the ethical, aesthetic, and philosophical issues of human-computer relations in life and art, and profoundly reveals that technology has deeply rooted in the transformation of human beings.

Returning to painting itself, painting has a dual logic of vision and interpretation. Viewing transforms the materiality of painting into meaning, and viewers and painters share the responsibility for the dissemination and communication of painting. In early Western painting, the primary task of painters was to reproduce, that is, to display universal visual experience, which was imagery rather than meaning. Therefore, early Western painting was seen as humble submission to the reproduction and reproduction of things. In this process, painting needs to strive to overcome many obstacles that are difficult for human and material resources to achieve. Each progress means that painting is moving forward with a heavy burden on the path of copying. Finally, the painter's experience stays between the retina and the brush, and "style as a concept is completely absent. Because of its lack of utilitarian value and clear intention, style does not need to be deliberately emphasized.". Drawing feature extraction analysis is shown in Fig. 1 below.

The introduction of multimedia into painting teaching can enable us to obtain knowledge in a relaxed and happy environment. This paper will also integrate sound, light,

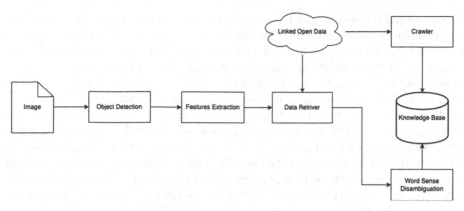

Fig. 1. Drawing feature extraction and analysis

electricity and characteristic music, dance and cartoon images into teaching with rich and colorful interfaces, and introduce the learning and understanding of basic graphics in painting, Make people realize that everything can be regarded as an understanding process from simple to complex and then to simple. Deduction to all things in the world is also a process from the simplest elements to complexity, and then to (highly refined) simplicity. Multimedia teaching fully embodies the advantages of modern teaching means, so it is easier to stimulate students' interest and produce good interaction [2]. It has unique functions, especially in enriching students' sensory materials, expanding teaching time and space, cultivating students' innovative consciousness, cultivating students' sense of learning responsibility and lifelong learning desire and ability. It fully embodies the idea that modern art education emphasizes student-centered, students are the subject of cognition and the active constructor of knowledge meaning. Multimedia teaching also helps to improve teachers' work efficiency, reduce labor intensity, and give teachers more time to organize discussion, counseling and Q & A, teaching discussion and innovation. In courseware making, teachers can optimize some contents for students of different levels. If students can't learn in class, they can continue to learn repeatedly after class. Students can combine their own needs for autonomous and exploratory learning, which greatly facilitates students. The application and promotion of multimedia teaching reduce the spiritual burden and pressure of parents [3]. Children no longer need parents to spend a lot of time and energy after class. They can spare more time to engage in other useful things, which has a very positive practical significance for social stability, progress, civilization and development.

2 Related Work

2.1 Multimedia and Multimedia Application

The term "multimedia" comes from the English word "multimedia", which is composed of "multi" and "media". Multi "comes from the Latin word "multiuse", which means "a lot", also extended to "many", and "media" means "media".

18   J. Sun

Multimedia is generally understood as the synthesis of multiple media. Multimedia is the combination of computer and video technology. In fact, it is two media; Sound and image, or in modern terms: sound and television. The original dual meaning of media refers to the entity storing information, such as magnetic disk, optical disk, magnetic tape, semiconductor memory, etc., which is often translated into media in Chinese; the second refers to the carrier transmitting information, such as digital, text, sound, graphics, etc., which is translated into media in Chinese [4]. The definition of multimedia technology can be summarized as follows: multimedia technology refers to the computer interactive comprehensive processing of multimedia information - text, graphics, image and sound, so that a variety of information can be logically connected, integrated into a system and interactive. In short, multimedia technology is an integrated, real-time and interactive technology for computer comprehensive processing of voice, text and image information. The multimedia application framework is shown in Fig. 2 below.

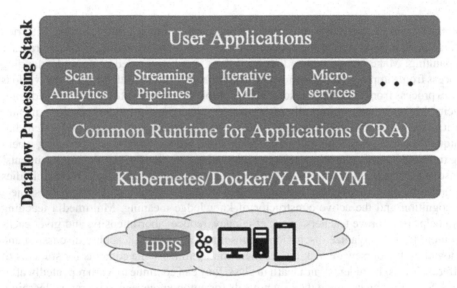

Fig. 2. Multimedia application framework

Multimedia is widely used in the following fields:

(1) Education and teaching. Multimedia is especially suitable for computer aided instruction (CAI). Through interactive multimedia assisted teaching, teachers can stimulate students' learning interest and initiative, and change the traditional indoctrination classroom teaching and counseling methods; Through multimedia assisted teaching courseware, students can carry out self-test and self strengthening, and improve their self-study ability. Network multimedia design can also be applied to distance teaching [5]. This kind of teaching has the characteristics of integration (multimedia information) and interaction (mutual communication information), so as to change the centralized and one-way traditional teaching method, which will have a great impact on the educational content, educational methods, the reform of educational institutions and the renewal of educational ideas. (2) Commercial advertising. The application of multimedia

in commercial advertising mainly includes stunt synthesis and large-scale demonstration activities. It includes film and television commercial advertisements, public poster advertisements, large display screen advertisements and print advertisements. (3) Medical treatment [6]. Because of the development of multimedia network, the means of network multimedia technology, network remote diagnosis and remote surgery are more and more widely accepted, so that local human resources can be maximized.

The development of modern society requires people to give full play to their subjectivity and creativity. Therefore, art courses should attach importance to cultivating students' individuality and innovative spirit. With the support of multimedia technology, modern multimedia teaching technology has shown great skill in the field of art education. In art education, teachers should encourage students to use computers to develop art creation and design.

Modern teaching equipment entering the classroom can enrich the forms and methods of classroom teaching, visually impart knowledge, and mobilize students' emotions. Teaching methods should reflect timeliness, and teachers should disseminate knowledge to students through certain media, namely, material carriers. In teaching, teachers use certain media to disseminate knowledge and act on students through certain material forms. This reflects the important characteristics of modern teaching methods, also enhances students' modern consciousness, and is conducive to cultivating people with modern knowledge and information literacy.

Under the previous teaching model, it is difficult for teachers to truly carry out art appreciation teaching. Due to restrictions on conditions, it is difficult for teachers to present original art works in class, making it difficult for students to fully experience the charm of famous paintings. Multimedia teaching methods have added new vitality to the teaching of art appreciation courses. For example, during the teaching process of "The Variety of Styles in Modern Architecture", teachers can use multimedia software to let students wander between famous Chinese and foreign buildings, allowing them to appreciate the richness and diversity of architectural styles, thereby guiding students to understand the composition and characteristics of buildings, and allowing students to deeply appreciate different architectural styles in a relaxed and pleasant atmosphere. For example, during the teaching process of "Chinese and Western Classical Fine Arts", teachers can play videos of the lives of Chinese and foreign art masters, as well as their learning process of painting, to stimulate students' enthusiasm for learning fine arts. At the same time, students can have "zero distance" contact with Chinese and foreign masters such as Wu Daozi, Fan Kuan, Da Vinci Picasso, and enjoy the rich thoughts of famous scholars.

2.2 Multimedia Teaching Application

The fundamental purpose of the application of multimedia means in college classroom teaching is to optimize the classroom teaching structure, effectively attract students' attention, stimulate students' interest in learning, solve practical problems in teaching and improve the effect of classroom teaching, such as: (1) using electronic teaching materials and self-made electronic teaching plans. Through various rich fonts, hypertext mode functions and powerful office components provided by PowerPoint. The electronic teaching materials with pictures, texts, sounds and images, combined with the difficulties of the text, made the electronic teaching plan, so that the teachers completely bid farewell to the chalk and blackboard [7]. The application block diagram is shown in Fig. 3 below.

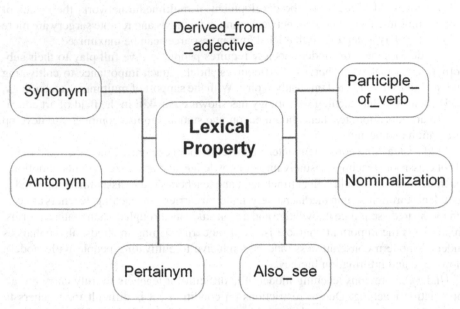

Fig. 3. Application Block Diagram

There are authentic text recordings, vivid historical figures, events, places and dynamic pictures in the electronic teaching materials. The after-school exercises with the combination of audio and video and controlled by time reflect that the multimedia function is the product of the combination of computer technology and cutting-edge technologies in the fields of graphics, images, animation, audio and video. (2) Use online resources. Computers equipped in classrooms, libraries and dormitories are connected with the network center, which greatly facilitates college students' review and completion of homework after class. During the review, students can not only browse the teaching contents of teachers in class, but also watch the teaching contents of other teachers and many relevant information. Especially in English listening, the online listening resources are rich in content and truly realize resource sharing. It is precisely because of this feature that multimedia computer is not only a means of teaching, And it has become an important factor to change the traditional teaching mode and even teaching thought. The application of multimedia has been accepted by teachers and students in Colleges and universities.

3 Feasibility of Multimedia Application in Painting Teaching

3.1 Multimedia Communication

As a new form of communication, multimedia communication presents distinctive characteristics in three aspects: production content, channel distribution and reading media. One is multi-modal presentation. The content of media reports is a collection of multimedia forms such as video, audio, text, pictures and animation; Second, multi-channel distribution. Publish and broadcast newspapers, radio, television, Internet and other media forms through traditional newspaper distribution network, Internet (including Wi-Fi), GPRS or CDMA and other transmission means of mobile communication operators, so as to realize multiple sales; Third, multi terminal reading. The audience can obtain information not only through traditional newsprint, TV screen and radio, but also through PC display screen, MP3, MP4, e-paper reader and mobile phone. Multi terminal reading meets the audience's requirements for information quickness, saves the time and cost of obtaining information, speeds up the speed of information transmission and enriches the forms of information reception, Increasing the fun of news consumption is a major feature of the information age.

3.2 Perception and Multimedia Experience

It refers to the direct perception of things in the human brain. There are many sensory organs in the human body, but the most important ones are vision, hearing, smell, taste, touch and other organs, namely eyes, ears, nose, tongue and skin. Perception refers to the objective feeling of things formed through the above sensory organs. Among the information collected by human senses, vision accounts for about 65%, hearing for about 20%, touch for about 10%, taste, smell and other senses account for about 5%. At present, the media that computers can process and apply are mainly visual and auditory media. In the application development of VR (virtual reality) and other systems, tactile media are used, such as pressure, motion, etc. the application of other sensory media is still under research. Multimedia experience: (taking vision and hearing as an example).

(1) Sensory Perception. Visual perception is divided into static and dynamic. Static visual perception: including picture appreciation, text description, etc. Research shows that the stimulation of visual organs through pictures and graphics helps deepen the impression. Pictures are suggestive and can help understand and remember. The picture style used in a courseware should be consistent, or photos or cartoons [8]. The use of pictures can promote art teaching. Firstly, it is difficult to accurately express the essence of pictures and paintings in oral or written expression; Second, because the writing or written expression is boring and contrary to nature, it is difficult to attract long-term attention. In addition, the use of pictures in teaching can provide learners with the means to obtain visual representation, which is considered to be a very important form of memory coding and storage.

(2) Dynamic Visual Perception. It refers to the communication in the form of animation, including TV programs, computer games, etc. The animation mode with small shaking amplitude is easy to be accepted by students, otherwise, it is easy to cause students' visual fatigue. Among the image arts that have the greatest impact on primary

school students, animation art is the most powerful. Comics and cartoons deeply attract them because of their unique charm in subject matter, form of expression, means of expression and content. It has its positive side to introduce the animation art loved by primary school students into all stages of basic art education. First of all, appreciating excellent animation works of art can have a certain positive impact on Pupils' aesthetic education psychological development, social psychological development, personality development and cognitive psychology. Secondly, under the influence of visual culture and visual art, contemporary art education is bound to expand into visual culture and art education.

In visual perception, a very important part is the perception of color. Bright pictures bring visual stimulation. At the same time, color also plays a role in distinguishing, classifying and prompting. Young people's preferences for color are generally unified. The use of color will affect students' psychology and effect. How to use it can be more conducive to teaching, which is worthy of our further study. As shown in Fig. 4, the picture shows a school's teaching website, which uses bright colors and has a strong contrast in the unified main tone, which makes a visual impact. With the vivid and interesting cartoon image, even boring educational websites will not feel boring.

Fig. 4. Multimedia painting experience

3.3   Characteristics of Art Education and Multimedia Teaching

Both art education series and art interest books have a common feature: The Legend of the whole book is more than words. Art, also known as "plastic art" or "visual art", expresses the author's environment and mood at that time through pictures, while the audience transmits a feeling and association to the brain through the perception of the picture and combined with their own experience. The teaching of art knowledge is inseparable from language, but the connotation of "art language" that can only be seen with eyes and felt with heart can only be spoken by art works. Sometimes it is unclear to use language as annotation.

In the current art classroom teaching, teachers often only spend 10–15 min to explain the subject according to the book, and let the students complete the classroom homework in the remaining two-thirds of the time. Many students hold the mentality that painting is a task to complete, only for speed, not quality. If the art class is only for the purpose of completing homework, it takes away the provision of image, the visual thinking activities that let students feel plastic art works, and the opportunity to obtain knowledge directly from art works. However, art education is not only the completion of works, but also the development of visual perception ability and aesthetic taste ability [9]. In the classroom, it is actually teacher centered, and all teaching design is carried out around how to "teach". Students are in a passive acceptance state most of the time, so it is difficult to give full play to students' initiative and enthusiasm, which is not conducive to the development of students' creativity and imagination in art learning.

Multimedia teaching means that in the teaching process, according to the characteristics of teaching objectives and teaching objects, through teaching design, reasonably select and use modern teaching media, and organically combine with traditional teaching means to participate in the whole teaching process, act on students with a variety of media information, form a reasonable teaching process structure and achieve the optimal teaching effect. Multimedia teaching adopts multimedia computer and carries out teaching activities with the help of pre-made multimedia teaching software. It can also be called computer assisted instruction (CAI) [10]. Multimedia computer assisted instruction refers to the use of multimedia computers to comprehensively process and control symbols, languages, words, sounds, graphics, images, images and other media information, organically combine various elements of multimedia according to teaching requirements, and display them through screen or projector projection, and add sound cooperation as needed, And the human-computer interaction between the user and the computer to complete the teaching or training process, which has the characteristics of interactivity, integration and controllability, as shown in Fig. 5. In the interactive learning environment such as multimedia computer, middle school students can choose the content they want to learn according to their learning foundation and learning interest, and can choose exercises suitable for their own level to make learning more like a game. In other words, students can give full play to their initiative and enthusiasm in this learning environment.

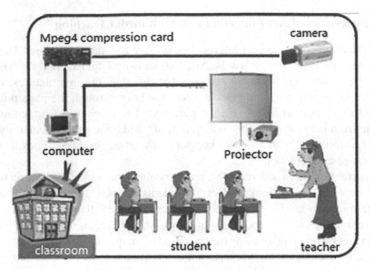

Fig. 5. Multimedia teaching mode

4 Effectiveness of Multimedia Painting Teaching

On this basis, teachers can also guide students to analyze the artistic creation characteristics and painting techniques employed by painters. With the help of multimedia teaching methods, teachers can convert static paintings into dynamic ones, or enlarge the details of the paintings, allowing students to better observe the artistic creation characteristics and painting skills of the paintings. For example, when appreciating the mural "The Painting of the Dynasty and the Yuan Dynasty", the painting teacher can use multimedia equipment to enlarge the details of the painting, allowing students to experience the essence of Chinese painting, that is, using line modeling and pen and ink as the main modeling means.

In the past, "cramming" teaching methods have often been difficult to effectively enhance students' innovative awareness and subjective initiative, and students' classroom learning mode is dominated by passive learning, resulting in a slight lack of artistic creativity and logical thinking abilities of some students. By properly applying multimedia teaching methods, painting teachers can effectively break students' thinking limitations, continuously activate students' innovative awareness, and promote the development of students' core literacy in the subject of painting.

For example, when appreciating Lebin's "The Tracker on the Volga River", the painting teacher can use multimedia technology to play relevant video materials, focusing on displaying the expression and state of the tracker under the scorching sun and suffering from wind and frost, so that students can understand the emotions contained in this work. Teachers can also appropriately integrate video images and music to create an atmosphere that matches the context of the painting, thereby further activating students' innovative awareness and improving their aesthetic ability.

5 Conclusion

Art education should be people-oriented, and we should pay great attention to the cultivation of intellectual and non intellectual factors. People's physical quality is multifaceted, such as self-confidence, patience, perseverance, the habit of focusing on things, and the spirit of not afraid of hardship, not afraid of fatigue, not disturbed by success or failure, and the spirit of positive and upward courage to explore. These factors play a key role in students' life growth. As the saying goes, "good habits benefit life." Only with the foundation of these good conduct can children thrive. The success or failure of students' painting is often not a matter of ability, but mostly affected by patience and willpower. Using multimedia technology to promote the development of students' image thinking mainly refers to promoting the establishment of students' image system through a variety of sensory stimuli, enriching the accumulation of image and original experience, so as to make students' mind flexible and thinking agile. The teaching goal of multimedia assisted students' painting is to improve the traditional education mode of teachers' "teaching" in students' art education, stimulate students' interest in painting and increase knowledge in games and happiness; Study whether multimedia technology can play this role in practical art teaching and better promote the development of students' thinking.

References

1. Wang, C.: Application value and applied research of diversified teaching based on big data analysis in oil painting teaching in chinese universities. J. Phys. Conf. Ser. **1648**(2), 022020 (2020). https://doi.org/10.1088/1742-6596/1648/2/022020
2. Jiang, C., Li, X., He, W., et al.: Research on teaching system for painting robot based on binocular stereo vision. In: 2019 IEEE 5th International Conference on Computer and Communications (ICCC), Chengdu, China, pp. 1754–1758 (2019). https://doi.org/10.1109/ICCC47050.2019.9064467.
3. Luo, H.: An analysis of difficulties and solutions in cultivating children's creativity in painting teaching activities 2022(4), 4
4. Song, Y., Niu, G.H.: The application of gamification teaching in preschool children's painting teaching—based on the physiology and psychology of children's games. J. Nanchang Coll. Educ. (2018)
5. Shi, Y.: On improving contemporary chinese painting teaching based on the cultivation of innovative thinking. J. Heihe Univ. (2019)
6. Niu, Y.: Penetration of multimedia technology in piano teaching and performance based on complex network. Math. Probl. Eng. **2021**, 1–12 (2021)
7. Zhang, K.: Research on the design of the multimedia intelligence teaching system based on the oral English curriculum **2018**(4), 3
8. Fang, B.T.: Exploration and research on project teaching of vehicle painting technology course based on work process. Educ. Teach. Forum (2019)
9. Liu, Q.J.: The advantage of applying multimedia technology in oil painting teaching. J. Hubei Corresp. Univ. (2016)
10. Zhang, S.S., Sun, X.L., et al.: Poetry and painting teaching: research on the new path of children's mathematics learning. J. Ningbo Inst. Educ. (2017)

Design of Multimedia Resource Search Service System for Preschool Dance Education

Menghan Wang[✉] and Yuezhou Wei

Weifang Engineering Vocational College, Weifang 262500, China
wangmenghan0420@163.com

Abstract. With the development of Internet technology, various pre-school education institutions or individuals have published their pre-school education resources on the Internet. These resources are more abundant than the resources of any single unit in the past. They can provide almost all the existing resources on pre-school education. This project aims to design a multimedia resource search service system for children's dance education. The main purpose of this study is to design and develop an information system to help teachers find appropriate resources related to dance activities and provide them with guidance on how to effectively use these resources. This will be achieved by developing an application that provides users with relevant information about available resources, including their content and format. In addition, the application will allow users to create playlists of suggested resources according to their needs and preferences.

Keywords: Pre school dance education · Multi-Media · Resource search service system

1 Introduction

The pre-school education major is established in response to the development and needs of the times. It aims to promote the comprehensive development of children and cultivate excellent preschool teachers and other personnel engaged in children's work based on the study of the laws of children's development and pre-school education. This major emphasizes the combination of theory and practice, as well as the combination of teaching and research. Preschool education majors at different levels of universities have different training objectives [1]. The undergraduate level preschool education majors aim to cultivate senior specialized talents engaged in preschool education with comprehensive development in moral, intellectual, physical, and aesthetic aspects, innovative spirit, and practical ability, including cultivating high-quality teachers, early education researchers, and management workers for kindergarten, and providing high-quality student resources for graduate education [2]. The specialty of preschool education at the higher vocational level aims to cultivate teachers or managers who master the basic theories, knowledge, and skills of preschool education and can engage in education, conservation, and research in preschool education institutions.

© ICST Institute for Computer Sciences, Social Informatics and Telecommunications Engineering 2024
Published by Springer Nature Switzerland AG 2024. All Rights Reserved
Y. Zhang and N. Shah (Eds.): BigIoT-EDU 2023, LNICST 584, pp. 26–37, 2024.
https://doi.org/10.1007/978-3-031-63142-9_3

Dance teaching is the process of purposeful and planned teaching, guidance, and inspiration by dance teachers, as well as autonomous learning by dance students, to gradually master the systematic knowledge and skills of various dances and improve students' ability to appreciate and create dance art.

Dance teaching is a unified activity process between dance teachers and dance students. Teacher teaching and student learning are two aspects of a whole. If students are the subject and object of dance teaching [3]; Then the dance teacher is the leader of dance teaching and the object of learning.

The forms of dance teaching can be divided into three categories: first, traditional on-site teaching; Second, information based distance learning; The third is the combination of online and offline teaching. In dance teaching for preschool education majors, most dance teaching is implemented through traditional on-site teaching. Live dance teaching involves dance teachers demonstrating each dance action and teaching dance knowledge, allowing students to observe, appreciate, and imitate the teacher's demonstration actions more closely. At the same time, it can increase classroom questioning and interaction, allowing dance teachers to conduct targeted teaching based on each student's own conditions.

Under the background of the rapid development of the Internet, with the development of multimedia technology, the multimedia resources in the network show a geometric growth trend. This trend is particularly obvious in the field of preschool education. The main reasons are as follows: first, with the in-depth study of children's cognitive characteristics by scholars, people pay more and more attention to children's preschool education, and the state has correspondingly increased relevant investment in this field; Second, multimedia resources directly stimulate the visual nerves of the audience, with rich expressiveness and more easily accepted by children; The rapid development of computer science, especially multimedia technology, has reduced the difficulty of developing multimedia resources, enabling more and more people to participate in the development of multimedia resources under the theme of preschool education. The massive growth of multimedia resources under the theme of preschool education is certainly a good thing, but it also brings a series of problems [4]. The most significant one is that it increases the difficulty for people to choose the multimedia resources they need. In other words, it is difficult for people to quickly and effectively obtain the resources they want from the massive multimedia resources. In the current network environment, there are hundreds of millions of multimedia resources under the theme of preschool education alone. Although search can be carried out to a certain extent through general search engines such as Baidu and Google, it is still a research hotspot in the field of search how to quickly locate those resources that are consistent with your own needs from these numerous resources [5]. The multimedia retrieval system based on the theme of preschool education is a service project to solve this problem. It is committed to integrating the multimedia resources in this field and the information characterizing the multimedia resources, so as to provide convenience for the multimedia retrieval in the field of preschool education and promote the development of preschool education [6].

On the basis of the system design, this paper improves the existing web page analysis methods to make the extracted text and multimedia resources have a higher degree of correlation; Summarize the characteristics of multimedia noise in web pages, design and improve the methods specially used to filter multimedia noise, and then improve the retrieval efficiency of multimedia search engine based on preschool education theme.

2   Related Work

2.1   Research Status of Multimedia Resource Search Service System

Based on the analysis and extraction of multimedia features, the Institute of computing technology of Chinese Academy of Sciences and the National Library jointly developed and designed the feature-based multimedia information retrieval system mires. The multimedia resources in mires come from the Internet. It provides content-based retrieval services for multimedia resources such as graphics, audio and video, and also provides full-text retrieval for text [7]. The system mainly includes the following parts: 1) shape based graphics document retrieval, which can find the similar graphics on the shape according to the example graphics input by the user; 2) image information retrieval based on the overall line characteristics, which can find the similar graphics on the line according to the example graphics input by the user; 3) Graphic information retrieval based on comprehensive characteristics and relevant feedback, i.e. comprehensively considering the characteristics of colors, lines, shapes and other aspects of graphics in a retrieval, and then communicating with users on this basis to find the most appropriate documents according to the user's retrieval objectives; 4) For text information retrieval, mires comprehensively uses different query methods. It not only uses traditional keyword matching methods, but also provides combination search conditions, fuzzy word segmentation and whole sentence matching. In addition, it also covers the characteristics of concept retrieval to a certain extent; 5) The concurrent processing method is adopted on the basis of the subject technology, that is, the retrieval system can split the user's query request, send the split results to different service subjects with respective responsibilities, and then integrate the data transmitted by each service subject and present it to the user. Through the mires system, the services that can be experienced by the searcher mainly include the following points: first, input a sample graph of the graph you want to retrieve to the system for retrieval; Second, inputting some text description information about the retrieval target image to the system for retrieval; Third, use the above two retrieval methods to query the target graphics; Fourth, in the retrieval method using the sample graphics, the searcher can set the weight values of different features by himself; Fifthly, for the retrieval results of the system, the searcher can give feedback to the system to help improve the retrieval results of the system and make them more consistent with the requirements [8]. The resource search service system is shown in Fig. 1 below.

Another domestic multimedia resource retrieval system corresponding to mires system is the multimedia news gathering and editing system of Xinhua news agency. The system has built-in cluster technology and load balancing technology, which can accommodate a certain number of users to use at the same time and provide corresponding search results for the user's operation continuously and quickly [9]. In addition, the system also reserves an interface for future function expansion. The multimedia news gathering and editing system uses UTF-8 encoding format to process all multimedia documents, and can analyze, store and find manuscripts in different languages. Currently,

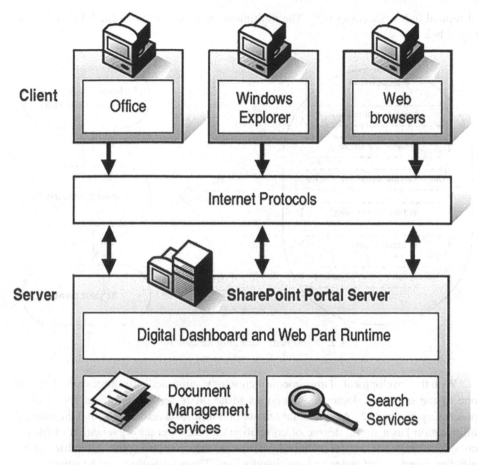

Fig. 1. Resource Search Service System

the languages that can be supported include English, Spanish, Japanese and Russian. At the same time, it also supports the issuance of multimedia manuscripts in different languages [10]. The multimedia news gathering and editing system was officially put into use in July 2005. It can comprehensively process text, graphic images, video, audio, animation and other documents.

2.2 Development Trend of Multimedia Technology

Under the influence of computer science and technology, multimedia technology presents the following development trends: first, the multimedia of computer system itself; Second, the combination of multimedia technology and other related technologies, such as digital TV and virtual reality, extends the application of multimedia technology to teaching, family life, business operation and other fields; Third, multimedia technology has entered the industrial field and combined with control technology to make the operation of related industries easier [11]. The multimedia teaching research model is shown in Fig. 2 below.

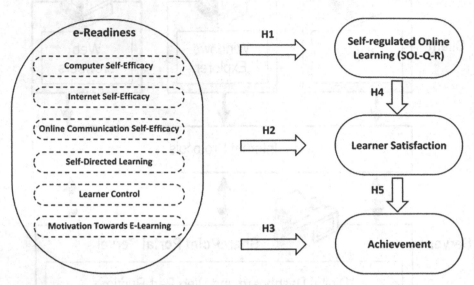

Fig. 2. Multimedia Teaching Research Model

With the development of multimedia technology, multimedia resources have become one of the important document categories to be processed by computer information processing system [12]. A significant feature of multimedia resources is that the internal information has a strong degree of correlation and the internal organization of files is complex. Under the current technical conditions, there are still some difficulties in the efficient management and use of multimedia files. These difficulties can be summarized as follows: first, multimedia files often contain a large amount of data, and there are many differences between colleague files, Making it difficult for the information system to organize and store effectively; Second, the file types of multimedia documents are increasingly rich, and different types often use different organizational structures, which further increases the difficulty of multimedia data processing; Third, the wide application of multimedia resources forces the database to change the corresponding interface so that it can store voice, text and multimedia files at the same time. Its colleagues also change the operation form of data [13]. The most significant here is the query mechanism and query method; Fourth, in the past, the business was usually short but full of content. However, multimedia resources could not do this [14]. For example, reading and playing a digital film from the dynamic video library; Fifthly, multimedia resources are made by using relevant software, and different versions of software may need different processing.

2.3   A Personalized Resource Search and Recommendation Algorithm for Dance

Business demand analysis shows that the platform has rich media resource management functions, so for the increasing amount of system data in the future, management can regularly maintain the data through the background, including uploading high-quality teaching resources, deleting defective teaching resources, and deleting or adding user data [15].

$$G\big(x(T_p)\big) = \sum\nolimits_{i=1}^{d} \frac{x_i(T_p)^2}{\|x(T_p)\|} c_a^b c_a^b \tag{1}$$

$$G''\big(x(T_p)\big) = \frac{2}{\|x(T_p)\|} \sum\nolimits_{i=1}^{d} \big(\frac{\|t\|x_i(T_p)}{\|x(T_p)\|} - \frac{1}{\delta_i}\big)^2 \geq 0 \tag{2}$$

This platform is intended to provide the management and learning of teaching resources related to books, and aggregate teaching resources based on the author's connectivity, knowledge map, and semantic web [16]. It uses personalized recommendation algorithms to recommend appropriate rich media teaching resources to learners, improving the depth and breadth of their learning.

$$Gini(\mathbf{x}(T)) = 1 - \sum\nolimits_{i=1}^{d} \big(\frac{x_i(T)}{\|\mathbf{x}(T)\|}\big)^2 \tag{3}$$

$$E(A) = \sum\nolimits_{j=1}^{r} \frac{s_{1,j} + \cdots s_{n_j}}{s} I\big(s_{1,j} + \cdots s_{n_j}\big) \tag{4}$$

Currently, in the relevant research on the teaching of this preschool dance course, there have been various teaching explorations such as case teaching, flipped classroom, and project modularization. Researchers generally believe that the current teaching of pre-school dance courses in search engines is still based on theory. Although there are also explorations of various teaching methods such as case teaching and project modularization, there is a general disconnect from practical application, and the teaching content is not highly consistent with the actual work content of the enterprise [17–19]. Some researchers believe that the cultivation of students' practical abilities should be enhanced in teaching, and suggest using the teaching method of case comparison, Deepen students' understanding of the working principles and optimization strategies of search engine optimization, and promote students' practical ability. In the research on the combination of search engine optimization preschool dance courses and OBE concepts, many different practical cases are designed for teaching in the classroom, and students need to complete multiple different tasks in one classroom [20]. Although such studies use students as the main teaching subjects for heuristic classroom teaching, some tasks or cases are relatively scattered and lack coherence, which can easily lead to fragmentation between various knowledge points in preschool dance courses and lack an understanding of the integrity of preschool dance courses.

3   Analysis of Characteristics of Multimedia Resources

Analyzing the file types contained in the multimedia resources, the distribution characteristics in the web pages and the nesting form in the web pages can provide some reference for the later web page analysis and noise filtering. It is an indispensable part of the system analysis in this system.

3.1 Teaching Significance of Multimedia Resources for Preschool Education

The objects of preschool education are children aged 0–6. According to Piaget's cognitive development theory, the cognitive level of children in this age group is in the perceptual motor stage and the pre operational stage. Their cognitive characteristics can be summarized as follows: first, At the stage of perceptual movement (0–2 years old, they know the surrounding world by feeling and action. At this time, they can not differentiate the subject and object, so "they show a fundamental self centralization" (Piaget, 1981). Second, children in the pre budget stage (2–7) begin to have symbolic (or symbolic) functions in their cognition (such as being able to represent things by means of language and various schematic means). It is precisely because of this process of eliminating self center and having symbolic function that the appearance or thinking becomes possible. But at this stage, children can not form correct concepts, and their judgment of objective things is dominated by intuitive thinking. For example, only when the two ends of two small wooden sticks are placed together, children at this stage think that they are like long; If one of them is moved upward, children will think it is longer than the other. Therefore, at this stage of cognitive development, children do not have the reverse nature of thinking, and there is no conservation at the same time. According to these two characteristics, it is very necessary to present the teaching content to children in the form of multimedia. This is more conducive to children's understanding of the content of education. If the educators in pre-school education can give full play to the role of multimedia resources in pre-school education, the effect of its education will achieve twice the result with half the effort.

3.2 Types and Characteristics of Multimedia Resources

Web multimedia resources are different from text resources in the Internet. They include pictures, audio, video and animation in form. Different forms of multimedia resources include different file formats, such as JPG, GIF and PNG for pictures, MP3, WAV and MIDI for audio, avi, RMVB and WMV for video and SWF and PPT for animation. The multimedia resources based on preschool education topics discussed in this paper refer to the pictures, audio, video, animation and other files related to preschool education topics distributed on the Internet.

The characteristics of multimedia resources in the web mainly include: 1) multimedia resources act directly on the audience's visual or auditory senses, and have stronger expressive power than text resources; 2) Multimedia resources generally use digital images or digital audio to represent the content to be expressed. Its content is easy to be understood by human beings, but it is not conducive to the "understanding" of computer programs. 3) even if a web page contains multimedia resources related to the theme, the number of multimedia is not large.

3.3 Pre School Dance Education Multimedia Resource Search Service System

Design and develop a search engine for preschool education topics, and provide classified retrieval of resources in various formats such as text, pictures and videos based on preschool education topics.

At present, there are many websites about preschool education on the Internet, among which the resources are mainly in the form of text documents, pictures and videos. These three forms also include many subclasses, such as text documents including PDF documents, word documents, web documents, etc., and videos including AV1, MPEG, flash, etc. The search engine based on preschool education must obtain and store the relevant information of these resources in advance and classify them in order to provide the classified retrieval service about preschool education.

The multimedia resource retrieval system based on the theme of preschool education provides users with classified retrieval services after automatic classification processing and Lucene technology indexing on the basis of accurate analysis of relevant information of multimedia resources. Its architecture is shown in Fig. 3:

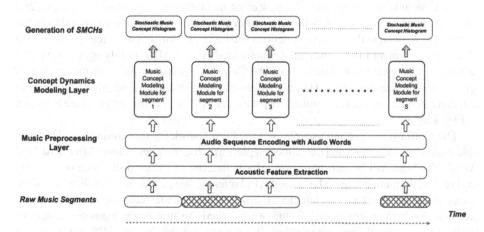

Fig. 3. Structure of multimedia resource search service system

Multimedia teaching resources theme search system "It is designed for searching the multimedia resources existing in the network." The architecture is the same as that of the conventional topic searcher. In this architecture, the web spider is the core of the whole search system. First, the teaching word set about a certain subject and a certain stage is established. These word sets are related to the contents of each subject, linked to the database engine, then input the seed website, start the web spider, and request to download the seed web through the HTTP protocol Stop the page, analyze the page and extract the link, determine the next crawling direction according to a certain heuristic strategy, and finally crawl to all the pages of the website, and store the crawled links in the database. The objects it deals with include: static web pages (text, multimedia information, etc.), web development dynamic web pages, and the internal structure of web pages. The topic searcher uses the close relationship between the three to extract the content representation information of multimedia teaching resources. The text in the web page is the representation of the basic content information of the multimedia web page and can be used as the proxy of the multimedia content. The whole searcher is divided into online part and offline part. The online training is mainly responsible for extracting web page information and selecting URLs in the queue to be crawled; Offline training is mainly responsible for URL rule training and web page relevance calculation.

4 Establishment of Preschool Dance Teaching System

The rich media preschool dance course resource management platform needs to achieve the upload, deletion, and display of various teaching preschool dance course resources, as well as in-depth aggregation and personalized recommendation of preschool dance course resources. Therefore, this article mainly uses the Java based Jfinal framework for development, which well reflects the advantages of MVC architecture, with low coupling, short development cycle, and other advantages.

Jfinal includes five components: a processor, an interceptor, a controller, a plugin, and a rendering function. Interceptor is used to filter and process requests transmitted from the client. Specifically, in this system, functions such as user permission settings, and filtering of adverse comment information are implemented; The handler mainly operates on data requests intercepted by the interceptor; The Controller performs business processing on specific requests and returns a Handle; After rendering specific js and other files, Render can convert them into corresponding display screens. The specific architecture is shown in Fig. 4 below.

The platform foreground uses the apicloud framework for foreground development. apicloud is a cloud integrated development platform that includes "cloud APIs" and "end APIs". The "end API" encapsulates some basic functions in a "modular" manner, greatly saving development cycles. The "cloud API" refers to the platform's cloudization of the background and database, which can automatically generate required service excuses. Because the background server in this article needs to implement complex functions such as personalized recommendation, it does not use the "cloud API" function, but uses an independent background framework for development. As can be seen from the execution process of the API Cloud engine, this framework uses html + css + js language for page code writing, which has the advantage of fast development, good adaptability to different screen sizes, and compatibility with both iOS and Android systems after integration using the API Cloud framework.

The platform carries online pre-school dance course resources for related books. Learners can directly learn by logging on to the platform, and can also scan the QR code in the book to directly obtain the required learning pre-school dance course resources. With the enhancement of learners' awareness of autonomous learning, it has become a trend to create an ubiquitous learning environment for learners, allowing them to obtain the resources and learning services they need to teach preschool dance courses anytime and anywhere. Therefore, this design uses two-dimensional code search technology to achieve the direct access function of teaching preschool dance course resources, while also providing a series of other learning services to create a ubiquitous learning environment around books for learners. These learning services specifically include teaching preschool dance course resource recommendations, notes, keyword search, community communication, and so on.

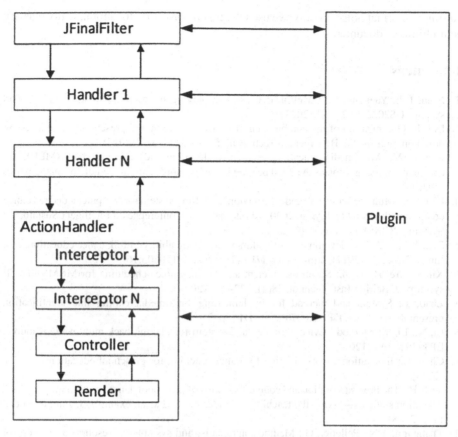

Fig. 4. Framework system

5 Conclusion

With the emergence and development of rich media technology, the multimedia resources contained in the Internet have made rapid progress in both quantity and quality. The multimedia resources mentioned here mainly include pictures, audio, video, animation and other resources, which are characterized by rich expressiveness and can express the teaching content in a more intuitive form, directly stimulate the senses of the educated and reduce the learning difficulty. Considering the cognitive level of preschool children, these characteristics of multimedia make it more important in preschool education activities. However, in the current environment, the multimedia resources based on the theme of preschool education still have some problems, such as the distribution of resources is not centralized, the interference information of multimedia resources is too much, various theme resources are mixed, the utilization rate of resources is low, and the resources are difficult to find. In view of the above problems, we designed a multimedia resource retrieval system based on the theme of preschool education, focused on the methods of capturing the multimedia resources related to the theme of preschool education and their related text information, and independently designed a rule-based filtering method of multimedia format noise. Finally, we used the text information to automatically classify the multimedia documents.

References

1. Nian, L.I., Yuepeng, L.I.: Multimedia resource playing method, apparatus, terminal, and system, US2022191287A1 (2022)
2. Liu, J.: Optimization of the combination of music education and preschool dance teaching based on multimedia. Bol. Tecnico Tech. Bull. **55**(19), 117–122 (2017)
3. Kaabar, M.: Multimedia education resource for learning and online teaching (MERLOT) certificate of recognition as the 2020 peer reviewer extraordinaire in the field of mathematics (2020)
4. Liang, X.: Multimedia system and information modelling system for computer aided red dance creation with virtual reality. In: 2020 3rd International Conference on Intelligent Sustainable Systems (ICISS), pp. 146–149 (2020)
5. Sun, X., Li, Y.: The development of children's aesthetic ability in folk dance education. Sci. Innov. **5**(5), 277 (2017). https://doi.org/10.11648/j.si.20170505.16
6. Xin, S., Ye, H., et al.: Spectrum-efficient and fair resource scheduling for MBMS in LTE systems. J. Beijing Inst. Technol. **28**(4), 777–782 (2019)
7. Zhao, J.: System and method for implementing multimedia calling line identification presentation service, DE602007002932 D1 (2017)
8. Li, N., Li, Y.: Method, device, terminal, and system for playing back multimedia resource, EP3930284A1. 120
9. Chen, L.: Innovation and exploration for dance teaching for preschool education in China (2019)
10. Yi, S.H.: The present situation and countermeasures of preschool dance creation for preschool education students—taking the teaching of ladder method as an example. J. Jiamusi Vocat. Inst. (2018)
11. Thangaraj, Y.N., Pelletier, G.: Methods, apparatus, and systems for resource allocation for multimedia broadcast multicast service (MBMS) in wireless systems, WO2021127069A1 (2021)
12. Liu, F., Linlin, M.A., Cai, Z., et al.: Design and implementation of the multimedia teaching resource management system based on PHP. Softw. Eng. **7**, 145–146 (2016)
13. Khodunova, V.: The use of multimedia resources to enhance the professional competence of pedagogical employees of preschool education institutions (2020)
14. Jichao, M.A.: Design of multimedia sharing system for multi-node networked intelligent teaching. Mod. Electron. Tech. **42**(14), 157–160 (2019)
15. Bao, B.: Constructing high quality public service system for preschool education—based on the investigation of the third-stage preschool education action plan in Guizhou. J. Teach. Educ. **5**(2), 53–62 (2018)
16. Ye, L., Li, Q., Tao, L.: A novel approach of constructing chinese handwriting mobile system and data service for elementary education domain. In: 2017 IEEE International Symposium on Parallel and Distributed Processing with Applications and 2017 IEEE International Conference on Ubiquitous Computing and Communications (ISPA/IUCC), pp. 1233–1240. IEEE (2017)
17. Huiling, C.: Practical teaching status and system establishment of preschool education under multimedia technologies environment (2016)
18. Sucipto, A., Bandung, Y.: Stereotypes based resource allocation for multimedia internet service in limited capacity network. In: International Symposium on Electronics & Smart Devices. IEEE (2016)

19. Feng, J.Y., Pang, L.J., Sun, Y.H.: Policy suggestions for improving basic public service system of preschool bilingual education in Xinjiang (2016)
20. Li. N., Li, Y.: Method, device, terminal, and system for playing back multimedia resource, WO2020207373A1 (2020)

The Transformation of Digital Media Art Design Talent Training Mode Based on AHP Algorithm

Xiaohu Wang[1,2]([✉]) and Ning Liu[1,2]

[1] Shandong Vocational College of Science and Technology, Weifang 261053, Shandong, China
w407132689@163.com
[2] Guangzhou City Construction College, Guangzhou 510925, China

Abstract. With the rapid development of the information industry, artistic creation continues to innovate in content, and the media of art also presents new forms. Digital media art is a product of the new combination of art and technology. This article mainly focuses on the research of Moodle based preschool education teaching system and its application. Moodle is a web-based education platform suitable for use in the field of preschool education. The article first introduces the advantages of building a preschool education teaching system based on Moodle, including centralized teaching resource management, rich and diverse online teaching and testing, enhanced social functions, and personalized evaluation. Subsequently, the article analyzed the possible problems that may arise during the application process and proposed improvement strategies. For example, teachers need to pay attention to the improvement of teaching technology and methods, as well as the optimization of teaching resources. At the same time, timely solutions are also needed to address the common problems of educational technology and children. Finally, this paper summarizes the application value of the preschool education teaching system based on Moodle, and puts forward suggestions, clearly pointing out that preschool education in the future should strengthen the application of information technology, provide comprehensive and high-quality education resources, so as to provide better protection and support for the growth and development of children. This study has important reference significance for expanding the teaching methods of preschool education and promoting the growth of young children.

Keyword: Digital media · Art design · AHP algorithm · personnel training

1 Introduction

With the rapid rise of cultural and creative industries has been promoted, and the demand for artistic design talents who are engaged in is also growing. The training of such talents also meets the common problems of the above. Through the extensive of the market, especially through the in-depth investigation of professional design companies, enterprise design departments, and the production front line, as well as the comprehensive feedback information from all walks of life, it is shown that the market demand for artistic

Y. Zhang and N. Shah (Eds.): BigIoT-EDU 2023, LNICST 584, pp. 38–49, 2024.
https://doi.org/10.1007/978-3-031-63142-9_4

design talents is comprehensive and multi-level, and it is far from enough to have only design skills [1]. In fact, "enterprises and the market are also in urgent need of a of talents with high comprehensive quality. Such talents need theoretical, but also to have solid operation skills. At the same time, they should have strong creative design ability and self-improvement ability." At present, the graduates of domestic art and design vocational colleges are often engaged in a single skill operation work when entering the society, and rarely get involved in the field of design, which is the goal of art and design talent training, but also to some extent shows the bottleneck of the general reform of domestic art and design vocational education [2].

Nowadays, traditional media, and continue to integrate and develop, and the era of information ecology, media pattern, and all media has quietly arrived. In addition to possessing multimedia means of expression, full media is mainly based on communication channels and media, usually including multiple media terminals such as newspapers, radio, television, the Internet, and mobile phones. It can fully utilize the advantages of different media forms in information dissemination, complement each other, and form a synergy to provide diverse services for the audience, Is an organic fusion of multiple media forms The formation of a new information and media ecology heralds the demands changes, and also for cultivating more digital media art talents to adapt and needs [3].

In the context of all media, it is to respect the laws of the times, adapt to the new media ecological environment, strengthen the importance attached to the construction, and cultivate new in the era of all media. Only in this way can we take the lead in the global information technology and cultural game process. In the context of the all-media era, how to adapt digital media art talent cultivation to the rapidly to address the slow pace of development of traditional and art education, as well as the talent cultivation and issue that needs to be considered by the media industry and education industry.

As a rapidly rising emerging specialty after the information technology revolution, the digital media art specialty has developed into a specialty offered by nearly 300 universities across the country in just 20 years. Nationwide, there are not only well-known art universities such as China Communication University, Beijing Film Academy, China Academy of Fine Arts, Nanjing Academy of Art, Jilin Academy of Art, Shandong Academy of Art, but also comprehensive universities as Tsinghua University, Beijing Normal, and Northeast Normal that have successively opened digital media art majors, shouldering the burden of cultivating new media talents in universities, Provide important talent guarantee for the implementation of the "network power" strategy [4]. This major applied the basic theories and methods information dissemination and artistic design in the digital context, and possess professional knowledge and skills in digital media production technology, media planning, and artistic design.

In the era of all media, we need to create a comprehensive talent echelon capable of mastering digital media technology, understanding information communication theory, and applying the laws and methods of art design, which is contemporary, practical, supportive, and adaptive [5]. The previous talent cultivation models have not been able to adapt well to the media, and the new and that arise in the process of all media layout. Therefore, it is necessary to reform the art professionals in order to follow the entire media era, adapt to the situation, and follow the trend. To reform the cultivation mode of digital media art talents, it is necessary to start with the establishment of advanced concepts in modern art education, strengthen the motivation art majors in optimizing the cross platform curriculum system and reforming and innovating the talent cultivation mode, and work hard to improve students' innovation awareness and ability, forming a complete set of integrated, innovative, comprehensive The innovative artistic education methods and practical achievements of the skilled and practical teaching system are deeply integrated with and culture in China, in order to adapt to the new and media ecological construction, and enable in the all-media environment to better serve society [6]. Therefore, the mode needs to be guided by scientific educational concepts, clarify cultivation concepts, set cultivation goals, build a stable cultivation structure and curriculum system, and build an excellent digital media art talent echelon.

Digital the combination art, which makes the boundary between and art disappear. It is a new art system with technology as the means and art as the goal. Because it uses digital technologies such as network media, it has certain interactivity. The technical elements in works of art are becoming more and more prominent, making the images of digital art become information, and the interactivity of digital art is becoming more and more important. Digital media art is essentially different from traditional art such as music, dance and painting [7]. It is a unique art form produced in the information age, which contains mechanical automation, mass, communication, interaction, entertainment and other characteristics.

2 Related Work

2.1 Overview of Digital Media

Digital media art is one of the emerging forms in the art field in recent years, covering various art forms such as music, movies, television, games, and the internet. Its characteristic is to use digital technology to enhance visualization and audibility of creativity. Analytic Hierarchy Process (AHP) is a decision-making analysis method that can be widely applied in the art field, suitable for helping decision-makers such as artists, curators, and students make decisions on artistic performance, exhibition venues, etc. This article will introduce the application of AHP algorithm for digital media art expression and management [8].

The basic principle of the AHP algorithm is to evaluate relevant problems based on certain standards, then layer the problems through the weight composition of different standards, and then collect the relative weights of attributes to determine the final weight. In digital media art, AHP can be used to calculate the relative weight of images, music, and videos. Digital media art can unify multiple art forms, so in its creation, AHP can evaluate, compare, and integrate works from different media.

Digital media art has great potential in achieving aesthetic innovation [9]. For example, in the field of digital music, artists can combine different types of instruments together and allocate weights through AHP to obtain more diverse forms of music expression. In the field of television and film, AHP can combine various elements such as painting, photography, film scenery, and special effects to ultimately create more distinctive, unique, and infectious works that resonate and enthrall audiences.

In addition, the display forms of digital media art are diverse, and AHP can also play an important role in this regard [10]. AHP can help exhibition curators classify, sort, and layer the works of different artists and creativity to achieve an overall artistic display. For example, in the Digital art exhibition, the works of different artists can be classified, sorted and layered according to different themes through AHP algorithm, so that the audience can better understand and appreciate the works.

In summary, in digital media art, the AHP algorithm can assist decision-makers such as artists, curators, and students in making decisions on artistic performance, exhibition venues, and other aspects, as well as evaluating the combination of various elements of multimedia [11]. The development direction of digital media art is diversification and comprehensiveness, and its display and management methods will become more diversified and diversified with the continuous progress of technology. In addition, multiple algorithm methods can be combined to achieve more optimized and accurate artistic creation and management.

2.2 Modes of Information Dissemination in Digital Media

As early as 1949, Shannon, the founder of information theory, and his colleague Weaver first proposed a communication mode for information transmission from the perspective of telegraph communication: source → coding → channel → decoding → destination. This mode is a one-way transmission of single information, which undoubtedly has limitations. So Shannon and Weaver added feedback on this mode. Source → coding → channel → decoding → destination → feedback → source. Although this extension seems simple, it reflects an important reflection on the two-way nature of information transmission. However, this mode is limited to the process of information transmission between communication systems, not between people [12].

The emergence of digital media has fundamentally changed the mode of information dissemination. The previous mode of communication was mainly through broadcasting, television, newspapers and other media for extensive promotion, while digital media provided a wider range of communication platforms, such as the internet, social media, video websites, mobile applications, etc.

Digital media has the characteristics of immediacy, interactivity, personalization, and multimedia, which can make information dissemination faster, wider, and more targeted. Taking the network as an example, its propagation mode has two modes: passive reception and active search [13]. Passive reception is the process of pushing information to users through channels such as websites, news clients, and social media, allowing users to easily view, share, or like it; Active search refers to users searching, following, and sharing information through search engines or social media to achieve the goal of targeted dissemination.

Social media is one of the most representative communication platforms in digital media, which can spread information through sharing, forwarding, or commenting. In social media, hot events, personal experiences, interests, and hobbies can all become popular information, thereby affecting more people [14]. Social media also has the advantages of high accuracy, strong interactivity, fast dissemination speed, and wide coverage, which can help information disseminators better locate audiences, find target groups, and improve the effectiveness and influence of information dissemination.

Art is an thing that can bring aesthetic feeling. Art is to create through artistic thinking and methods, not only to solve problems, but also to bring people aesthetic, spiritual and emotional needs.

There are three main fields art design. Web based design, such as web animation design; Design based on communication media, such as multimedia publication design, etc.; There are also software based interaction design, interface design, and so on.

At present, the talents in China has always been a problem of valuing art over technology, and valuing knowledge over ability. It is necessary to combine the objective needs of regional economy and the for talents in different levels, specifications, and types of specialized positions, guide talent cultivation based on industry needs, and appropriately position the objectives of the art specialty [15]. Currently, most of the goals for art professionals in China specify that they should master the relevant theories and basic skills of digital media art, and have requirements for the application capabilities required by the industry. At the same time, they specify the specific employ. However, few universities have specified the the cultivation of artistic talents in the training goals of digital media art professionals [16]. On the contrary, in order to distinguish from technology majors, often restricts the achievement of corresponding technology goals in order to "avoid suspicion" in talent cultivation goals. However, in order to cultivate qualified digital media and art professionals, relevant professional construction universities must.

In an all media environment, the concept of media has been redefined. "Everything is media," and media has become ubiquitous. The talent demand for media related majors is not only from certain media institutions or platforms, but also integrated into various industries. Many conventional positions require digital media art talents. The formulation of talent cultivation goals should take into account that the normal state of media development in the future is a process of continuous integration and breakthrough, which is fluid and changing [17]. Therefore, the demand for media practitioners with professional education backgrounds is not limited to the field of media employment. In the process of setting the training goals for digital media professionals, it must be clearly seen that the digital layout of media does not only exist in the past media industry, but also permeates the entire industry ecosystem. Therefore, the art not only focus on certain media professional groups, but also aim at the characteristics of universities and professional construction positioning, and take the position as the guiding direction. It is not only to cultivate specialized talents in the field of digital media, but also to cultivate comprehensive all-media talents who can master digital technology, have artistic aesthetic vision, and have media skills [18]. Let digital media art talents not only have the employment competitiveness in a certain position, but also have the adaptability to adapt to the development of the position. Colleges and universities should, according to their training objectives, refine the direction of professional training, select and implement training approaches, and a comprehensive talent training.

3 AHP Algorithm

3.1 Introduction to AHP Hierarchical Model

Analytic Hierarchy Process (AHP) is a decision-making analysis method mainly used to deal with complex decision-making problems, and needs to consider the relative importance of multiple influencing factors. AHP is usually composed of Hierarchical database model and a group of judgment matrices.

Hierarchical database model is the basis for building the AHP analysis framework. It decomposes problems and hierarchizes them, expands from high-level concepts, gradually refines them into more specific sub levels, and finally reaches the specific decision-making scheme at the bottom [19]. The AHP Hierarchical database model usually consists of four parts:

(1) Goal: The overall goal or vision of a strategy.
(2) Criteria: Various considerations used to achieve goals, usually divided into multiple dimensions or levels of criteria.
(3) Subcriteria: Each criterion can be decomposed into more specific subcriteria to reflect the considerations in greater detail.
(4) Decision Plan: Under each sub criterion, list all feasible decision plans that need to be compared and selected to clarify the effectiveness of each decision plan in achieving goals and each criterion.

In the AHP Hierarchical database model, the relationship between the levels is usually a tree structure, where the top level is the target level and the bottom level is the decision scheme level. In AHP analysis, decision-makers weigh the information at various levels to determine the final weight of each decision plan, and rank them to ultimately determine the priority level and the best decision plan.

The AHP Hierarchical database model usually uses the 1–9 scale for punishment, that is, 1 indicates the relative weight between the two, and 9 indicates the importance of one party to the other is very important. Each element in each judgment matrix needs to be normalized to reflect its relative importance. By calculating the final weight of each decision plan, the achievement of each decision plan in achieving goals and various criteria can be accurately evaluated [20].

In general, AHP Hierarchical database model is a systematic and effective decision-making analysis method, which can be used to deal with complex decision-making problems and is widely used in business, government, science and other fields.

The evaluation system of talent is shown in Fig. 1 below.

As shown in Fig. 1, the interpretative structural model is divided into three model blocks, and the indicator weights of each block are studied by constructing a judgment matrix. The formula for calculating the weight, maximum characteristic root, consistency index, and random consistency index proportion is shown in the following formula.

$$\cos\theta = \frac{A_1 \times B_1 + A_2 \times B_2}{\sqrt{A_1^2 + A_2^2} + \sqrt{B_1^2 + B_2^2}} \tag{1}$$

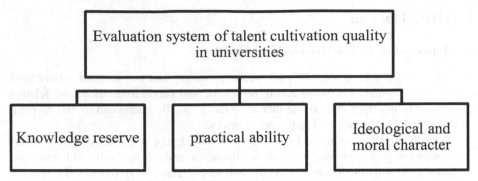

Fig. 1. Evaluation system of talent cultivation quality in universities

The pre-similarity calculation method in N-dimensional space: let vector A = (A1, A2,... An), B = (B1, B2,...., Bn). The cosine value formula is:

$$\cos\theta = \frac{\sum_1^n A_i \times B_i}{\sqrt{\sum_1^n A_i^2} \times \sqrt{\sum_1^n B_i^2}} \tag{2}$$

$$d_{12} = \sqrt{(x_1 - x_2)^2 + (y_1 - y_2)^2} \tag{3}$$

The calculation method of Euclidean distance in 3D space: let a (xl, yl, z1), b (x2, y2, z1) be any two points in 3D space, then the distance d12 between two points of a and b is:

$$d_{12} = \sqrt{(x_1 - x_2)^2 + (y_1 - y_2)^2 + (z_1 - z_2)^2} \tag{4}$$

3.2 Steps of AHP Algorithm

The development pattern of all media will overturn the previous forms of media communication, and at the same time will reverse the change in the form of talent cultivation. How to cultivate talents with cross platform and cross industry composite capabilities while highlighting the advantages of talent specific skills to adapt media socialization and social is a difficult problem facing the the AHP algorithm. Adopting the teaching organization form of interdisciplinary joint training of talents in different cross directions of digital media art based on AHP the training effectiveness of specialized talents in different cross directions with higher efficiency. According to industry development and social needs, joint experimental classes can be jointly held in different professional directions, and the composition of the teaching team can be arranged in a coordinated manner to bring into play the expertise of teachers in different professional directions. This is beneficial for universities to establish the development characteristics of digital media art majors under the AHP algorithm, as well as differentiated talent cultivation paths. Teaching activities can be carried out through the guidance of industry mentors, joint experimental class teaching, integrated studio system, and participation in simulated actual combat projects, as well as cross professional course selection, credit mutual recognition, etc., to the teaching reform art majors under the AHP algorithm, promote the integration, cross media platforms, and cross industry capabilities, and innovate the high-end talent cultivation mode under the AHP algorithm. In the process of organizing interdisciplinary "consortium" teaching, the case teaching mode and the operation mode of combining "simulation actual combat" are used to make up for the imbalance in talent ability cultivation caused by the span of majors in the process of integrating "teaching, learning, and doing", and to serve interdisciplinary practical projects based on their own majors. According to the teaching methods such as group learning and discussion, team division of labor simulation and practical project operation can be actively adopted, and digital media technology education methods based on AHP algorithm can be fully utilized to carry out teaching. Internet technology can be actively used to achieve digitization and based on AHP algorithm.

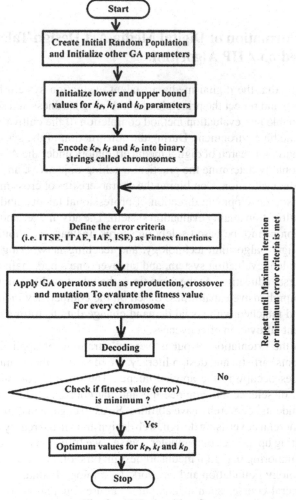

Fig. 2. AHP algorithm flow

The analytic hierarchy process is generally, as follows:

(1) Determine the overall. That is, through in-depth study of the system, we can analyze the measures taken for decision-making, the criteria for achieving goals, various constraints, etc.
(2) Build judgment matrix. Under the specified criteria, the elements of each layer have a weight ratio relative to the elements of the same layer. First, build the weight ratio matrix of the same layer. Then build the weight ratio relative to the overall goal [17].
(3) Calculate the weight and adjust the matrix. Then, the judgment matrix is adjusted according to the consistency test results, and the process is repeated until the judgment matrix meets the consistency.
(4) Analyze the calculation results. After obtaining the optimal judgment matrix, analyze the scientificity and objectivity of the results.

The AHP algorithm flow is in Fig. 2.

4 The Transformation of Digital Media Art Design Talent Training Mode Based on AHP Algorithm

In the era of all media, the digital media art talent evaluation system based on AHP algorithm the times and reflect the principle of combining hardness and softness. Establishing and reasonable and evaluation method completion of the cultivation of versatile talents in the all-media environment. During the construction of the system, it is necessary to take the market research of digital media art majors under the AHP algorithm as the premise, reasonably determine the practical teaching objectives, and break through the traditional talent evaluation. Combining the characteristics of cross majors, integrating the characteristic development direction of professional talents, and establishing a complete talent cultivation quality evaluation system. The advantages and disadvantages of talent cultivation cannot be based solely on scores. Instead, we should use big data technology, intelligent algorithm technology, and teaching networking technology to build a dynamic talent evaluation system, and tap everyone's personalized potential on the basis of universal education. At the same time, the talent evaluation process of indicators of and comprehensive capabilities. Based on the competency index required for, the cultivation and matched with social demand change data to form a comprehensive evaluation of talent cultivation effectiveness.

According to the orientation of our university's training of applied talents, while focusing on students' artistic and design literacy, we recognize that computer and communication courses occupy in the applied talents. The organic combination of these technical courses of science and engineering and the courses of design specialty can better cultivate students' comprehensive abilities. So as to engage in digital video, audio processing, commercial advertising design, web design and virtual reality in the future. In the process of setting up a series of computer courses, we fully considered the characteristics of students majoring in digital media art design. First of all, we set up two courses, Computer Technology Foundation and Network Technology Foundation, to effectively connect with general courses such as computer culture foundation for undergraduate students. Then two courses, Digital Signal Processing Technology Fundamentals and

Communication Technology Fundamentals, are set up to enable students to better understand the implementation technology. Considering that the theoretical basis of students majoring is relatively weak, the above courses mainly focus on teaching basic concepts and basic applications, accounting for only 18 class hours. Then we set up Computer Language Design to introduce the relevant concepts of computer programming language. Let students understand the implementation method of digital media works with program control when referring to and borrowing from them. Finally, we have set up Virtual Reality and Implementation and Computer Aided Design, so that learned after mastering the computer series courses required by their major.

Digital media art is a new form of art that is mainly based on digital technology and is expressed through forms such as sound, images, and animation. Digital media art and design talents need to possess comprehensive abilities in artistic creation, technological research and development, visual communication, and user experience. Therefore, the cultivation of digital media art and design talents needs to focus on interdisciplinary education and studio style practical education methods, and establish a professional training system closely integrated with practical work, as shown in Fig. 3.

(1) Comprehensive Education

The cultivation of digital media art and design talents requires interdisciplinary education to cultivate students' comprehensive abilities, including various disciplines such as art, technology, media, psychology, etc. Therefore, the curriculum should focus on the combination of core courses and interdisciplinary courses, as well as Transdisciplinarity and practice. Cultivate comprehensive digital media art and design talents with solid technical, theoretical, and other basic knowledge, while also being sensitive to artistic creativity.

(2) Studio Style Practical Education

The cultivation of digital media art and design talents needs to focus on the method of studio style practical education, that is, conducting practical education through simulating studios. Through studio practical education, students can be exposed to practical digital media art and design work, and learn basic design, research and development, and production techniques, thereby improving practical and team collaboration abilities.

(3) Practice Oriented Education

The cultivation of digital media art and design talents requires a focus on practical oriented educational methods. The education model needs to be based on actual needs and social positioning, through the improvement of assessment methods and teaching methods, in order to cultivate design talents that meet the needs of the talent market, meet the needs of social development, and truly contribute to society.

(4) Enterprise Cooperation Mode

The cultivation of digital media art and design talents needs to focus on cooperation models with enterprises. Students should have the opportunity to integrate with enterprise project practice, engage in enterprise practice and practical project development.

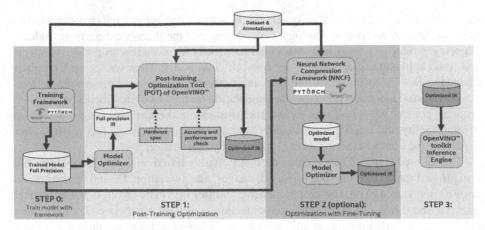

Fig. 3. Training mode for digital media art and design talents

5   Conclusion

The transformation of digital media art and design talent cultivation mode based on AHP algorithm emphasizes four training methods: comprehensive education, studio style practical education, practice oriented education, and enterprise cooperation. This model cultivates students' interdisciplinary education and comprehensive quality cultivation, cultivating their cross disciplinary and teamwork abilities, enabling them to truly possess various abilities such as digital media art and design. At the same time, in studio style practical education, students can be exposed to practical digital media art and design work, and learn basic design, research and development, and production techniques, thereby improving practical and team collaboration abilities. Practical oriented education methods and enterprise cooperation models can also effectively improve students' practical abilities and employment competitiveness. In short, the digital media art and design talent cultivation model based on the AHP algorithm can better meet market demand, cultivate design talents with practical, innovative, and comprehensive abilities, and make great contributions to the development of digital media art and the prosperity of the industry.

References

1. Wu, Z., Zhou, C.: Prediction model of internationalized talent training based on fuzzy neural network algorithm. In: Hung, J.C., Yen, N.Y., Chang, J.-W. (eds.) Frontier Computing: Proceedings of FC 2021, pp. 416–423. Springer, Singapore (2022). https://doi.org/10.1007/978-981-16-8052-6_51
2. He, T., Lin, S., Chen, X.: Research on the Training Mode of Innovative and Entrepreneurial Thinking of Design Talents — A Case Study of Digital Media Arts (2020)
3. Chen, Y., Liu, X., Hu, G.: Design of arbitrary shaped pentamode acoustic cloak based on quasi-symmetric mapping gradient algorithm. J. Acoust. Soc. Am. **140**(5), EL405–EL409 (2016)

4. Li, X., Zhou, J.: A sliding mode control design for mismatched uncertain systems based on states transformation scheme and chattering alleviating scheme. Trans. Inst. Measur. Control **40**(8), 2509–2516 (2017). https://doi.org/10.1177/0142331216680351
5. Wang, R., Cheng, H., Ye, L., et al.: Reproduction transformation rule-based sound generation for film soundtrack. J. Comput. Aided Des. Comput. Graph. **34**(10), 1524–1532 (2022). https://doi.org/10.3724/SP.J.1089.2022.19727
6. Lei, Z., Xu, F.: Design and implementation of course arrangement model based on reforming deep reinforcement learning. J. Phys. Conf. Ser. **1846**(1), 012052 (2021). https://doi.org/10.1088/1742-6596/1846/1/012052
7. Cui, Q.: Research on transformation of industrial building heritages based on lattice point algorithm. Revista De La Facultad De Ingenieria **32**(13), 133–137 (2017)
8. Yang, G., Wang, L.: Quality evaluation algorithm based on ahp and utility theory. In: 2019 6th International Conference on Systems and Informatics (ICSAI), Shanghai, China, pp. 573–578 (2019) https://doi.org/10.1109/ICSAI48974.2019.9010592
9. Huimin, M.A., Shao, X.: Research on the training mode of "three-quality talents" in application-oriented universities based on OBE. Asian Agric. Res. **14**(12), 3 (2022)
10. Zhang, Z.W., Sui, P., Xie, W.Y.: Research of the innovative talent training mode based on subject contest. Lab. Sci. (2016)
11. Tang, C., Guo, X., Gao, J.: Design of text-image separation algorithm based on FIR filter and its application in photocopying equipment (2018)
12. Zhu, X.: Study on construction and development paths of major of digital media art design in higher vocational colleges. Jiangsu Vocat. Inst. Architect. Technol. (2018)
13. Zhang, N.: Construction cost optimization system based on AHP-BP neural network algorithm. In: Macintyre, J., Zhao, J., Ma, X. (eds.) The 2021 International Conference on Machine Learning and Big Data Analytics for IoT Security and Privacy: SPIoT-2021 Volume 1, pp. 121–129. Springer, Cham (2022). https://doi.org/10.1007/978-3-030-89508-2_16
14. Xie, J.: Research on the talent training mode for visual communication design—based on intelligent computing via project in studio project. In: Hung, J.C., Chang, J.-W., Pei, Y., Wei-Chen, Wu. (eds.) Innovative Computing: Proceedings of the 4th International Conference on Innovative Computing (IC 2021), pp. 597–604. Springer, Singapore (2022). https://doi.org/10.1007/978-981-16-4258-6_74
15. Zhou, J., Gong, S., Chen, J.: Reform and practice of textile design talent training in line with "fashionable textile". J. Zhejiang Sci-Tech Univ. (Soc. Sci. Ed.) (2018)
16. Zhang, W.W., Xu, F., Huang, et al.: Digital transformation of insurance industry based on k-means algorithm. Digit. Technol. Appl. (2019)
17. Wang, W., Zhou, K., Wang, Y., et al.: Design of convolutional neural networks accelerator based on fast filter algorithm. J. Electron. Inf. Technol. **41**(11), 2578–2584 (2019)
18. Lin, H., Huang, W., Hu, X.: Research on the design of talent training mode based on the ordered class for certain majors in vocational education. In: International Conference on Arts (2017)
19. Sun, F.F., Li, Y.: Thinking and practice of course construction in studio training mode—a case study of digital media art in Suzhou University of Science and Technology. Educ. Teach. Forum (2016)
20. Zhao, S.L., Wang, N., Chen, J.Y.: Curriculum design research based on knowledge-to-capability transformation. J. Hebei Univ. Eng. (Soc. Sci. Ed.) (2019)

A Study of New Media Technology in Foreign Literature

Yumeng Yang[1,3(✉)] and Shiyu Wu[2,3]

[1] Sichuan University, Chengdu 610200, Sichuan, China
OliviaYYM0929@163.com
[2] Ningbo University of Finance and Economics, Ningbo 315000, Zhejiang, China
[3] City University of Macau, Macau 999078, China

Abstract. The 21st century is the era of new media, which makes people in the information dissemination and communication, has been inseparable from the network, cell phones and other emerging media. At the same time, Internet technology and information technology are developing rapidly. Literature as a special foreign literary commodity has its own unique charm, it is processed through the work to get the public's favorite and can resonate with the reader to promote reading interest to produce consumer behavior or effect; at the same time, literature is also a specific form to reflect social life, reveal the author's inner world for the purpose, so it has a unique in the dissemination process. New media technology provides more channels for this uniqueness. Therefore, this paper takes Japanese literature as an example to explain the study of new media technology in foreign literature.

Keywords: New Media Technology · Foreign Literature · Communication

1 Introduction

In the era of economic globalization, the links between countries in education have become increasingly close. While learning our own national culture well, it has become a requirement of the new era to base ourselves on tradition, take a broad view of the world, and actively absorb all excellent cultures. In the process of Chinese language teaching in secondary schools, it is necessary to enhance the recognition of the national culture, while cultivating students to recognize cultural diversity with a more inclusive and open attitude, and to understand the rapidly changing world in a holistic and comprehensive way of thinking. As the mother tongue curriculum in China, Chinese curriculum not only bears the function of disseminating the native language, but also is an important way to carry out humanistic education. The president of Notre Dame University in the United States believes that education should include two parts, "One is to learn to do things, and the other is to learn to be a person. Here, learning to do things means that the educated should cultivate a scientific spirit while receiving scientific education. Learning to be a person means that the educated should cultivate a humanistic

Y. Zhang and N. Shah (Eds.): BigIoT-EDU 2023, LNICST 584, pp. 50–60, 2024.
https://doi.org/10.1007/978-3-031-63142-9_5

spirit while receiving humanistic education." "He emphasizes the integration of science education and humanistic education, and while science education is developing rapidly, it is necessary to attach greater importance to students' humanistic education, so that students strive to be a person who pursues truth, goodness, and beauty. In order to adapt to the requirements of the new era, give full play to the educational function of Chinese courses, and cultivate comprehensive talents that meet the needs of social development, it is necessary to carry out humanistic education in the teaching of secondary schools. As an important component of world culture, foreign literature is an important component of world culture It contains rich humanistic values and plays an important role in improving students' personality and humanistic literacy. Therefore, this article will explore the teaching strategies of Chinese and foreign literature in middle schools from a humanistic perspective.

The proportion of foreign literature in Chinese teaching is not small, but the effectiveness of foreign literature teaching is unsatisfactory, and there is still a large room for improvement. From the current situation of foreign literature teaching, there are the following problems: First, the model is "exam oriented". All teaching work in the middle school stage is always carried out around the middle school entrance examination, and language teaching is no exception. Almost all students' interest in learning foreign literature is focused on completing the tasks assigned by the teacher. Teachers are lazy to talk about content beyond the scope of the examination, and students are also lazy to learn, This has also indirectly led to the ossification of the teaching methods and content of foreign literature, which is a devastating blow to highlighting the value of foreign literature teaching. During the process of educational internships and internships, the author was fortunate to learn about the actual process of classroom teaching of Chinese and foreign literature in some middle schools. It was generally found that most foreign literature teaching is presented in the form of lecture and reading classes, with most of the class hours being one class hour. The teaching focus is on knowledge and ability goals, while the exploration of interpretation texts and humanistic connotations is still insufficient. Secondly, the teaching form is unitary. When teaching foreign literature, some teachers have limited foreign literature literacy, often superficial interpretation of texts, and superficial exploration of the humanistic spirit contained therein, resulting in poor teaching effectiveness of foreign literature. In addition, the distribution of the works itself is relatively scattered, and the links between the works are not close enough. Most Chinese teachers teach the text on the topic, ignoring the systematic nature of foreign literature teaching.

The rapid innovation and social penetration of information technology, represented by the Internet and cell phones, has created a new space for social communication that differs significantly from the traditional mass communication process centered on television and newspapers. The new media are expected to build a new world alongside social and economic globalization, and their recent progress has been remarkable. Since the birth of the media, people's lives have been inseparable from the Internet, and literature has been integral to it. With the continuous development and popularization of new media technology, the Internet and other information dissemination tools are rapidly changing the way people appreciate literature. In particular, new media mass reading represented by microblogging, Twitter and Facebook has become one of the most popular and influential topics used by contemporary people. At the same time, the proliferation of various forms of works on the Internet makes readers curious and gradually accept them, and the unique charm of literature attracts more readers to join them, so it is obvious that the combination of new media and foreign literature will produce wonderful changes.

2 Related Work

2.1 Concept and Characteristics of New Media

In contemporary society, people attribute digital multimedia such as digital TV, outdoor digital electronic large screen advertising and digital broadcasting to the category of new media. From this level, we believe that new media are media that rely on cutting-edge science and technology, especially digital technology, and are different from traditional media communication forms. In the broad definition of new media [1], certain traditional media can also be classified as new media due to their transformation by using digital technology, like in-car TV, digital TV, digital broadcasting, etc. Although both new media and traditional media are used for information dissemination and both belong to media, there are major differences between them as carriers and tools for information dissemination. Compared with traditional media, new media is "new" because the form of communication and receiving platform are incomparable to traditional media. Any media form related to the Internet, computers, mobile communication and the latest digital technology can become new media. With the introduction of new communication technologies, print media, mainly newspapers and books, have receded, while visual media, which make extensive use of electronic technology, have developed. However, some argue that the emergence of new media will bring "print media" back into power. This is because the new media are able to transmit textual information extremely efficiently, which is quite different from the traditional "print" method. In other words, the new media can be described as the emergence of "letters" with electronic wings. The traditional process of printing large quantities of type, collating, binding and delivering it in the printing press may disappear. Instead, letters will be symbolized, digitized, fed into computers, and transmitted via radio waves and cables. Digitized text messages can be viewed and printed at home, in the office, or anywhere else a signal can be transmitted. To the selectivity and storability of newspapers, magazines and books, the mass and instantaneous communication of radio is added a new element of "interactivity", the ability to "process information", which is equivalent to writing. This can also be said to be an important factor in the rapid popularity of new media in the media world in a short period of time.

The advantage of using new media to disseminate books instead of print is that the cost of transmitting information is greatly reduced in exchange for the elimination of procedures such as printing, binding and delivery. In addition to the significant reduction in cost, the speed of dissemination can be greatly increased in the context of the Internet [2], which is considered an important factor in the use of new media as a means of book dissemination. Of course, traditional audiovisual media, such as television and radio, have changed considerably with the advent of new media, but the main change has been "multi-channel" rather than fundamental. However, it can be argued that the emergence and development of new media has revolutionized the way books were traditionally disseminated through the print medium. A typical example of using new media to disseminate books instead of print is the Internet library, or e-library, for example, the most famous e-library in Japan is Aozora Bunko.

The "newness" of new media is intuitively reflected in its advantages, or characteristics, compared to traditional media [3]. New media has the following characteristics (Fig. 1).

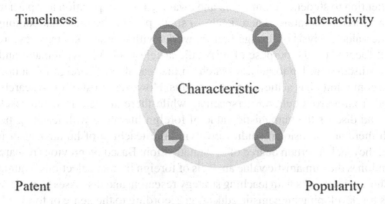

Timeliness   Interactivity

Characteristic

Patent   Popularity

Fig. 1. Characteristics of New Media

2.2 Development of Curriculum Teaching Resources

Curriculum resources are rooted in the center of curriculum and teaching, and are an indispensable link in curriculum development. In her master's thesis "Research on the Development and Teaching of Chinese and Foreign Literature Curriculum Resources in High Schools", Dai Menglin attempts to explore the development and effective use of foreign literature curriculum resources and teaching in high schools from four aspects: the development of text resources in foreign literature, the enrichment of teaching environments, the utilization of homework resources, and the utilization of teaching processes. The classification of text resources focuses on text types, themes, genres, and author situations in order to have a rational and objective complete understanding of foreign literary works. In the comparative study of foreign literature text resources between China and the United States, it is necessary to reflect on the current development situation of foreign literature text resources in China, accelerate the construction of a text resource system for foreign literature teaching in China, and enhance the flexibility of the system through the construction of "online classroom".

The author searches for relevant literature using foreign literature and humanism as keywords, and some literature studies use foreign literary works as research objects to analyze the humanistic value contained therein. In her analysis of the emotional value of modern and contemporary foreign literature, Haizhen mentioned that she should deepen the connotation and artistic expression of foreign literature and explore its humanistic value. In terms of specific methods, it is not limited to the description of the author's inner emotions, and it is also a good way to conduct close reading of the text in combination with the introduction of cultural background.

The other part of the study is to apply specific teaching methods to the teaching of foreign literature by infiltrating the idea of humanistic education. For example, Wang Wanqiu advocated a problem-oriented and text-based foreign literature teaching model in his "Problem Oriented Chinese Textbook Interpretation: Teaching Reform and Practice of Foreign Literature Courses Based on the" Problem Oriented "Teaching Method, emphasizing a teacher led, student led learning approach in the teaching process, while paying attention to students' enthusiasm and awareness of cooperation and participation in learning foreign literature. There is also a small part of research that combines the humanistic value analysis of foreign literary works with teaching strategy research, but most of it focuses on the purpose of a specific article, lacking a systematic and comprehensive discussion. Up to now, research on the teaching of foreign literature in the academic community has achieved certain results. However, most of the research is still conducted from a cross-cultural perspective, while there are few research results that combine and discuss the humanistic value of foreign literature with teaching practice. Although there are occasional studies involving the teaching of humanism in foreign literature, they lack a certain degree of systematization. Based on previous research, this paper combines the humanistic value analysis of foreign literary selections in junior high school Chinese textbooks with teaching strategy research, and discusses specific feasible measures for developing humanistic education according to the genre of foreign literary works. In order to explore the humanistic value of foreign literature and use foreign literary works to cultivate students' humanistic spirit in teaching practice, this article has conducted statistics and classification of foreign literary works appearing in junior high school textbooks, classified and summarized the humanistic values contained in different foreign literature, and combined the teaching strategies of foreign literature previously studied with the humanistic teaching of junior high school Chinese foreign literature, Making the teaching of foreign literature no longer limited to indoctrination teaching, enables students to experience the rich and colorful heterogeneous culture while improving their aesthetic taste, and become happy learners. In response to the requirements of quality education, modern and contemporary Chinese courses pay more attention to the unity of instrumentality and humanity, and focus on giving full play to the humanistic function of the language discipline. The author combines the humanistic value of foreign literature with humanistic teaching strategies, providing a new perspective for teachers to teach foreign literature and students to learn foreign literature, striving to improve the dull and tedious teaching situation of foreign literature. At the same time, it is hoped that some of the teaching strategies proposed in this article can provide assistance to frontline teachers in conducting humanistic teaching of foreign literature.

2.3   Research on Foreign Culture of New Media Technology

The Influence of "New Media Plus" on Foreign Literature Classroom Teaching.

In traditional foreign literature classrooms, due to the limited access to information for students, students have little knowledge of foreign literature in terms of its creative background, creative intent, and cultural differences between the East and the West. This undoubtedly leads to frequent misunderstandings or misunderstandings among students during classroom learning, which hinders the classroom teaching of foreign literature. At the same time, due to the complex and diverse forms and extensive coverage of foreign literary works, it is difficult for teachers to comprehensively teach students the connotation or related knowledge of literary works within a short classroom time. It has become the norm for many foreign literature classroom teaching to choose only the key points in the classroom or to explain the content simply. Such teaching methods will undoubtedly have a serious impact on students' learning outcomes, and may even dampen students' enthusiasm for learning foreign literature.

In the "new media+" environment, due to the advantages of new media such as abundant information, access to information, and information sharing, the application of new media in foreign literature classrooms can just help teachers overcome the above difficulties and enable students to find effective ways to understand foreign literature more comprehensively. Teachers can also improve classroom teaching models through new media, displaying and teaching more teaching content in the classroom, There can also be a deeper analysis of the teaching content. The arrival of the era of "new media+" can undoubtedly effectively help foreign literature classrooms overcome teaching difficulties.

The Relationship between "New Media Plus" and Foreign Literature Classroom.

Although the "new media+" model of foreign literature classroom can effectively help teaching in the classroom teaching mode, with the continuous deepening of the new curriculum reform, the reform of foreign literature classroom should always comply with the requirements of the new curriculum reform. This requires foreign literature teachers to clarify the relationship between "new media+" and foreign literature classrooms. On the premise that the teaching model has been greatly improved, the content and objectives of classroom teaching are the most important things that foreign literature teachers need to pay attention to. Many classrooms have benefited from the help of new media in their teaching models, but the content is still outdated and unchanged, without keeping pace with the times. Such classrooms are also difficult to attract students' attention, and the teaching effect will not be significantly improved. Foreign literature teachers should first clarify that "new media+" is only an effective means of assisting teaching, and what is really important is to use the advantages of "new media+" to reshape and improve the teaching content. Classroom teaching should clearly take students as the main body of the classroom, arouse students' enthusiasm for classroom participation through new media, stimulate students to actively participate in the classroom, and conduct benign interaction between students, teachers, and students. Emphasizing the active participation of students in the classroom is also an effective way to improve the humanistic atmosphere in foreign literature classrooms.

3 New Media Technology Has Expanded the Content and Form of Foreign Literature Communication

3.1 New Media Technology Enriches the Disseminated Foreign Literature

The development of new media has made the content of foreign literature become popular and popularized, and many people are no longer just the main recipients of foreign literature, but have become the "media people" of foreign literature, in this case, the content of foreign literature has also changed. In the traditional media, such as the traditional paper media, are reported by professional journalists after interviewing and printing, and finally appear in front of the reader's eyes, but now due to changes in the communication media, the content of foreign literature has become very diverse, from national events, down to parents, all can become the content of foreign literature to be disseminated. Therefore, the content of communication has become richer and more diversified. Because the new media has brought people unprecedented convenience, the public's ability to accept the new media has become stronger and stronger, thus, the impact on the traditional media is even greater, but the advantage of the new media is that it brings the traditional foreign literature dissemination effect is also better and better. Both men and women, young and old, have felt the great role of new media tools in their lives. It has also changed the whole pattern of foreign literature. Human society cannot be separated from information, and then the dissemination of information cannot be separated from media, so the rapid development of new media can be said to be the requirement of the times [4]. The richness of new media communication lies in the fact that new media greatly enriches the communication environment of foreign literature, the way of foreign literature communication and the dissemination of more foreign literature contents.

Human society is a complex system organization, with various groups, and everyone has complex social relations, so it is also a complex social environment that the new media faces. But its emergence makes foreign literature more convenient and efficient because it has more channels and ways to spread people's ideas and foreign literature. Before the emergence of new media, people never thought that they could transmit their thoughts and values with just a single move of their fingers, and that they could cross the limits of time and space. In the past, literary scholars and artists had to go through various institutions, such as publishing houses, exhibition halls, etc., to disseminate their ideas and show their works, and not only that, their autonomy was also limited. But nowadays, everyone can be a disseminator and can spread information freely on their own initiative, just by posting it on websites or social platforms, and then it can be quickly promoted, and this way of dissemination makes foreign literature more widely available [5].

The new media has broken through the geographical limitation, and the scope of its dissemination is so wide that if they want to spread a certain information, they only need to publish it, without considering the speed and scope of its dissemination, as small as one's "space dynamics", "WeChat" This is a characteristic of the Internet, which is virtual. It can bring people the convenience and special emotion that they cannot enjoy in the real world.

One of the reasons for the speed of development of new media is its unique way of communication and the effect it produces, which is a height that traditional media cannot reach. For example, today's reading is not only limited to paper media, but can also be done through iPad, Kindle and other electronic books or "listening books" (a form of audio reading), and the number of books in the library, the convenience of purchasing books [6], smaller cities of readers are no longer confused by the lack of local bookstore supplies. According to the latest National Reading Survey, the number of digitally read books in China has reached a crescendo and has been rising for eight consecutive years. In 2016, this figure reached 68.2%, an increase compared to the previous year. New media have changed the way people read and the way foreign literature is read. The openness of foreign literature provides good conditions for the use of new media, and this good condition, in turn, has a good impact on the development of foreign literature, through the dissemination of which people perceive things differently, have a broader vision, and do not have a biased understanding of things. However, workers engaged in new media should pay attention to grasp the opportunity to analyze the trend of the development of the times, not to spread randomly, but to take the right way and spread the right content, which is the way to win. This is something that the traditional paper media cannot compare with [7].

There are various ways to disseminate foreign literature, such as interpersonal communication, mass communication and so on, especially interpersonal communication. This is one of the most common forms of communication. In the past, interpersonal communication was limited by technology, so it was not thorough enough, but in the new media environment, Internet technology is developing rapidly, and the ways and means of foreign literature are more advanced, so foreign literature is more effective [8]. A variety of dissemination methods is conducive to promoting the communication and integration between different foreign literature, maintaining the diversity of foreign literature and promoting the diversification of foreign literature.

3.2 New Media Technology Diversify the Way of Communication

New media can take various forms, as long as it invests in digital technology and uses cutting-edge technology, it can be called new media and used for the communication and dissemination of foreign literature. At present, in addition to the Internet, smart phones, outdoor digital electronic large screen advertising are also considered important forms of new media. Especially, the emergence of smart phones and their rapid popularity have greatly increased the activity of mutual communication of foreign literature. In the face of traditional media, people want to communicate and express their opinions, they can only communicate with their friends around them in a limited way, while the emergence of new media makes the dissemination and communication of foreign literature has no such restrictions, and can even communicate across national boundaries, so that everyone can express their views and know the views and opinions of others through new media, which makes foreign literature in the new media environment and This makes foreign literature and communication in the new media environment more active and prosperous than ever before.

The rise of new media has been able to quickly occupy the market and change the media needs of the audience because it has captured the psychology of society at large. The emergence of high-tech means makes people's thinking habits change implicitly, people are becoming more and more "inert" both psychologically and physiologically, and the new media have seized this characteristic and let news appear in people's lives in various forms and ways, such as cell phone clients. According to the survey, more than 83% of the people in today's society will have negative emotions such as panic and anxiety without cell phones [9]. It can be seen that the cell phone has become one of the necessary tools in people's lives, and the emergence of smart phones has further weakened the function of cell phone calls and communications, and receiving information, transmitting information and finding information through clients has become one of the main functions of cell phones, for example, people get knowledge of a professional field through the public number of WeChat's circle of friends, and the top three mobile applications downloaded by cell phones are "Mobile phone WeChat" one [10]. New media has penetrated people's production life in many forms, making people rely on and favor new media far more than traditional media, which is also the rapid development of new media brought by the continuous technological update changes of modern advanced and convenient smart phones, iPads and other mobile communication tools. Smart phones, now almost a handful, also bring great convenience to foreign literature. WeChat clients make everyone have the opportunity to become a media person, and this means of spreading in various forms, such as text, pictures and videos, anytime and anywhere, makes the speed of foreign literature and the cycle of updating foreign literature content greatly shortened, and is a more convenient medium for foreign literature than computer networks.

4 A Platform to Learn a Foreign Literature

4.1 Overall Platform Architecture

On the basis of the analysis of the basic functions of the platform, we carry out the overall architecture of the platform. Because the platform mainly uses J2ME, J2EE and other JAVA technologies, the mobile client is implemented as a MIDlet, which is connected to the WEB server through the wireless network. The Servlet in the WEB layer gets the request information from the mobile client, the relatively simple logic is processed by JavaBean, the complex logic and data access by SQL Server, and then returns the result to the Servlet, which sends the processed result to the client. The client is a variety of mobile smart devices containing MIDP applications, mainly for end-users, providing UI interaction functions and passing user data to the back-end server; MIDP programs can store and process data locally, so they can save network traffic, save bandwidth and reduce latency, thus effectively alleviating the problem of long time and high cost.

The middle layer is isolating the specific details of database connection and management, which provides an I/O interface for the client and an efficient access service for the back-end database server.

From the system architecture, we see that the system follows a typical three-tier architecture, distributing computing resources reasonably among the client, middle tier, and database tier. It makes full use of the computing power of the client, effectively reduces the load on the server, supports the local storage function, reduces the dependence on the network, and realizes offline operation. The middle tier shields the more time-consuming database I/O operations, which improves the operational performance of the client and also effectively improves the access efficiency of the database.

4.2 Platform Development Environment

J2ME is built on top of J2SE, so you need to install J2SE first before developing J2ME.

Install JDK1.6.0 to the E: disk, the directory named E:\ jdk1.6.0_12. Set the Windows XP environment variable: path = ".;E:\ jdk1.6.0_12\bin;"

classpath = ".;E:\jdk1.6.0_12 \lib\dt.jar;E:\jdk1.6.0_12 \lib\tools.jar".

NetBeans is a full-featured open-source Java IDE built by Sun, written entirely in Java, that helps developers write, compile, debug, and deploy Java applications, and incorporates version control and XML editing among its many features. NetBeans supports the creation of J2SE applications, 2-tier Web applications using JSPs and Servlets, and core groups of APIs and software for 2-tier Web applications, making it easier for developers of J2ME applications to track and troubleshoot problems. After downloading the Netbeans IDE6.5 file from the official website, install Netbeans IDE6.5 to E:\ Netbeans IDE6.5 and the installation system will automatically check if the previous JDK installation is correct. After installation, test Netbeans: Start Netbeans, create a new project, select "Sample \javaME(MIDP)", select a sample (for example, select "SUN sample"), follow the Follow the prompts to set up each step, enter the program interface, select "Run" on the project, and the simulator will appear.

4.3 Design and Implementation of the Network Connection

The platform uses a combination of Servlet and SqlServer2000 communication. Two methods in the Servlet, one is doGet(), which is responsible for responding to HttpGet requests; the other is doPost(), which is responsible for responding to HttpPost requests. doGet() or doPost () method is called by the default implementation of the Service() method and passes the request object and response object as parameters to the function. The HTTP workflow between the client and the server is shown in Fig. 2.

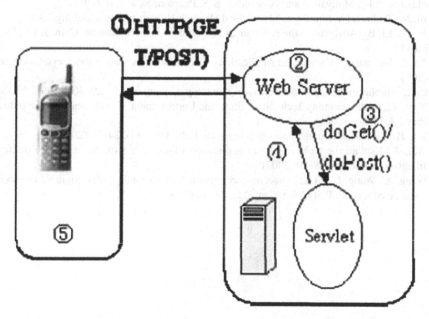

Fig. 2. HTTP workflow between client and server

(1) The client sends a request to the server
(2) The server receives the request from the client
(3) doGet()/doPost() is used to access the Servlet
(4) Servlet responds to the request, calls the database sent to the server, the server sends the content to the client
(5) The client gets the requested content and closes the data stream

5 Conclusion

With the rapid development of Internet technology, the era of new media has also come. Many new media are used in the dissemination of foreign literary works in China. Among them, network communication is one of the most influential and prominent factors. The effective communication between Chinese literature and foreign literature requires the use of new media to achieve effective information. Since new media technology is highly interactive and has a wide audience, foreign literature can better attract readers' attention with its help. Thus, new media technology has a positive effect on the dissemination of foreign literature in China.

References

1. Hu, J.: Analysis on the characteristics and development trends of New Media. J. Beijing Print. Inst. (10), 22–24 (2014)
2. Maslow, A.H.: Motivation and Personality, p. 8. Pearson, New York (1954)
3. Ju, N.: Technical Valtheory, p. 72. National Defense University Press, Beijing (2012)
4. Ju, N., Li, B.: Analysis on the root causes of technical value alienation. Chin. J. (3), 50–53 (2011)
5. Jie, Z.: Streaming Principle and Applications. China Radio and Television Press, Guangzhou (2007)
6. Li, I.: Mobile streaming business review. Contemp. Commun. (15), 29–30 (2005)
7. Yong, L., et al. Streaming Technology Entry and Improvement of. National Defense Industry Press, Arlington (2006)
8. Wu, B.: Mobile streaming application research. Publ. Print. (3), 24–26 (2006)
9. Wei, T.: Explain the technology and application of streaming media in the 3G platform. Jiangsu Commun. **6**, 48–50 (2007)
10. Wang, X., Wang, J.: 3 The impact of G communication technology development on modern distance education. Party Wen Yuan (12), 78–80 (2007)

The Advantages of Introducing Multimedia Technology into College Students' Physical Education

Siyu Zhou[✉] and Shufen Yang

Ministry of Sports, Nanguo Business School, Guangdong University of Foreign Studies and Foreign Trade, Guangdong 510545, China
94158592@qq.com

Abstract. With the development of the times, multimedia technology is playing an increasingly important role in the field of education. Introducing multimedia technology into college physical education teaching has the following advantages. Firstly, multimedia technology can stimulate students' interest in learning. Through visual display methods such as images and videos, physical education knowledge and skills can be presented intuitively, increasing students' interest and participation in physical education teaching. Secondly, multimedia technology is beneficial for improving learning outcomes. Through multimedia display, abstract concepts can be concretized, deepening students' understanding and memory of sports knowledge. Furthermore, multimedia technology can provide richer teaching resources. Through the internet and multimedia software, students can have access to rich teaching materials and cases to enhance their ability to learn independently. In addition, multimedia technology can also provide real-time feedback and evaluation mechanisms, helping teachers timely understand students' learning reactions and development, and providing support for personalized teaching. In summary, introducing multimedia technology into college students' physical education teaching can help stimulate students' interest, improve learning effectiveness, enrich teaching resources, and promote personalized teaching, which is worth promoting and applying.

Keywords: Multimedia technology · Cloud computing · Physical education teaching · advantage

1 Introduction

The purpose of this study is to investigate and compare the impact of students who use multimedia technology (such as video, audio-visual) in physical education class and those who do not use such technology on students' learning outcomes, which are measured by their performance in physical education courses.

In recent years, not only has the emphasis on professional knowledge continuously increased, but students have higher requirements in many aspects such as morality,

Y. Zhang and N. Shah (Eds.): BigIoT-EDU 2023, LNICST 584, pp. 61–71, 2024.
https://doi.org/10.1007/978-3-031-63142-9_6

intelligence, physical fitness, beauty, and labor. In particular, the teaching of physical education in most schools is also constantly being strengthened. Excellent physical education teaching methods can help students relax their psychology and build a strong physique. But this is a very big teaching challenge for physical education teachers. With the development of society, science and technology are also making continuous progress. The teaching methods of physical education teachers are also constantly innovating [1].

Compared with traditional teaching methods, the most obvious effect of multimedia information technology is that it can display sports knowledge more intuitively. In the initial stage of physical education teaching, students' mastery of some sports actions is not complete, so they are easily injured. Teachers can use multimedia information technology to teach and play difficult sports actions in the form of videos, allowing students to observe and accumulate experience before taking action. Through careful analysis of the structure of the human body, the characteristics of muscles, the positions of exertion, and the order of exertion, students can change the teaching method of talking on paper, allowing them to experience practical effects in practice, and making physical education more vivid and intuitive [2]. Traditional oral teaching is relatively simple, and for students, a single language teaching cannot intuitively express the content of physical education teaching.

When students face multimedia teaching equipment, they will gradually transform from listening to what the teacher says in traditional education to thinking about what they want to do and how to do it in the guidance and demonstration of the teacher [3]. This will also be a qualitative leap forward in the concept of sports. Therefore, when students use multimedia teaching methods such as electronic courseware to obtain skill information and complete sports skill actions, they must closely integrate rational thinking and perceptual visual judgment, and complete the learning process with the direct participation of seeing and thinking. This teaching method can fully mobilize the subjective initiative of students, thereby improving their participation and learning interest and awareness. It will achieve twice the result with half the effort for successfully completing learning tasks and familiarizing themselves with skill movements.

It helps students quickly form correct emotional cognition, thereby effectively cultivating sports skills. One of the main tasks of sports courses is to enable students to quickly understand the corresponding sports technology. Students often need to read and understand the dynamic process of related technology to generate a new skill dynamic. The application of multimedia information technology has an important effect on training students' good psychological observation ability, and also has a positive impact on students' rapid formation of correct emotional understanding. In sports courses, there are many sports skills and movements that are not only complex in structure, but also require a series of repetitive skill movements in an instant, such as the air dynamics of track and field high jump events, the coherent dynamics of gymnastics support takeoff, and the roll over of skills. By using multimedia, teachers can help students see the technical details of each moment of action clearly, and they can also explain the skill points of each decomposition action, which greatly improves the classroom effect of animation teaching at the cognitive stage and greatly simplifies the classroom teaching process. The design idea of multimedia physical education curriculum is shown in Fig. 1 below.

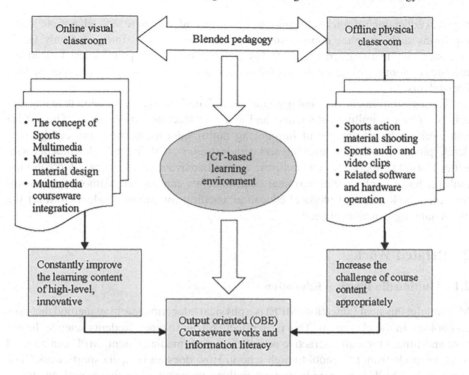

Fig. 1. Curriculum Design Ideas for Multimedia Physical Education Teaching

Introducing multimedia technology in college physical education teaching has many advantages. Firstly, multimedia technology can provide richer and more diverse teaching content. Through various media forms such as images, videos, and audio, students can have a more intuitive understanding of sports techniques, tactics, and rules. This multimedia presentation method can stimulate students' interest and improve their understanding and memory of sports knowledge.

Secondly, multimedia technology can create interactive and dynamic learning environments. By using interactive teaching software and virtual reality technology, students can participate in sports activities, simulate actual competition scenes, and provide real-time feedback and interaction. This interactivity can help students better understand and apply their sports knowledge, jointly solve problems, and explore innovation. At the same time, the dynamic nature of multimedia technology can also increase the fun and attractiveness of learning, enhance students' learning enthusiasm and participation.

In addition, multimedia technology can provide instant feedback and evaluation mechanisms. By collecting and analyzing students' exercise data, video recordings, etc., teachers can accurately evaluate and guide students' performance. This personalized feedback can help students better understand their strengths and improvement directions, and achieve personalized learning and skill enhancement.

Most importantly, multimedia technology can break through the limitations of traditional classrooms and regions, providing flexible learning methods. Students can access physical education resources and guidance anytime and anywhere through remote learning forms such as online courses and video teaching. This flexibility not only facilitates students' learning arrangements, but also expands the scope of access to learning resources, promoting cross-cultural communication and cultivating a global perspective for students.

Through multimedia technology, college students' physical education teaching can achieve a more intuitive, interactive, and dynamic teaching environment. This article will explore the advantages of introducing multimedia technology into college students' physical education teaching and demonstrate how it can provide students with better learning experiences and cultivate comprehensive sports literacy. By combining multimedia technology with physical education, we can further promote the innovation and development of physical education teaching for college students to meet the ever-changing educational needs.

2 Related Work

2.1 Multimedia Physical Education

Multimedia Physical Education (MPE) is a physical education teaching method that uses technology in the classroom. This is an effective way to teach students science, health care and fitness through interactive activities of multimedia content. MPE can be used in every grade from preschool to high school. How does multimedia sports work? The main goal of MPE is to provide students with an interesting learning experience while actively participating in active games and learning.

Multimedia sports refers to the combination of multimedia technology and sports to create a rich and immersive sports experience. Through the application of multimedia technology, audiences can participate and enjoy sports activities in a new way.

In multimedia sports, video playback and live streaming play important roles. Viewers can watch live broadcasts, replays, and highlights of competitions through television, internet video platforms, or mobile applications. Technologies such as high-definition image quality, multi camera angles, and slow motion playback can provide a better viewing experience, helping viewers better understand and appreciate the details and exciting moments in sports.

In addition to video playback, multimedia technology can also provide real-time data statistics and analysis to help viewers have a more comprehensive understanding of the competition situation. For example, real-time score updates, player statistics, tactical analysis, etc. can be presented to the audience through charts, real-time images, and textual information, enhancing their participation and understanding of the game.

In addition, virtual reality (VR) and augmented reality (AR) technologies have also brought new possibilities to multimedia sports. Through wearable devices or mobile applications, viewers can immersively experience competitions or interact with athletes. They can watch games in virtual venues, compete with virtual athletes, or use AR technology to overlay real-time data and images on actual competition venues to enhance the viewing experience.

Multimedia sports provide viewers with richer and more personalized ways to watch sports, and promote the development of the sports industry. By integrating multimedia technology and sports, people can better participate, appreciate, and share the joy of sports.

The schematic diagram of the design concept of "cloud space" in physical education is shown in Fig. 2.

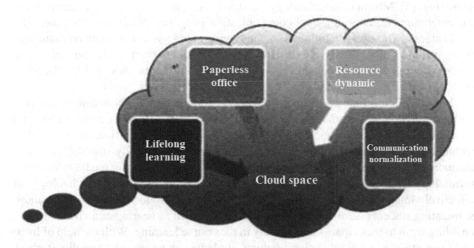

Fig. 2. Schematic diagram of design concept of "cloud space" in Physical Education

Using multimedia technology to integrate text, shapes, images, colors, sound, video, animation, and other features, teachers can quickly present teaching images to students in an intuitive, multi angle, and multi lateral manner; Using the non-linear characteristics of teaching materials and the network organizational structure, teachers can divide the course into units, knowledge points, and other materials. At each knowledge point, they can also use some text, pictures, audio, video, and other materials for analysis and display. They can also achieve mutual transformation through information linking functions, using a large amount of knowledge information, very detailed and vivid to deepen the understanding and memorable nature of teaching content; Using the interesting and real-time characteristics of courseware, teachers can design exercises at a certain knowledge point, enabling students to consolidate and improve in a relaxed and pleasant environment.

Informatized sports classroom is a comprehensive, efficient, three-dimensional sports model. Teachers use multimedia information teaching to greatly enrich teaching methods, and students also have different learning senses. Multimedia information teaching can provide teachers with rich teaching resources, and for students, physical education learning will no longer be affected by time, environment, and other factors. Students can study and exercise whenever they want. Most traditional teaching methods of teachers are based on teaching tasks, ignoring students' learning psychology [4]. The learning effect cannot reach the desired standard. Multimedia information teaching is a new learning and teaching experience for both students and teachers, which can simultaneously improve students' learning efficiency and teachers' teaching methods.

2.2 Multimedia Technology

Multimedia technology is the application of audio, video and computer technology to create multimedia products. The term "multimedia" was first used by IBM in the 1970s to describe a new generation of computers that can display graphics, sound and text at the same time [5]. Multimedia technology has developed into a wide range of applications for entertainment, education and communication purposes. What does this mean for my business? The use of multimedia technology can help your company communicate with customers more effectively than ever before. With the right tools, you can contact potential customers in an engaging way through social media sites such as Facebook [6].

Multimedia information technology has the characteristics of convenience, diversified presentation of information, novelty and order, which is very consistent with the psychological needs of students in the new era. Integrating multimedia information technology with high school physical education teaching can fully stimulate students' autonomy and enthusiasm for physical education learning, and using media information technology will also effectively attract students' attention. Multimedia technology can effectively integrate relevant information resources such as videos, pictures, and audio, stimulating students' senses in multiple dimensions such as hearing and vision, thereby enabling them to participate more actively in the course learning. With the help of lively and interesting physical education teaching, students can understand and digest physical education knowledge, which will effectively improve the teaching effect of physical education courses [7]. From the analysis of traditional physical education teaching, it can be seen that a single teaching method and mode, as well as a low degree of student participation, all lead to unsatisfactory teaching results. Introducing multimedia technology into the curriculum, presenting physical education teaching content in various forms such as illustrations and text, audio and video, as well as careful explanation and intuitive demonstration by teachers, can continuously enhance students' interest in learning and create a better classroom atmosphere, which will motivate students to actively participate in physical training, thereby effectively improving the quality of physical education teaching. For example, during the knowledge teaching process of "track and field sports", high school physical education teachers can use multimedia technology to present diverse track and field sports videos to students, thereby helping them understand the basic concepts of field and track sports. After that, multimedia can be used to display some pictures and action skills of track and field sports, and then guide students to judge field and track sports, To further deepen students' sensory experience and understanding [8]. The application of multimedia technology will stimulate students' better interest in learning, inspire students' thinking through diversified information presentation methods, promote students' effective understanding and digestion of the content learned, and ultimately achieve the development of sports ability.

3   Research on the Advantages of Introducing Multimedia Technology into College Students' Physical Education

Physical education is the practice of sports activities, which can help a person develop and maintain good health. Physical activities can be carried out in many different ways, including sports, dancing, hiking or gardening..Cloud computing is a new way of working. You can use the resources you need anytime, anywhere. This is about using technology as the enabler of your work, not limited by it. All this is to make things easier, faster and more efficient. This means that whenever possible, we can use it to provide services and make our lives easier, just as mobile phones have changed the way we communicate with each other in recent years. Cloud computing offers us these opportunities, but it also gives us the freedom to choose the tools we want to use and how they should be used. The multimedia mixed teaching method is shown in Fig. 3 below.

To carry out physical education teaching, it is necessary to first stimulate students' interest in learning and simply impart theoretical knowledge, which can lead to boring classroom teaching [9]. Combining traditional teaching methods and multimedia technology can better break through the limitations of time and space, and combining pictures and videos. Guide students to understand sports culture through watching sports stories, and to visualize sports spirit through the combination of hearing and vision when watching sports news and major sports events, in order to cultivate students' strong willpower, a spirit of struggle that is not afraid of hardship, and a sense of unity. At the same time, it can also integrate scientific sports knowledge into their growth experience, continuously increasing the scope of students' learning sports knowledge, and helping students develop good habits of balanced diet and scientific fitness.

There is a lot of knowledge in physical education teaching, and physical education teachers in colleges and universities must have certain expertise and knowledge skills. In the process of implementing physical education teaching in the classroom, multimedia technology can be used to assist teaching work, which will have better teaching effects. First, standard demonstration actions. During the teaching process, for the analysis of teaching highlights and difficulties, teachers can choose multimedia technology to demonstrate standard actions, and play slow actions from multiple angles and spaces. This allows students to learn these action essentials according to the videos played by multimedia, and under the guidance of physical education teachers, can better enhance the effectiveness of actual physical education classroom teaching. Second, compare demonstration actions with practice actions to correct errors. Students can improve their motor skills by watching correct demonstrations, recording videos after practice, and playing back and comparing videos to find out the problem [10].

Strengthen and extend classroom content and guide extracurricular exercises. Teachers can upload teaching videos to the multimedia platform to guide students in and after class exercises [11]. When students practice, they can record videos to enable teachers to understand their learning progress and intensity in a timely manner, and better adjust teaching content based on the effects of physical exercises. They can also design teaching methods in a reasonable manner to actively maintain good interaction with students, guide students' extracurricular exercises Monitoring and correct evaluation.

Online teaching can indeed better showcase sports content, including high difficulty and high difficulty movements. In order to ensure that important information in the

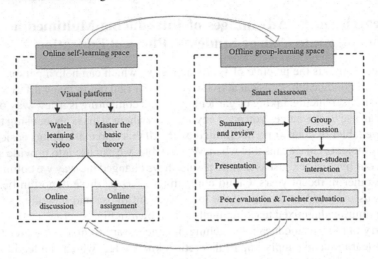

Fig. 3. Multimedia mixed teaching method

school website is not leaked, ordinary university physical education teaching systems can use HTTPS protocol. HTTPS is an HTTP channel that protects website security through encryption and authentication [12].

By using the HTTPS protocol, ordinary university physical education teaching systems can provide a more secure network environment. HTTPS protects the transmission process of data between the client and server by using SSL/TLS encryption protocol. This means that during the transmission process, data will be encrypted, making sensitive information less susceptible to theft or tampering.

In addition, HTTPS also provides authentication functionality to ensure that users establish connections with the correct website [13]. This can prevent malicious attackers from stealing user information by forging websites.

By using the HTTPS protocol, ordinary university physical education teaching systems can improve website security, prevent information leakage, and protect the privacy and data security of teachers and students. The system structure of the school is shown in Fig. 4.

The system structure mainly consists of six parts:

1. Operating system: As the core of the system, you can choose an operating system that is suitable for your needs, such as Windows, Linux, etc. Operating system management and coordination of system resources, providing a stable operating environment.
2. Database system layer: used to store and manage data, providing efficient data access and queries. Common database systems include MySQL, Oracle, MongoDB, etc. [14].
3. Server side: responsible for processing requests and providing services, which can use server software such as IIS, Apache, Nginx, etc. The server mainly processes user requests and coordinates and interacts with other system components for data exchange.

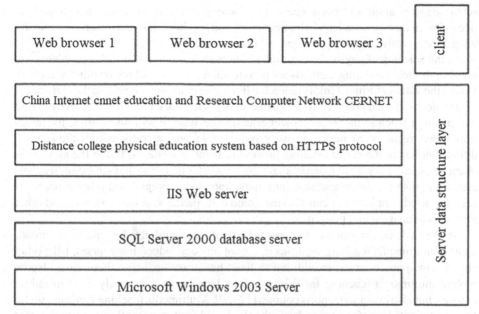

Fig. 4. System structure of College Physical Education Network Education Platform

4. Application service layer: Provides various functions and services, such as user authentication, data processing, data analysis, etc. The application service layer implements the core business logic of the system, providing users with rich functions and interactive experiences [15].
5. Network interaction layer: connecting the system with external networks, including network protocols, API interfaces, etc. Through the network interaction layer, the system can communicate and exchange data with other systems, platforms, and devices.
6. User interface: including user client and user interface design. The user client can be a web page, mobile application, or desktop software, which interacts with the system through the user interface.

The above six parts collaborate with each other to form the overall architecture of the system, providing a reliable operating environment, efficient data management, powerful functions, and a good user experience.

4 Functional Modules of Sports Online Education Platform

Because multimedia teaching information technology can achieve comprehensive application management of multimedia teaching such as text, audio, including video, graphics, images, and animation, teachers should select appropriate multimedia teaching information for classroom teaching when designing multimedia teaching software systems, and set these information contents as classroom teaching elements into different course practice units. In this way, students' characteristics and teachers' abilities can be organically integrated, greatly improving the level of teaching quality [16].

In the teaching of physical education, teachers should first clarify what problems and goals multimedia teaching methods are used to solve, and should not be blindly applied. Due to the various forms of information feedback dissemination available through multimedia means, if used properly, it can enable students to concentrate more, thereby giving the finishing touch to the improvement effect. Otherwise, it will divert students' attention, which requires teachers to visually, multi-angle, and laterally display the key and difficult points in the entire teaching process in front of students; Using the non-linear characteristics of teaching materials and the network organizational structure, teachers can distinguish the entire teaching into units, knowledge points, and other aspects. At each knowledge point, they can also use some text, pictures, sounds, videos, and other materials to analyze and present.

In the basic construction of the campus, attention should also be paid to the investment in multimedia teaching facilities in school physical education courses. Like other courses, in sports courses, in addition to fixed hardware facilities, there must also be mobile multimedia teaching facilities, such as laptops. It is not only used in indoor courses, but also in outdoor sports courses [17–20]. Multimedia teaching facilities are far from sufficient. Therefore, secondary schools should further strengthen their investment in multimedia teaching projects and install appropriate multimedia teaching facilities in response to the current educational situation. Only in this way can they truly use multimedia in sports courses more deeply.

5 Conclusion

This research aims to develop a new physical education teaching method, in which multimedia technology is introduced into the classroom. The purpose of this study is to study the advantages and disadvantages of introducing multimedia technology into college students' physical education. What are the advantages and disadvantages of using multimedia technology in college physical education? Advantages: 1) it will help teachers improve their teaching skills because they can easily access information on any topic they want. This will enable them to enhance their understanding of various disciplines, especially when teaching science related topics, such as anatomy and physiology or other scientific mattes.

References

1. Zhai, X.: The application model of multimedia technology in college physical education (2017)
2. Zhang, F.: The Function of Introducing Multimedia Technology into Badminton Teaching in Colleges and Universities (2018)
3. Guo, Q.: Role of AI physical education based on application of functional sports training. J. Intell. Fuzzy Syst. Appl. Eng. Technol. **40**(2), 3337–3345 (2021)
4. Wang, X.: The application of multimedia and network technology on college physical education (2018)

5. Metwaly, D.: The effects of multimedia computer assisted instruction on learning the swimming basic skills for physical education students (2016)
6. Da-Wei, W.F.: Research and application of multimedia digital platform in the teaching of college physical education course. J. Intell. Fuzzy Syst. Appl. Eng. Technol. **34**(2), 893–901 (2018)
7. Da-Wei, C., Chao, L., Shun, W., et al.: Research and application of multimedia digital platform in the teaching of college physical education course. J. Intell. Fuzzy Syst. **34**(2), 893–901 (2018)
8. Fu, W.: The Integration Mechanism of Multimedia Computer Technology and College English Education (2021)
9. Liu, Y., Chengfu, S.U., Chunyue, H.U., et al.: Research on integrating traditional Chinese medicine into college students' ideological and political education under the new media environment. Chinese Medicine Modern Distance Education of China (2019)
10. Suchyadi, Y., Safitri, N., Sunardi, O.: The use of multimedia as an effort to improve elementary teacher education study program college students' comprehension ability and creative thinking skills in following science study courses. Universitas Pakuan **4**(2), 201–205 (2020)
11. Liu, H.: Research on the Innovation of College Students' Educational Management under the New Media Technology (2019)
12. Sun, M., Wang, B., Hao, R., et al.: Research on college students' ideological education based on computer multimedia (2017)
13. Chen, X.: An improved method for physical education guiding paradigm by using computer assisted multimedia technology. Revista de la Facultad de Ingenieria **32**(9), 166–173 (2017)
14. Yan, W., Hui, S., Cui, X., et al.: The advantages of multimedia technology in the teaching of biochemistry experiment. Modern Commun. (2016)
15. Min, Z.: Research on the effect appraisement of multimedia teaching in physical education classroom based on information platform. Int. J. Eng. Model. **31**(1), 15–22 (2018)
16. Ye, H., Ma, Z., University, Z.: Research on the teaching strategy in college physical education to solve the problem of college students' internet addiction. Bull. Sport Sci. Technol. (2018)
17. Chen, Z.: On the advantages of the chaoshan red culture in establishing college students' core values. Sci. Educ. Article Collects (2016)
18. Liu, R., Zhu, Q.: Research on the implementation of data mining application in multimedia physical education and track and field teaching based on network data. Boletin Tecnico/Tech. Bull. **10**(4), 19–28 (2017)
19. Liang, R.: Analysis of the influence of multimedia network hybrid teaching method on college students learning ability in physical education. Int. J. Contin. Eng. Educ. Life-Long Learn. **29**(1/2), 1 (2019)
20. Huang, R.: Application of multimedia technology in the teaching of physical education in colleges and universities. J. Huaibei Voc. Tech. College (2018)

Construction and Analysis of Dance Teaching System Based on Digital Media Technology

Xiaoxuan Gong[1,2(✉)] and Yanyan Cao[1,2]

[1] Yunnan College of Business Management, Yunnan 650106, China
gongxiaoxian23@163.com
[2] Yan'an University, Yan'an 716000, Shaanxi, China

Abstract. There are many kinds of dances. It is a new problem to organically combine all kinds of dances into a teaching system in dance teaching in Colleges and universities. Based on the digital media technology, this paper constructs a dance teaching program system, which provides a new teaching mode to improve the quality of dance teaching and competitive level.

Keywords: Digital media technology · Dance teaching · System construction

1 Introduction

The dance is rich in content, with its pleasing dancing posture and moving music, which has great attraction to college students and makes college students have a strong desire and enthusiasm for learning. Dance is divided into two categories: modern dance and Latin dance. Modern dance is divided into five types: Waltz, Vienna waltz, tango, trot and Foxtrot. Latin dance is divided into five types: Rumba, Cha Cha, samba, cowboy and bullfight. There are ten kinds of dances in total. How to organically combine these ten kinds of dances to build a dance teaching program system and improve the quality of dance teaching, This puts forward a new topic for dance teachers in Colleges and universities.

2 Digital Media Technology

2.1 Concept of Digital Media

Digital media is a highly integrated interdisciplinary subject of science and art, which is dominated by information science and digital technology, based on mass communication theory and guided by modern art, and applies information communication technology to the fields of culture, art, commerce, education and management. Digital media technology integrates many technologies and creative links, such as computer graphics and images, network technology, communication technology, digital art, digital audio, media interaction, two-dimensional animation, three-dimensional animation,

Y. Zhang and N. Shah (Eds.): BigIoT-EDU 2023, LNICST 584, pp. 72–78, 2024.
https://doi.org/10.1007/978-3-031-63142-9_7

digital video audio processing and so on. Digital media involves a wide range of industries, including film and television, publishing, news, entertainment, games, advertising and other industries, as well as television stations, network companies and other units [1]. Its products include animation, online games, mobile games, digital movies, digital TV, mobile TV, digital publications, digital education and other research institutions. According to a recent research report released by strategy analytics, global digital media revenue will exceed film entertainment revenue for the first time in 2008. In the media industry, the revenue growth from traditional distribution channels will slow down, and the digital media business model will provide crucial growth opportunities for the whole industry. It can be said that the digital media industry is full of opportunities.

2.2 Development of Digital Media Technology

As we all know, the market determines the rise and fall and development future of the industry. In fact, the emergence and rise and fall of each technology are adapted to the degree of economic development at that time. From the perspective of China's situation, national policies, capital flows and attention determine whether the industry can be regularized. Generally speaking, China started relatively late in the field of digital media, but it has developed relatively fast and there is still a lot of room for development. This is not only a progress, but also a breakthrough. All over the country, whether advertising departments or radio and television systems, are making a steady transition to digitization. Therefore, digital media technology belongs to a sunrise industry, which is very promising in the long run. From the current development trend, there will be greater development in the field of digital media. The large space occupied in a wide range of fields such as visual design, product design, advertising design, architectural design, online games, animation, mobile phone value-added, digital television, digital broadcasting, digital film and online media shows that the social demand for digital media technology professionals is growing steadily, The maturity of digital media technology can also promote and promote the better and faster development of China's media industry.

In short, the development prospect of this major is like the emergence of computers ten years ago. It is needed everywhere, but no talents can be found everywhere. It develops very fast. According to the current growth rate of Internet users and the popularity of network media and digital TV in China, this major will have a good employment situation in a few years. However, a good major does not mean a good job. There are many things to learn in this industry, and it is continuous learning, because perhaps today's very high-end production technology has become the basic knowledge popularized by the whole people in five years. Especially in recent years, with the growth of people's demand for animation and other content and the intensification of the demand for highly skilled professionals, it is difficult for Chinese graduates of relevant majors to really meet the needs of enterprises.

2.3 Digitization of Global Life

The world Internet has gone through more than 20 years. Until 2010, the world's total population was 6.9 billion, and the number of Internet users has exceeded 2 billion. With the acceleration of digital processing time and access speed, the improvement of storage capacity, the emergence of high-definition screens and the connection between various electronic devices, global life has entered the digital era. The number of users of Facebook and twitter, the two major social networks in the world, has reached 650 million, the number of video visits to YouTube has reached 2 billion every day, and the number of apps' downloads on smartphones has surged 7.9 billion, of which 71% comes from Apple's online store. Mobile subscription, pay HD TV and broadband services are also developing rapidly, with a total use of more than 6 billion. The consumer groups of smart phones, tablets and video game consoles are growing day by day. People spend more time shuttling through social networking sites than those large portals. Social networks are more localized [2]. The way of watching news and obtaining information is gradually transferred from traditional computers to smartphones and tablets. Looking forward to the future, the market prospect of smart phones is broad, and its development speed will surpass the traditional notebook computers and become the core equipment of people's digital life in the future, which means more mobile phone application development and wider data M2M transmission. The future digital life will be composed of a broader multimedia platform. Logistics will be gradually replaced by download and information flow. The services of cloud technology will enable more devices to achieve seamless connection.

3   Construction and Analysis of Dance Teaching System

3.1   Necessity of Constructing Dance Digital Teaching System

(1) Expand demonstration methods. The traditional dance teaching process is embodied as: demonstration - imitation - display. That is, the teacher first makes demonstration actions, and then the students imitate learning according to the demonstration. Finally, the learning results are displayed under the guidance of the teacher. The first two links, namely "demonstration" and "imitation", are inseparable from the demonstration guidance of teachers. Therefore, the level of teachers' demonstration will directly affect the learning effect of students. The demonstration level of dance teachers is often restricted and affected by age, health, mentality and other factors. The influence of any factor may lead to the inaccuracy of demonstration and bring learning errors. If we use the dance digital teaching system, in the teaching process, the teachers play relevant dance video materials according to the teaching needs, which is like inviting the best dancers to the classroom for demonstration, so that students can see the standard demonstration and accurate action specifications, and then accept the demonstration and explanation of the teachers, Realizing the synchronous influence of multi-point visual perception and action form analysis will greatly improve the effect of dance teaching.

(2) Improve the limitations of self-examination. In the process of traditional dance teaching, students' observation and cognition of their own learning status can only be realized by looking at the mirror. The disadvantages brought by the mirror are: first, students can only see their own plane image, but can not see the complete body shape; Second, due to too much focus on the mirror, resulting in action error. Through the

dance digital teaching system, students' performances can be recorded from different angles in the teaching process and saved digitally. Students can play back and self-examination at any time to help students comprehensively observe and analyze their learning status and correct existing problems in time.

(3) Promote creative practice. Creative practice is an important part of dance teaching. The traditional creative practice is limited by the dual problems of physical technology and thinking ability. Students can only use limited physical skills to approach the infinite action ideal, and often get twice the result with half the effort. Through the dance digital teaching system, whether it is the creation and analysis of movements, or the setting and Deconstruction of the environment, it can be realized through digital technology, so that the realization of imagination in dance creation practice can be infinitely expanded. At the same time, the combination of dance and digital images, as well as the cooperation with various motion acquisition and 3D software, also stimulate the germination of new creative ideas. Some countries in Europe and the United States began to explore the combination of dance and image as early as the 1960s. At the end of the 1990s, moss and kanningham's "hand drawn space" and bill T. Jones's "soul capture" all used the expression of the combination of dance and image, realized the integration of body and virtual image, and effectively promoted the creation and practice of dance.

Today, a large number of performances are using digital technology, which embodies the creative concept of the combination of virtual and real. Through digital technology, the creation and practice of dance can explore new creation and enjoy completely different fun of creation and practice.

3.2   Possible Problems and Solutions in System Construction

(1) The confusion caused by lack of financial resources and talent. Dance digital teaching system can bring many benefits, but the high-end development of digital technology brings the soaring price of digital equipment. The high price of a dance digital teaching system may also deter many dance teaching units. In the face of possible financial constraints, it is very important to formulate a long-term development plan. No system project can be achieved overnight. For several levels that need to be achieved in the dance digital teaching system, formulate a detailed equipment planning scheme, and then promote it step by step in stages and batches [3]. At the same time, to ensure the smooth operation of the dance digital teaching system, we need to train professional technicians to participate in it, and we need to carry out special training for teachers who use the dance digital teaching system. This is not easy, and we need to implement it step by step in a planned way.

(2) The confusion of using dance digital technology. Some people worry that after the adoption of dance digital teaching system, although dance communication extends and expands people's perception by multiple means, it also weakens the imagination and ability to analyze the essence of things of students who lack a positive attitude. Therefore, many people have reservations about the use of dance digital teaching system. But in fact, when the digital dance two-dimensional and imitation three-dimensional world planarizes all dance information, it is also constructing the

diversified field of dance education in another way. In the process of dance digital teaching, it does not deviate from the core proposition of body technology. Only through physical skill training can all information be digested and absorbed, so that dance teaching can move from closed art learning to open life exploration.

4 Construction of Dance Teaching System Based on Digital Media Technology

4.1 Basic Teaching System of Dance Teaching

Different from the previous dance teaching, which is only limited to professional teaching, the dance teaching system theory first takes a strategically advantageous position and pays attention to the overall situation. That is to pay enough attention to the basic teaching system as ecological engineering, environmental engineering and space engineering, and establish its necessary position.

Just as people in modern society pay more and more attention to the purification and optimization of living environment, dance teaching must first pay attention to the basic teaching system and take it as a necessary condition for the whole dance teaching. Specifically, the basic teaching system, a subsystem of dance teaching, mainly includes the following subsystems:

(1) Character system. Including cultivating students' thought, character, morality, character and so on. That is, to achieve both morality and art, to avoid the occurrence of phenomena such as emphasizing specialty over morality and having art without morality, and to get out of the misunderstanding of the lack of Ideological and moral education.
(2) Psychological system. It includes cultivating students' psychological qualities such as learning interest, desire, will, inspiration, emotion and understanding, and improving students' psychological endurance and psychological regulation.
(3) Cultural system. Standing at the height of "big culture" and observing dance teaching, we will fully realize that dance art is bound to be restricted and affected by dance culture, and cultural atmosphere and cultural conditions directly determine the professional level and artistic creativity of dance artists, so we will pay full attention to the creation of cultural heritage and cultural taste in dance teaching, And the construction of dance culture.

4.2 Professional Basic Teaching System of Dance Teaching

The professional basic teaching system of dance teaching belongs to the "foundation engineering system", and is also the "intermediary system", "bridge system" and "link system" between the basic dance teaching system and the professional system. Its schematic diagram is shown in Fig. 1:

Specifically, the subsystem of dance teaching, professional basic teaching system, also includes the following subsystems:

(1) Knowledge system. Including literary knowledge, historical knowledge (Chinese and foreign dance history), artistic knowledge, music knowledge, dance knowledge and so on.

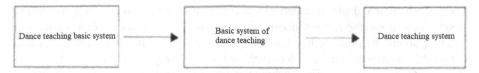

Fig. 1. Sketch of dance teaching system

(2) Capability system. Including literary understanding, artistic perception, dance perception, emotional expression and so on. The ability system should be listed as the core and focus of the basic teaching system of dance teaching specialty, because the great transformation from examination oriented education to quality education is mainly reflected in the transformation from knowledge to ability. The soul of dance teaching is the training and cultivation of dance ability, not just the inheritance, teaching and learning of dance knowledge. It serves the formation of ability. We must always take the cultivation of dance ability as the starting point and destination of dance teaching.

(3) Create systems. Including thinking creativity, artistic creativity, dance creativity, etc. Like all artistic activities, dance art is also an artistic creation project, rather than imitation and learning to walk in Handan. It is not a simple painting of gourds and gourds. We should focus on creation and train students not only to dance, but also to choreograph. Even dancing should be integrated into your own creative thinking and contain your own artistic creativity.

4.3 Professional Teaching System of Dance Teaching

The professional teaching system of dance teaching is the "main engineering system" in the whole dance teaching system, and it is also the most important and key subsystem. Specifically, the professional teaching system of dance teaching can also be divided into the following subsystems:

(1) Teaching policy system: we should cultivate dance talents with all-round development of morality, intelligence and beauty. At the same time, according to the needs of the talent market, we should cultivate compound and generalist dance talents integrating editing, creation, performance, teaching, counseling and theoretical research.

(2) Teaching principle system. We should take humanized teaching as the principle, give full play to students' learning enthusiasm, creativity and subjective initiative, change "want me to learn" into "I want to learn", and truly implement "teachers are the leading and students are the main body" At the same time, the traditional teaching principles of teaching students according to their aptitude, step-by-step, practice first and teaching in fun should also be well inherited and carried forward.

(3) Teaching content system. The teaching content system is not only the carrier and support of the whole dance teaching system, but also an important means and reliable guarantee. The author believes that the reform of the teaching content system of dance teaching is imperative. It is necessary to change the old puppet state of traditional content and replace it with new and dynamic teaching content with large amount

of information and strong update of information, such as women's solo dance The spirit of sparrow, the group dance thousand hands Guanyin, modern dance and street dance should be incorporated into the formal teaching content system as soon as possible, so as to make the dance teaching full of vitality and strong vitality.

(4) Teaching means system. The teaching means system serves to implement the teaching content and achieve the teaching purpose. The means system of the dance teaching system must also be updated in an all-round way, introduce new modern teaching means, such as video tape, CD, disk, multimedia, network and other teaching means, give full play to its convenient and fast advantages, and make the conventional teaching complement each other make the old and new contrast and complement each other.

(5) Teaching evaluation system. Teaching evaluation system is an effective way and way to test teaching effect and achievement. We must strengthen reform, achieve fairness, openness and justice, realize scientific evaluation system and democratic evaluation methods, and abolish the traditional "dictatorship" of one teacher scoring In order to prevent the unhealthy trend of black box operation and disgraceful behind the scenes trading, and return a pure land on the campus and a clear sky on the side of dance art [4].

5 Conclusion

In the process of the rapid growth and rapid development of the digital media industry produced by the integration of digital media, network technology and cultural industry all over the world, the application and development of digital media technology is also extremely rapid, which has become the highlight of the development of information industry and has a very broad prospect. The construction of dance digital teaching system is to combine the traditional dance education mode with advanced digital technology The combination of dance and art will explore a new development path for dance education. After the completion of dance digital teaching system, it will realize the digitization of dance image acquisition and preservation, editing and reproduction, analysis and research, and then realize the digitization of dance communication, arrangement and research. The construction of dance Digital Teaching system can also be expanded to realize dance music acquisition and dance composition The digitization of dance image and music synthesis. Further practice will open a profound unknown field. The active exploration of this field will promote the improvement of dance teaching level and in-depth research, promote the development of dance discipline construction, and promote the further prosperity and development of dance art.

References

1. Zhang, L., Jia, Q.: Application of traditional culture in modern stage art design. Cult. Ind. (09), 332–340 (2021)
2. Xie, C.: Design of dance teaching resource management system based on computer assistance. Mod. Electron. Technol. (16) (2018)
3. Xu, J.: Design and implementation of online dance teaching system. Jiangxi University of Finance and Economics (2018)
4. Chai, W., Liu, X., Lin, Q.: Analysis on the application of folk cultural elements in modern stage art design. Chin. Foreign Entrep. (11) (2020)

Design of Vocal Music Teaching Assistant System Based on Android Technology

Gu Xiao[1,2](✉) and Ying Gao[1,2]

[1] Zaozhuang College, Zaozhuang 277000, Shandong, China
guxiaomusic@163.com
[2] Wuhan Business School, Wuhan 430000, Hubei, China

Abstract. With the continuous progress of mobile devices and network technology, the vocal teaching assistance system based on Android technology has become a promising small-scale application architecture. This article proposes a design scheme for a vocal teaching assistance system based on Android technology. Through the sound processing function provided in the system, students can learn vocal music more comprehensively, meticulously, and scientifically. The main content of this plan includes mobile applications, music instrument laboratories, music libraries, and online explanations. Mobile applications are the core of students' interaction with vocal teaching systems. It provides a controller through the Android platform to send students' recorded sounds and videos to the server, which can help students achieve remote monitoring of the laboratory and exchange audio and video data with data on the server. The music instrument laboratory is where students can perform virtual flipping in the music laboratory after mastering a certain foundation, in order to better utilize the timbre of the sound; Music library is a database for students to learn music; Online explanation is a platform that provides students with online listening guidance. In the design process, the system fully considers the requirements of mobility, scalability, and interactivity. Its main advantages include: 1) Through the internet function of mobile devices, teaching and guidance can be more convenient and fast; 2) The self-learning function of the application can enhance students' enthusiasm and effectiveness in autonomous learning; 3) Adapt to the common problems in current music education and improve the teaching quality and effectiveness of vocal music courses.

Keywords: Vocal music teaching · Android technology · Auxiliary system

1 Introduction

The popularization of mobile learning has also changed the mode of online education. Previously, computer platforms were used for education, but now mobile platforms are used for teaching various skills. Many educational related APP applications have been born. With the advantages of mobile technology products and the Internet, this form can control the place and time of education at any time, and can use sporadic time

© ICST Institute for Computer Sciences, Social Informatics and Telecommunications Engineering 2024
Published by Springer Nature Switzerland AG 2024. All Rights Reserved
Y. Zhang and N. Shah (Eds.): BigIoT-EDU 2023, LNICST 584, pp. 79–89, 2024.
https://doi.org/10.1007/978-3-031-63142-9_8

for teaching at any time. It does not require occupation of work and class time, and acquiring knowledge is flexible [1]. According to APP STORE's statistics on the current situation of the education application market, as of the end of 2017, there have been over 500 education applications on the market, which are a large number of application types besides game applications. Education apps are the carrier of mobile education, with many convenient advertisements. It does demonstrate the practical role of flexible learning [2]. With the increasingly widespread application of intelligent terminal products and services in human daily life, online education accompanied by mobile intelligence is slowly affecting human life. Whether it is higher education, early childhood education, or more high-end popular science education, it can be achieved on the APP, bringing new educational environments and increasing learning interest. This kind of application software about active learning will also guide the new trend of learning [3].

As time enters the 21st century, internet information technology has also entered a new stage. Computer digital products are increasingly inseparable from human daily life. Digital technology is profoundly affecting our lives, both in terms of entertainment and the convenience it brings to our daily lives. It is inseparable from human life. For example, using mobile software to edit various music and other images and videos [4]. They are all familiar functions to us. In addition to using built-in adjustment functions to adjust the system's timbre, sound size, and sound accuracy, music production software can also produce excellent music clips. At present, there are also many phenomena in vocal education and teaching in China that utilize digital technology for music teaching, accompanied by multimedia technology and physics classroom teaching by teachers. Jointly forming vocal teaching. In many music classes, music theory teaching, music vocal teaching, and music composition [5]. It is an important aspect of adopting digital teaching, improving the overall quality of music teaching and expanding the scope of music education. This type of music teaching also meets the needs of most people for music teaching and improves the efficiency of music teaching. And be able to flexibly utilize their spare time, enabling people to improve their autonomy in learning phonetics.

With the gradual development of music education, vocal teaching has gradually become an important component in music education. However, in traditional vocal education, the teaching method is single, the operation is cumbersome, and it is difficult to grasp real-time practice situations during the learning process. With the continuous development of mobile devices and network technology, a vocal teaching assistance system based on Android technology has emerged, aiming to provide vocal learners with a more comprehensive, detailed, and scientific teaching assistance system.

Use mobile intelligent terminals for autonomous learning, especially for vocal autonomous learning application software. In response to this situation, the auxiliary system developed in this article can quickly utilize the resources of the system platform and enrich users' vocal knowledge [6]. Whether it's vocal learners or beginners of vocal courses, students who have undergone professional studies in school, or users who are only interested in vocal music, this is more interesting than traditional teaching courses.

From another perspective, this system has practical significance for autonomous vocal learning, and its functional operations are also applicable to highly professional teachers and students [7].

The purpose of this study is to explore the design of a vocal teaching assistance system based on Android technology, and to improve the effectiveness and quality of vocal teaching by implementing this application. The design of this system is based on Android platform development technology, combined with the characteristics of popular music education, fully utilizing the characteristics and advantages of mobile devices, integrating real-time practice situations and teaching materials into the system platform, thereby better meeting the personalized needs of vocal learners.

At present, the rise of mobile internet and the popularization of intelligent devices have made people's educational needs more precise and professional. The vocal teaching assistance system based on Android technology can take advantage of the characteristics of mobile devices, providing students with more convenient and efficient learning methods. At the same time, it can also provide more music learning resources, providing more choices and convenience for people who need to learn vocal music. The vocal teaching assistance system based on Android technology can provide more comprehensive and detailed listening videos and materials, as well as more professional online discussions and Q&A functions, thereby improving students' self-learning ability and learning effectiveness. In addition, the system can also facilitate teachers to develop courses and arrange teaching plans, improving the efficiency and quality of vocal education.

2 Related Work

2.1 Android Development Environment

When China borrows mobile intelligent products for flexible learning, the most commonly used carrier is mobile application software products. The representative research project is AppBlackboard. This project is the result of a typical school enterprise cooperation research, with the main technical participant being Zhejiang University and the participating enterprise being Blackboard Company. The mobile terminal carrier used in the AppBlackboard project is the iPad, which has received high praise for its excellent operability and good user experience since its inception in 2012. At the beginning of the AppBlackboard project design, the main users were the EMBA student group. The system's function was to send key information to users at any time, and students could use mobile terminals for electronic learning. Through the learning of electronic products, students could communicate and discuss before. Another form is the system software app developed by students on campus as the center user, which was released in Shenzhen in June 2013. Analyzing the functional structure of this app, it is mainly used to address the online reading needs of students and experience the different experiences brought by mobile learning through mobile terminal platforms.

The development of Android technology in this article is based on JAVAEE technology. At present, the development technology of mobile terminals mainly includes two aspects: Android technology and IOS technology, both of which are mature and stable technologies accumulated in the user market for many years. JAVAEE provides two powerful development methods for mobile developers, SDK and NDK. The auxiliary question answering system studied in this article adopts the SDK development method. This development allows you to improve the response method for multithreaded data and provides good excuse support for multi-platform docking. Meanwhile, during the development process, it is possible to effectively parse program code and achieve data validity [8]. During the system development process, use Eclipse for simulation and ADT for rapid program development.

The system development uses the Android system platform to achieve mobile terminal functions. According to the classic Android development architecture, the system architecture is divided into four levels: application, application framework, Libraries, and Android runtime. Both the Android platform and the IOS platform can fully support the JAVAEE protocol and data management protocol used by the system studied in this article, which can well analyze data and can be ported to both platforms for application [9].

The recall rate or is the given by the following formula:

$$Rec = \frac{TP}{TP + FN} \qquad (1)$$

The accuracy the following formula:

$$Prec = \frac{TP}{TP + FP} \qquad (2)$$

FP is a false positive, that is, F-measure is an indicator that combines precision and recall, as shown below:

$$FM = \frac{2 * recall * precision}{recall + precision} \qquad (3)$$

Because F metrics are calculated, as shown below:

$$W - FM = \frac{(F_m N_m) + (F_b, N_b)}{N_m + N_b} \qquad (4)$$

A streaming technology that accomplishes video/audio playback through mobile terminal devices. Therefore, the concept of mobile streaming media relies on mobile terminals and streaming media data transmission protocols. Through mobile streaming media, video/audio files are converted into a specific data packet, which is processed by the server and transmitted to the user through the Internet. The user only needs to perform a simple decompression operation on the data packet to obtain a complete video/audio. The emergence of streaming media technology has made online video playback programming a reality. Moreover, streaming media technology can also cache current files while playing, facilitating users to play them again in the future [10].

In terms of the types of data transmission protocols for mobile streaming media, there are generally two categories: one is that in a prescribed order, and the other is that in accordance with time series, i.e. real-time transmission. The latter needs to meet both the bandwidth requirements of the network and the transmission rate requirements of the hardware.

2.2 Android Platform Architecture

Due to historical reasons, China's informatization started late. As of 2017, China has been struggling on the road of informatization construction. However, with the economy and good policy guidance, China's scientific and technological level is also improving with each passing day. During the 13th Five Year Plan period, China put forward the strategic goal of education informatization, which is the initiative to promote the transformation of the new education model. The birth of the concept of networked teaching in China dates back to the end of the last century. In Shanghai, the economic capital, for the first time, some scholars put forward the view of mobile intelligent teaching. This view is also introduced from the relevant research results of Desmond Keegan. After the concept was put forward, some new research results and applications on mobile teaching emerged in China.

In the Modern Education Center of Peking University, the first mobile education research center in China was established. And gradually started the practice and project construction of mobile teaching. It is precisely because of the promotion of this project that China has continued to establish multimedia mobile teaching project research and CETA mobile website pilot. These off duty items have not been tried before in China, and have also caused topic discussion nationwide. Especially when China's mobile Internet is developing rapidly, the technology level of mobile learning mode is also improving rapidly.

When China borrows mobile intelligent products for flexible learning, mobile application software products are the most used carriers. The representative research project is AppBlackboard. This project is the result of a typical school enterprise cooperation research. Its main technical participant is Zhejiang University, and the participating enterprise is Blackboard. The mobile terminal carrier used in the AppBlackboard project is the iPad. Since its birth in 2012, it has been highly praised for its excellent operability and better user experience. At the beginning of the design of the AppBlackboard project, the main users were EMBA students. The function of the system was to send key information to users at any time. Students could use mobile terminals to learn about electronics, and through learning about electronic products, they could communicate and discuss with students before. Another form is the system software App developed by students in the school as the central user, which was released in Shenzhen in June 2013.

Figure 1 shows the of the Android system.

3 Vocal Music Teaching Assistant System Based on Android Technology

3.1 System Development Objectives

The vocal teaching assistance system based on Android technology is a convenient mobile application that can achieve real-time monitoring and transmission of audio, video, course materials, and online tutoring during the vocal teaching process. A vocal teaching assistance system based on Android technology should have the following objectives.

(1) Response speed

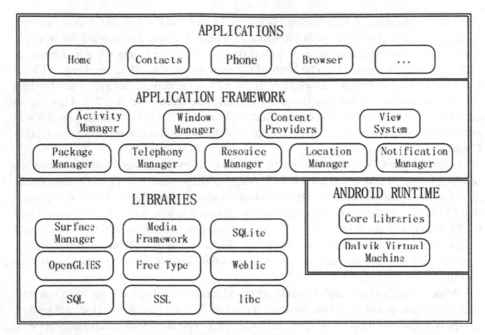

Fig. 1. Android architecture

In the actual server interface of a vocal self-learning assistance system, developers should ensure that the redesign process is fast and not too long, and that the system can provide response response in the shortest possible time when users perform query tasks. In the process of publishing information and data content under network conditions, these resource data should also be protected to ensure the accuracy of the data and information content transmitted to clients. In an online learning system, the following points should be achieved:

Firstly, the system should ensure that the initial response time of the system client interface does not exceed 3 s before transmission;

Secondly, during the transmission process, the system should ensure that the transmission response time of the system server interface does not exceed 5 s;

Finally, when users query information and data, the feedback response time of the system database cannot exceed two seconds.

(2) Scalability

In the auxiliary and operational process developed in this article, it is not only necessary to complete all internal functions of the system, but also to use the most popular information technology to provide solid support for the system, in order to complete the central task of scalability. The specific operating steps are as follows: During the system construction process, developers and designers must first prepare an extension port in advance that can accommodate the addition of new modules. Secondly, develop appropriate functional interfaces for the actual needs of the auxiliary system, so that the system can operate normally and successfully complete the upgrade or update tasks in the later updates.

(3) Provide rich music learning resources

Good music learning resources are a key element for the success of vocal teaching. A vocal teaching assistance system based on Android technology should have rich music resources, including music libraries, audio, video, and other materials, which can be played online or downloaded to mobile devices for learning.

(4) Provide real-time teaching guidance

The vocal music teaching assistance system based on Android technology should support real-time teaching guidance, which can guide online courses, real-time Q&A, and other forms, allowing students to quickly receive help and support from teachers and other classmates in their learning.

(5) Practicality

The first consideration in the development process of the vocal self-learning assistance system is its practical value. Otherwise, the cost of software and development may not be very useful, which will lead to a significant waste of resources. Therefore, when developing a system, it is necessary to ensure that its functionality can fully meet actual business requirements after implementation. Therefore, the practicality of the system requires a deep understanding of the system's business content and processes in the early stages.

(6) Provide teachers with convenient analysis tools

The success of vocal teaching lies not only in the learning of students, but also in the guidance and evaluation of teachers. A vocal teaching assistance system based on Android technology should provide teachers with convenient analysis tools that can track students' learning process and performance, such as homework progress, evaluation reports, etc.

(7) Ease of use and scalability of applications

Vocal education applications based on Android technology need to be user-friendly and scalable. Currently, mobile devices and applications focus on user experience, so they should adopt simple, clear, and user-friendly interfaces and interactive methods. At the same time, it should have scalability and better openness, and be able to expand and modify system architecture, functional integration, and other aspects in the future.

In short, the design goal of a vocal teaching assistance system based on Android technology should be to meet the personalized learning needs of students; Provide rich music learning resources; Provide real-time teaching guidance; Improving the educational effectiveness and quality of vocal education; Provide teachers with convenient analysis tools; Ease of use and scalability of applications. These goals are the key to truly achieving intelligence and optimizing vocal teaching in a vocal teaching assistance system based on Android technology.

3.2 System Architecture Design

The vocal teaching assistance system based on Android technology is an application program that relies on the Android platform, mainly used for real-time monitoring and transmission of vocal teaching. Its architecture design is crucial, and the currently popular architecture design pattern is the MVC (Model View Controller) pattern. The following is the architecture design of a vocal teaching assistance system based on MVC mode. as shown in Fig. 2.

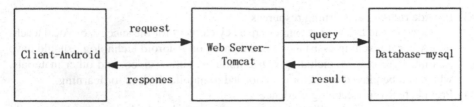

Fig. 2. Framework of Vocal Music Teaching Assistant System

(1) Model layer

The model layer is the basic layer of the vocal education assistance system, mainly responsible for tasks such as sound processing, data storage, and management. In the vocal teaching assistance system, the model layer needs to provide many interfaces for manipulating sound, such as real-time recording, audio playback and editing, real-time processing, and improving sound quality. At the same time, in order to facilitate data management and storage, full consideration should be given to storing data and parameters in local databases for the convenience of system data management and retrieval.

(2) View layer

The view layer is the user interface layer of the vocal education auxiliary system, mainly providing various visual outputs of the application. In this layer, special attention should be paid to the design of user experience and interactive effects, including font color, image size, and the selection of user interaction methods. At the same time, this layer also needs to be responsible for the interaction flow and control of the application program, as well as the responsibility for information transmission and interaction between users and the system.

Let a be the target application and Cat be its category. Let dt be one of the data types under consideration, and let Vdt a ∈ Sa and Vdt Cat ∈ SCat be vectors. The risk estimates for data type dt applications are as follows:

$$\mathcal{DF}^{dt}(a) = \frac{\sum_{i \in V_a} df(V_a^{dt}[i], V_{Cat}^{dt}[i])}{\|V_a^{dt}\|} \tag{5}$$

where df(Vdt a [i], Vdt Cat[i]) is computed as follows:

$$\begin{cases} 1 - WP(V_a^{dt}[i], ccd(V^{dt}[i])) & \text{if } V_a^{dt}[i] = 1, V_{Cat}^{dt}[i] = 0 \\ 0 & \text{otherwise} \end{cases} \tag{6}$$

Let's consider again the signature for app1 and the signature for the entertainment category shown in Fig. 3. According to Example 1, the most recently collected data item with an element set of 1 (i.e., Vmedia app1 [G] = 1) for the frst app1 signature is Node J. Therefore, we calculate the similarity value between Wu and Palmer. Media. tv) as follows:

$$WP(G, J) = \frac{2 \times depth(lca)}{dist(G) + dist(J) + 2 \times depth(lca)} \tag{7}$$

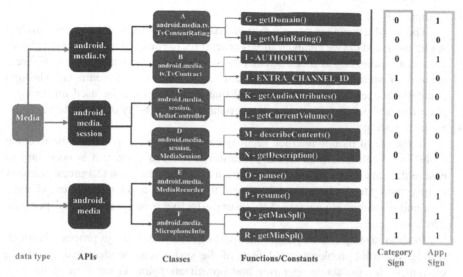

Fig. 3. Part of a data type taxonomy

System users of this functional module can either play online or download files before playing. Generally, it is recommended to choose to download to the local location and play it again to avoid the problem of poor playback caused by network instability. During playback, you can select the playback mode and perform volume adjustment operations.

4 Test Method

After the design of a vocal teaching assistance system based on Android technology is completed, testing is an indispensable part. Through testing, it is possible to verify whether the system meets design requirements and goals, identify potential problems and defects, ensure stable operation of the system, and provide users with a good user experience. During the testing process, the following aspects need to be considered.

(1) Functional testing

   The functional testing of the vocal teaching assistance system mainly includes checking basic functions such as logging in, registering, viewing materials and resources, watching teaching videos, listening to teacher explanations, and conducting online Q&A. Through functional testing, it is possible to verify whether the various functions of the system are functioning properly, meeting design requirements, and setting goals.

(2) Performance testing

   After confirming the normal operation of the system through functional testing, performance testing is very important. Performance testing mainly includes testing the system's response speed, data transmission speed, load testing, and other aspects, aiming to verify whether the system's performance indicators such as running speed, load-bearing performance, and screen resolution meet the requirements, to ensure that the system can still operate stably under high frequency and high load conditions.

(3) Compatibility testing

The vocal teaching assistance system based on Android technology is a mobile application, and device compatibility is crucial for user experience. In compatibility testing, it is necessary to check whether the system can operate normally on different versions of Android platforms, devices, and various network environments. Through compatibility testing, it can be ensured that the system can be used on multiple platforms and devices, improving the popularity and stability of the system.

(4) Security testing

In the era of mobile internet, security has become an important issue in using mobile applications. In the vocal education assistance system, it is necessary to ensure the data security of user information and user education resources. Security testing mainly tests whether the security of the system's login, registration, viewing data and resources is guaranteed to ensure effective protection of users' personal education data.

In short, testing is a very important part of the system design process. Through testing, potential problems and defects of the system can be identified, providing guarantees for the stable operation and optimization implementation of the system. The testing process of the vocal teaching assistance system based on Android technology should also include testing the system's usability, experience, and user satisfaction to ensure that the system can be widely applied and praised among the user group. The test results are as follows:

(1) Functional test results

It can be seen from the function test case in the previous section of this chapter that when a user logs into the system, the system can automatically verify the validity of the data entered by the user according to the security requirements. If no items for the account or password have been read, the user cannot log in to the system. Access is only allowed if all information is entered correctly. The test results indicate that the system has achieved the design objectives.

Then, based on the actual functions of the auxiliary system, corresponding tests were conducted on functional modules such as music theory self-learning management, management, training singing management, training singing video playback management, system rating management, and user management.

The auxiliary display of function test results on the Android system has the ability to support various operations in the functional modules, and the operation results of various functions are consistent with expectations.

(2) Performance test results

The results of this test section indicate that the system requirements can meet the requirement of fast response, which is less than 3 ms. When the user exceeds 150, the system is significantly longer, but it can still be maintained within 6 ms. When the maximum value is 1000, it remains within 9 ms and there is no significant fluctuation in the data tested multiple times.

The above test results indicate that the self-learning assistance system studied meets the user's requirements in terms of functionality and performance, and can be put into normal use.

5   Conclusion

The vocal teaching assistance system based on Android technology is a mobile application designed for the needs of vocal learners, aimed at helping students better learn and master vocal knowledge. The design goal of this system is to meet the personalized learning needs of students, provide rich music learning resources, provide real-time teaching guidance, improve the educational effectiveness and quality of vocal education, provide convenient analysis tools for teachers, and make the application program easy to use and scalable. In the system, it is necessary to provide rich music education resources, such as music libraries, audio, videos, etc., to provide students with more choices and convenience. In addition, the system should also provide real-time teaching guidance to facilitate interaction between students and teachers. In the design of the system, emphasis should be placed on usability and scalability to meet the continuous development and progress of education. In practical applications, vocal teaching assistance systems can improve the educational effectiveness and quality of vocal education, provide learners with richer and more real-time educational services, and improve learning efficiency and teaching experience. With the continuous deepening and popularization of mobile internet consumption and intelligent mobile terminals, the application of voice teaching assistance systems based on Android technology will become more widespread and important. In the future, it is expected to promote more innovation and upgrading of music education methods, better meet the diverse learning needs of students, and improve the quality and level of music education nationwide.

References

1. Dai, D.D.: Design of online music teaching system based on B/S architecture. Sci. Programm. **2021**, 1–6 (2021)
2. Wang, M.: RETRACTED: design of college physical education teaching system based on artificial intelligence technology. J. Phys. Conf. Ser. **1852**(4), 042005 (2021). https://doi.org/10.1088/1742-6596/1852/4/042005
3. Tian, G., Darcy, O.: Study on the design of interactive distance multimedia teaching system based on VR technology. Int. J. Contin. Eng. Educ. Life-Long Learn. **31**(1), 1 (2021)
4. Zhou, H.: Optimization of the rapid design system for arts and crafts based on big data and 3D technology. Complexity **2021**, 1–10 (2021). https://doi.org/10.1155/2021/7906047
5. Li, B., Yang, B., Xiang, F., Guo, J., Li, H.: The source structure design of the rotating magnetic beacon based on phase-shift direction finding system. Sensors **22**(21), 8304 (2022). https://doi.org/10.3390/s22218304
6. Dong, L., Wang, Z.: Design and implementation of an intelligent classroom teaching system for music class based on internet of things. Int. Assoc. Online Eng. (IAOE) **16**(18), 171 (2021)
7. Zhang, J.: Design and implementation of sewage monitoring system based on internet of things technology (2021)
8. Molli, S., Durante, D., Boscagli, G., et al.: Design and performance of a Martian autonomous navigation system based on a smallsat constellation. Acta Astronautica **203**, 112–124 (2023)
9. Nafise, S., Ranjbar, A.A., Gorji, T.B.: Design and implementation of a new portable hybrid solar atmospheric water-generation system. Clean Energy **6**, 6 (2022)
10. Lee, C., Koo, B.-H., Chae, C.-B., Schober, R.: The internet of bio-nano things in blood vessels: system design and prototypes. J. Commun. Netw. **25**(2), 222–231 (2023). https://doi.org/10.23919/JCN.2023.000001

Design and Development of College Aerobics Network Teaching System Based on "Internet+"

Huixing Zhou[✉]

Sports Major, Ningxia Institute of Science and Technology, Ningxia 753000, China
zhouhuixing0729@163.com

Abstract. With the continuous development of Internet technology, the requirements for cultivating and enhancing students' innovative ability are also increasing. This article uses aerobics teaching as a basis for in-depth research, constructing a college aerobics network teaching system, and effectively combines traditional aerobics teaching And diversified teaching modes, in the process of teaching interactive activities integrated inside and outside the aerobics class, realize the network modular teaching mode, and provide an applied teaching mode with a sense of the times. Based on the deepening development of online teaching of aerobics in colleges and universities as the research objective, this paper takes the research and development of online teaching system of aerobics in ordinary colleges and universities as the research object, and adopts research methods such as literature review, investigation, software development, and logical analysis. Based on the investigation, analysis, and research of the existing elite online physical education courses in ordinary universities in China, a large number of documents and books were consulted. According to the actual situation of aerobics teaching, Dreamweaver was used as a website production tool, PHP was used as a scripting language, MySQL was used as a back-end database, and B/S architecture was adopted. WEB services were implemented through Apache, combined with flash, Photoshop Fireworks and other software for the preparation of aerobics network teaching system. A relatively in-depth study was conducted from the design of teaching content, the design and implementation of functional modules, curriculum art design, database design, and other aspects.

Keywords: Colleges And Universities · Aerobics · Diversification · Network Teaching System

1 Introduction

The popularization and application of 5G technology will provide a smoother and higher-definition experience for online video teaching. Virtual reality technology VR will provide learners with immersive learning experience and further enhance the interest and effectiveness of learning. The development of artificial intelligence AI will make personalized recommendation of learning resources more accurate. Emerging technologies

Y. Zhang and N. Shah (Eds.): BigIoT-EDU 2023, LNICST 584, pp. 90–98, 2024.
https://doi.org/10.1007/978-3-031-63142-9_9

such as intelligent assisted teaching robots will provide more diversified and personalized services for teaching and learning. At the same time, with the popularization of lifelong learning concept, the college aerobics network teaching system will not only be limited to students in school, but also attract more people to participate in aerobics learning and exercise. It will play a positive role in promoting the development of national fitnessWith the coming of "Internet+" era, the application of information technology in the field of education is more and more extensive. In order to meet the needs of college students for aerobics learning and promote the digital process of aerobics teaching, this paper aims to explore how to use "Internet+" to build a network teaching system of aerobics in colleges and universities. The system will rely on Internet technology to provide students with a convenient and efficient learning platform, further enrich aerobics teaching resources and improve teaching quality [1–3].

2 Related Work

2.1 Analysis of Network Teaching of Aerobics in Universities

The diversified teaching model of aerobics is based on cultivating students' language and manual skills, creative and organizational teaching skills, appreciation and autonomous learning skills, referee and competition organization skills, and skills to analyze and solve problems [4]. The purpose is to improve students' abilities, based on testing and evaluating teaching effectiveness and quality, with the goal of improving initial teaching, teaching process, and teaching results, fully tap students' personality and creativity, and make them become innovative, complex, and application-oriented aerobic teaching models.

In aerobics teaching, lectures and lectures are combined, guidance and self-learning are combined, traditional teaching and online teaching are combined, comprehensive teaching objectives and targeted teaching objectives are combined, online teaching environment is combined, theoretical teaching and practical teaching are combined, theoretical knowledge and practical ability are combined, and students' independent ability, innovation ability, practical ability, arrangement ability, and teaching ability are strengthened and cultivated Competitive training ability, independent thinking ability, logical thinking ability, and other comprehensive abilities [5].

The evaluation of diversified aerobics teaching uses qualitative and quantitative evaluation methods, based on the basic principles of evaluation between teachers and students, peer teachers, and students. It focuses on the evaluation and feedback of the teaching process and teaching effectiveness, emphasizing the timeliness and authenticity of the evaluation, and the accuracy and importance of information feedback, which will ultimately complete the comprehensive evaluation results of stage evaluation, formative evaluation, and summary evaluation [6, 7].

$$M_i = \prod_{j=1}^{n} a_{ij}, i = 1, 2, \ldots, n \tag{1}$$

Compute the nth root of Mi.

$$\overline{W}_i = \sqrt[n]{M_i} \tag{2}$$

Normalize the vector $\overline{W} = [\overline{W}_1, \overline{W}_2, \dots, \overline{W}_n]^\mathsf{T}$.

$$W_i = \frac{\overline{W}_i}{\sum_{j=1}^n \overline{W}_j} \tag{3}$$

$$\tilde{p}(n, m) = p(n, m) * h(n) = \sum_{L=-N_1}^{N_1} p(n - l, m)h(l) \tag{4}$$

Under the background of "Internet plus", the effective intervention of information technology can help aerobics teachers effectively solve the above problems. College aerobics teachers can use multimedia teaching equipment to present aerobics to students [8]. For the explanation of the "step" technique, aerobics teachers can use multimedia to decompose the step technique, and use the multimedia repeat playback function to show students external skills such as side crossing, step touching, and step sucking. In this process, teachers can also use the multimedia slow down function to present coherent movements to college students in the form of slow shots, ensuring that students truly master movement skills [9]. Under the influence of multimedia videos, college students can not only master various movement skills of aerobics, but also obtain visual enjoyment according to the video presentation method, truly experiencing the special charm of aerobics. This has important value significance in stimulating students' enthusiasm for learning, promoting students to absorb aerobics knowledge, and mastering aerobics sports skills [10].

2.2 Overall Framework Design of Aerobics Network Teaching

The overall framework design of aerobics online teaching is based on the characteristics of aerobics projects and online teaching, and the aerobics online course is divided into six modules for design (see Fig. 1). The modules include login and registration module, course introduction module, learning module, communication and question answering module, exam related module, and knowledge development module. The aerobics course introduction module includes three sub modules: aerobics teaching plan, syllabus, and teacher introduction [11]. The aerobics learning module consists of six sub modules: basic knowledge, basic exercises, routine practice, aerobics creation, technical action scoring standards, and basic quality scoring standards. Communication and Q&A consists of three sub modules: aerobics course announcements, FAQs, discussion forums, short messages, and instant messaging tools. The aerobics examination module consists of two sub modules: theoretical examination and score announcement [12]. Aerobics knowledge development includes three sub modules: related downloads, excellent aerobics website, and excellent aerobics thesis.

Through an understanding of the difficulty of the course, aerobics teachers should appropriately divide the course into multiple modules, allowing students to watch teaching videos in detail through slow playback and playback modes, in order to strengthen their understanding and digestion of difficult movements [13]. In addition, students can also watch simple actions repeatedly and learn from videos to make the actions more standardized and standardized. Secondly, it is beneficial to assist students in correcting incorrect actions in training [14]. In the past, during the development of aerobics teaching activities, aerobics teachers will directly demonstrate aerobics movements to students,

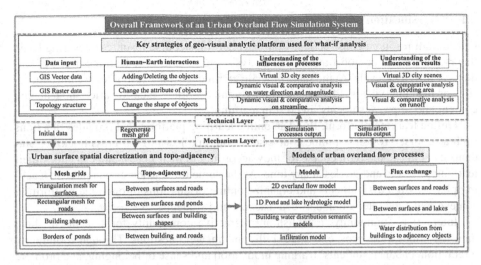

Fig. 1. Overall Framework of Aerobics Network Teaching System

demonstrating and introducing the essentials of movements. In the classroom, students' standing, learning foundation, and understanding abilities are different, so when students learn the same action, they will produce different results [15]. For example, when performing series actions, some students rely on their own senses to perform series actions. In this process, due to the lack of professional knowledge among students, it is difficult to ensure the standardization and correctness of the action series.

3 College Aerobics Network Teaching Design

The diversified aerobics teaching model is composed of six teaching parts: the diversification of classroom teaching, the autonomy of student learning, the diversification of teaching methods, the systematization of teaching practice, the networking of teaching process, and the integration of test scores. As shown in Fig. 2.

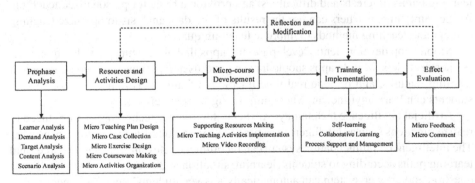

Fig. 2. Network Teaching Mode of Aerobics in Colleges and Universities

3.1 Diversification of Aerobics Classroom Teaching

Curriculum resource construction: Construct aerobics course resources covering basic theory, movement demonstration, skill analysis, etc., to meet the learning needs of students at different levels. At the same time, diversified teaching resources are introduced, such as teaching videos, PPT courseware, graphic tutorials, etc., to enrich the teaching content and improve students' interest in learning.

Online learning platform: Build an online learning platform that provides functions such as course browsing, online course selection, and learning progress tracking. Students can choose the right course to study according to their needs, and can check their learning progress and grades at any time. At the same time, teachers can publish teaching plans, assign assignments and organize online discussions through the platform to achieve real-time interaction between teachers and students.

Interactive Community: Establish an interactive community for students to share their learning experiences, exchange skills, and answer questions. Through community interaction, enhance students' learning motivation and sense of belonging, and promote the sharing and dissemination of knowledge.

Intelligent evaluation system: An intelligent evaluation system is designed to track and evaluate students' online learning in real time. The system can give personalized suggestions according to students' learning progress and grades to help students adjust their learning strategies in time. At the same time, comprehensive teaching feedback is provided to teachers so that they can optimize teaching content and methods.

3.2 Student Learning Autonomy

Cloud computing technology: Leverage the distributed storage and computing capabilities of cloud computing to build an efficient and stable teaching resource management and online learning platform. Through cloud computing technology, the safe storage and rapid processing of data can be realized, and the scalability and availability of the system can be guaranteed.

Big data analysis: Use big data analysis technology to analyze and mine students' learning behaviors. Through the analysis of learning data, we can understand students' learning habits, interests and difficulties, and provide a basis for personalized teaching. At the same time, teachers can use the results of big data analysis to optimize teaching content and teaching methods to improve teaching quality.

Mobile app development: Develop mobile apps that allow students to learn on their phones or tablets. Mobile apps should have a good user experience, provide convenient learning features, and provide real-time interactive features. Through the mobile app, students can learn anytime, anywhere, improving learning efficiency.

Artificial intelligence technology: Artificial intelligence technology is introduced to realize functions such as intelligent recommendation and intelligent question answering. The intelligent recommendation system can recommend relevant learning resources and learning paths according to students' learning situation and interests, and the intelligent question and answer system can automatically answer students' questions encountered in learning to improve students' learning efficiency.

3.3   Networking of Aerobics Teaching Process

Demand analysis: in-depth understanding of the needs of teachers and students in colleges and universities for aerobics online teaching, and clarify the functional positioning and development direction of the system. Through communication with teachers and students, opinions and suggestions are collected to provide a basis for the design and development of the system.

System design: According to the results of demand analysis, design the overall architecture, functional modules and technical implementation scheme of the system. Ensure that the system has characteristics such as stability, scalability, and ease of use. At the same time, formulate corresponding development plans and resource requirements.

Development and implementation: Carry out development work according to the system design scheme. In the development process, pay attention to the standardization and maintainability of the code. Adopt agile development methodologies and develop and test systems in phases to ensure that the results of each phase meet the expected requirements.

Testing & Optimization: Conduct comprehensive testing of the developed system, including functional testing, performance testing, and security testing. According to the test results, the system is optimized and improved to ensure the stability and reliability of the system. At the same time, user feedback is collected to further improve the functionality and user experience of the system.

Deployment and maintenance: Deploy the optimized system to the production environment to ensure the normal operation and service quality of the system.

4   Research on the Construction of Diversified College Aerobics Teaching Network System

4.1   The Design Process of the Network Teaching System

10 evaluation item indicators can be set, and 7 levels are used to evaluate students' aerobics learning achievements. The 10 evaluation items include: aerobics skills homework, autonomous learning, autonomous learning ability assessment, class and class Offline learning attitude, online and offline learning attitude, attendance, teaching ability assessment, creative ability test, level complete set of action assessment, open and closed book test. The 7 level assessment indicators include: A+, A−, B+, B−, C+, C−, D. Teachers pass the 10 item scores of the evaluation system, and finally score an average score for students learning aerobics courses, and objectively and comprehensively evaluate the learning results of students' aerobics courses. The evaluation system of this system is scientific and open. It can feed back effective information from students' learning in time, and can realize the integration and automation level of evaluation, data collection, sorting and analysis.

4.2   Design of Aerobics Network Teaching System Module in Colleges and Universities

According to the educational goals, the construction of aerobics network teaching system in colleges and universities includes five basic modules: data module, teaching module, expansion module, evaluation module and communication module. Under these 5 modules, theoretical knowledge, teaching videos, and teaching files are set up respectively., Video zone, music zone, picture zone, text zone, innovation ability, fitness zone, communication and interaction, teacher evaluation and mutual evaluation between teachers and students, and 12 sub-modules (see Fig. 3).

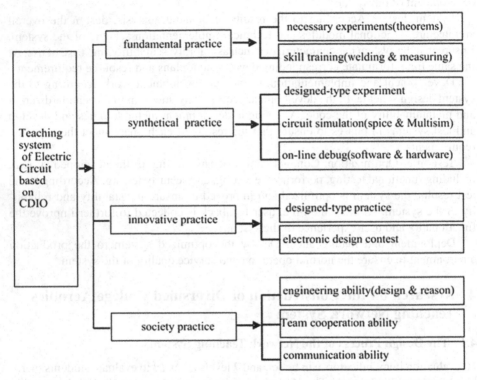

Fig. 3. The construction of aerobics network teaching system in colleges and universities

The evaluation module includes two parts: teacher evaluation and mutual evaluation between teachers and students and students: ① The teacher makes an objective and fair evaluation of students' attendance, open and closed paper exams, homework and task completion and level complete set of action exams, that is, outcome evaluation. ② In-class and out-of-class learning attitude, online and offline learning attitude, autonomous learning ability, autonomous learning, teaching ability and creative ability the mutual evaluation method between teachers, students and students is a process evaluation; such an evaluation the system not only pays attention to the importance of students' learning process and learning results, but also better guarantees the quality of teaching and teaching effect.

5 Conclusion

The construction of aerobics network teaching system in colleges and universities is based on the application-oriented teaching combining traditional aerobics teaching and network teaching system, which reflects the guiding ideology of "the combination of the leading and the main body", and is based on a good integrated teaching interactive activity inside and outside the class Process, realize the network modularized teaching mode, and provide an applied teaching mode with a sense of the times. The teaching and learning process of aerobics network resources has many advantages, but there are also some shortcomings. The teaching application research of network courses still lacks the guidance of systematic and complete scientific research methods, and the design process of network courses is due to the teachers' own information technology skills. The shortcomings still need the help and support of professionals.

References

1. Li, P., Zhang, H., Tsai, S.B.: A new online and offline blended teaching system of college English based on computer internet technology. Math. Probl. Eng. Theory Methods Appl. **2021**(2021-Pt.50), 1–12 (2021)
2. Ma, H.: Design of Chinese linguistics teaching system based on K-means clustering algorithm. In: Xu, Z., et al. (eds.) CSIA 2022. LNDECT, vol. 123, pp. 424–431. Springer, Cham (2022). https://doi.org/10.1007/978-3-030-96908-0_53
3. Nie, A.: Design of English interactive teaching system based on association rules algorithm. Secur. Commun. Netw. **2021**, 1–10 (2021). https://doi.org/10.1155/2021/9275363
4. Yuan, X.: Design of college English teaching information platform based on artificial intelligence technology. J. Phys. Conf. Ser. **1852**(2), 022031 (2021)
5. Ma, C.: Design and practice of aerobics teaching design based on data fusion algorithm. Wirel. Commun. Mob. Comput. **2022**, 1–14 (2022). https://doi.org/10.1155/2022/1275508
6. Liu, M.: Piano playing teaching system based on artificial intelligence - design and research. J. Intell. Fuzzy Syst. Appl. Eng. Technol. **40**(2), 3525–3533 (2021)
7. Shao, J., Li, X.: Design of distance learning system for dance movement based on wireless network communication technology. J. Interconnect. Netw. **22** (2022)
8. Huang, Q., Wang, F.: Design method of aerobics teaching assistant platform based on 5G technology. In: Sugumaran, V., Zheng, X., Zhou, H. (eds.) MMIA 2020, vol. 2, pp. 75–81. Springer, Cham (2021). https://doi.org/10.1007/978-3-030-51556-0_12
9. Wang, L.: The design and implementation of the university network education information monitoring system based on big data technology. In: Pei, Y., Chang, J.W., Hung, J.C. (eds.) IC 2022. LNEE, vol. 935, pp. 201–207. Springer, Singapore (2022). https://doi.org/10.1007/978-981-19-4132-0_23
10. Aju, W.: Design and implementation of key modules of English teaching system based on J2EE. In: Jan, M.A., Khan, F. (eds.) MIND 2022. CCIS, pp. 37–45. Springer, Cham (2023). https://doi.org/10.1007/978-3-031-23950-2_5
11. Wu, X.: Design of Taijiquan multimedia distance teaching system based on ASP technology. In: Jan, M.A., Khan, F. (eds.) BigIoT-EDU 2022. LNICS, SITE, vol. 466, pp. 146–155. Springer, Cham (2023). https://doi.org/10.1007/978-3-031-23947-2_16
12. Wang, J.: Research on college English teaching system based on computer big data. J. Phys. Conf. Ser. **1865**(4), 042141 (2021). (10pp)

13. Mao, Y.: Design of calisthenics choreography and recording system based on action recognition algorithm. In: Liu, S., Ma, X. (eds.) ADHIP 2021. LNICS, SITE, vol. 416, pp. 186–193. Springer, Cham (2022). https://doi.org/10.1007/978-3-031-24367-7_19

14. Liu, Y., Huang, Z.: Recognition of aerobics movement posture based on multisensor movement monitoring. In: Liu, S., Ma, X. (eds.) ADHIP 2021. LNICSSITE, vol. 416, pp. 167–178. Springer, Cham (2022). https://doi.org/10.1007/978-3-030-94551-0_14

15. Wang, S., Zhang, H., Meng, X.: Design of video teaching system based on virtual reality technology. Electron. Sci. Technol. Appl. 7(4), 72 (2021)

Research on the Application of Internet+In Environmental Design Teaching

Dong Lina$^{(\boxtimes)}$, Luo Kunming, and Feng Weizhou

Jiangxi Vocational College of Tourism and Business, Jiangxi Province,
Nanchang City 330100, China
36003413@jxlsxy.edu.cn

Abstract. While Internet technology has changed people's lives, it has also had a profound impact on the evaluation of environmental design teaching. The evaluation tools used for traditional environmental design teaching evaluation are limited to offline paper versions, while the rapid development of the Internet has caused a subversive change in the evaluation methods of environmental design teaching. The appearance of online environmental design teaching evaluation and digital curriculum quality evaluation has enriched the evaluation methods of environmental design teaching. Teachers and students face the problem of how to correctly evaluate the teaching of environmental design through the school's independent campus intelligent education platform, WeChat official account, online education platform and other network interactive environmental design teaching. Therefore, in the "Internet+Education" environment, how to make a scientific and reasonable evaluation of these emerging environmental design classroom teaching and integrate them into the environmental design teaching evaluation system is a problem worth discussing. This paper adopts the methods of literature, case analysis, interview and comparative analysis to explore the form of environmental design teaching evaluation under the environment of "Internet+education".

Keywords: Internet+ · Environmental design · Teaching research

1 Introduction

Since entering the new century, with the rapid change of science and technology, Internet technology has penetrated into all aspects of the economy and society, and the Internet has gradually developed into an important hub to promote global economic development and social and environmental progress. "Internet+Environmental Design Teaching Evaluation" is a product of the times.

Environmental art design originates from interior design, which is an independent major and began to teach in the world in the middle of last century. Environmental art design is a complex subject with strong practicability and great market demand. Therefore, how to improve the education level of this major is crucial [1]. It is necessary to reconcile with the bottom of the market, find out the investigation and research points

Y. Zhang and N. Shah (Eds.): BigIoT-EDU 2023, LNICST 584, pp. 99–109, 2024.
https://doi.org/10.1007/978-3-031-63142-9_10

in the environmental design education system itself, and establish a fairly perfect new model and control system. In view of the problems described above, it is necessary to develop a teaching and evaluation system of universal value.

The concept of "Internet+" is fully used in the application of environmental design teaching evaluation form, constantly playing the intelligent role of intelligence, data integration and sorting [2]. The concept of "Internet+" has become more and more popular. Combining different fields of education with new Internet achievements, and exploring new forms of environmental design teaching evaluation will help to continuously enhance the quality of environmental design teaching evaluation forms, and form a new development trend of the application of environmental design teaching evaluation forms under the network environment [3].

The teaching system and research methods of environmental art in China were actually introduced from the West and focused on interior decoration design around 1980. After being introduced into China, Chinese educators and artists have been named "environmental art" based on social needs and professional development directions. And it integrates teaching content related to landscape architecture, urban planning, geographic information, ergonomics, and even architecture, interweaving and evolving into an environmental construction activity related to people and space [4]. In the decades from the introduction to the subsequent development, environmental art has only derived from the design teaching content, but the specific teaching implementation and academic research are still the integration of the names of relevant disciplines under the western knowledge system. Although it still absorbs the essence and develops independently into a professional discipline, the theoretical research of environmental design is relatively separate, and only landscape architecture, urban planning Relevant theories such as civil engineering have been transformed, and some even remain at the surface of design activities. The boundaries between disciplines are relatively unclear, and most of the research results are still copied from the West. This has also led to the perception by outsiders that environmental art is only a abridged version of other disciplines [5]. At the same time, these disciplines are also ambiguous in the domestic education system. Through this paper, the author hopes to conduct research on the development of environmental design education in the context of the digital media era, based on the understanding and achievements of predecessors in this field, and combining his own learning curriculum and teaching theory perspective. The current research situation in foreign countries began as early as the early 20th century, and European scholars and artists have continuously deepened their exploration of the mode of art education, which has also prompted researchers to expand the scope of the object of art research. At this time, art is not confined to the form of space and separation. For example, the walls integrated into the overall building and the alleyways formed by the city have slowly begun to form an action of integrating art and design, resulting in the environment becoming art. In foreign countries, artistic concepts have been discussed and become an open system. However, in the Western teaching system, the attitude towards things is a nodal and segmented approach, and the study of environmental art is still a conceptual fusion of architectural art, landscape architecture, ceramic art, and public art. However, it does not incorporate educational practice into comprehensive research, but only focuses on the promotion of environmental aesthetics at the philosophical level [6]. Some Western scholars have also attempted to integrate aesthetics with ergonomics, and although they have achieved some good results, environmental art in practice is still an interdisciplinary discipline in comprehensive practice. Therefore, exploring the details of the turning point in the localization of environmental design education is of practical significance in the field of environmental art.

2 Related Work

2.1 Research on Internet plus Environment Design Teaching System

Internet+education has achieved a series of changes, including not only the transformation of the educational environment from "intervention means" to "teaching ecology", but also the gradual transformation of curriculum teaching from closed to open and integrated, from "traditional closed" teaching to "semi open connected" flipped classroom teaching and the reform of socialized and self-organized open curriculum teaching; At the same time, it includes the transformation from knowledge construction to core quality cultivation, from teacher centered to student centered, from individual learning to group construction, from direct teaching to independent discovery, and from multimedia demonstration to exploration tools [7]. Internet+ promotes educational innovation, which not only reconstructs traditional social relations, subverts the basic structure of traditional schools, combines the characteristics of the Internet, such as development, sharing, equality and freedom, with the essential laws of education and teaching, and forms a re positioning and thinking of learners, courses, schools, educational policies, mechanisms and systems and other relevant factors [8].

All the majors we college students study need to be developed and adjusted with the progress of the times, because the purpose of the university is to cultivate many technical talents who can contribute to the times. The same is true of the environmental design major, which attaches great importance to keeping pace with the times and applies a famous saying: everything in the world is changing [9]. Therefore, in order to establish a relatively stable model, we can serve the times and the market for a longer time, which makes the new model meaningful in the new era.

It's like installing cameras in the classroom to monitor students' learning. In a professional teaching, teachers need to timely understand the content of each link of teaching, and through collection and analysis, understand what needs to be improved, including curriculum content, learning plan, teacher work, student learning, etc. So as to judge its origin and find out the solution [5]. Through this comprehensive evaluation system, we can explain the reason why students lack the ability of design innovation, and enable teachers to guide students more specifically. If students can often be fed back their learning achievements, they will be encouraged and satisfied psychologically, which can stimulate their enthusiasm for progress [10]. At the same time, it can also supervise and urge teachers.

The cybernetics gives the definition of control: to improve the development of a controlled object by obtaining the required use information. This information based function used on the object is called control. It can be concluded that control needs information as the basis, and control feedback its effect through information. Figure 1 below shows the teaching system of environmental design.

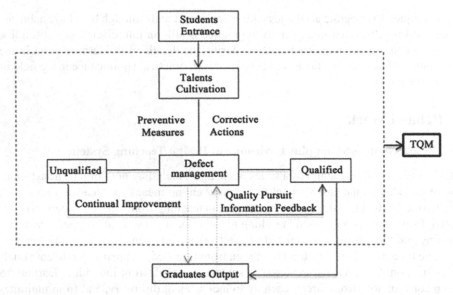

Fig. 1. Environmental Design Teaching System

Since it is a control system, just as the state needs to be controlled by the government, the system also needs to be controlled by institutions. The nature of the company is the same [11]. There are superiors, employees, judges, etc. Everyone can represent different environmental art design practice organizations in China, so that many horticultural materials in China can be well mastered, and then through the division of labor and cooperation within the organization, such as who formulates standards, who raises funds, who is responsible for review, who is responsible for implementation, and so on. Managing this control system in the form of a company can change the teaching situation again and again according to the market demand, and improve the social status of the profession.

2.2 Prospects for the Development of Internet Technology in Teaching

Environmental design is a major that discusses the integration and artistic composition of spaces within and outside buildings. In the past, environmental design teaching has tended to focus on the understanding and mastery of design performance and construction techniques. The Internet teaching model of "BIM + VR" focuses on how to make environmental design in the Internet era an integrated form that is both an output port and the most advanced port through information digitization, data modularization, and standardized design. This is also the core idea for forming the teaching curriculum system of environmental design in the Internet era [12].

The application of the "BIM + VR" model in the teaching practice of environmental design majors can fully realize the practicality of teaching. In the process of teaching practice, those who do not leave home can truly feel how people exist in the environment and space in the design, to what extent, proportion, and type of materials, and many subtle experiences in the design process can be unified through the "BIM + VR" Immersive and experiential to create a true feeling. Fully experienced the aesthetics of design, the essence and process of design, and also enhanced the interactive experience with people during the design process [13].

StyleGAN successfully applied Adaptive Instance Normalization (AdaIN) to a progressive generation model that distributes features to potential variables. Inspired by this, we have introduced several ARBs to finely reconstruct body components, using AdaIN to reconstruct the spatial distribution information of semantic maps and the content information of component images. AdaIN is calculated as:

$$\text{AdaIN}(x, y) = \gamma(y)\left(\frac{x - \mu(x)}{\sigma(x)}\right) + \mu(y) \tag{1}$$

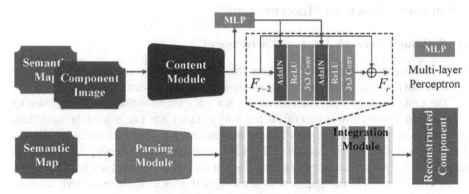

Fig. 2. SMIAN Structure Overview

As shown in Fig. 2, the feature processing operations in the entire Internet teaching can be defined as:

$$F_{r-1}^{\text{mid}} = \phi_{r-2}\sigma_{r-2}\text{AdaIN}(F_{r-2}, F_m) \tag{2}$$

$$F_r^* = \phi_{r-1}\sigma_{r-1}\text{AdaIN}(F_{r-1}^{\text{mid}}, F_m) \tag{3}$$

After the standard ResNet block, a skip connection structure has been added for merging input and output feature maps using:

$$F_r = F_{r-2} + F_r^* \tag{4}$$

"BIM + VR" applied to the teaching of environmental design will be a brand new teaching mode. With a realistic interactive interface, the virtual interactive learning mode is close to the real display of teaching details that could not have been directly observed in the form of stereoscopic visual sensory effects and autonomous control interaction [14]. Through "BIM + VR", students can participate in the learning process from multiple dimensions such as a brand new design thinking, emotion, and behavior mode. "BIM + VR" The teaching model is also more suitable for the demands of future social development.

In the Internet era, How to Develop "BIM + VR at a High Speed" "Making it a leading teaching system and development model will definitely become the core issue of environmental design education and teaching. At the same time, while deeply promoting innovation in the education and teaching development of environmental design in the Internet era, we will build a new Internet-based, structural, and forward-looking design and teaching information supply system, strengthen the leading role of innovation in the transformation and upgrading of environmental design teaching, and achieve the transformation of environmental design teaching model in the Internet era." Type upgrade [15].

3 Reconstruction of Teaching Methods of Environmental Design Specialty Based on "Internet plus"

3.1 Building a Network Teaching Environment

Driven by Internet thinking and technology, the original teaching environment and teaching mode can no longer meet the current needs of massive knowledge teaching and learning. The emergence of new teaching modes not only changes the process of learning and teaching, but also turns part of the teaching content into extracurricular activities, making the classroom more a place to help students answer questions and solve doubts. Moreover, with the changes in students' learning methods such as learning first after class and flexible learning time, static teaching content and teaching methods have also been greatly challenged. The development of teaching activities that aim to achieve teaching goals is no longer limited to fixed class hours and classroom spaces, but extends to more diverse time, space, and online media as students' learning styles change.

In order to overcome excessive distortion, we introduce a sampling interval consistency loss Lsic in GMN to limit the spacing between sampling points; It is given by the following formula:

$$\mathcal{L}_{\text{sic}}(\widehat{G}_x, \widehat{G}_y) = \sum_{i=-1,1} \sum_x \sum_y | \widehat{G}_x(x+i, y) - \widehat{G}_x(x, y) | \tag{5}$$

The teaching environment of teachers and the learning environment of students are no longer completely overlapping, but developing towards a new teaching environment built by artificial intelligence technologies such as virtual reality and augmented reality. Therefore, using modern virtual environment and educational technology to build a network teaching environment and a cloud service platform, to achieve in-depth communication and interaction between teachers and students in teaching, optimize the teaching process, improve teaching effectiveness, and reconstruct the teaching method of environmental design specialty. It is not only a means for the environmental design specialty to keep pace with the times and constantly optimize the education and teaching environment in the "Internet plus" era, but also based on the "Internet plus" thinking, The direct embodiment of the "student centered" teaching method is shown in Fig. 3.

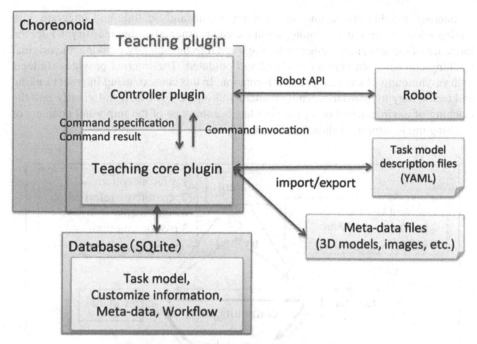

Fig. 3. Network Teaching Environment

3.2 Accelerate the Role Transformation Between Teachers and Students

The existing teaching of environmental design majors mainly focuses on "The disadvantage of teaching with a master and apprentice model is that it ignores the interest and awareness of students in active learning. The maturity of Internet thinking and technology has enabled college teachers to rethink the role of teachers and students in teaching and learning from a student oriented perspective while reexamining the teaching environment, providing a driving force for the deepening of teaching reform and accelerating the transformation of the roles of teachers and students in teaching." The numerous open education platforms on the Internet provide far richer teaching resources than teachers' classroom teaching; On the other hand, students can obtain learning resources anytime and anywhere according to their own needs, and can learn according to their own plans and importance. Teachers are more likely to act as guides for students' learning directions and answer learning questions. Students are both the subject of learning and the subject of teaching. In the process of role transformation, although the role of teachers has been weakened, students' enthusiasm, initiative, and creativity in the learning process have been stimulated.

3.3 Teaching Content

The establishment of teaching content for environmental design majors is determined based on the requirements of industry development for talent capabilities. The current stage is an era of "Internet of Everything", with the continuous expansion and extension of Internet thinking and technology, making it constantly collide and integrate with cutting-edge concepts and technologies in the environmental design industry. Under the influence of modern cutting-edge technology and interdisciplinary thinking, the original teaching content often appears outdated and outdated. The Internet provides students with vast amounts of knowledge and information. In this context, using Internet thinking and technology to innovate teaching content and inject new blood and vitality into the teaching of environmental design majors has become one of the important contents of teaching mode reform, as shown in Fig. 4.

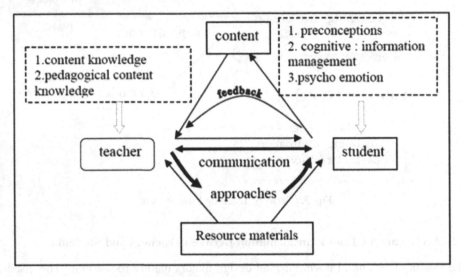

Fig. 4. Teaching Content of Environmental Design

According to a survey of the ability needs of existing industries, it is found that while the requirements for students' practical abilities are increasing, they also need to have a lifelong and continuous learning ability to cope with possible problems in the work process. The changes in students' learning styles have shown that using the Internet and modern information technology, open resources can be obtained to ensure their continuous exploration of problem-solving methods. Therefore, innovating teaching content and cultivating students' habits and awareness of lifelong learning is a beneficial teaching model to meet the needs of social industries.

4   Research on the Application of Internet+In the Teaching of Environmental Design

Although the development of the new curriculum reform continues to deepen, the transition period from theory to practice of curriculum teaching mode and various aspects related to environmental design teaching still needs a long time. The limitations of teaching evaluation doomed the teaching effect of environmental design to run counter to the original intention of the new curriculum reform.

Under the influence of the traditional teaching form of environmental design, students can usually only accept the assessment of environmental design teaching within the specified time limit and in the specified site. More often, teachers will require the assessed objects to take the completion of the task under the unified standard as the basis for evaluation, so as to carry out on-site paper registration and evaluation of relevant scores, and then input them into the computer system. For students with a slightly poor foundation in environmental design, if they cannot reach the unified standard or have just reached the standard, they are likely to have a sense of gap in their psychology, unable to give play to what they are good at, and unable to meet their internal requirements.

The evaluation of traditional environmental design is made by a special environmental design teacher, including the specified time limit, designated items, unified standards, etc. of the evaluation requirements. All evaluation objects can be regarded as having completed the evaluation only if they have completed the designated evaluation items within the time limit set by the evaluator. In this case, students only regard the completion of the assessment as a task, but do not care about the quality of the task. This is because the teachers did not mobilize the students' autonomy and enthusiasm for learning, and the students' sense of subjectivity was weak. The examination was conducted to complete the task, resulting in poor evaluation results and unsatisfactory results. The details are as follows:

(1) The subject of evaluation is not clear enough: in the traditional teaching of environmental design, the only value evaluation standard in the teaching process of environmental design is usually a number of charts with specific evaluation criteria, detailed statistical charts and other charts. However, few evaluation criteria have been formulated for the contribution of the evaluation object in the teaching process of environmental design, as well as the development and change of psychology, students' specialty and ability, and hobbies, which weaken the role of environmental design teaching evaluation in these aspects. It is not conducive to the development and cultivation of students' autonomous learning environment design skills and sports expertise.

(2) The traditional teaching goal setting of environmental design is relatively rigid: the teaching goal of environmental design is a measurement index of environmental design teaching evaluation. The goal setting of modern environmental design teaching must be error free, objective and scientific. The goal setting of different age groups of students should also be differentiated. The clock should focus on different aspects of students' body, mind, and social interaction. The content of traditional environmental design teaching goal setting is more about the convenience of operation. The organizational form of environmental design teaching does not reflect the students' subjective consciousness, and relatively lacks the emphasis on individual differences.

(3) The traditional teaching evaluation process of environmental design is easy to ignore the process: in the past, the most common traditional teaching evaluation process of environmental design is easy to ignore the process characteristics of students. The past evaluation process of environmental design teaching has the following shortcomings: First, the description of the evaluation results is too qualitative and lacks innovation. Second, the teaching process of environmental design is more focused

on quantitative evaluation, lacking consideration of students' personalized development. Third, in different teaching links of environmental design, the unified rules of standards are implemented, lacking guidance and giving full play to students' autonomy. The above contents are all related defects existing in the past environmental design teaching evaluation process, which cannot meet the requirements of modern environmental design teaching evaluation in terms of keeping the results objective, respecting the scientific laws of the process, and considering the development of students comprehensively. Therefore, the validity of the evaluation results generated in the past environmental design teaching evaluation process is difficult to be convincing.

In the era of the Internet, the application of Internet technology itself in environmental design teaching has also become a key component that cannot be ignored. In the face of the continuation and continuous development of traditional Chinese aesthetic thinking, environmental design education still needs to face the rapid development of the times, the international evolution of design education, and cultural soft landing, and many other demands. The old environmental design education model is gradually unable to meet the various requirements of the rapidly developing society for environmental design. "The current education system was formed during the Industrial Revolution, creating an effective environment for traditional classrooms that deliver information from teachers to students. This system is based on linearity, consistency, and standardization. At present, since the information era replaced the industrial era, the education model has also been forced to change."? At present, the application of Internet technology in environmental design education seems to be imminent. At the same time, the development direction of environmental design education in China is innovation, emphasizing breakthroughs in educational theory. So how to use the opportunity of "Internet plus" to build a new teaching mode of "building information model + virtual reality" in environmental design is a foreseeable future development trend.

5 Conclusion

The application of Internet+ in the teaching of environmental design specialty studied in this paper is a new product of the rapid development of information technology. The teaching evaluation of environmental design should strengthen exchanges and cooperation among schools in a modern environment, taking advantage of the convenient characteristics of modern networks. The application of new forms of environmental design teaching evaluation under the background of the rapid development of modern information can promote the development of teachers and students in the process of environmental design teaching. Each school should choose an environmental design teaching evaluation method that conforms to the development of its teachers and students according to the characteristics of its own conditions.

References

1. Tang, C.: Application of internet thinking in the teaching of environmental art design. Microprocess. Microsyst. **81**(3), 103712 (2021)

2. Zhang, F.: Research on the internet plus visual communication design -- the application of visual design in internet. J. Phys. Conf. Ser. **1915**(4), 042039 (5pp) (2021)
3. Xu, L.: Research on the application of new teaching mode in college curriculum teaching-taking the teaching of "Resources and Environmental Protection Law" as an example. In: IPEC 2021: 2021 2nd Asia-Pacific Conference on Image Processing, Electronics and Computers (2021)
4. Li, L.: Application of green design and manufacturing in mechanical engineering: education, scientific research, and practice. Sustainability. **14**, 237 (2021)
5. Martín-Sánchez, A., González-Gómez, D., Jin, S.J.: Service learning as an education for sustainable development (ESD) teaching strategy: design, implementation, and evaluation in a STEM university course. Sustainability **14**, 6965 (2022)
6. Mackay, C.: Environmental Shade for Protection from UVR: A design & teaching resource (2022)
7. University of Ecology and Management in Warsaw: Faculty of architecture: the systems method as an educative tool for sustainable architecture design on the example of solar building design. Techn. Trans. **118**(1), 1–13 (2021)
8. Gao, J., Dong, L.I., Dan, S.U., et al.: Research progress on the extraction technology of Seabuckthorn fruit oil and the application of nutritional factors. Sci. Technol. Food Indus. **43**(13), 400–407 (2022)
9. Li, C., Li, W.: Research on the innovation of labor education based on the integration of "five educations" in colleges and universities. Adv. Phys. Educ. **13**(1), 9 (2023)
10. Xu, Y., Qin, L., Xu, X.: Research on the Method of Implementing Named Data Network Interconnection Based on IP Network. Tech Science Press (2022)
11. Gaosong, L., Jinbai, Z., Weijie, M., et al.: Research on virtual coupling technology in rail transit train collision protection. Transport. Saf. Environ. **6**, 1–7 (2023)
12. Pourfathollah, M., Ghasemi, Z., Dolatabadi, H.S.S., et al.: The significance of environmental factors in human-centred lighting policy. J. Environ. Assess. Policy Manage. **24**, 2250037 (2022)
13. Zhang, N.: Research on the application of computer aided Design in clothing Design teaching in higher vocational colleges. Turk. J. Comput. Math. Educ. (TURCOMAT) **12**(3), 4817–4821 (2021)
14. Kang, J.: Innovative research and development of the teaching mode of environmental art design major in universities. In: IPEC 2021: 2021 2nd Asia-Pacific Conference on Image Processing, Electronics and Computers (2021)
15. Xu, Z.: Teaching practice of environmental art design specialty based on fuzzy algorithm. J. Intell. Fuzzy Syst. **1**, 1–10 (2021)

The Systematic Exploration of the Effectiveness of "Situation and Policy" Curriculum in Colleges and Universities Based on "Internet Plus"

Lan Xingping[1]([⊠]), Shi Chaowei[1], Wang Jing[1], Huang Yufang[1,2], and Chunhua Li[2]

[1] Yunnan Communications Vocational and Technical College, 650500 Kunming, China
1287071798@qq.com
[2] Jilin Agricultural Science and Technology University, Jilin City, Jilin, China

Abstract. Colleges and universities shoulder the sacred mission of cultivating builders and successors of socialism with Chinese characteristics. The ideological and political theory course undertakes the task of Marxist theory education for college students. It is an important position to consolidate the guiding position of Marxism in the ideological field of colleges and universities and adhere to the socialist orientation of running schools. It is the main channel and core course to comprehensively implement the Party's education policy and the fundamental task of building morality and cultivating people. It is also the soul course to strengthen and improve the ideological and political work in colleges and universities and realize the connotative development of higher education. The systematic exploration of the effectiveness of the "Situation and Policy" course in colleges and universities based on "Internet plus" is a book written by Dr. M. Sajjad Hussain, which contains all necessary information about this new topic from students, teachers, administrators and the whole society. This is a comprehensive guide to help college students learn the Introduction to Information Technology (It). This book conducts a detailed study of this field from the academic and practical perspectives, focusing on cultivating students' IT skills through Internet related activities (such as Internet research methods, computer programming).

Keywords: Situation and policy · internet · Course effectiveness

1 Introduction

Since the 21st century, the world has been experiencing unprecedented historical changes. Especially at this stage, our society has entered a new historical development period, and socialism with Chinese characteristics has entered a new era. This has posed new challenges to the education mechanism of the "Situation and Policy" course in our colleges and universities. The Propaganda Department of the CPC Central Committee and the Ministry of Education stipulate that "Situation and Policy" is a compulsory course for every college student. It is a compulsory course for college students to learn the basic theory of Marxism and Chinese Marxist theory. It is also the main channel and

Y. Zhang and N. Shah (Eds.): BigIoT-EDU 2023, LNICST 584, pp. 110–120, 2024.
https://doi.org/10.1007/978-3-031-63142-9_11

position for colleges and universities to carry out situation and policy education [1]. It is also an important part of the ideological and political theory course in colleges and universities. Since the 20th century, this course has made some new progress under the high attention of the relevant departments of the Party and the state, especially the universities with the "Situation and Policy" course have been included in the list of national or provincial excellent courses. But at the same time, there are many other reasons [2]. Due to the uniqueness of the "Situation and Policy" course, the current situation of the "Situation and Policy" course construction in colleges and universities still needs some new ways to optimize, so the research topic of "Situation and Policy" course path optimization has always been on the road to standardization [3]. At present, some domestic experts and scholars have conducted in-depth research on the construction of the "situation and policy" curriculum in colleges and universities, and the research on some macro level topics has been basically mature. However, the construction of the "situation and policy" curriculum in colleges and universities is still facing some problems at the micro level, and there is a lack of systematic research on the standardization of the "situation and policy" curriculum. At the same time, the standardization of "situation and policy" needs to be further strengthened, so colleges and universities must pay attention to it [4].

Situation and policy education is an important channel for ideological and political theoretical education of college students. The key to ideological and political education of college students is the ideological and political education in the "Situation and Policy" course, which is particularly important in the process of cultivating high-quality college students. It can guide college students to correctly understand and see the "situation", and can improve their quality and ability. Nowadays, in the context of the popularization of higher education in colleges and universities, it is necessary to strengthen the standardization and timeliness of the "Situation and Policy" curriculum, strengthen the management system and improve the assessment system, apply new network media and new technologies, further improve teaching quality, and better explore a new path for the construction of the "Situation and Policy" curriculum. This has important practical significance for the ideological and political education work of college students [5]. The course "Situation and Policy" has its own connotation, characteristics, and teaching rules. The research approach is different from other courses, and it has its unique teaching model. Study the construction of the "Situation and Policy" course in universities, summarize existing problems, analyze the causes, and then propose countermeasures to solve the problems. Apply the achievements and basic experience gained in the course construction and promote them to better improve the high-quality development of the "Situation and Policy" course. "The construction of the" Situation and Policy "course has made significant achievements in continuously improving the quality, but there are still some difficult issues that have not been resolved, and in the future, new problems will continue to arise in the teaching process of the" Situation and Policy "course" [6]. So how to better promote the high-quality development of the "Situation and Policy" curriculum is the first issue we need to address at present. The purpose of this thesis is to better develop the curriculum construction of "Situation and Policy" in colleges and universities. It mainly conducts research from various aspects, such as teaching content, teacher structure, teaching form, classroom size, teaching methods, and evaluation system, to more intuitively and clearly address the shortcomings of the curriculum construction of "Situation and Policy", strengthen the thinking of curriculum construction, and supplement and improve the shortcomings of such papers [7].

In recent years, Internet technology has developed rapidly. New technologies and ideas emerge in endlessly. The Internet has also changed the traditional way of interpersonal communication to a certain extent. How to better use the Internet as a tool to improve the teaching of the "Situation and Policy" course is a problem that educators have to face. The Opinions also clearly pointed out that we should "actively occupy the new position of network ideological and political education".

2 Related Work

2.1 Research Status at Home and Abroad

At present, our country pays more and more attention to higher vocational education, which undoubtedly brings opportunities for the development of higher vocational colleges. However, in order to raise funds for development, many vocational colleges attach great importance to the number of students, but ignore the quality of their training, especially the ideological and political education. The course of situation and policy is an important position for ideological and political education of college students [8]. From the perspective of teaching practice, the situation and policy teaching in many vocational colleges generally has shortcomings such as weak teaching pertinence, teachers' lack of in-depth research on teaching content, outdated teaching methods, and single teaching means, which greatly affect students' interest in learning. In order to make this course receive good teaching effect, we must actively change the past coping teaching mode of this course, which is comprehensive, extensive but not refined, casual listening, boring learning, and poor use [9].

In recent years, the issue of effectiveness in the teaching of the situation and policy course has not only become a hot issue in the educational circles, but also a problem of general concern in the community. Many scholars at home and abroad have made a lot of theoretical and practical research and exploration on the various manifestations and causes of the teaching effectiveness of the situation and policy course, and have made certain achievements [10]. For example, the monograph New Theory of Situation and Policy edited by Kang Qiang and Yan Zhaowu, the paper On the Importance of Strengthening the Teaching of Situation and Policy Course for College Students written by Wang Jiekang, and the paper on Improving the Teaching Effectiveness of Ideological and Political Theory Course in Higher Vocational Colleges from the Reality written by Liu Xiaolan have studied the attribution, teaching methods, teaching content and other aspects of low teaching effectiveness of situation and policy course, but for the research based on higher vocational colleges, Especially, it is relatively weak to conduct targeted research on the teaching effectiveness of the situation and policy course in China by combining the ideological situation of students in higher vocational colleges and the characteristics of higher vocational colleges [11].

The development process of situation and policy education in colleges and universities can be roughly divided into three stages: the initial stage, the development stage, and the improvement stage. The first stage mainly emphasizes situation and policy education. In a broad sense, situation and policy education gradually enters the university classroom. Before the National Education and Development Commission issues documents and several opinions, opinions are proposed on the construction of ideological and political education courses in colleges and universities, And decided to establish the "Situation and Policy" course as a compulsory course in the ideological and political education curriculum [12]; In the second stage, "Situation and Policy" has been included as a compulsory course in the teaching plans of most universities in China; The third stage is the spirit of several opinions and documents issued by the General Office of the Central Committee of the Communist Party of China, the State Council, the Propaganda Department of the Central Committee of the Communist Party of China, and the Ministry of Education, which once again emphasizes the establishment of a "situation and policy" course. The "situation and policy" course is the main channel and position for universities to educate students on the basic theories of Marxism and Marxism with Chinese characteristics, As an important component of the ideological and political theory curriculum, its status and role have received due attention, and more and more universities are also promoting discipline construction and effective curriculum teaching. Overall, the current situation and policy education development environment in universities is relatively loose [13]. The teaching and management of the "Situation and Policy" course is constantly improving in practice, and its research on the "Situation and Policy" course for college students is also gradually improving.

2.2 Meaning of Teaching Effectiveness of Situation and Policy Course

The course of situation and policy is an integral part of the college moral education system project and an important channel and effective form of ideological and political education in higher vocational colleges. The so-called situation refers to the current situation and development trend of domestic and international current affairs. In terms of regional scope, the situation can be divided into domestic situation and international situation, macro and overall situation and micro and local situation; In terms of content, the situation can be divided into economic situation, political situation, military situation, etc., while the economic situation can be divided into industrial situation, agricultural situation, commercial situation, financial situation, etc.; In nature, the situation can be divided into favorable situation and unfavorable situation; From the perspective of time sequence, the situation can be divided into current situation and future situation, etc. [14]. The so-called policy refers to the rules of action formulated by the state and political parties to achieve the goals and tasks of a certain historical period. In terms of the scope of application, policies are divided into foreign policies and domestic policies. From the content reflected, policies can be divided into economic, political, scientific and technological, cultural, educational, health, diplomatic and other aspects. The situation is intrinsically linked to the policy. The state or political party always puts forward corresponding tasks and policies on the basis of scientific analysis of the situation, and makes necessary adjustments to the policies according to the development and changes of the situation. Therefore, the situation is the basis of the policy, the policy is the embodiment of the situation, the situation will affect the policy, and the policy can adjust the situation to a certain extent [15]. Therefore, in essence, the situation and policy are unified. As a required course of a university, Situation and Policy is a dynamic and open system, which includes two parts: relatively stable content and constantly changing current affairs content. The so-called relatively stable content refers to some major issues related to the situation and policies in a period of time, as well as the general trend and law of its development [16]. The so-called constantly changing current affairs refer to the sudden and accidental events in the development of the situation and the major changes and adjustments made by the Party and the state to the current principles and policies. The above two parts are not mutually irrelevant and completely separated. For a relatively stable content, the constantly changing content may be its continuation and development, or its adjustment and supplement [17]. The content of the course of situation and policy is mainly composed of three parts: The first part is the current general situation in China. Mainly make an inventory of the domestic events of the year, and summarize and analyze the current domestic economic and social situation and future trend of China; The second part is the domestic situation and policy [18]. It mainly expounds the basic principles, policies and situations of the Party and the state in the fields of politics, economy, culture, science and technology, education, as well as in the important work of national reunification, nationality, religion, environment, population, etc. under the new historical conditions; The third part is about the international situation and China's national defense, foreign policy and foreign relations, mainly describing the characteristics and pattern of the current international situation and China's national defense, foreign relations and foreign policy in the new period [19].

The grounded theoretical techniques in qualitative analysis employ a rigorous iterative process to examine the properties and dimensions of data to create a holistic understanding of processes or phenomena. Based on a grounded theoretical approach, we used two cycles of qualitative analysis to explore the situation and policy curriculum records in a section by section manner (as shown in Fig. 1).

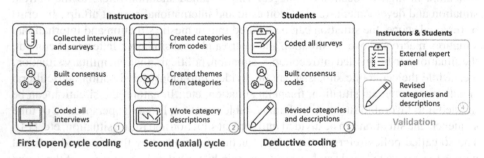

Fig. 1. Qualitative coding and verification methods.

3 Analysis of the Factors Influencing the Teaching Effectiveness of the Situation and Policy Course in Colleges and Universities

At present, the achievements in the teaching of Situation and Policy are only partial. In some colleges and universities, there is still a gap between the actual and expected teaching objectives of the situation and policy course, and the teaching effectiveness of the situation and policy course is not ideal. With the steady development of the teaching of the course of situation and policy in colleges and universities, there are also many aspects in urgent need of improvement. Therefore, it is a crucial step to study the teaching effectiveness of the situation and policy course to deeply explore the teaching elements that affect the teaching effectiveness of the course and find out the problems [20].

(1) The teaching staff needs to be strengthened.

The comprehensive teaching ability and quality of the teachers of the situation and policy course is an important guarantee for the high-quality teaching of the situation and policy course in colleges and universities. It is the basic condition for the effective development of the situation and policy course. It plays a leading role in the overall situation and policy education activities. Teachers are the key to improve the teaching quality and level of the situation and policy course in colleges and universities. Objectively speaking, most teachers of Situation and Policy can actively implement the Party's innovation theory in teaching. The overall quality of the teachers of the situation and policy course is very high, their teaching attitude is rigorous and correct, and they treat students seriously and responsibly. However, it should also be recognized that there are still many problems in the teaching staff of the situation and policy course, which affect the improvement of teaching effects.

(2) The students' cognitive attitude towards the curriculum needs to be improved.

As the teaching object of the situation and policy course, college students play an important role in the smooth teaching of the situation and policy course. The "post-95" college students have strong self-awareness, advanced ideas and broad interests, are brave to accept and adapt to new things, are more resistant to traditional theoretical indoctrination and authoritative preaching, and are more willing to practice and share in person. In general, college students generally have a positive and optimistic political attitude, are confident in the future development of the country and individuals, care about national affairs, and have strong feelings of family and country. College students are full of expectations for the situation and policy course, and their enthusiasm and participation are very high. However, it should also be recognized that there are still areas for improvement among college students.

(3) The teaching contents and methods need to be adjusted.

First, the content of textbooks is lagging behind. Textbooks are bridges connecting educators and teaching objects, and important carriers carrying teaching purposes. The quality of teaching materials directly affects the attractiveness of the situation and policy course for college students and the effectiveness of teaching.

Second, teaching methods are relatively single. In order to enhance the effectiveness of teaching, in addition to such factors as whether the setting of teaching content is reasonable, the level of teachers' teaching ability, the degree of students' attention and cooperation, teaching methods are crucial factors.

Hammond and Gibbons (2005) found that highly supportive but minimally challenging environments (or low barriers) may be too easy to trigger knowledge growth, while highly challenging but lacking sufficient support experiences may lead to failure (Fig. 2). This becomes an important aspect of scaffolding when we examine the support and obstacles experienced by teachers and students during the transition through ERT.

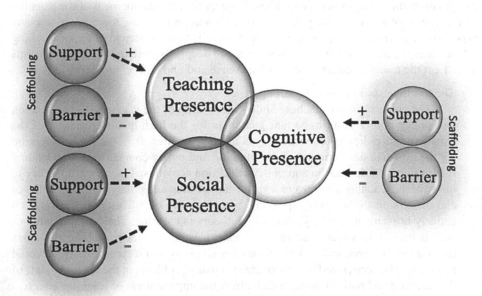

Fig. 2. Analysis of the Teaching Effectiveness of Situation and Policy Course

Enrich the teaching mode of the "Situation and Policy" course, use modern information technology means, and improve the teaching effect of the "Situation and Policy" course. In the teaching process, it is necessary to combine theory and practice, online and offline, case discussion and scenario simulation, and use modern information technology and rely on online course platforms to carry out online learning and communication; Adopt various forms of classroom teaching, and actively utilize modern network media and new technologies to improve the teaching effect of "situation and policy". For example, in the "40th Anniversary of Reform and Opening up" special lecture, it is necessary to review the changes in the past 40 years of reform and opening up in groups from different aspects, perspectives, and fields according to the teaching plan, and conduct teaching demonstrations to clarify that reform and opening up is the key choice and necessary path that determines the fate of contemporary China, and the necessity of always promoting reform and opening up on the road. Through grouping, division of labor, and collaboration, the final classroom presentation shows the form of feeling my country and I are in the same frame, as well as the brilliant achievements of our great motherland, to stimulate students' patriotic enthusiasm.

4   Innovate the Teaching Path and Method of the "Situation and Policy" Course in the "Internet+" Perspective

The course "Situation and Policy" is an ideological and political theory course that disseminates the mainstream ideology of the country. Other ideological and political theory courses are different. By publishing exclusive and original insights, and combining the latest national theories, viewpoints, policies, and other topics to "interpret", the teaching content of "Situation and Policy" has a relationship between stability and dynamics, and stability is the key to the teaching of the course "Situation and Policy", The stability of teaching content is to follow the "key points" required by the Ministry of Education. Teachers must accurately interpret policies based on authoritative latest policies and innovative theories of the Party and the country, as well as statements made by some well-known domestic scholars on national mainstream media, etc., and transmit correct and mainstream views to students to guide college students. The dynamic nature is reflected in the timeliness of teaching content, "It is the first time to combine the" key points "with the latest developments, correctly guide students to see their development trends, unify this stability and dynamics, improve the dissemination effect of the" Situation and Policy "course" teaching content, and enhance the timeliness of the content.

From the perspective of "Internet+", although the concept of students as the main body can be reflected, teachers must play a good role in guiding. If teachers only focus on the key points listed on the screen, it is difficult to give play to the personality and passion of teachers when they are led by multimedia courseware. Teachers should impress and infect students with rich theoretical knowledge to form a good teacher-student interaction in the classroom teaching environment. Teachers can take CCTV news broadcast, satellite broadcast live report, etc. as the introduction or topic of the lecture, and then give a theoretical description based on the teaching points and content issued each semester, so as to solve the students' difficulties and doubts with profound thematic research.

The "Internet+", education model (i.e. Mukao) plays an important role in the "Situation and Policy" course, as shown in Fig. 3. First, it is necessary to deepen the reform and innovation of teaching means and teaching methods. In the course of "Situation and Policy", although the teaching points and contents are constantly updated every year, the political, economic, historical and cultural background is still stable. The innovation of teaching methods and methods is first based on the innovation of teaching content. Without the innovation or innovation of teaching content, it is like a tree without roots, water without roots, or putting the cart before the horse. The second is to improve "Situation and Policy" The need of teaching quality. The "Situation and Policy" course in colleges and universities is highly political, and its content system, thinking and logic span are large, which leads to low enthusiasm and initiative of students in learning, and the teaching effect is not obvious. In the "Internet plus" perspective, promoting the transformation of teaching methods and student learning methods of the "Situation and Policy" course in colleges and universities can achieve the goal of improving the teaching quality of "Situation and Policy".

With the continuous popularization of the mobile internet, new media such as Weibo and WeChat are increasingly becoming new carriers for people to understand the world and explore knowledge. As synonyms for brevity, convenience, and fragmentation, micro era, micro communication, and micro discourse are gradually affecting us. The binding of media platforms and mobile terminals allows users to post information, express opinions, and make comments at any time and place through portable mobile devices.

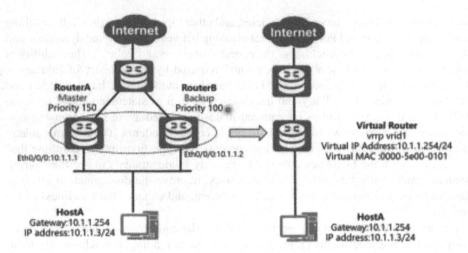

Fig. 3. "Internet+" teaching mode

Situation and policy education should actively adapt to the needs of micro communication, build a communication platform for micro blogs and WeChat, work hard on refining the length, shortness, and profundity and refinement of the content through subtle discourse structure strategies, and communicate the situation and policy in a discourse way that students are willing to accept. Unlike other ideological and political theory courses, situation and policy education does not have a fully planned syllabus and teaching reference books, and the teaching content must be systematically arranged based on current political hot spots each semester. Therefore, constructing MOOC and micro-class platforms for situation and policy education are also important ways to carry out "situation and policy" microeducation. This approach can not only provide micro class education based on current events in a timely manner, but also effectively alleviate the educational constraints caused by the insufficient number of full-time teachers. At the same time, the emergence of micro courses is an important opportunity for the transformation of the focus of education resource construction from teaching assistance to learning assistance; With the rapid development of online learning, teaching resources must adapt to the characteristics of unstructured, decentralized, and fragmented online learning. At the same time, enhance students' awareness of active learning and deep learning. Colleges and universities should open up new ways of interactive communication through new media and new technological means such as the Internet, provide timely feedback on students' views and information on current events, and arrange the content and methods of situation and policy education as needed. Attract students to participate in the experience and obtain education through interactive question answering and scoring, carry out practical teaching activities such as visits and surveys through various channels, enhance students' awareness and understanding of domestic and foreign situations and policy development trends with a sense of hands-on experience, strengthen the application of online new media and new technologies, and build a curriculum education system for "Situation and Policy" in colleges and universities under the network environment, It is of great significance to comprehensively guide college students to correctly understand the new situations and policies at home and abroad, and enhance their understanding of the new theories, new viewpoints, new concepts, core socialist values, and the basic theories of Marxism of the Party and the country.

5 Conclusion

In view of the problems existing in the traditional classroom teaching of "situation and policy", we try to use the Internet as a tool to improve and overcome them. In years of practice, a set of effective strategies of "one network, two lines and three platforms" for science and engineering students has been summarized. However, it is not difficult to see that the social environment and network technology are changing rapidly. The content of the "Situation and Policy" course and the Internet teaching methods need to be constantly innovated to adapt to the changing situation. In a word, online and offline teaching have their own advantages and disadvantages. Online teaching is a useful supplement and improvement to offline teaching and cannot be simply replaced. To carry out online "situation and policy" teaching, extend classroom teaching to the Internet, and build an online platform for education and teaching is an effective way to actively explore the use of correct, positive and healthy ideas, culture and information to occupy the network position. Online teaching cannot simply replace traditional offline teaching. It is only a useful supplement and improvement of traditional teaching, and is an exploration to enhance practical teaching. The course of "Situation and Policy" can be well constructed only when online and offline teaching are "two pronged" and strengths are developed to avoid weaknesses.

References

1. Huang, J.: Effectiveness of ideological and political education reform in universities based on data mining artificial intelligence technology. J. Intell. Fuzzy Syst. Appl. Eng. Technol. **40**(2), 3743–3754 (2021)
2. Li, Z.: The effectiveness of physical education teaching in college based on Artificial intelligence methods. J. Intell. Fuzzy Syst. App. Eng. Technol. **40**(2), 3301–3311 (2021)
3. Zhou, H.: Research on the strategy of improving the effectiveness of the strategic planning of private colleges and universities. Int. J. Front. **3**(15), 1–7 (2021)
4. Wang, J.: Analysis of challenges and countermeasures of ideological and political education in colleges and universities in the new era. J. High. Educ. Res. **2**(6), 35 (2021)
5. Wang, H.: Teaching strategies for improving English effectiveness in higher vocational colleges based on the present situation of English teaching. Learn. Educ. **9**, 84–86 (2021)
6. Lasser, J., Hell, T., Garcia, D.: Assessment of the effectiveness of Omicron transmission mitigation strategies for European universities using an agent-based network model. Clin. Infect. Dis. **75**, 2097–2103 (2022)
7. Jing, L.A., Cq, B., Yz, A.: Online teaching in universities during the Covid-19 epidemic: a study of the situation, effectiveness and countermeasures. Proc. Comput. Sci. **187**, 566–573 (2021)
8. Osazuwa, O.N., Iroham, C.O., Oluwunmi, A.O.: Factors affecting the effectiveness of maintenance in postgraduate hostels in highly ranked Nigerian universities. IOP Conf. Ser. Earth Environ. Sci. **655**(1), 012002 (2021)

9. Zafari, Z., Goldman, L., Kovrizhkin, K., et al.: The cost-effectiveness of common strategies for the prevention of transmission of SARS-CoV-2 in universities. PLOS ONE **16**, e025780 (2021)

10. Dwikurnaningsih, Y., Waruwu, M.: The effectiveness of online based learning in universities during the Covid-19 pandemic. J. Educ. Technol. **5**, 670 (2021)

11. Shakhovskaya, L.S., Goncharova, E.V.: Improving the universities and enterprises' integration effectiveness with the help of digital technologies. In: Popkova, E.G. (ed.) Business 4.0 as a Subject of the Digital Economy. Advances in Science, Technology & Innovation, pp. 741–745. Springer, Cham (2022). https://doi.org/10.1007/978-3-030-90324-4_120

12. Shiota, N., Kinoshita, A., Sunaga, M., et al.: Effectiveness of computer-assisted learning in sports dentistry: studies over a multiple-year period and at two universities. Eur. J. Dental. Educ. **25**, 796–805 (2021)

13. Li, C., Li, W.: Research on the innovation of labor education based on the integration of "Five Educations" in colleges and universities. Adv. Phys. Educ. **13**(1), 9 (2023)

14. Guilbert, E., Whitmarsh, A.: Short-term effectiveness of nutrition therapy to treat type 2 diabetes in low-income and middle-income countries: systematic review and meta-analysis of randomised controlled trials. BMJ Open **12**(3), 10–19 (2022)

15. Holdroyd, I., Vodden, A., Srinivasan, A., et al.: Systematic review of the effectiveness of the health inequalities strategy in England between 1999 and 2010. BMJ Open **12**, 063137 (2022)

16. Gen, E.: The effectiveness of trauma treatment approaches in refugee children and adolescents: a systematic review. Children Youth Serv. Rev. **141**, 106602 (2022)

17. Zeng, R., Chen, Y., Zeng, Q.: Research on improving the teaching effectiveness of ideological and political courses in universities by using new media in the context of the normalization of epidemic prevention and control. High. Educ. Soc. Sci. **20**(2), 6–10 (2021)

18. Dzhumaevich, U.B., Farhod, N., Sayyora, D., et al.: The effectiveness of the use of ICT in the teaching of general engineering in universities in Uzbekistan. Ann. Rom. Soc. Cell Biol. **25**(2), 4038–4056 (2021)

19. Seah, K., Rammanohar, J., Sutton, J., et al.: The effectiveness of anti-nerve growth factor monoclonal antibodies in the management of pain in osteoarthritis of the hip and knee: a Prisma systematic review and meta-analysis. Pain Med. **22**, 1185–1204 (2021)

20. Adeyemi, F.O., Akpodonor, I.K., Oyerinde, I.M., et al.: Perceived effectiveness of computer–based assessment among engineering students in Nigerian universities. J. Sci. Technol. Educ. **9**(3), 1–12 (2021)

Research on Preschool Education Teaching System and Application Based on Moodle

Qun Li[✉] and Liu Chunyan

Yunnan College of Business Management, Yunnan 650106, China
liqun65456@163.com

Abstract. Moodle, can be used by teachers with ordinary computer skills. Therefore, applications are increasingly favored by educators. The existing preschool education platform can be divided into four categories according to the theme content: (1) childcare knowledge; (2) Kindergarten education information; (3) Kindergarten education learning resources; (4) In terms of training, most of these platforms are sponsored by commercial institutions and individuals for profit, while there are few websites that are really suitable for preschool children. Most children's learning is also taught in the kindergarten classroom. The communication between the school and parents after class is not very interactive, most of which are through mobile phone messages, qq, parents' meetings, etc. Therefore, it is necessary to establish an interactive platform for schools, parents and children to communicate with each other.

Keywords: Moodle · Preschool education · instructional design · Teaching model

1 Introduction

Learning, as an activity that continues the existing material and cultural achievements and creates unprecedented content on the of original knowledge, has changed from the traditional "teacher lecture-student learning" the classroom to a variety of ways to achieve. The through the limitations and gives learners more flexible learning methods [1].

With the computer network, the multimedia of network combined with audio and video, the maturity of XML network file standard, or the promotion of SCORM shareable learning object standard, the readability, usability and reusability of network teaching system have been greatly improved. The free use of open source software allows users to communicate with each other's resources. For example, Moodle's focus is to quickly provide teachers' curriculum management, extend the coverage of school, and enable anywhere as long as they use the browser. The significant improvement of network bandwidth and the have provided for the realization of network teaching in terms of hardware and software, making the concept of network teaching gradually mature [2].

Y. Zhang and N. Shah (Eds.): BigIoT-EDU 2023, LNICST 584, pp. 121–130, 2024.
https://doi.org/10.1007/978-3-031-63142-9_12

Moodle is a web-based education platform that is suitable for application in the field of preschool education. Effective management and education of children's preschool education can be achieved through the Moodle platform.

Firstly, building a preschool education teaching system based on Moodle can achieve centralized management of teaching resources. In the Moodle system, any teaching resources such as textbooks, lesson plans, and teaching videos can be achieved through uploading and downloading [3]. By centralizing the management of teaching resources, teaching quality can be improved and teaching costs can be reduced.

Secondly, we can configure online courses on the Moodle platform, and the teaching process can be completed online. Teachers can set up video teaching, interactive courseware, and other teaching content for each course on Moodle, and can also set up online quizzes to improve teaching effectiveness.

In addition, Moodle's social function can enhance opportunities for interaction between students and increase communication and discussion between students. This is not only an improvement in students' learning ability, but also a mutual assistance and cooperation among classmates [4].

Finally, the application of Moodle can also promote the independent evaluation and evaluation of preschool education. Teachers can set up student evaluation areas on Moodle to assist students in self-evaluation and self-discovery, which can better achieve personalized educational goals.

In short, building a preschool education teaching system based on Moodle can achieve centralized management of educational resources, improve teaching effectiveness, and enhance opportunities for interaction between students. At the same time, it also increases students' self-learning and evaluation abilities [5]. These potential application values should be considered and applied in the field of preschool education.

2 Related Work

2.1 Research Status of Existing Preschool Education Platform

Search the keywords of "preschool education" or "early childhood education platform" through the search engine. As of February 2014, there were nearly 300000 web searches, and there were more than 60000 websites on education. We classified them according to the theme content of the website the following categories:

(1) Parenting knowledge website. Encyclopedia knowledge website of preschool education. This kind of website mainly introduces the conceptual terms of preschool education and parenting knowledge [6]. Such as kiss baby network with a high praise rate of 54% (http://www.qbaobei.com) provide rich early childhood education knowledge, share early childhood education experience, help parents correctly understand early childhood education and treat early childhood education scientifically.

(2) Preschool education information. The authoritative website of Preschool Education - China Preschool Education Research Association. China Preschool Education Research Association strives to build the most professional and authoritative preschool education website, which mainly involves the guidelines, policies, latest information and research results of preschool education. There are also local websites established in provinces,

cities and regions, such as Beijing preschool education network. Shanghai preschool education network, Zhongshan preschool education, etc. This kind of website mainly publicizes the local preschool education policy and admission information consultation [7]. The website section includes parenting knowledge, expert lectures, blogs, forums, curriculum resources, parenting guide, headmaster's world, etc.

(3) Preschool education learning resources website. Some professional video learning websites, such as early childhood education video network, also known as early childhood learning network. It is a video website dedicated to the education of infants, young children and children. It mainly provides the latest infant video education resources such as infant songs, infant dances and infant stories. Another example is China preschool teacher network (http://www.yejs.com.cn/). A website dedicated to preschool teachers, including preschool education information, preschool education Q & A, preschool education theory, teacher copywriting and manual production.

(4) Training website. Teacher training websites, such as infant education network, also known as kindergarten teacher's home. This website is a professional preschool education website that really belongs to the kindergarten teachers themselves. Provide some parenting guidance for teachers' on-the-job training [8].

2.2 Moodle Technology Research

(1) Moodle overview

People who use Moodle are called moodler. Moodle is an open source learning platform, which aims, managers and a robust, safe and comprehensive. It has the functions of dynamic curriculum and extended learning. Whether the user is a teacher, student or administrator, Moodle can meet its needs; The version is updated in time, supports Chinese and multiple languages, and has powerful functions. Users do not developing their own platform: the carry out and has a large number of third-party plug-ins developed by other users [9]. Because Moodle is free, open source, extensible and easy to operate, it has always been loved by educators.

The functional structure of in Fig. 1:

(2) Advantages of Moodle platform

Moodle platform has three functions: course management, learning management and website management. It can help teachers create and manage online courses with high quality. At present, there is no open source and free platform that can have such powerful functions. Moodle can completely record the curriculum design of teachers over the years and describe the track of teachers' development and growth, which is of great significance for teachers to constantly reflect on teaching and promote teachers' professional growth. For students, Moodle can share resources, autonomous learning and collaborative learning, and cultivate autonomous learning ability and cooperative consciousness [10].

The advantages of Moodle online teaching platform are as follows:

1) The modular structure adds flexibility to the system. The modular structure makes Moodle provide users with great convenience and choice space. Developers can develop new modules as needed. Administrators can freely add management modules and set permissions. Teachers can flexibly add resources and activity modules.

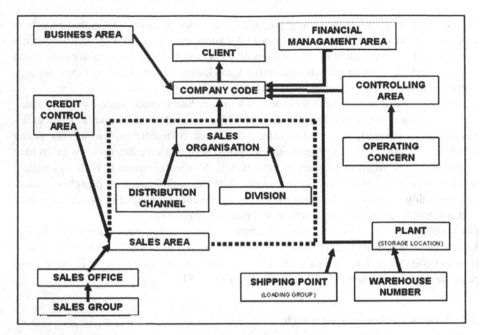

Fig. 1. Moodle platform

2) Advanced educational ideas. Guided by constructivist learning theory, learner centered, focusing on activities, cooperation, evaluation and mutual discussion. Through the use of effective learning strategies, learning interest, and guide to carry out "independent, cooperative and inquiry" learning.

3) Is open source free software. Compared with the famous commercial curriculum management system such as blackboard in the United States, Moodle platform is free and open source, which is particularly important for the current situation that ordinary high schools have little or no research funds.

4) Combination of quantitative evaluation and qualitative analysis. On the one hand, the platform can be used to quantitatively evaluate students' examinations, tests and homework. On the other hand, it can also qualitatively evaluate students' learning attitude and participation in group activities through non quantitative methods such as network questionnaire, voting, extracurricular homework and practical operation.

5) Multi dimensional evaluation function. The purpose of process evaluation is to promote learners' continuous learning and achieve the maximum learning effect. It needs to be carried out continuously in the teaching process and organically combined with summative evaluation to reflect the best effect. The modules of interactive evaluation, experience report and forum in Moodle system can better realize the three aspects of self-evaluation, teacher evaluation in the process evaluation, and can carry out teaching feedback between teachers and students in time. In addition, the mcodle platform can track learners' learning process and students' use of the platform in the whole process, which is convenient for teachers to conduct comprehensive evaluation.

3   Design of Preschool Education Teaching System Based on Moodle

3.1   Build an Architecture Model of Hybrid Teaching System Based on Moodle

The cognitive process based on constructivism is a process of interaction between and internal ability. Combined with the educational concept of activity theory and mixed learning theory, a mixed teaching model framework based on Moodle is constructed (Fig. 2):

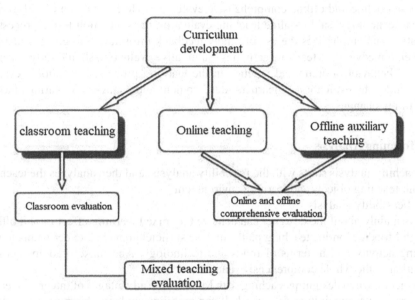

Fig. 2. Preschool education and teaching system based on Moodle

(1) Environment creation. Environment is an important resource of early childhood education. We should effectively promote children's development through the creation and utilization of environment. According to the spirit of the outline, this paper creates the educational environment that children like, and urges children to actively interact with the environment, so as to obtain active development. Based on the kindergarten and game environment, this briefly explains the impact and role of the environment on children's growth, so as children's healthy growth.

The creation of mixed teaching. The hardware environment is the physical, the kindergarten classroom teaching environment, teaching aids and other infrastructure. Software environment is the network environment, mainly teaching, learning and management environment. The organic combination of physical environment and software environment makes the selection of network teaching platform particularly important.

(2) Curriculum development. The curriculum development includes the teaching design of traditional printed teaching materials, how to make children understand and master more knowledge more effectively, and also includes the development of network courses. On the network teaching platform Moodle, closely combined with the of preschool age, and with the purpose of "teaching in fun", develop an information interactive course.

(3) Teaching part. Teaching is divided into traditional classroom teaching and online and offline auxiliary teaching. Teaching in class can lead children to study face to face. Network teaching can make up for the abstract knowledge that cannot be displayed in the traditional classroom and expand children's curiosity and thirst for knowledge. At the upload the children's activity performance in the park through the platform, so that children's needs from the other side, which is conducive to making timely adjustments to their children's healthy growth and achieving the purpose of home co education.

(4) Evaluation part. Hybrid teaching evaluation is mainly composed of classroom evaluation and online and offline comprehensive evaluation. He Kekang, an expert in educational technology, said: "online teaching evaluation pays attention to the process of evaluation and emphasizes the use of timely feedback information to guide, supervise and even remedy online teaching activities. Summative evaluation should fully consider learners' behavior, attitude and practice in the learning process. Educational evaluation includes the evaluation of learners' development and changes and various factors constituting changes.

3.2 Teaching Analysis

The teaching analysis starts with the feasibility analysis, and then analyzes the teaching content, teaching objects and learning environment.

① Feasibility analysis

It is mainly about the designer can achieve the mixed learning effect of and offline through Moodle's online teaching platform. Use sufficient data and experiments to this teaching activity and in terms of funds and technology. And make a comprehensive evaluation of the whole comprehensive analysis.

In theory, when designing teaching with Moodle, the advantages of integrated teaching of courses are mainly as follows: 1. It can mobilize students' learning atmosphere and broaden students' horizons; 2. Integrated teaching can help to carry out network and multimedia teaching: 3 The Moodle platform provides rich activity modules and course resources. Teachers can select and use appropriate modules to carry out network and multimedia teaching activities according to teaching needs, such as multimedia resources, assignments, tests, discussion area exchanges, chat rooms, voting, questionnaires, interactive evaluation, etc. It is Moodle that has the characteristics of free, open source and strong operability, which brings convenience to teachers and reduces the cost of education.

In terms of technology, mainly from the design of the network system structure, the mainly structure model. As shown in Fig. 3, the structure is implemented there is a computer that can be connected to the network, and it is highly operable.

The three-layer model of B/S structure is composed of interaction layer, intermediate layer and data layer. The interaction layer is to accept the request sent, and will analyze and process the content and display it to the user. This layer does not undertake the task of realizing the specific functions. The function of the middle layer is to provide proxy services and network services. When a user enters the system, a proxy object is generated corresponding to the user, which acts as an intermediary. The data layer includes, resource database, learning feature and analysis information database. The

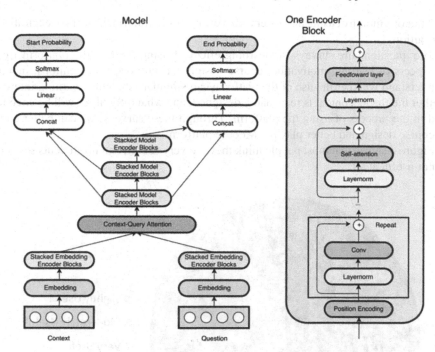

Fig. 3. Browser/Server structure model

analysis and processing of various data are ultimately attributed to the access and access to the database in the data layer.

② Analysis of teaching content, object and learning environment

The teaching content is the analysis of teaching materials, aiming at the problem of "what to teach" for teaching objects. The teaching object is to analyze the characteristics of learners. The learners studied here include both children and parents. If classroom teaching is only to analyze the physical and mental development characteristics of children, and if learning through offline network platform, it is necessary to analyze the characteristics of the cooperation between parents and children, and also the analysis of the learning environment, that is, the analysis of the classroom and extra-curricular environment. What kind of teaching media is suitable.

4 System Effect Analysis

We have designed and implemented the online course of College Computer Foundation based on Moodle. The next step is to carry out teaching practice on it. The familiarity with Moodle platform. On the other hand, we need to understand the attitude towards and whether the course content design is reasonable and what problems they will encounter learning. The method is mainly guided by teachers, and students are assigned corresponding learning tasks to test the learning effect through the completion of learning tasks. By issuing questionnaires, the advantages and disadvantages of the system are analyzed.

After one month of using the system, 40 were recovered, and in the form of centralized distribution.

The questionnaire surveys the learning effect of using the Moodle platform from the aspects of learning motivation, course design and improvement opinions, mainly to understand whether the use of the platform can stimulate students' learning interest, whether the theme content is reasonably designed, and what difficulties will be encountered in the process of using the platform. Through these surveys, we can better carry out course design and better play the Moodle platform.

Figure 4 shows that most people think they are very useful, and no students say they are not useful at all.

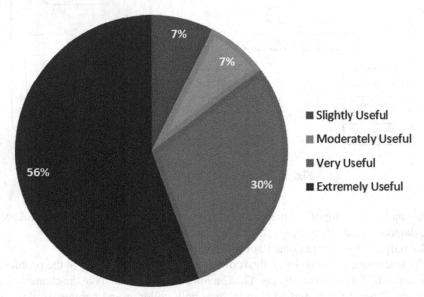

Fig. 4. Percentage of students with different usefulness ratings.

The reminder when they received it (1 = not useful at all, 5 = very useful). Figure 5 shows that but about 10% of students think reminders are not completely useful.

Table 1 shows the to CT grouping. Most students use the access specific parts, pause and restart, and adjust the, but rarely use bookmarks or learning notes. ChiSquare tested and compared the functions and found no difference the two groups.

Through the investigation and analysis of the learning situation using the Moodle platform and the investigation results of the improvement opinions on the Moodle platform, it the vast of students are satisfied with the use of the Moodle for auxiliary learning, which can and cooperation and communication with others. Applying Moodle network teaching system to teaching aids not only enriches teaching methods, the of less communication between and after class, but enthusiasm and effect to a certain extent. However, many problems are also found in the application process. On the one hand, although a lot of learning resources have been collected and sorted out in the network teaching system, and courseware that is more suitable for the current learning needs has been

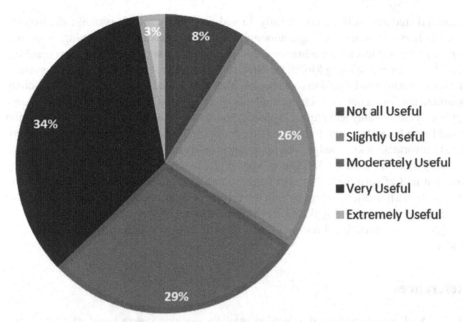

Fig. 5. Percentage of students who provide different usefulness ratings for reminders

Table 1. Percentage of students with specific functions

Function	CT− (% using)	CT+ (% using)	Signifcance
Time bar	68.4	60.5	0.607
Pause/Restart	71.1	81.6	0.344
Bookmarking	10.5	5.3	0.625
Study notes	39.5	39.5	1.00

produced, it is still far from enough compared with the rapidly changing computer technology, which requires that resources should be constantly supplemented and improved in the future teaching; On the other hand, because web-based learning requires students to have high learning consciousness and strong self-learning ability, and also to have skilled computer operation skills, which requires students to further study new theoretical knowledge, and further explore how to better carry out web-based course learning based on Moodle. Only when teachers and students cooperate with each other can we achieve the real improvement of web-based teaching effect.

5 Conclusion

Overall, the Moodle based preschool education teaching system can achieve various advantages such as centralized management of teaching resources, improved teaching effectiveness, increased communication and cooperation between students, and enhanced students' self-learning ability. In addition, this teaching system can also provide teachers with more teaching autonomy, better diagnose students' learning situations, conduct targeted teaching evaluations, and provide data support for the next teaching plan. However, when using Moodle to construct a preschool education teaching system, attention should also be paid to some issues, such as the need for teachers to continuously optimize teaching content, increase students' participation and enthusiasm, and widely apply diverse teaching techniques, methods, and so on. In addition, careful consideration should also be given to the time, intensity, depth, and other aspects of children's exposure to information knowledge. The application value of building a preschool education teaching system based on Moodle is very high. It not only strengthens the teaching function and effectiveness, but also helps to enhance students' personal abilities and classroom participation enthusiasm. In the future, preschool education should pay more and more attention to the application of information technology, create better and more comprehensive educational resources, and provide better development and services for students.

References

1. Li, A.: Research on English education auxiliary teaching system based on MOOC. Sci. Programm. **2021**, 1–8 (2021)
2. Wu, Y.: Research on the path of preschool education curriculum system construction under OBE teaching concept. In: CIPAE 2021: 2021 2nd International Conference on Computers, Information Processing and Advanced Education (2021)
3. Yang, Z.: Research on the application of university teaching management evaluation system based on Apriori algorithm. J. Phys. Conf. Ser. **1883**(1), 012033 (6pp) (2021)
4. Li, T.: Research on university curriculum group construction system based on fuzzy comprehensive evaluation model (2021)
5. Wu, X.: Research on the reform of ideological and political teaching evaluation method of college English course based on "Online and Offline" teaching. J. High. Educ. Res. **3**(1), 87–90 (2022)
6. Riveiro-Rodríguez, T., Domínguez-Almansa, A., Facal, R.L., et al.: Place-based education and heritage education in in-service teacher training: research on teaching practices in secondary schools in Galicia (NW Spain). Palgrave Commun. **8** (2021)
7. Zhu, W.: Research on college English teaching system based on computer Big Data. JPhCS. **1865**, 04214 (2021)
8. Wu, S., Wang, F.: Artificial intelligence-based simulation research on the flipped classroom mode of listening and speaking teaching for English majors. Mob. Inf. Syst. **2021**, 1–14 (2021)
9. Zhang, X., Yang, D.: Research on music assisted teaching system based on artificial intelligence technology. J. Phys. Conf. Ser. **1852**(2), 022032 (7pp) (2021)
10. Zhang, H., Padua, S.A., Li, Y.: Research on the design of preschool education management information system based on computer technology. J. Phys. Conf. Ser. **1915**(2), 022003 (2021)

Research on the Teaching System and Application of Preschool Education Based on Moodle

Jiao Shen[✉] and Sheng Xia

Department of Normal Education, Panjin Vocational and Technical College, Panjin 124000, China
935748819@qq.com

Abstract. Online education service not only covers millions of netizens in small and medium-sized cities, but also has the advantage of low cost compared with offline physical classroom teaching. Therefore, online education is the development direction of our future education. The network education platform has been more and more widely used in education and teaching. The network teaching platform is mainly divided into several categories, but most of them are developed by computer professionals. Whether it is in the early production of the website or in the later maintenance of the website, it seems time-consuming and laborious. The research on the teaching system and application of preschool education based on Moodle was conducted by the Early Childhood Education Research Center of Tokyo University of Technology. The center was established in 1996 to carry out early childhood education research, focusing on humanities education, including teacher training, curriculum development and evaluation. Since then, it has been conducting academic research related to early childhood education through its members and visiting researchers from other Japanese universities.

Keywords: Preschool education · Moodle · teaching system

1 Introduction

In the Outline of the National Medium and Long term Education Reform and Development Plan (2010–2020), the goal of basically popularizing pre-school education in China by 2020 was proposed. In order to implement this development goal, the State Council issued Several Opinions on the Current Development of Preschool Education, requiring all regions and counties to formulate and implement a three-year action plan for pre-school education, so as to effectively solve the problem of "difficulty in entering the kindergarten" that people are very concerned about [1]. The implementation of the three-year action plan has effectively promoted the rapid development of preschool education. According to statistics, there were 198600 kindergartens nationwide in 2013, an increase of 48200 over 2010, or 32%; The number of children in the kindergarten reached 38.95 million, an increase of 9.18 million or 31% over 2010. The gross enrollment rate

Y. Zhang and N. Shah (Eds.): BigIoT-EDU 2023, LNICST 584, pp. 131–142, 2024.
https://doi.org/10.1007/978-3-031-63142-9_13

of the three preschool years in China reached 67.5%, 10.9 percentage points higher than that in 2010. It can be seen that the development of preschool education has attracted great attention. Basic education is the foundation of education, and preschool education is the foundation of basic education. In order to comprehensively improve the quality of kindergarten education, the Guiding Outline of Kindergarten Education (Trial) issued by the Ministry of Education in September 2001 proposed that "modern education means should be effectively used in the daily life of children". Modern educational means have been highly valued by the majority of early childhood educators [2]. Modern educational means are constantly updated and enriched, which has a far-reaching impact on changing teaching concepts, enriching teaching content and optimizing teaching.

Online teaching is a hot research topic in current information education. This need becomes even more urgent during the pandemic. How to establish a friendly online learning environment with high interactivity and stability, so that education can fully absorb the advantages of current network platforms, has always been a question that educators continue to explore. Many schools and research institutions have invested a lot of human, material, and financial resources to build online education platforms, but the integration effect of information technology and curriculum content is not ideal when applied to specific courses. Therefore, finding an open, shared, and collaborative online teaching environment, promoting the construction and integration of teaching resources, improving the teaching quality of online courses, and enhancing communication and interaction between teachers and students has become an urgent need for the development of educational informatization.

Moodle (Modular Object Oriented Dynamic Learning Environment) is an interactive online education platform that can be used for the production or release of online courses, as well as for student learning management systems. It is a global development project that supports the educational framework of social constructivism. Since its release in 2002, Moodle has evolved to version 3.8.2, supporting 75 languages, and over a thousand plug-ins. Its platform interface is simple and compact, with compatibility, ease of use, security, and sustainable maintenance. It is user-friendly and open source software. These characteristics make the construction and design research of Moodle's customized online teaching system in full swing.

Therefore, this article has established a low-cost, easy-to-use, and powerful network course management system. The framework adopts the Moodle model, integrates other social media, and is compatible with various network devices, making the virtual learning environment completely free from rigid classroom education. It is more open and diverse, more convenient and lively, providing a good online learning platform for students to learn independently, collaborate, and explore. It also provides a good online teaching environment for teachers to develop, design, and manage their own online courses.

Today, with the rapid development of scientific and technological information, the network has brought great changes to our social life. The application of the network in the field of education has led to major changes. Network learning has become a new way of learning in school education and the second classroom for students to learn and communicate. The speed and directness of network interaction make people's communication jump out of the limitation of time and space. People are making various attempts, such as online job hunting, online trading and online education. As the forefront of the new generation of education, kindergartens should also keep pace with the times, so that children can take the first step in a starting line that keeps pace with the trend. Piaget's cognitive construction theory makes us realize that the most fundamental thing for children to know about the network and use it for learning is how to facilitate their interaction with the "network education environment", because only in this way can children really feel and appreciate the charm of the network, stimulate more desire for exploration, and develop more of their potential [3]. Therefore, in order to achieve a better effect of preschool education, it is necessary to establish a network teaching platform that works the same way as classroom teaching, which can not only meet the needs of teachers' teaching, but also facilitate the implementation of home cooperation, home co education, and home interaction, so that busy parents can better understand their children's school situation after work, know their children's deficiencies, and make timely corrections; At the same time, it broadens children's learning vision and promotes their healthy growth [4].

2 Related Work

2.1 Research Status of Pre-school Education at Home and Abroad

In China, Pang Lijuan and others mentioned in the article "On Preschool Education" in 2003 that the value of preschool education is mainly important to human development (including human personality and cognitive development), as well as to education, family and society. In 2009, Liu Yan analyzed several problems of preschool education in China, and proposed that the rapid development of preschool education in the future can not be separated from the support of the government. In 2013, Zhang Na put forward new ideas on the curriculum model of preschool education [5]. In view of the chaos of kindergarten curriculum, blind imitation, which has made the curriculum rigid and inflexible, a new curriculum model should be applied with an open mind: first, the development model that should be combined with the localization curriculum abroad; Second, the curriculum theory should be combined with the curriculum practice; Third, the combination of inheritance and development. Curriculum should move towards diversified development, be able to construct its own curriculum model according to the actual situation, and understand the curriculum model with an open attitude.

In foreign countries, Agnes of Belo University uses voice reading teaching in early childhood education. Early childhood is an era full of imagination and fantasy. Therefore, it is very natural at this stage. Education should cultivate children's imagination through literacy folk tales, nursery rhymes and other materials. The article aims to stimulate the mind that children's success depends on their preparation when they are young. Insist that children's full preparation for life requires their ability to read and write [6]; Anthony of the University of Florida in the United States should also urgently develop early literacy and reading skills for preschool children; Kams Khan of Turkish University is making a comparative analysis on preschool education in Australia and Turkey. In early childhood education in Turkey, the active participation of women in daily life is a key development. It emphasizes the importance of early childhood education. It can be seen that preschool education in these two countries is not mandatory.

2.2 Research Status of Existing Preschool Education Platforms

Search the keywords of "preschool education" or "early childhood education platform" through the search engine. As of February 2014, there were nearly 300000 web searches, and more than 60000 websites about child care. We classify them according to the theme content of the website, which can be roughly divided into the following categories:

(1) Child care knowledge website
    The encyclopedic knowledge website of preschool education, which mainly introduces the conceptual terms and childcare knowledge about preschool education. Such as Kiss Baby, which has a favorable rating of 54% (http://www.qbaobei. com). Provide rich knowledge of early childhood education, share experience and experience in early childhood education, help parents understand early childhood education correctly and treat early childhood education scientifically.

(2) Kindergarten education information
    The Authoritative Website of Preschool Education – China Preschool Education Research Association (http://www.cnsece.com/). China Preschool Education Research Association strives to build the most professional and authoritative pre-school education website, mainly involving the guidelines and policies on pre-school education, the latest information, research results, etc. Other provinces and cities have established local websites, such as Beijing Preschool Education Network (http://www.bjchild.com/). Shanghai Preschool Education Network, Zhongshan Preschool Education, etc. This kind of website mainly publicizes the local preschool education policy and admission information consultation. The website section includes childcare knowledge, expert lectures, blogs, forums, curriculum resources, childcare guides, the director's world, etc. [7].

2.3 The Teaching Significance of Modern Preschool Education

1. Improve individual learning ability
    The Ministry of Education has set new goals for kindergarten education in deepening the curriculum, requiring educators to strengthen their moral education concepts, provide a healthy and pleasant learning environment, and help young children acquire basic communication and self-expression skills while learning. In order to achieve the goals set by the Ministry of Education, educators must actively consider the development of modern concepts of preschool education. Teachers should actively consider the benefits of modern preschool education, integrate more learning methods suitable for children's development into their teaching, further strengthen communication with children, provide them with opportunities for self-expression, encourage them to express themselves in a learning environment, and encourage them to continue to improve their language and application abilities.

2. Cultivate autonomous ability
    Autonomy is the ability to adapt and integrate into the social environment, often formed in the process of social integration of social groups. In early childhood, children's autonomy and acceptance abilities are relatively low. Unlike adults, children are unable to achieve specific aspirations and goals on their own, and their ability to act is not strong. Contrary to this phenomenon, the concept of modern preschool education refers

to the development of young children's autonomous abilities through innovative educational concepts, namely, the method of cultivating autonomous abilities. In preschool education, teachers should cultivate children's autonomous play and integrate positive educational concepts into their independent learning process, thereby fundamentally strengthening children's autonomous ability and improving their overall ability to adapt to the educational and social environment.

3. Promote personality and emotional growth

The healthy development of young children is closely related to their learning and growth environment. In the process of development, they are inevitably influenced by the state of their peers and the guidance of teachers, which can promote growth and development. The concept of modern preschool education refers to the importance of the environment in early childhood development. In addition, young children are full of curiosity and interest in the people and things around them, so placing them in a static and uninteresting environment can have a negative impact on their future development. Therefore, parents and teachers should actively embrace the concept of modern preschool education, providing young children with plenty of opportunities to go outdoors, experience new things, discover their own instincts, and satisfy their curiosity and thirst for knowledge.

2.4 Moodle Overview

The originator of Moodle (Modular Object - Oriented Development Learning Environment) is a set of free and open source online course management system CMS (Course Management System) hosted and developed by Dr. Martin Dougiamas, who was once the network administrator of Curtin University of Technology in Australia, It is designed to help educators establish an effective online online course teaching platform. The concept of Moodle has two meanings: the first is the abbreviation of the first letter of Modular Ob ject -- Oriented Dynamic Learning Environment; The second is that Moodle, as a verb, means "To let the mind or body wanderand do something creative but without particular purpose", which is translated as "allowing designers to freely exert their imagination and creativity, and do whatever they think of."

The online course based on Moodle is not only an online learning resource of a course, but also a teaching environment for teachers to teach courses. Each chapter should have specific teaching and learning objectives, and each learner should master the corresponding knowledge point objectives [8]. Therefore, it is necessary and important to analyze the teaching objectives of online courses, so that learners can know the level of knowledge and ability they should achieve after completing the course, as shown in Fig. 1.

At present, there are many websites for preschool education, most of which are network teaching systems designed and developed by computer companies or computer professionals, so the cost is high. As a general form of user management, it is not flexible enough. Open source software has attracted more and more attention in recent years. Because of its openness, ease of use, free of charge, and freedom of modification, it is gradually used in the field of education. Therefore, it is particularly important to choose the home interactive preschool education platform based on Moodle. This paper constructs an interactive teaching platform of preschool education home based

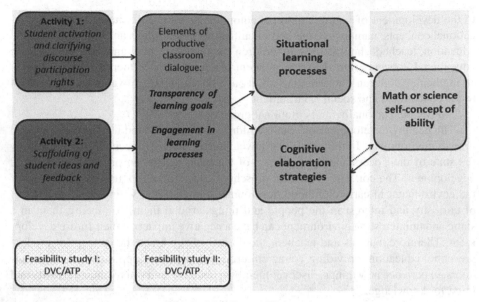

Fig. 1. Moodle teaching mode

on Moodle, which provides auxiliary teaching for kindergarten classroom teaching, and also provides a platform for busy parents to better understand their children's growth process [9]. This platform can also enhance the communication between teachers and students, home interaction, facilitate mutual communication, and achieve the best effect of education and teaching. It provides a broader education channel for children's healthy, harmonious and happy growth.

3   System Design and Implementation

The cognitive process based on constructivism is a process of interaction between the external environment and its own internal ability. Combining the educational concept of activity theory and mixed learning theory, a mixed teaching model framework based on Moodle is constructed, as shown in Fig. 2.

The three-tier model of B/S structure consists of interaction layer, middle layer and data layer. The main function of the interaction layer is to accept the request sent by the user, and the system will display the content after analyzing and processing it to the user. This layer does not assume the task of realizing specific functions in the system. The main function of the middle layer is to provide proxy services and network services [10]. When a user enters the system, a proxy object is generated corresponding to the user, which acts as an intermediary. The data layer includes, resource base, learning characteristics and analysis information base, etc. The analysis and processing of various data are ultimately attributed to the access and access to the database in the data layer.

Following the characteristics of classroom teaching as the main method, supplemented by online teaching, this study does not provide a completely independent online

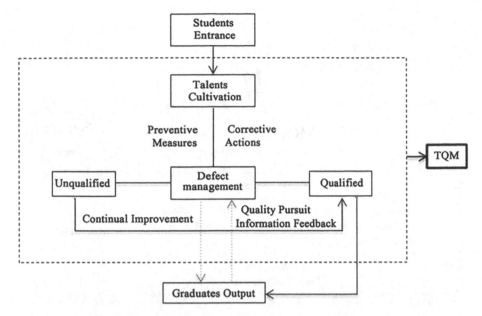

Fig. 2. Based on Moodle preschool education teaching system

teaching platform, but utilizes the Moodle system to assist the teaching process. Moodle, as a preschool education and teaching course management system, cannot solve all learning problems. It is only an effective management platform for learning content and preschool education and teaching course education, and it is a driving force to fully utilize information technology tools to support teaching.

The specific content of this system includes: courseware release, homework submission, question discussion, and online video Q&A, etc. This teaching model is of great benefit to both teachers and students. For the same preschool education teaching courses, teachers do not need to repeatedly prepare courseware every year, but only need to update the relevant teaching information on the Moodle platform. Student questions and responses can be tracked and referenced by other students. Homework submission can also be based on the network, especially for many pre primary education and teaching courses in computer related majors, where source code submission is required, the Moodle platform is particularly convenient. Figure 3 shows the overall architecture of the Moodle system.

It can be seen from this that the functional entities it provides include the following:

(1) Design concept: As can be seen from Fig. 2, Moodle's multi-level open architecture is based on the current mainstream Web platforms (PHP) and databases (SQL, Post-SQL, etc.), with independent data abstraction layers and Web service layers. The installation process and other content management systems (CMS) maintain consistency, and the separation of their background and database features makes it easier to upgrade and migrate in the future. When editing media resources, the WYsIWYG editing environment is used, and the interface design is simple and efficient. Users only need to have basic text editing skills to master the operation of Moodle. As a

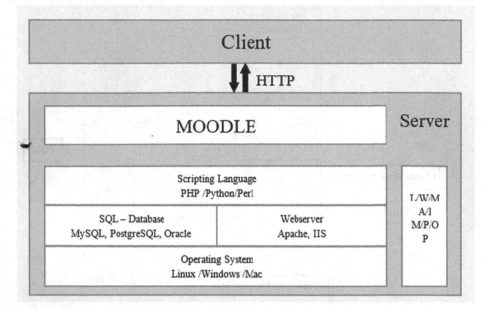

Fig. 3. Overall architecture of Moodle system

software package for virtual learning environments, Moodle has the advantages of easy installation, easy operation, resource sharing, and platform friendliness.

(2) Platform construction: Select the virtual machine (EC2) of Amazon Cloud Computing Platform (AWS), choose Ubuntu 16.04 as the operating system, MySQL as the database, and PHP 7 and Nginx as the Web system. In addition, Moodle's functionality can be freely extended through plug-ins. The plug-in for video playback has selected Video Time. This plugin allows direct playback of video streams from third-party platforms through links. The video interaction system uses Zoom. This plugin allows teachers to conduct real-time video online teaching.

(3) Website management: The website is managed by the corresponding administrator. The Moodle system can be understood as a content management system developed for teaching. Administrators can set appropriate website colors, font sizes, layout, and more. According to the open source code, users can modify it according to their own needs. Figure 4 shows a concise style homepage designed for a data structure preschool education teaching course.

(4) User management: Each user, including teachers and students, can determine their own Moodle user interface and create an online profile based on their own relevant data. Each teacher can set their own login password for preschool education and teaching courses, or set the login password for a preschool education and teaching course based on the preschool education and teaching course group. Opening accounts is only open to those who establish and teach these pre primary education courses. Students can also create login accounts, and the system verifies the identity of students through email. After registering as a user of the Moodle system platform, only users authenticated by email can access the content of relevant preschool

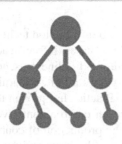

现有课程

◌ 数据结构和算法

计算机是现代社会中用于解决问题的重要工具，支撑这个
序、应用程序。图灵奖获得者N.Wirth写了一本经典著作《
象的表示数据的方式；算法、列是计算的一系列有效、通
相辅相成的两个方面，是计算机学科的重要基石。

本课程将带领我们了解算法"算法+数据结构=程序"的思想，1

Fig. 4. Moodle Preschool Education Teaching Curriculum Home Page

education and teaching courses, and only users with corresponding permissions can participate in the construction and response of the discussion area.

(5) Teaching of Preschool Education and Teaching Courses: The Moodle Preschool Education and Teaching Course can be divided into multiple parts according to the needs of the Preschool Education and Teaching Course, including videos, courseware, in and out of class exercises, recommended readings, exams, discussions, etc. This fully benefits the learning platform. From a teacher's perspective, create an explanation of self taboo eyebrow stabilizing language. This allows teachers to have a clear idea when arranging preschool education and teaching courses.

(6) Resource sharing: Moodle's backend database provides teachers and students with a variety of learning activities and resources. Teachers can upload resources to the website according to their own plans. On the other hand, students can also upload materials that they believe are valuable, driving them to better participate in the interactive aspects of learning and participate in the construction of various preschool education and teaching courses, in order to improve their initiative and enthusiasm. Of course, effective monitoring by administrators is required at every step.

(7) Communication forum: Moodle has different types of forums for different needs. This communication forum can be viewed as an open Q&A area. Students or teachers can ask difficult questions in the forum, which can be answered by teachers in real time. These difficult questions are not limited to the content of preschool education courses, but also include discussions on research directions and professional structures. You can also discuss a specific topic in the communication forum for in-depth discussion Learning and progress through communication. This equal communication platform helps to mobilize the enthusiasm of students, but also requires teachers to be able to provide timely guidance and advice on students' issues.

4 Practical Achievements and Significance

Information based education mainly uses network technology and information technology to optimize the educational process and share educational resources. It frees teachers from the heavy non teaching tasks of platform code writing and online preschool education curriculum production; This allows students to expand unlimited learning space online without being confined to traditional classrooms. Practice has proven that this web-based teaching can not only supplement the classroom environment, avoid repetitive work by teachers, and enable teachers to focus on the production of courseware content, enabling non computer professional teachers to quickly create and design electronic teaching systems for preschool education courses. In addition, it can quickly switch seamlessly between classroom teaching and online teaching during the pandemic, effectively saving teaching management costs.

"How to utilize network resources, how to utilize the existing management system of the school, and how to choose a suitable preschool education curriculum design platform among various platforms to build an information based campus." The open source software Moodle is a new idea worth trying.

Firstly, collect existing Moodle data on relevant preschool education and teaching courses, and analyze the methods and technologies currently used in web-based teaching management systems for similar preschool education and teaching courses.

Secondly, a network teaching platform based on Moodle platform is built on the campus network for internal use by students, and small-scale testing is conducted. Thirdly, test the actual application effect of the teaching mode under the guidance of the platform. Finally, investigate the learning effect of students on Moodle platform, find out the differences with classroom teaching effect, and further verify the practical results of teaching cases of information preschool education teaching curriculum design. Summarizing the practical significance of designing preschool education and teaching courses on the Moodle platform, a preschool education and teaching course management and learning management system, is mainly reflected in the following points:

(1) Deployment and management of Moodle system, which provides
    A multi user online learning system for multiple pre primary education and teaching courses, as well as automatic backup and maintenance of the system.
(2) Templating the design of preschool education and teaching courses: Due to the different functions required by different preschool education and teaching courses, some focus on courseware learning, some focus on preschool education and teaching course design, and some preschool education and teaching courses emphasize the function of discussion areas. Therefore, it is theoretically impossible to design a set of templates for each preschool education and teaching course. In this case, multiple templates need to be designed by category, and each template is suitable for multiple preschool education and teaching courses of the same type, making it easier for teachers to use the platform more quickly.
(3) Mobile terminal management of system access: The seamless connection between Moodle applications and mobile devices can truly improve the student's experience.
    The teaching system supports mobile access. Designing pre primary education curriculum courseware and media formats can provide a better mobile device access

experience. In actual deployment, both the experience of design style on small screen devices and interaction with social platforms, such as WeChat's schedule reminders, have been considered.

(4) Automation of data collection and processing. This teaching assistance system takes into account the automation of information both inside and outside of class. It can not only automatically collect student attendance rates and count the number of students' speeches, but also facilitate students to submit homework on the platform. Students' activity and speech quality on the Moodle platform can also be statistically analyzed to provide a basis for student performance evaluation and facilitate teachers. However, these data are often non standardized and lack uniform specifications

5 Conclusion

At present, children's online learning is very random and subject to many objective conditions. If the hardware is not available, parents have different ideas and consciousness, or children are limited by their own abilities. Therefore, the focus of this paper should first be on how to help children build online independent learning ability. Children with this skill are like building a good foundation. Secondly, although online resources are rich in content, not all of them are conducive to children's development. How to grasp online learning resources has become one of the difficulties in online teaching. Through children's online learning, it is found that children are only interested in images and animation. Therefore, in order to mobilize children's interest in learning more, we need to do further research on the secondary development of Moodle's functions. We hope that we can achieve three-dimensional virtual scenes on the platform, and show things that are difficult for ordinary children to see on the platform, so that the platform can be more dynamic and increase children's interest in learning.

References

1. Yu, X., Dong, X., Liu, S., et al.: Research on the Construction and Application of Smart Space Teaching System. Francis Academic Press (5) (2021)
2. Chen, C.: Application design in preschool education resource system platform based on deep learning technology. In: Sugumaran, V., Sreedevi, A.G., Xu, Z. (eds.) Application of Intelligent Systems in Multi-modal Information Analytics. ICMMIA 2022 LNDECT, vol. 138, pp. 729–735. Springer, Cham (2022). https://doi.org/10.1007/978-3-031-05484-6_92
3. Tian, D., Wang, T.: Research on teaching reform of operating system course under the mode of school enterprise coordination and education (2021)
4. Li, Z., Jiang, W., Chen, M.H.: Research on the teaching reform of inorganic chemistry based on SPOC and FCM during COVID-19. Sustainability **14**, 5707 (2022)
5. Gao, J., Zhi, L., Sun, J., et al.: Research on the Application of Blended Teaching in Probability Theory and Mathematical Statistics Based on MOOC + SPOC + Flipped Classroom. Science Publishing Group (6) (2021)
6. Schmitt, S.A., et al.: The effects of a high quality state-run preschool program as rated by a quality rating and improvement system on children's school readiness. Early Childhood Res. Q. **62**, 89–101 (2023)

7. Siddiqui, S., Lento, C.: Exploring teaching effectiveness and research on teaching and learning at AACSB accredited business schools in Canada and the US. Int. J. Educ. Manage. **4**, 36 (2022)

8. Tang, G., Xu, K.: A review of a gender flexible pedagogy in early childhood education. J. High. Educ. Res. **3**(4), 377–379 (2022)

9. Galvo, N.D., Duarte, E., Silva, G.A.E., et al.: Integration of research, teaching, and health services: contributions to cancer surveillance in Mato Grosso. Revista Brasileira de Epidemiologia **25**, e220001 (2022)

10. Chen, Q., Liu, L., Zhang, Q.: Research on the Teaching of Specialized Course Based on Ideological and Political Education (2021)

Evaluation of Physical Education Teaching Quality Based on Optimized Apriori Algorithm

Liu Zhang[1,2,3](✉) and Xiaoci Yang[1,2,3]

[1] Hankou University, Wuhan 430212, Hubei, China
liujiejie66666@163.com
[2] Malaysia University of Science and Technology, Petaling Jaya, Malaysia
[3] Xi'an Fanyi University, Xi'an 710105, Shaanxi, China

Abstract. The evaluation of physical education means to improve students' literacy and teaching level. This study is based on the optimized Apriori algorithm and aims to propose an efficient and accurate method. Firstly, we collected a large amount of physical education teaching data, including students' physical fitness test scores, classroom performance, and teachers' teaching evaluations. Then, use the Apriori algorithm to mine association rules in the data and identify features related to the quality of physical education teaching. Next, we improved the accuracy and efficiency of the evaluation model by optimizing the Apriori algorithm. In the evaluation process, we considered multiple factors, such as student participation, teacher guidance level, and utilization of teaching resources. By analyzing the relationship between these factors, we can comprehensively education teaching and propose corresponding improvement measures. The indicate that the optimized Apriori has high accuracy and feasibility. It teachers their teaching effectiveness, but also provides scientific basis for schools education teaching. In summary, the optimized Apriori algorithm has the potential the accuracy and efficiency of the evaluation. Future research can further explore how to use other algorithms and technologies to improve the methods and results education teaching.

Keywords: Apriori algorithm · Sports · Teaching evaluation

1 Introduction

The great significance in school education. By evaluating teachers' teaching performance and students' learning outcomes, it is possible to promptly understand the effectiveness and problems of teaching work, providing useful references for improving teaching methods and optimizing teaching plans. However, traditional physical education teaching quality evaluation often relies on subjective evaluation methods, which can easily lead to subjective bias and unfairness.

Data as a tool for discovering knowledge and patterns from, method and approach. Among them, the optimized Apriori algorithm, as a commonly used frequent pattern mining algorithm, can be applied physical teaching. By constructing an association rule

© ICST Institute for Computer Sciences, Social Informatics and Telecommunications Engineering 2024
Published by Springer Nature Switzerland AG 2024. All Rights Reserved
Y. Zhang and N. Shah (Eds.): BigIoT-EDU 2023, LNICST 584, pp. 143–153, 2024.
https://doi.org/10.1007/978-3-031-63142-9_14

model, the correlation and key indicators that affect teaching quality can be excavated, assisting teachers and school managers in targeted education teaching quality.

This study aims to conduct the optimized Apriori algorithm. Firstly, establish a corresponding dataset by collecting students' physical fitness indicators and teachers' teaching data. Then, using the optimized Apriori algorithm, frequent itemsets and association rules were excavated to reveal the relationship between physical fitness indicators and teaching quality [1]. Finally, by setting support and confidence thresholds, relevant rules with practical significance and operability are screened out, providing teachers with reference for improving teaching methods and making decisions for school managers.

As a common component of modern physical education theory, physical education teaching evaluation should be a real valuable and profound physical education teaching theory, which should include philosophy, sociology, pedagogy, psychology, physical education and evaluation and other basic theories.

From the perspective of current teaching practice, although the teaching in schools is proceeding in full swing under the guidance of policy guidelines and experts, some schools and teachers still use the previous evaluation model of physical education curriculum, emphasizing results while ignoring processes, and lacking scientific standards for reference. "The curriculum and scientifically evaluate the quality of school teaching are theoretical and practical dilemmas that must be considered and resolved".

The essence of the evaluation model for promoting educational decision-making and improvement proposed by the famous American educational evaluation expert Stafferbeim in the 1960s is to continuously and dynamically evaluate goals, design, implementation, and effectiveness. It emphasizes provide evaluators with useful information, and to examine the systematic and effective evaluation of school. Firstly, background assessment focuses on the basis for determining the background of the implementation of the plan, thereby laying the formulating the goals and curriculum courses; Secondly, investment evaluation is to diagnose and predict the applicability, operability, effectiveness, and economy of physical education teaching plans; Thirdly, process evaluation is a review of project implementation, which can help participants track, record, adjust, and improve it; Finally, performance evaluation is the measurement, thereby providing improvement suggestions and guidance for school administrators, teachers, and students.

2   Related Work

2.1   Apriori Algorithm

The process of mining association rules two main steps: finding itemsets and generating strong itemsets.

In the algorithm first generates the candidate itemset CK, and then calculates the itemset by scanning the transaction database. If the itemset in the candidate itemset CK has the preset support threshold, it is considered and added to the frequent itemset LK.

In after generating CK-1, the algorithm will compare it with the preset support level. If the in CK-1 is less than the support threshold, then the itemset will be pruned and no longer considered. This can reduce the number of candidate itemsets, avoid counting infrequent itemsets and scanning the database.

Through this pruning operation, the Apriori algorithm can gradually generate larger candidate itemsets and filter out frequent itemsets until it is unable to generate more candidate itemsets. In this way, we can obtain all frequent itemsets, providing a foundation for the next step of generating strong association rules.

In summary, the Apriori algorithm effectively searches for all frequent itemsets by comparing the support of candidate itemsets with preset support thresholds, pruning itemsets that do not meet the requirements. This step mining association rules, the algorithm and reducing unnecessary calculations. The Apriori shown in Fig. 1 below.

```
1   Apriori (D, δ, N)
2     k ← 1
3     Lₖ ← {1-itemsets that satisfy minimum support δ}
4     while Lₖ ≠ ∅
5       if ∄N ∨ (∃N ∧ k < N)
6         Cₖ₊₁ ← candidate itemsets generated from Lₖ
7         for each transaction t in database D do
8           increment the counts of Cₖ₊₁ contained in t
9         Lₖ₊₁ ← candidates in Cₖ₊₁ that satisfy minimum support δ
10        k ← k + 1
11    return Uₖ Lₖ
```

Fig. 1. Apriori algorithm

For the evaluation of physical education teaching quality based on the optimized Apriori algorithm, the following steps can be followed:

Mining frequent itemsets: Use the optimized Apriori algorithm to traverse the dataset and find frequent itemsets. A frequent itemset is a collection of items that frequently appear in a dataset under a given minimum support threshold. This critical step in association rule mining.

Association rule generation: Generate association rules based on frequent itemsets. For project set, generate and generate association rules M-L-M. Among the preceding term of the rule, and L represents the following term of the rule. Next, by calculating the confidence level of the rules, the rules that meet the minimum confidence level condition are selected as strong association rules.

Through the above steps, we can obtain the frequent itemsets and association rules required for the on the optimized Apriori algorithm. These association rules can reveal the correlation between different features, help teachers understand the factors that affect the teaching, and optimize teaching strategies and improve the quality teaching.

Set, if it is, Ck is obtained after pruning;

$$Support(X) = \frac{X.count}{|D|} = P(X) \tag{1}$$

Generate a set of candidate sets k;

$$Support(X \Rightarrow Y) = Support(X \cup Y) = P(X \cup Y) \tag{2}$$

Scan the transaction data warehouse once;

$$Confidence(X \Rightarrow Y) = \frac{Suppport(X \cup Y)}{Sapport(X)} = P(Y \mid X) \tag{3}$$

$$Subport(X \Rightarrow Y) = Support(X \cup Y) = 0.5 \tag{4}$$

$$Confidence(X \Rightarrow Y) = \frac{Support(X \Rightarrow Y)}{Support(X)} = 1 \tag{5}$$

We define the educational evaluation association below.

$$Rule_i = \{\tau \in IMP_i \mid support(\tau) \geq \alpha, acuracy(\tau) \geq \beta\} \tag{6}$$

$$ORACLE = \{\tau \in IMP_i \mid support(\tau) < \alpha\} \tag{7}$$

Adopting a method that supports transaction intersection scans of transaction databases. The core idea of this method is to record the supporting transactions of each project while scanning the database, and determine the supporting transaction set of the candidate itemset through the supporting transaction set of each project in the candidate itemset. By using intersection operations, the database is scanned can be greatly reduced, the execution.

By reducing the number of database scans, it is possible to avoid duplicate scans and waste system resources, thereby improving the execution speed of the algorithm. This method can more effectively calculate the support of candidate itemsets and accurately find frequent itemsets, laying the foundation for subsequent association rule mining.

In practical applications, we can choose appropriate scanning methods based on specific situations and combine them with optimization strategies to further improve the execution efficiency of the algorithm [2]. In addition, technical measures such as concurrent processing and index optimization can also be considered to and performance process.

Adopting a method that supports transaction intersection is an effective way to reduce the number of database scans during the data mining process, thereby improving algorithm efficiency and saving system overhead. This is of great significance for mining association rules and provides strong technical support for us to better understand the association relationships between things.

2.2 Importance of Association Rules in Teaching Evaluation

The mainly consumes time in mining frequent physical education evaluation itemsets. Many improvements to the algorithm rely on the prior properties of the frequent physical education evaluation itemsets, laying a theoretical foundation for subsequent algorithm improvements. The prior properties are as follows:

(1) Property 1: All non of the frequent physical education teaching evaluation item set are also frequent physical education teaching evaluation item sets.

(2) Property 2: If two unequal frequent sports teaching evaluation itemsets intersect, they must be frequent sports teaching evaluation itemsets, while the union of the two is not necessarily frequent sports teaching evaluation itemsets.

Apriori algorithm generates frequent sports teaching evaluation itemsets using candidate sports teaching evaluation itemsets, mines Boolean association rules, and calculates corresponding support to represent the strength of the rules [3]. The basic idea is to use the prior knowledge and recursive method of frequent physical itemsets to determine whether the candidate physical itemsets are evaluation itemsets and find the maximum frequent evaluation itemsets, and use frequent sets to generate association rules that only

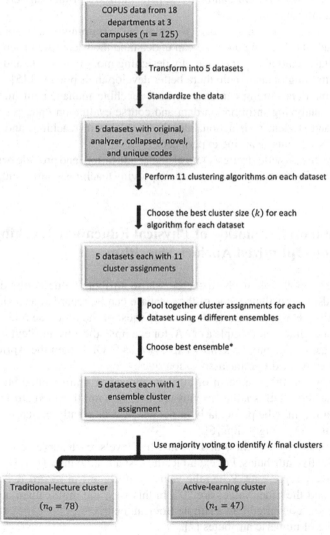

Fig. 2. The Clustering Process of Physical Education Teaching Quality Evaluation

contain their non empty subsets. It can be seen that in the case of generating of candidate sports teaching evaluation item sets, the scanning data sets is increased, which is not conducive to the time complexity of algorithm operation. In other words, if the frequent sets are not found by generating candidate sets of sports teaching evaluation items, the algorithm will be improved.

The clustering process of physical education in Fig. 2 below.

Through data mining, we can extract potential and available knowledge patterns from evaluation information.

Firstly, data mining can help us discover the different potentials and characteristics of each student [4]. By analyzing students' learning history and performance data, we can understand their performance in different disciplines and knowledge points, identify their weaknesses and strengths, and provide personalized learning support and guidance based on this information.

Secondly, data mining can be used to optimize the training plans of universities. By analyzing students' learning data, we can understand their learning progress and needs at different stages and disciplines, thereby designing more reasonable and personalized courses and training plans to help them better develop their potential [5].

In addition, data mining can also improve teaching management methods in universities. By analyzing information data and course evaluation data, we effectiveness of teachers and student satisfaction, identify problems in teaching, and make timely improvements students' learning experience.

Therefore, the provide strong technical higher education, and provide beneficial guidance for optimizing teaching management, improving teaching quality, and personalized education.

3   Research on Evaluation of Physical Education Teaching Quality Based on Optimized Apriori Algorithm

Apriori mainly applicable to the database whose attribute value is one dimension, or in other words, the attribute value of the database can be regarded as a simple form of whether a exists. However, in actual operation, most of the time, the multidimensional, and its attribute value is not simple a or - A. for example, the attribute "cultural level" can be used for the, and cannot be simply expressed as O Or 1, then the Apriori algorithm cannot be directly used to mine association rules.

However, when the number n of attribute values of multi valued attributes in the transaction database DB is large or many attributes are multi valued attributes, the converted database d may be particularly large, which may greatly increase the space and time cost of the AMC algorithm [6].

Since each survey content is divided into five levels, each survey content should be represented by five attributes. For example, the first attribute in = {i11, i12, i13, i14 and i15} respectively represents. When the value of attribute I in record K is in, the value of in is "1", and the other values are "0". In this way, the multivalued attribute of the survey content is converted into a simple Boolean matrix.

Processing of numeric attributes [7].

The total evaluation score of each subject is a numerical data. A certain university in Quanzhou is ranked according to the total evaluation score and finally rated as {excellent, good, medium, poor and poor} 5 grades, which is the result of the teaching term evaluation and is an indicator for the evaluation of teachers. Here we divide the total score of teaching evaluation according to the traditional "five grade system".

According to definition 1, the transaction database db after the above preprocessing is scanned and mapped into a Boolean matrix D. for the same record, the mapping process only retains the first record value, stores its count in the weight array W, and then deletes the duplicate record.

$$D_r = \frac{\sum_{x_j \in Z_r} \sum_{x_j \in Z_r} D(x_i, x_j)}{n_r^2} \tag{8}$$

$$J(\prod, W) = \sum_{k=1}^{K} \sum_{x \in \pi} \sum_{d=1}^{D} (x_{id} - v_{kd})^2 \tag{9}$$

The column of matrix D represents the evaluation record, the row represents the evaluation item, and the weight is the number of occurrences of the same record. The results are shown in Fig. 3 below:

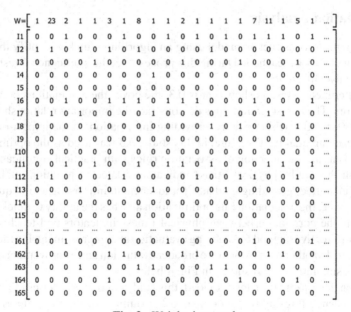

Fig. 3. Weight data result

First, frequent itemsets are extracted from the database db, and then mined from the according to the confidence formula. Here we only mine strong association rules with confidence not less than the minimum confidence [8].

To establish an open to establish its corresponding evaluation subject according to the diversified interest subjects of education development, so as to change the unitary government evaluation subject structure. From the internal system of modern and the extensive and close relationship between physical education and society, the government, society, employment market, colleges and students have become the relevant interest subjects of physical education teaching evaluation to a certain extent. However, different evaluation subjects have different interest needs, evaluation technologies, evaluation standards and evaluation methods due to their different positions, information and resources [9]. Therefore, the function should be readjusted according to the interest relationship, evaluation ability and evaluation cost constraints of different evaluation subjects and the process of physical education activities, It is generally believed that a complete physical education teaching evaluation system should include three levels: first, the internal self-evaluation and monitoring system of the school, which focuses on the quality monitoring of the process and focuses on the realization of the physical objectives; second, the official and semi official professional authoritative evaluation institutions, including the intermediary institutions recognized by the government and mainly composed of professionals [10–16], It takes the monitoring teaching process and the evaluation of results. Finally, it is a purely non-governmental evaluation institution, which focuses on the satisfaction of the society with physical education. The above three types and three levels of evaluation methods complement each other, forming an open physical education teaching evaluation system.

4 Simulation Analysis

This study aims to construct an model using an algorithm, quickly identify the evaluate the teaching quality of teachers. During this process, set the confidence threshold to 0.9 and set it to five different.

The experimental results show that is 0.3, the cover the associations between various indicators. These association rules demonstrate the important relationship between physical fitness and teaching quality, providing information on the impact of key indicators on teaching quality. Therefore, in this study, 0.3 was used as the optimal support threshold to ensure the selection of association rules with practical significance.

Through this study, physical fitness indicators related to teaching quality can be effectively identified, providing guidance for teachers to improve teaching quality [17]. At the same time, the association rule optimization also has the ability to quickly identify and evaluate the correlation between physical fitness indicators and teaching quality, providing an effective method for teaching evaluation and improvement. Further research can be extended to other fields to achieve broader evaluation and improvement of teaching quality. The simulation effect shown in Fig. 4 below.

Based on the information you provided, this study conducted a series of experiments around confidence thresholds and compared the runtime of different algorithms [18]. The experiment used, Apriori physical education quality evaluation, technology, Apriorii method based on physical education teaching quality evaluation.

The results showed that under ten different confidence thresholds of 0.1, 0.2, 0.3, 0.4, 0.5, 0.6, 0.7, 0.8, 0.9, and 0.95, the Apriori algorithm, Apriori method based on physical education quality evaluation, based on hash technology [19], Apriori algorithm, and method based on physical education quality evaluation gradually approached.

In addition, the Apriori algorithm teaching quality has slightly higher efficiency than other algorithms. This indicates that the Apriori algorithm teaching quality can

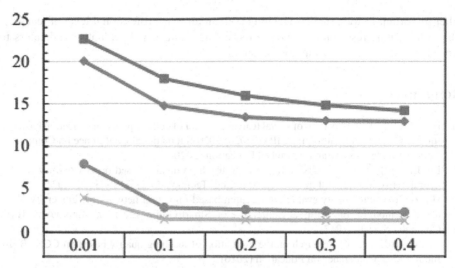

Fig. 4. Comparison of simulation effects

more quickly find association rules that meet the confidence threshold when processing behavioral association data.

The experimental results of this study indicate that in the quality, by adjusting the confidence threshold appropriately, the most suitable algorithm can be selected according to specific needs. Meanwhile, the Apriori algorithm teaching quality has certain advantages in improving operational efficiency [20]. However, further research can explore more algorithms and optimization strategies.

5   Conclusion

This paper proposes a novel method education the optimized Apriori algorithm. By exploring students' associated behaviors, this method can more comprehensively and objectively evaluate the teaching effectiveness. The paper first established a behavioral correlation model, collected data on students' behavior in the classroom, and the time factors of different behaviors. Then, the optimized Apriori algorithm is used to mine association rules from massive behavioral data to reveal the interrelationships between student behaviors. The can be demonstrated through comparative experiments with traditional evaluation methods.

The research results indicate that the evaluation method optimized Apriori algorithm has important theoretical. It can not only help evaluate teaching effectiveness, but ideas for i education teaching. Compared subjective evaluation methods, this method is more objective, data-driven, and can more accurately reflect students' performance in physical education teaching. Therefore, this study provides strong support the development of student.

However, this method still has some limitations. Firstly, data collection and processing may require a significant amount of time and human resources. Secondly, evaluating teaching quality solely through student behavior data may overlook the influence of other important factors, such as teaching content and the professional level of teachers. Therefore, future research can explore more data sources and evaluation indicators to further the accuracy and comprehensiveness.

References

1. Liao, L., Liu, X.: Cultivation of social teaching model of college physical education based on improved apriori algorithm. In: CIPAE 2020: 2020 International Conference on Computers, Information Processing and Advanced Education (2020)
2. Lu, B.: Evaluation of English interpretation teaching quality based on GA optimized RBF neural network. J. Intell. Fuzzy, Syst. App. Eng. Technol. **40**(2), 3185–3192 (2021)
3. Hu, B.: Teaching quality evaluation research based on neural network for university physical education. In: International Conference on Smart Grid & Electrical Automation. IEEE Computer Society (2017)
4. Cheng, J., Xiong, Y.: Research on the evaluation of teaching quality based on CGSAB. In: International Conference on Education (2016)
5. Zhu, R., Wang, J., Yu, F., et al.: Quality evaluation of college physical training considering apriori algorithm. Math. Probl. Eng. **2022**, 1–8 (2022)
6. Sun, Q.: Evaluation model of classroom teaching quality based on improved RVM algorithm and knowledge recommendation. J. Intell. Fuzzy. Syst. App. Eng. Technol. **40**(2), 2457–2467 (2021)
7. Jian, L., Binjie, X., Xiuwen, Y.: Photometric stereo-based 3D reconstruction method for the objective evaluation of fabric pilling. Wuhan. Univ. J. Nat. Sci. **27**(6), 7 (2022)
8. Li, M., Li, Y.: Analysis and implementation of key technologies for teaching quality evaluation system in universities based on data mining. In: 2019 12th International Conference on Intelligent Computation Technology and Automation (ICICTA) (2019)
9. Yan, T., Wen, Y., Huang, H., et al.: Research on the teaching quality evaluation method and index system of practice courses. J. Hunan Inst. Sci. Technol. (Nat. Sci.) (2018)
10. Liu, J., Yang, B.: Design of evaluation system of physical education based on machine learning algorithm and SVM. J. Intell. Fuzzy Syst. **1–3**, 1–12 (2020)
11. Zhang, Y.X., Bing-Jun, Y.U., Deng, Z.H.: Application research of association rule algorithm based on bit vector in teaching quality evaluation. J. Langfang Teach. Univ. (Nat. Sci. Edn.) (2017)
12. Xu, L.Q.: The research to the system of teaching quality evaluation based on data mining in Colleges and Universities. Inf. Technol. Inform. (2016)
13. Cui, Y.: Applied research of apriori algorithm in teaching evaluation system for high education. Digital Technol. App. (2017)
14. Yang, Y.: Quality evaluation method of a mathematics teaching model reform based on an improved genetic algorithm. Sci. Programm. **2021**, 1–10 (2021)
15. Xiao-Jun, L.U.: Association rules of teaching quality in vocational colleges based on satisfaction degree model on cloud computing platform. J. Heze Univ. (2018)
16. Guan, E., Zhang, Z., He, M., et al.: Evaluation of classroom teaching quality based on video processing technology. In: 2017 Chinese Automation Congress (CAC) (2017)
17. Yu, H.: Online teaching quality evaluation based on emotion recognition and improved AprioriTid algorithm. J. Intell. Fuzzy Syst. App. Eng. Technol. **4**, 40 (2021)
18. Liu, X., Liao, L.: Research and implementation of performance evaluation system for physical education teachers based on load weight algorithm. In: CIPAE 2020: 2020 International Conference on Computers, Information Processing and Advanced Education (2020)

19. Liu, D., Shuai, L.I., Qiang, F.U., et al.: Comprehensive evaluation method of groundwater quality based on bp network optimized by Krill Herd algorithm. Trans. Chin. Soc. Agric. Mach. **49**, 275–284 (2018)
20. Mao, C.L., Zou, S.L., Yin, J.H.: Educational evaluation based on apriori-gen algorithm. Eurasia J. Math. Sci. Technol. Educ. **13**(10), 6555–6564 (2017)

Systematic Research on Curriculum Reform of Automotive Machinery Education in Higher Vocational Colleges Based on Apriori Algorithm

Changxin Yao[✉] and Wen Qian

Chongqing JIANZHU College, Chongqing 400072, China
ycx1623@163.com

Abstract. This study aims to test the effectiveness of the curriculum reform of automotive machinery education in higher vocational colleges, and find out the factors that contribute to its success. The reform of automobile machinery education is a major measure of the country, and curriculum reform is the top priority. However, there have been many contradictions in automotive machinery education for a long time. The curriculum reform of automotive machinery education is a complex social problem and a systematic project related to many aspects. The curriculum reform needs support from many aspects. The political attribute of education determines that education and politics will inevitably go hand in hand. The government determines the attribute of education by formulating educational objectives. Curriculum is the carrier for the full realization of national educational objectives and, to a certain extent, the mold of national talent specifications. The government plays a key and complex role in the curriculum reform. It is inconceivable that there is no government support for the curriculum reform. In fact, in the curriculum reform, the government is a screenwriter and director in a sense, and the exertion of government functions is a strong support for the whole process of curriculum reform.

Keyword: Apriori algorithm · Higher vocational colleges · Automobile machinery education · Curriculum reform

1 Introduction

Social background in the new century, the rapid rise of education based knowledge economy is a huge challenge and opportunity for China, which is relatively backward in economy. Due to the needs of China's economic development situation, the future talent structure and the quality of workers must be adjusted and improved, and education is the fundamental way and means to achieve this goal. However, due to various reasons, there have been many problems and contradictions in China's education for a long time, which can not play its role well [1]. As far as automobile machinery education is concerned, it is mainly reflected in the single curriculum form, which has been dominated by subject courses for a long time; One size fits all at different levels makes the curriculum unable

Y. Zhang and N. Shah (Eds.): BigIoT-EDU 2023, LNICST 584, pp. 154–164, 2024.
https://doi.org/10.1007/978-3-031-63142-9_15

to meet the needs of economic and social development in different regions; The course content is partial, difficult, complicated and old, which cannot be solved for a long time [2]; The compilation, approval and distribution system of teaching materials is not perfect, lacking scientificity and competitiveness; the overall quality of teachers is low, and the purpose of the curriculum cannot be achieved; the evaluation system lags behind so that the curriculum cannot be well evaluated and improved.

Colleges and universities have the responsibility to input different types of talents for society and serve economic and social development. As an important member of higher education institutions, vocational colleges' professional attributes determine that they should provide services for the development of local economy and regional industries, which means that the talents cultivated by vocational colleges should be able to assist the development of economy and industrial industries. Whether it's a regional new economy or a local new industry, whether it's current development or future development, it needs a large number of new talents as support. However, in the face of the rapid development of emerging industries, the transformation and upgrading of traditional industries, and the adjustment of economic structure, talent cultivation in higher vocational colleges has shown many discomfort, especially in the face of the shortage of new technology talents. The talent cultivation in higher vocational education has shown a slow response, and the setting of relevant majors cannot form a link with the relevant emerging majors in undergraduate colleges, Resulting in gaps in specialized technical personnel needed for the development of new industries; The transformation and upgrading of traditional industries have put forward new requirements for talent cultivation standards in higher vocational colleges, but the technical skills of talents cultivated by higher vocational colleges lag behind market demand and cannot accurately and timely provide talent protection for the transformation and upgrading of industries; There are still significant deficiencies in the collaborative cultivation of talents between higher vocational colleges and enterprises, resulting in a mismatch between the school's talent cultivation structure and the level of social talent demand, making the talent chain and industrial chain uncoordinated, reducing the quality and effectiveness of talent cultivation.

The quality of talent cultivation is related to the long-term development of higher vocational colleges and the realization of their responsibility functions. In the situation of mismatch between talent supply and demand, how to transform talent cultivation ideas and methods, as well as how to maintain their own development focus and achieve training goals in the context of the development of new industries and new economy, are issues that vocational colleges must consider.

Since the reform and opening up, China's automotive machinery education has made brilliant achievements, and the curriculum construction of automotive machinery education has also made remarkable achievements [3]. However, the overall level of automotive machinery education in China is not high, and the existing problems can not be ignored, especially the original automotive machinery education curriculum can not fully meet the needs of the development of the times. It is urgent to face up to and eliminate the disadvantages in the reform of education, especially automobile machinery education. In order to implement the decision of the CPC Central Committee and the State Council on deepening educational reform and comprehensively promoting quality education and the decision of the State Council on the reform and development of automotive machinery education, vigorously promote the curriculum reform of automotive machinery education, adjust and reform the curriculum system, structure and content of automotive machinery education, and build a new automotive machinery education curriculum system that meets the requirements of quality education [4]. The implementation mode of curriculum resource reform is shown in Fig. 1 below.

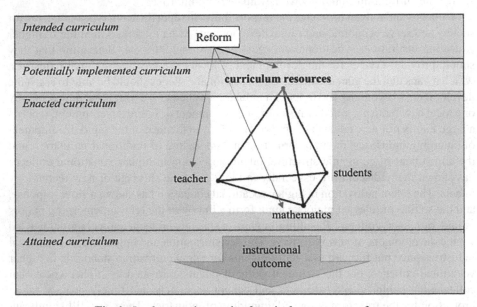

Fig. 1. Implementation mode of curriculum resource reform

In a sense, all educational purposes can only be achieved through curriculum, that is, curriculum reform is the way out of educational reform. The reform of automobile machinery education is a major measure of the country, and curriculum reform is the top priority. The curriculum reform of automotive machinery education is a complex social problem and a systematic project related to many aspects. The smooth implementation of the curriculum reform requires various support.

2   Related Work

2.1   Teaching Reform Puts Forward New Requirements for Specialty Construction and Curriculum Reform

The training goal of higher vocational colleges is to cultivate students' enterprise post skills. In today's increasingly fierce competition, although our theoretical study time has been reduced, we must not reduce the training specification. On the contrary, we should strengthen the training of post skills and highlight the practical ability of higher vocational students [5]. In order to adapt to the change of the new training mode, the courses are set up in two categories and four modules. Two categories: compulsory courses and elective courses; Four modules: vocational quality course, vocational ability course, vocational skill course and vocational development course.

(1) Vocational quality course: it is a general education course designated and set according to the talent training objectives and basic specifications. General education has become an indispensable part of the university education process, especially in the field of higher vocational education, the implementation of humanistic general education is an inevitable choice. Vocational quality course is a public course that lays a universal foundation for students' vocational knowledge, ability and quality and realizes the cultivation of students' basic quality. It usually includes ideological and political theory courses, public English, physical education, computer culture foundation, etc.

(2) Vocational ability course: it is divided into two parts: one is the course of basic knowledge, basic theory and basic skills of the major that students must master; The second is to deepen the professional foundation and learn professional skills, which are the core courses that reflect the characteristics of majors and professional directions. The course structure of professional courses adopts sub module combination, which has the flexibility of choice and the adaptability of professional posts [6]. Two or more directions can be set to change the single talent training mode.

(3) Vocational skills course: refers to the link of creating conditions for students and cultivating students' practical ability. Including entrance education, military training, internship (Internship), production labor, social practice activities, graduation thesis (Design), etc.

(4) Career development courses: students are allowed to choose courses to study. It is divided into vocational elective courses (also known as limited elective courses) and public elective courses (also known as optional courses).

In order to adapt to the change of the new training mode, the urgent task is to reform the existing curriculum system and achieve the talent training specification with less class hours [7]. Job skills are often measured by the vocational qualification certificates obtained by students, so we urgently need to find out the relationship between professional basic courses and professional courses, find out the dependence of job skills (evaluated by the acquisition rate of vocational qualification certificates) on professional basic courses and professional courses, and strive to design a reasonable sequence of classes, arrange an appropriate proportion of class hours and teachers, and achieve a reasonable allocation of teaching resources, Meet our talent training specifications with the minimum number of class hours and improve the acquisition rate of vocational qualification certificates.

2.2 Curriculum Reform of Apriori Algorithm

Apriori is a recursive algorithm based on the idea of two-stage frequent itemsets, which is the core algorithm. That is to say, Apriori algorithm is the most influential algorithm used by people to mine frequent itemsets of Boolean association rules.

The basic idea of Apriori algorithm is to first find all frequent itemsets from all itemsets. The so-called frequency means that the frequency of these itemsets should not be less than the predefined minimum support level. On this basis, strong association rules are generated from frequent itemsets. Of course, these rules must also meet the constraints of minimum support and minimum confidence. Then we use the frequent item set found in to generate the association rules we want, which is to generate all rules that contain only the items in the set. Each rule in these rules has only one item on the right, which is what we call the definition of a rule in. As long as these rules are generated, that is, only those rules that are greater than the minimum confidence level given by the user will be retained. In order to generate all frequent itemsets during mining, we use a recursive method to process them.

The two biggest drawbacks of Apriori algorithm are that it can generate a large number of candidate sets and may require repeatedly scanning the database many times during mining.

The Apriori algorithm is essentially a hierarchical iterative method for searching frequent itemsets. The search at each level is divided into two steps, namely, the connection and pruning of itemsets. The connection step is to find the k-term frequent itemset L_k. We can use the k-1 term frequent itemset L_{k-1}. A connection to itself to generate a set of candidate k-itemsets C_k. The second step, the pruning step, is to scan the transaction dataset and remove those transaction items that do not meet the support constraint, i.e. are less than the specified minimum support.

The algorithm starts by filtering from the simplest 1-item to find the L_1. After 1, we'll let L_1 and L_1. The self connection generates C, and then we filter all transaction items of C to generate L_2. By analogy, continue iterating until the final L_ Until k is an empty set.

$$support(\mathbf{A} \Rightarrow \mathbf{B}) = P(A \cup B) \tag{1}$$

$$confid(A \Rightarrow B) = P(A) \tag{2}$$

According to different classification standards, association rules can have the following classification forms:

(1) According to the type of data processed, association rules are often divided into Boolean and curriculum numerical types. Boolean association rules are used to handle discrete values, that is, these values are categorized; Unlike Boolean association rules, curriculum numerical association rules can be combined with multi-dimensional or multi-level association rules to process curriculum numerical fields and then dynamically segment them. There are also some methods that directly process the original data without segmentation. Of course, it should be noted that curriculum numerical association rules can include curriculum numerical variables, You can also handle containing category variables like Boolean association rules.

(2) According to the abstraction level of the data processed in our rules, we can divide association rules into two types: single level association rules and multi-layer association rules. The variables in the single level association rules do not consider the multi-level problem of real data; On the contrary, in multi-level association rules, people should fully consider the multi-level nature of data.

(3) If we divide the association rules based on the dimensions of the data involved in the rules, we can divide the association rules into two types: single dimensional and multidimensional.". In the former, which is a single dimension of association rules, we often only involve one dimension of data; However, in multidimensional association rules, the data we need to process usually involves multiple dimensions. In other

words, single dimensional association rules are used to handle some relationships within a single attribute; Multidimensional association rules are used to handle the association relationships between multiple attributes.

2.3 Systematic Stratification of Curriculum Reform

Nowadays, the competition among countries is essentially the competition of comprehensive national strength, and science and technology is an important factor of comprehensive national strength, so the improvement of comprehensive national strength depends on science and technology. The development of science and technology cannot be separated from education. In the final analysis, the development level of science and technology is determined by education. Today's education determines tomorrow's productivity development level, which has become the consensus of all countries in the world [8]. Curriculum is the core of school education. In order to reflect the value of education, enhance the competitiveness of the country, and give full play to the role of basic education in cultivating qualified construction talents, it is necessary to reform the old and backward basic education curriculum content, curriculum structure and management mode. In order to carry out the reform smoothly and achieve the expected results, the government must pay attention to the curriculum reform of basic education and try to play its own role in this process. The curriculum reform evaluation tool and data set are shown in Fig. 2 below.

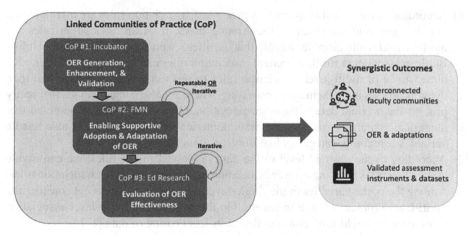

Fig. 2. Curriculum Reform Assessment Tools and Datasets

The deepening of the reform of educational system, educational thought, educational content and educational methods has updated and developed people's understanding of the nature, tasks and training objectives of basic education, and put forward the topics of educational reform and curriculum reform. The central task of curriculum reform is to innovate teaching content, actively carry out the reform of curriculum management mode, and strive to build a curriculum system with the goal of comprehensively improving students' quality [9].

Curriculum reform is a complex system engineering, which involves curriculum planning, textbook compilation and production, curriculum implementation, curriculum evaluation and curriculum improvement. Among them, curriculum planning, curriculum implementation and curriculum evaluation are the basic processes of curriculum reform. These processes require the participation of all kinds of personnel and factors. In order to make the overall dynamic system of curriculum reform achieve its set goals, we must optimize the structure of all levels and coordinate and manage all factors. Curriculum reform covers a wider range and contains more factors than the curriculum itself. In order to make the curriculum reform system advance smoothly, it is necessary to analyze the basic characteristics of the curriculum reform system to clarify the factors it contains, so that we can look at specific things as a whole, and then mobilize the enthusiasm of each factor, so that each factor can perform its own duties and do its best to ensure the realization of the purpose of the system.

3   Curriculum Reform of Automotive Machinery Education in Higher Vocational Colleges Based on Apriori Algorithm

3.1   Apriori Algorithm

According to different classification standards, association rules can have the following classification forms:

(1) According to what kind of quantity is processed, association rules are often divided into Boolean and numerical types. Among them, Boolean association rules are used to deal with discrete values, that is, these values are categorized; Unlike Boolean association rules, numerical association rules can be combined with multi-dimensional or multi-level association rules to process numerical fields, and then dynamically segment them after processing. There are also some methods to directly process the original data without segmentation. Of course, it should be noted that numerical association rules can contain numerical variables, You can also handle variables containing categories like Boolean association rules [10–12].

(2) According to the abstract level of the data processed in our rules, we can divide association rules into single-layer association rules and multi-layer association rules. Among them, the variables in the single-layer association rules do not consider the multi-level problem of data in reality; On the contrary, in multi-level association rules, people should fully consider the multi-level nature of data [13].

According to different classification standards, the classification of association rules is shown in Fig. 3.

Apriori is a recursive algorithm about the idea of two-stage frequent itemsets, which is the core algorithm. That is to say, Apriori algorithm is the most influential algorithm used by people to mine the frequent itemsets of Boolean association rules.

The basic idea of Apriori algorithm is to find all frequent itemsets from all itemsets first. The so-called frequency means that the frequency of these itemsets should not be less than the predefined minimum support. On this basis, strong association rules are generated from frequent itemsets. Of course, these rules must also meet the constraints of

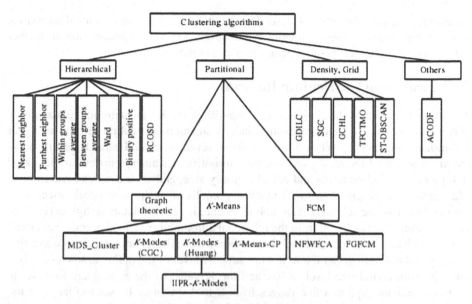

Fig. 3. Classification of association rule algorithm

minimum support and minimum reliability [14]. Then we use the found frequent itemset to generate the association rules we want to get, that is, to generate all rules that contain only the items of the set. There is only one item on the right of each rule in these rules, which is the definition of what we call the rule in. As long as these rules are generated, that is to say, only those rules that are greater than the minimum confidence given by the user will be retained. In order to generate all frequent itemsets during mining, we use a recursive method to deal with them.

$$\|\Delta x_{k+1}(t)\| \leq \int_0^t e^{(pk_f + m_2 + m_3)(t - \tau)}(m_1\|\Delta u_k(\tau)\| + pd)d \tag{3}$$

The two biggest disadvantages of Apriori algorithm are that it may produce a large number of candidate sets, and it may need to repeatedly scan the database many times during mining.

3.2 Application of Apriori Algorithm in Curriculum Reform of Automotive Machinery Education in Higher Vocational Colleges

At present, the vast majority of information in Colleges and universities is stored in the form of relational databases. The association rules in relational databases and transaction databases have different characteristics. This chapter combines some student performance data of Vocational and technical colleges, first converts the relational database into a Boolean based transaction database, and then studies the transaction database [15].

This kind of database is built according to the relational model, and the fields are based on certain The basic unit of organization is the data table. Therefore, mining association rules in relational database is the process of finding strong association rules in several tables of relational database. This section first discusses relational databases, analyzes the characteristics of relational databases, and then discusses how to further extend the related concepts of association rules to relational databases.

4   Research on Curriculum Reform

This article is based on the classic Apriori algorithm to mine the automotive machinery curriculum data of the automotive machinery education curriculum reform in higher vocational colleges [16]. When mining, you can set the threshold value for each course based on actual needs, set the amount of automotive machinery curriculum data read into memory based on needs and actual memory size, and click the Read Automotive Machinery Curriculum Data to Memory button, Read in the automobile mechanics course data from the relational automobile mechanics course database SglServer2005, and complete the conversion from the relational automobile mechanics course database to the Boolean based transactional automobile mechanics course database according to the threshold setting. Set the minimum support level of the main parameters to 0.2, the minimum confidence level to 0.6, and the K value of the K frequent item set to 2. The minimum support value ranges from 0 to 1. "Cannot be set too large or too small. If the value is set too low, the algorithm may take a long time to process and require a lot of memory;"; If the setting is too large, many rules and knowledge may be omitted. The minimum confidence value ranges from 0 to 1 [17]. The values of the above parameters should be set based on actual situations and expert experience. Setting them too small can lead to too many rules being generated, making it difficult to discover useful knowledge. Setting them too large can lead to too few rules being generated, and also loss of useful knowledge. Maximum Itemset Specifies the value of the maximum itemset. Reducing the maximum itemset value will reduce processing time, because when the size of the candidate set reaches this limit, the mining algorithm does not need to further iterate over the automotive machinery course dataset. Therefore, the minimum support threshold and minimum confidence threshold and minimum confidence threshold should be determined not only based on experience and the opinions of domain experts, but also mainly based on the size of the automotive machinery course dataset. The main reason for determining which threshold is appropriate is through experiments, because there is a significant relationship between the threshold and the automotive machinery course dataset.

The transactional automotive machinery curriculum database contains items that only come from the same dimension, so we can consider the relational automotive machinery curriculum database to be a broader form of transactional automotive machinery curriculum database [18]. The relational automotive machinery curriculum database has been expanded in dimension compared to the transactional automotive machinery curriculum database. Therefore, we can consider that the mining technology of association rules in the relational automotive machinery course database is more extensive and generalized than the mining technology of Boolean association rules in the transactional automotive machinery course database. From the above comparison, it can be seen that the mining technology of association rules in the relational automotive machinery course database based on Boolean transformation can obtain correct strong rules, However, due to the fact that the relational automotive machinery course database we are dealing with has many multivalued classification attributes, numerical values, and other type attributes, our discretization of these attributes inevitably increases the time overhead caused by the preprocessing of automotive machinery course data during the entire mining process. We have also increased the storage space occupied by the conversion of the relational automotive machinery course database by a lot [19]. Therefore, it can be said that although the mining method of association rules in the relational automotive machinery course database based on Boolean transformation is theoretically feasible, it is actually at the cost of sacrificing the running time and storage space of the entire mining process.

When the program is running, the minimum support level is set to 0.2, the minimum confidence level is set to 0.6, and the K value of the K frequent item set is set to 2. The minimum support value range is 0–1, and the minimum confidence value range is 0–1. "These values cannot be set too low, otherwise the algorithm may result in significantly longer processing times and require a significant amount of memory.". Of course, the setting of the above parameters should be based on actual experience and the opinions of domain experts. If the setting is too small, it will lead to too many rules generated, making it difficult to discover useful knowledge. If the setting is too large, it may lead to too few rules generated, and also lead to the loss of a lot of useful knowledge [20]. Reducing the maximum itemset value will reduce processing time, because when the size of the candidate set reaches this limit, the Apriori algorithm does not require further iterations on the automotive mechanics course dataset.

5 Conclusion

On the premise of introducing the related concepts and research status of data mining, this paper describes the origin, definition and classification of association rules in detail, and studies the methods and processes of data mining. It analyzes two classical algorithms apriori, which are used to mine in transaction database, and then extends the problem to relational database, The algorithm of mining association rules in relational database is analyzed. Combined with the score data of some students in Vocational and technical colleges, the relevant knowledge and rules are mined in the experiment, which provides theoretical guidance and data support for our curriculum reform and professional construction.

References

1. Yu, H.-T.: A research of differentiation education mode in chorus class in higher vocational colleges. DEStech Trans. Soc. Sci. Educ. Hum. Sci. (2017)
2. Hu, Y.: Discussion and research on the professional english reform of automotive major in vocational colleges based on ability. In: Proceedings of the 2018 International Workshop on Education Reform and Social Sciences (ERSS 2018) (2019)
3. Guo, Q.C., Zhao, L.I., Tian, D.J.: Research on curriculum reform of "municipal engineering map drawing and recognition" in higher vocational colleges based on outcome based education. Heilongjiang Sci. (2018)

4. Chen, J.H.: Research on the curriculum reform of logistics cost management in higher vocational colleges based on the cultivation of sustainable competitiveness. Logist. Eng. Manag. (2018)
5. Xie, H., Yuan, C.: Research on the reform of music appreciation curriculum system in higher vocational colleges based on CBE. Sci. Technol. Vis. (2018)
6. Chen, X.Q., Zhao, H., Hao, J.: Research on curriculum reform of market investigation and forecast in higher vocational colleges based on career-oriented orientation. J. Hubei Ind. Polytech. (2018)
7. Xiang, W.: Research on the curriculum reform of "computer application foundation" in higher vocational colleges. Sci. Educ. Article Collects (2019)
8. Bao-Yu, L.I., Ling, Y.E.: Research on the necessity and importance of physical education curriculum reform in higher vocational colleges from the perspective of professional physical development. J. Beijing Coll. Finance Commer. (2019)
9. Zhou, H.Q., Chen, Y.Q.: Research on optimization of higher mathematics curriculum system and reform of teaching content in higher vocational colleges. J. Jiamusi Vocat. Inst. (2018)
10. Yi, Z.: Vocational college automotive marketing project curriculum reform based on skills competition. Guide Sci. Educ. (2016)
11. Xu, S., Zhang, X., Amp, V., et al.: Teaching reform and exploration of automotive machinery foundation course in higher vocational college. Automob. Appl. Technol. (2019)
12. Zhang, S.: Research on the reform of curriculum assessment for tourism management majors in higher vocational education based on the flipped classroom. Times Agric. Mach. (2017)
13. Wu, D., Wang, J.: Research on the reform of public physical education teaching in higher vocational colleges based on club system. Sci. Educ. Article Collects (2019)
14. Tang, G.F.: Research on practical path of "ideological and political education in curriculum" in higher vocational colleges based on problem orientation. J. Hubei Open Vocat. Coll. (2019)
15. Chen, Y.C.: Research on curriculum reforming practice of preschool education in higher vocational colleges. Educ. Teach. Forum (2018)
16. Zhou, C.X., Fang, S.L., Zhang, Z.H.: Research on curriculum reform of port and waterway engineering in higher vocational education. J. Heilongjiang Vocat. Inst. Ecol. Eng. (2018)
17. Wang, H.: Research on informationalized teaching reform of computer specialty in higher vocational colleges based on the education cloud platform. J. Qingdao Tech. Coll. (2019)
18. Zhong-Wen, H.U.: A research on the teaching reform of "automobile maintenance technology" in higher vocational colleges based on micro-lectures. Jiangsu Educ. Res. (2017)
19. Liu, Y.L.: Research on the curriculum reform of the profile of guest source country course in higher vocational school based on innovation angle. J. Heilongjiang Coll. Educ. (2019)
20. Liu, X.G.: Research on the reform of software testing courses in higher vocational colleges based on mobile technology. Educ. Teach. Forum (2018)

The Role of Internet of Things Educational Technology in Improving the Teaching Quality of Normal Students

Ding Miao[1,2(✉)] and Wentong Zhang[1,2]

[1] Yunnan College of Business Management, Yunnan 650106, China
dingmiao212@aliyun.com
[2] Lijiang Culture and Tourism College, Yunnan 674199, China

Abstract. At present, there is a big gap between the educational technology ability of normal students and the development of basic education. Relying on only one public course of educational technology, it is difficult to ensure that normal students systematically and deeply master educational technology skills, Reforming the teaching method of educational technology public course is an important way to achieve the goal of cultivating normal students' educational technology ability.

Keyword: Internet of things educational technology · Normal students · Teaching quality

1 Introduction

With the rapid development of information technology, teachers who are responsible for the dissemination of knowledge and skills should have good information literacy. At present, normal colleges train front-line teachers for basic education in rural areas. Due to the relative lack of modern teaching equipment for basic education in rural areas, especially in the western frontier minority areas, the teaching task of exam oriented education is still relatively heavy, and there is still a large gap with the requirements of modern educational technology. It is necessary to train "go down, stay and use" For normal students, they will face the problem of how to effectively integrate the limited information technology resources with the knowledge courses taught. Combined with the research on the curriculum reform of modern educational technology, they put forward the following ideas of teaching reform, hoping to provide help to the cultivation of normal students' educational technology ability.

The Ministry of Education officially launched the "development of educational technology competence standards for primary and secondary school teachers" project in April 2003, and officially promulgated the educational technology competence standards for primary and secondary school teachers (Trial) (hereinafter referred to as the standards) in December 2004, which is the first professional competence standard for teachers issued by China since the founding of the people's Republic of China [1]. The promulgation of

Y. Zhang and N. Shah (Eds.): BigIoT-EDU 2023, LNICST 584, pp. 165–170, 2024.
https://doi.org/10.1007/978-3-031-63142-9_16

the standard also provides an important basis for the current public curriculum reform of educational technology for normal students, which puts forward normative requirements for teachers and future teachers' educational technology ability from the four dimensions of consciousness and attitude, knowledge and skills, application and innovation and social responsibility. In this way, we can change the current curriculum teaching. Due to the different reference standards of teaching materials and teaching contents selected by various schools, there are great differences in training objectives. Since the standard has put forward perfect training objectives for normal students' educational technology ability, the problem that schools need to solve is how to carry out teaching reform to achieve this training objective.

2 Related Work

2.1 Overview of the Internet of Things

Internet of things (IOD), also known as sensor network, is the extension of the Internet from people to things. It refers to the deployment of connected chips and software systems with certain perception and information processing capabilities in the real physical world to realize information transmission and real-time processing through network facilities, so as to realize the communication between things and people. R. As the "skin" of building the Internet of things, RFID is essentially a non-contact automatic identification technology. It automatically identifies the target object and obtains relevant data through RF signals, so as to realize the automatic identification and management of various objects in different states (moving, stationary and harsh environment). By pasting RFID electronic tag on mobile learner's mobile phone SIM card, when mobile learner carries mobile phone SIM card with RFID electronic tag through the tag identifier, the electronic tag is automatically sensed by the tag identifier, and the information in the electronic tag is transmitted to the information processing center through wireless network. After processing, the processing result is sent to the tag identifier, So as to realize flexible and efficient automatic identification and information management.

2.2 Main Features of the Internet of Things

According to people's understanding of the Internet of things, the Internet of things refers to the deployment of some software and embedded chips with certain computing ability, perception ability and execution ability on the actual objects in the real world, so as to make the objects become "intelligent objects", and realize information transmission, collaboration and processing through some network facilities, Realize the interconnection between objects and people and between objects. The hierarchical structure of the Internet of things is shown in Fig. 1. The Internet of things has the following three main features:

1) Comprehensive perception refers to the real-time collection and acquisition of object information by using some sensing, capture and measurement technologies, such as sensor QR code and radio frequency identification; Sensing devices are particularly important to the Internet of things, such as radio frequency identification (RFID),

infrared sensors, global positioning system, laser scanners and other information sensing devices, which are particularly important to the Internet of things. They are important components in the Internet of things. With these sensing devices, data readout and data transmission can be realized, as well as some automatic sensing without contact at a long (short) distance.

2) Reliable transmission is to send some information about objects accurately and in real time through the integration of some Internet and telecommunication networks; For the Internet of things, it is an integration, an integration of a variety of networks and connecting and application technologies. At the same time, it is also a platform that enables objects to communicate with people, nature and people, and objects and objects. Therefore, under the requirements of relevant protocols, implementing the collaborative work of multiple networks and the co-existence of collaborative and distributed is an important feature of the Internet of things. Compared with the Internet, the Internet of things is very open and has some new capabilities, such as being able to accept new components and provide new services at any time, that is, the Internet of things has the ability of self-organization and self adaptation. This is the key to the realization of Internet of things technology, and it is also an aspect that people value.

3) Intelligent processing is one of the core contents of the Internet of things. It uses some intelligent computing (such as fuzzy recognition, cloud computing, etc.) to analyze and process a large amount of information and data, so as to intelligently control objects. "Intelligence" refers to the comprehensive ability of an individual to make some purposeful behaviors through analysis and judgment of objective things, and to effectively and reasonably deal with matters in the surrounding environment. The Internet of things is the product of the continuous development and integration of computer network technology, microprocessor technology, wireless communication technology and sensor technology. The Internet of things can represent or even replace people to reasonably analyze and judge objective things, act purposefully, and then deal with the surrounding environmental matters. "Intelligence is a manifestation of the comprehensive ability of the Internet of things.

3   Improvement of Teaching Quality of Normal Students by Internet of Things Educational Technology

3.1   Application of Internet of Things in Educational Technology

The application of Internet of things in education can be roughly divided into the following fields, with different applications in different fields

(1) Information teaching. Use the Internet of things to establish a ubiquitous learning environment. Smart tags can be used to identify the objects to learn, and adjust the learning content according to the students' learning behavior records. This is an expansion of traditional classroom and virtual experiment. In terms of space and interaction, it enhances students' experience through field investigation and practice.

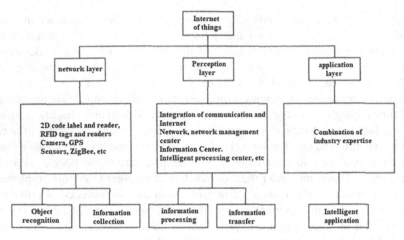

Fig. 1. Hierarchy diagram of Internet of things

(2) Education management. The Internet of things can be used in personnel attendance, book management, equipment management and so on. For example, a student card with RFID tag can monitor students' access to various teaching facilities and their action route. As another example, RFID can be used for book management, books can be easily found through RFID tags, and book information can be easily obtained when borrowing books without taking out and scanning books one by one.

(3) Smart campus. As shown in Fig. 2, the intelligent teaching environment and the control of the Internet of things can also be used in the fields of campus traffic management, vehicle management, campus safety, teacher-student health, intelligent buildings, student life services, etc. For example, install light sensors and controllers in the classroom to adjust the illuminance in the classroom according to the light intensity and the position of students. Another example is to install cameras and

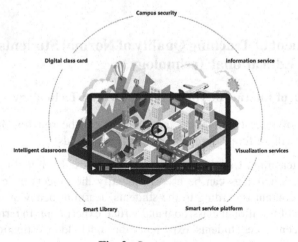

Fig. 2. Smart campus

infrared sensors in areas with potential safety hazards in the school to realize safety monitoring and automatic alarm.

3.2 Public Courses in Educational Technology

Opening public courses of educational technology for all normal students is the main channel to Cultivate Normal Students' educational technology ability. Educational technology is a new marginal discipline, involving many fields of knowledge, but the main goal of public course teaching is not to cultivate experts in educational technology, but to cultivate the practical application ability of ordinary normal students. Therefore, in the arrangement of teaching content, remember "Large and comprehensive", we should reasonably adjust the teaching content and highlight the cultivation of practical application ability. In teaching, we should select the teaching content, reasonably arrange the curriculum structure and strengthen the practical links of teaching according to the future teaching needs of different scientific students.

In the arrangement of the specific content of the public course of educational technology, it generally includes the following main parts: the core content of educational technology ability is teaching design, so teaching design is also the focus of the teaching content of the public course of educational technology; the application of conventional media, computer multimedia and network technology is the teaching focus of the skill part [2]. Because the basic technology of computer and network is in the public course of computer It has been learned in, so this part focuses on the design and production of special multimedia teaching software and network teaching software, and the teaching software selected for students of different disciplines is also different and focused. For example, the geometric sketchpad teaching software is only taught for students majoring in mathematics.

4 Internet of Things Educational Technology Strengthens the Teaching Content of Information Retrieval and Curriculum Integration

(1) Clarify the teaching objectives and highlight the teaching contents of "information retrieval" and "curriculum integration" After the teaching focus of public courses, the key lies in how to implement it in the teaching process. Teachers should guide students according to the efficiency and quality of information retrieval, so that students can master how to find and collect the required knowledge content through the Internet as soon as possible, and guide students how to organically combine the found knowledge with the teaching content they may engage in in in the future, Achieve the teaching goal of improving students' information literacy and realize the deep integration of information technology and curriculum [3].

(2) Combined with students' professional characteristics, make full use of network resources to carry out curriculum design. The professional classification of normal universities determines the general direction of teaching that normal students will engage in in in the future When the public course of modern educational technology is taught to students of different majors, it is necessary to carry out targeted

training on the curriculum design of relevant majors, which will improve students' interest in learning and their ability to use modern teaching media.

(3) Strengthen extracurricular practice and comprehensively improve students' information literacy. Relying solely on Modern Educational Technology In the limited time in the classroom, it is difficult for students to really master how to complete relevant curriculum teaching tasks through information retrieval and curriculum integration, which requires teachers to increase the training of how to carry out curriculum design ability by using network resources in the after-school and assessment content, so that students can strengthen extracurricular learning and improve their personal information through their own efforts The purpose of literacy [4].

5 Conclusion

At present, the construction of normal students' educational technology ability is still in the development stage, the examination and certification need to be completed independently by each school, and the evaluation standards are still different. However, with the passage of time and the further improvement of teachers' educational technology ability certification system, the assessment of normal students' educational technology ability will also step into the standardized stage, so as to realize the integration with in-service teachers' educational technology ability certification Like the current computer and English level examination, it is certified by a unified organization, and the results can be recognized by all schools, so that normal students do not need to participate in similar repeated training after working. Improving normal students' educational technology ability is a systematic project, which involves the school's curriculum system, teachers, experimental and practical training conditions and so on Therefore, it is not a career that can be completed in a short time, but also needs to be continuously explored and improved in practice.

References

1. Yuan, D.: Investigation and training strategy of educational technology ability of normal students in local colleges and universities. J. Shangrao Normal Univ. (6) (2010)
2. Luo, L., Qu, W.: Investigation and reflection on the cultivation of educational technology ability of normal students -- taking southwest university as an example. J. Southwest Agric. Univ. Soc. Sci. Ed. (2) (2010)
3. Yang, Z.: Research on strategies to enhance the effectiveness of training normal students' educational technology ability. Mod. Educ. Sci. (2011)
4. Cheng, L.: Reflections on the problems existing in the cultivation of normal students' educational technology ability. Teacher growth (2008)

Evaluation of Technical Ability of High-Level Table Tennis Players Based on Multimedia Video

Xiaomei Sun[1]([✉]), Li Lu[2], and Minfa Shi[2]

[1] Yunnan Normal University Business School, Kunming 650051, China
meizibang8@163.com
[2] The Academy of Marxism of Hefei Technology College, Hefei 230012, Anhui, China

Abstract. In view of the technical characteristics of table tennis matches and the shortcomings of traditional evaluation methods, a technical ability evaluation system for high-level table tennis players based on multimedia video is constructed. The purpose of this study is to evaluate the technical ability of high-level table tennis players based on multimedia video. We will use a 3D motion analysis system, Kinect for Xbox 360, to measure the technical performance of each player in a real-time environment, and then use statistical software (SPSS) for analysis. The competition data collection software was developed, and the technical data of high-level athletes at home and abroad were collected by using competition video to achieve the continuity and systematicness of data collection. The PSO algorithm combined with neural network was used to evaluate the technical ability of high-level table tennis players on the spot. The model accuracy and convergence were good, which provided a certain decision-making reference for guiding athletes' training and competition.

1 Introduction

In China, there are many researches in the field of sports psychology related to the theory of task self goal orientation, including those that test the theory and those that apply the theory to guide practice. These studies have achieved certain results. However, there are still some unsolved problems, such as the concept and relationship between "task" and "self"; The function of "task" goal and "ego" goal; In the existing research, few studies distinguish the goal orientation from the goal state. At present, most of the studies involve the individual tendency of goals, and in sports practice, the state goals of athletes are more interesting to applied sports psychologists [1]. The friction between the existing research status and the new theoretical guidance has aroused the discussion spark of this researcher.

Many coaches and athletes still use traditional training methods in training, and they think what they used in the past is what they should use now. Some coaches are completely unable to distinguish the quality of athletes' movements, or why some movements are safer and more efficient than others, or why some movements are more likely to cause injury and make athletes unstable. Some coaches like to use trial and error training methods. In the absence of sports biomechanics knowledge, the coach will guess the

Y. Zhang and N. Shah (Eds.): BigIoT-EDU 2023, LNICST 584, pp. 171–182, 2024.
https://doi.org/10.1007/978-3-031-63142-9_17

way to improve or enhance sports skills. Sometimes they can get good results, but most of the time they have no harvest. This misguided experiment will also cause physical injury to athletes. Many coaches will carry out skill training for athletes according to the sports skills of world champions, but they do not take into account the differences in body shape, ability and maturity between them.

For training athletes' sports skills, it is very important to distinguish safe, mechanically correct actions and invalid actions. Coaches and athletes who blindly imitate other people's training methods and sports skills cannot improve. Perhaps this limited attention to sports technology is a reflection of the contents of publications in the field of sports science. A survey of sports science pointed out that physiology - a subject that studies the response of sports to human body structure and physiological function - is the most worthy of in-depth study. Sports biomechanics studies how the human body moves and can best describe sports technology. This book can help people correct wrong exercise methods. Through understanding the principles of mechanics, readers can analyze the characteristics of motion and learn to use more efficient ways of motion, so that they can have better performance.

Table tennis is a national sport in China, which undertakes the important task of winning gold medals in major events such as the Olympic Games, the World Championships and the World Cup. However, at present, the level of top players at home and abroad is very close, the competition is becoming increasingly fierce, and the situation of winning gold medals is becoming increasingly severe. Athletes' technical ability, tactical ability, on-the-spot psychological state, physical function state, coaches' guidance level, competition venue, and even competition equipment will affect the outcome of the game. These factors interact and combine, showing disorder, uncertainty and randomness, Among them, the athletes' on-the-spot technical and tactical ability is the main factor determining the outcome of the game, and the physical function and psychological factors are finally reflected through the athletes' on-the-spot technical and tactical behavior. Since the 1980s, many experts and scholars at home and abroad have devoted themselves to the research and practice of the evaluation and diagnosis of the on-the-spot technical and tactical abilities of high-level table tennis players. The major influential and widely used methods are the segmented index evaluation method proposed by Wu Huanqun and the ten index evaluation method proposed by Li Jinliang [2]. The traditional technical and tactical evaluation method is easy to operate and fast, and can timely feed back the technical and tactical statistical data to the coaches. However, it is greatly affected by the subjective influence of coaches and experts, and there are few evaluation indicators, so it is easy to miss some important technical and tactical ability information. Based on the multimedia video database of major competitions, this paper collects the technical data of high-level athletes at home and abroad, and realizes the continuity and systematicness of data collection [3]. It uses particle swarm optimization algorithm and neural network to evaluate the technical ability of high-level table tennis players on the spot. The model has high precision and good convergence, and can further combine the facial expressions, emotional actions Language is used to evaluate the psychological ability of athletes in competitions.

2 Related Work

2.1 Construction of Evaluation Indicators

Establishing a scientific and reasonable evaluation index system of table tennis players' ability is the key to building the model. The determination of the indicator system is related to whether it can accurately reflect the actual work situation of table tennis players. Improper selection of indicators will bring certain deviation to the results of the evaluation method. Considering the impact of various factors existing in the reality on the evaluation results, this paper believes that a relatively scientific and objective indicator system should be established by following the principle of combining importance and comprehensiveness and combining quantitative and qualitative indicators.

There are a lot of uncertainties in the table tennis player cycle of the software project, including short-term projects and long-term projects, so it is not necessary to evaluate the ability of the project personnel after the project is completed, but can divide the table tennis player process into several stages, and evaluate the ability of the table tennis player personnel in each stage [4].

Calculate index weight.

The weight value of the evaluation index can be obtained by ranking the index system model by the judgment matrix and relevant calculation. For judgment matrix A, calculate formula $AW = \lambda_{max} W$. The maximum eigenvalue and eigenvector, where λ_{max} x is the largest characteristic root of the judgment matrix A, and w is A corresponding to λ_{max} The eigenvector also represents the weight set corresponding to the index set, and its component w is the weight value of the corresponding index of the level. This paper selects the sum method to calculate the weight value, and the specific steps are as follows.

It is obtained after normalizing matrix A;

$$\overline{A} = (\overline{x}_y), \overline{x}_y = \frac{x_y}{\sum_{i=1}^{n} x_0}, i,j = 1, 2, \cdots, n \tag{1}$$

Add A by line to get:

$$\overline{W} = \sum_{j=1}^{n} \overline{X}_{ij} = \begin{bmatrix} w_I \\ w_2 \\ \vdots \\ w_n \end{bmatrix} \tag{2}$$

Normalize w to obtain:

$$W = \begin{bmatrix} w_I \\ w_2 \\ \vdots \\ w_n \end{bmatrix}, w_i = \frac{\overline{w}_i}{\sum_{i=I}^{n} w_i} \tag{3}$$

Because there is a certain correlation between the data of various indicators reflecting the ability of table tennis players, it is impossible to accurately select specific indicators to measure the ability of table tennis players. If too few indicators are selected, some important information may be omitted, thus reducing the accuracy of the evaluation model. If too many indicators are selected, it will not only increase the corresponding amount of calculation, but also increase the difficulty of analysis due to the large amount of duplicate information between the evaluation indicators [5]. Therefore, the factor analysis method is selected to reduce the dimension of the index. This method transforms the problem of multiple index variables in the original high-dimensional space into the low-dimensional space, and forms a new factor variable to replace the original variable for subsequent correlation processing. The new variable obtained is a linear combination of the original variables, which can retain the original information to the greatest extent [6]. The factor analysis method has the advantages of strong objectivity and independent of the subjective attitude of the decision-maker, but it is easy to appear that the determined weight of the index is inconsistent with the actual situation. Therefore, it is considered to set the corresponding weight value for the original evaluation index by combining the analytic hierarchy process with expert experience before it, so as to improve the recognition rate of the sample data.

2.2 Domestic Research Status

There are four papers on technical play in China. Li Bo's Synergistic Analysis of the Evolution of Table Tennis Technical Play System uses the essence of synergetics theory to analyze the evolution law of the table tennis technical play system, emphasizing that the evolution power of the open system should be based on the non-linear organizational vitality within the system. Li Tie's Discussion on the Technical Play of Table Tennis in Heilongjiang Province, Wang Fei's Analysis on the Technical Play of Table Tennis among Teenagers in Heilongjiang Province, and Huang Xuelin's Analysis on the Technical Play of Table Tennis among Teenagers in Heilongjiang Province are mainly aimed at discussing the phenomenon of imbalance between the way of my racket and the type of play, and putting forward corresponding countermeasures [7]. This paper is mainly from the perspective of driving the evolution of table tennis techniques.

There are 20 papers on the development trend of table tennis in China. Huang Qi's Talking about the Way Out and Analysis of Table Tennis Slicing has studied how to break through and improve itself in the rapid development of attack technology today, analyzed the unfavorable factors affecting the chopping in terms of training and technical and tactical awareness, and put forward corresponding suggestions.

Qi Kexin investigated 33 excellent table tennis teams registered by the General Administration of Sport of the People's Republic of China in the article "The construction and development trend of the playing style of China's excellent table tennis players", and learned the proportion of each playing style. Then through the statistics of the distribution of the playing style of the top three male and female sports teams who participated in the large group competitions from 2001 to 2005, a reasonable proportion of the future sports teams in China was constructed.

Liu Fengde, in the Analysis of the Technical Development Trend of Women's Doubles and Mixed Doubles in Table Tennis – Research Report on Women's Doubles and Mixed Doubles in the 48th World Table Tennis Championships, through on-site statistics of women's doubles and mixed doubles in the 48th World Table Tennis Championships, obtained the scoring rate and utilization rate of the main players in the service and snatch stages, reception and snatch stages, stalemate stages and other data. On this basis, it analyzes the technical reasons for the victory of women's doubles and mixed doubles players in China and the development trend of women's doubles and mixed doubles technology in the world in the future [5].

Chinese scholars have also conducted other types of research on table tennis. Yu Fangliang and others analyzed and studied Wang Hao's technical and tactical application in the French snatch, catch snatch and stalemate in the men's singles final of table tennis in the 29th Olympic Games, providing a reference for the future training and competition of our table tennis team. Zhang Wei provided some ideas for the development of table tennis professionalism in China by analyzing the process of table tennis professionalism and the characteristics of the management system in Germany [8]. The research on the importance and training methods of table tennis players' psychological training conducted by Li Yueling and others provides a reference for improving the psychological quality of table tennis players in China.

2.3   Research Status Abroad

Compared with our country, there is relatively little research on table tennis abroad. On the spring foreign language periodical website, in the search with the theme of "Table tennis", there were two papers on table tennis and four book chapters. Most of the research focuses on mechanics, film and television production and computer software development. However, there are few articles that really study the techniques, tactics and playing styles of table tennis. Physicist Carole's Dynamic Analysis of Table Tennis uses the relevant theory of fluid mechanics to timely create a reasonable arc in the game and improve the internal mechanism of hit rate. In the article "Research on Film and Television System of Table Tennis Class", scholar Tony developed the shortcomings of gesture recognition technology in processing video of table tennis matches, introduced a more efficient method (gesture based), and realized the gamification of table tennis matches. In a chapter of the book "Research on Dynamic Control Robot and Human Playing Table Tennis", David, a scholar, put forward some ideas, that is, to program all the information of table tennis players of different styles, use robots as companions, and improve the competition ability of players in the form of man-machine practice [9].

To sum up, the articles of experts and scholars on technical play are mainly limited to the research on the adverse phenomena of technical play in a certain province or city. The trend paper only talks about the development trend of table tennis from the research on the current situation of a certain playing method or a certain competition [9]. However, on the basis of summing up the historical laws, this study reveals the internal impetus to promote the evolution of table tennis techniques, and discusses the future development trend from the aspects of playing methods, technical and tactical patterns and guiding ideology [10]. Therefore, this study has some new ideas and has certain theoretical and practical value in promoting the development of table tennis.

3 Technical Ability Evaluation of High-Level Table Tennis Players Based on Multimedia Video

3.1 General Characteristics of Table Tennis Competition Techniques

The implementation process of table tennis competition technology is actually a process of control and counter control. It combines the changes of rotation, line, speed, arc, impact point, strength and rhythm to effectively mobilize the other party, increase the difficulty of the other party's hitting, reduce the technical quality of hitting, and force the other party to make mistakes in hitting [11]. Table 1 below shows the technical ability characteristics of high-level table tennis players.

Table 1. Characteristics of technical ability of high-level table tennis players

Scale type	Comprehensive scales	Number of gauges	Reasonableness	threshold
Technical value	synthesis	500M	0.85	0.6
	So so	1G	0.65	0.6
Capacity scale	synthesis	500M	0.75	0.6
	So so	1G	0.69	0.6
Personality scale	synthesis	500M	0.75	0.6
	So so	1G	0.92	0.6

There are many kinds of hitting techniques in table tennis, and they are complex, random and flexible. The technical type, playing method, psychological situation and physical function of opponents are closely related to the selection and play of on-site techniques. Generally speaking, table tennis techniques can be divided into restrictive and non restrictive techniques Non restrictive technology means that the use of players' technology is not affected by the other party, that is, serving; The restrictive technology refers to that in the course of competition, the use of players' technology will be limited by the conditions of the opponent's arrival. The restrictive technology can be divided into three categories: offensive technology, control technology and defensive technology [12]. The offensive technology includes loop, fast attack, smash and hit. The control technology includes split length, swing short, block and short shot. The defensive technology includes chop, block and high shot.

After the weight of each index is obtained by the analytic hierarchy process, it is not suitable to train the neural network directly. Because more evaluation indicators will increase the complexity of the neural network model and slow down the convergence speed, thus reducing the accuracy of the evaluation results. If the index with lower weight is discarded directly and the index with higher weight is used to train the neural network, the result will have strong subjective color and destroy the integrity of the original data information [13]. Therefore, the factor analysis method is selected to reduce the dimension of the original multi-indicator system, and several new factor indicator variables are generated to replace the original variables for the next step. The new factor variables are a linear combination of the original variables, which can save the original information of the data to the maximum extent. While reducing the dimension of the multi-indicator data, it can also complete the reduction operation of the statistical characteristics of the indicator data set. The set of variables thus obtained provides favorable conditions for the establishment of the mathematical model to be carried out in the next step [14]. The simulation results of technical capability scoring processing are shown in Fig. 1 below.

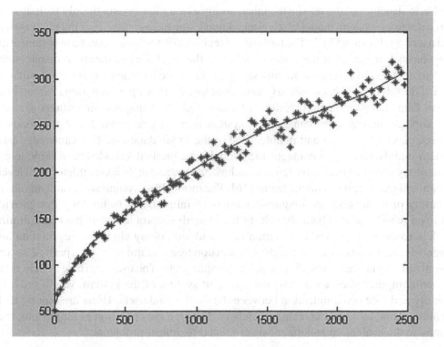

Fig. 1. Technical ability score processing simulation results

It can be seen from the table that for KMO test, the test value obtained is 0.836, which is suitable for factor analysis according to the judgment criteria described above. According to Bartlett's sphericity test results, the sphericity test reached a significant level, so the factor analysis method can be used for analysis. Among them, the significance value is 0.000, which means that each subsystem rejects the assumption that each indicator variable is independent of each other [15].

There are a variety of influencing factors in the ability evaluation of table tennis players, including qualitative factors and quantitative factors. Because of the different dimensions between the two, it is impossible to compare, so the first task is to eliminate the impact of different dimensions between the indicator data in this method. The indicator data set is standardized according to formula (4).

$$X_{ij} = \frac{x_{ij} - \overline{x}_i}{\sigma_i}, (i = 1, 2, \cdots, n) \tag{4}$$

The goal of factor analysis is to use as few factors as possible to produce a large variance contribution rate, and to achieve the goal of using a few common factors to express enough information of original capacity indicators.

3.2 Basic Structure of Evaluation System for On-site Technical Ability of High-Level Table Tennis Players

Based on the technical characteristics of high-level athletes, combined with user needs, the basic structure of the on-site technical ability evaluation system mainly includes five parts: database system, model base system, knowledge base system, user interface system and users, as shown in Fig. 2. The table tennis technical information database system is the most basic component of the system, including the database and database management system, in which the database mainly stores the multimedia video and other information data of the Olympic Games, World Championships, World Cup, International Grand Prix, Asian Cup, Eurasian Games, National Games and other major competitions at home and abroad; the database management system is mainly responsible for the creation, access, playback, editing and maintenance of the video database. The knowledge base system mainly stores and manages the explicit and implicit knowledge of table tennis technology obtained from table tennis coaches, experts and high-level athletes at all levels of national teams and provincial teams [16]. The model base system stores and maintains a variety of evaluation and diagnosis models of table tennis technology that provide decision reasoning, comparative selection and analysis problems, such as data mining models based on improved association rules and ant colony algorithm, evaluation and diagnosis algorithms based on rough sets, decision trees, neural networks, particle swarm optimization, genetics, annealing, system dynamics, etc. The user interface system is the human-computer interface and its management system of the system, which provides friendly and safe communication between the system and users. Users are mainly table tennis coaches, athletes and team researchers. Through the operation of the system, they complete the evaluation and diagnosis of related technical problems.

4 Table Tennis Technical Data Acquisition System Based on Multimedia Video Library

Compared with traditional words and statistical data, the competition multimedia video integrates images, graphics, actions, sounds and video images, which is more vivid, vivid, clear, orderly and comprehensive to reflect all kinds of information of athletes in the field competition. It is an important means for many high-level sports teams at home and abroad to provide pre competition technical and tactical guidance, psychological regulation, and post competition analysis and summary. According to the technical characteristics of high-level table tennis players, combined with the knowledge of table tennis coaches and relevant experts, the video data collection system for table tennis singles matches developed is shown in Fig. 3, which collects the key technical information of each shot of the game video, and can realize the storage, editing and management of each shot of video. It includes the name of the game and the information of the players, the information of the way the players hold the racket, service, loop, fast break, smash,

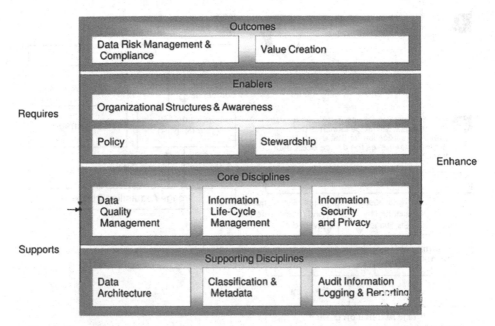

Fig. 2. Structure of evaluation system for table tennis players' on-the-spot technical ability

and pick [17]. There are 12 kinds of hitting technical information, such as split length, swing short, block ball, chop, drop ball, and loft ball; 5 kinds of hitting rotation degree information, such as strong topspin, medium topspin, non spin, medium underspin, and strong underspin; 4 kinds of hitting position information, such as forehand position, backhand position, side position, and reverse side position; 5 kinds of hitting effect information, such as good, good, average, poor, and poor.

In order to find out the relationship between the on-the-spot technical abilities of high-level table tennis players in major competitions and their scores, an evaluation model of on-the-spot technical abilities based on neural network and particle swarm optimization algorithm was constructed. Based on the principle of combining hitting point with special technology, the input indicators of on-site technical ability of this model include serving short, serving half billiards, serving long balls, forehand loop - forehand, forehand loop - middle road, forehand loop - backhand, backhand loop - forehand, backhand loop - forehand, backhand loop - backhand, backhand loop - backhand, backhand loop - middle road, backhand loop - backhand, backhand loop - backhand Pick - the other side's middle, pick - the other side's backhand, split long - the other side's forehand, split long - the other side's middle, split long - the other side's backhand, swing short - the other side's forehand short, swing short - the other side's forehand half comes out [18]. It can also be seen from the table tennis skill evaluation as shown in Fig. 4 that the curve before component 6 is relatively steep, while the curve after component 6 is relatively stable. Therefore, the five factors extracted in this paper can contain most of the data information contained in the original indicators to a certain extent.

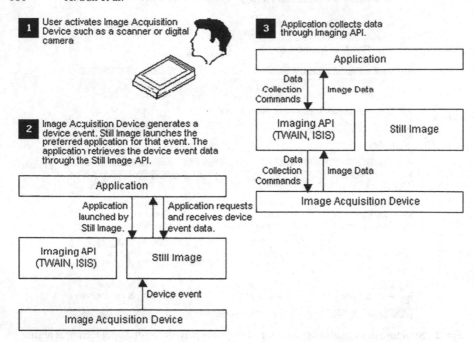

Fig. 3. Structure of competition video data acquisition system

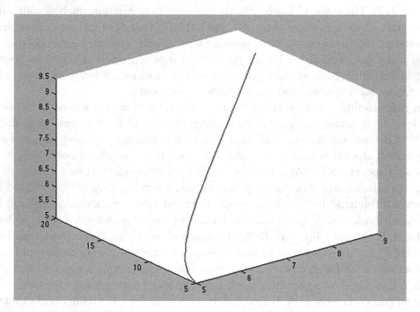

Fig. 4. Table tennis skill evaluation curve

The scoring rate, utilization rate and error rate of the short middle short ball, short backhand short ball, short backhand short ball, short backhand half ball, block forehand, block middle ball, block backhand are 56 sub indicators in total, and one output indicator is the score rate of the game [19]. The three-layer BP (back propagation) neural network is used to establish the input and output framework of the model, and the particle swarm optimization algorithm is used to optimize the weights and threshold parameters of the neural network.

5 Conclusion

Taking high-level table tennis players at home and abroad as the research object, based on the multimedia video database of major table tennis matches, the paper collects the on-site technical data, and constructs a high-level table tennis players' technical ability evaluation model based on neural network and particle swarm optimization algorithm. The model has high accuracy and convergence, which provides a certain decision-making reference for targeted guidance of athletes' training and competition.

References

1. Cao, S.: The ways of high level table tennis players use raw rubber by pen-hold grip and analysis of training techniques. Bull. Sport Sci. Technol. (2016)
2. Hou, X., Jiang, J.: Analysis on the mental quality and performance of table tennis players based on the cloud computing big data. Boletin Tecnico/Tech. Bull. **55**(19), 348–354 (2017)
3. Qi, R., Li, R.: Network multimedia table tennis teaching design based on embedded microprocessor. Wirel. Commun. Mob. Comput. (2022)
4. Huang, W., Lu, M., Zeng, Y., et al.: Technical and tactical diagnosis model of table tennis matches based on BP neural network. BMC Sports Sci. Med. Rehabil. **13**(1) (2021)
5. Šlosar, L., Šimunič, B., Pišot, R., Marusic, U.: Validation of a tennis rating score to evaluate the technical level of children tennis players. J. Sports Sci. **37**(1), 1–8 (2019)
6. Kang, L.: Empirical research on the hitting ability of tennis players based on computer vision. Revista de la Facultad de Ingenieria **32**(13), 300–305 (2017)
7. Liang, C.M., Zhou, X.D., Zhang, Y.Q., et al.: Current situation of amateur high-level table tennis playerss—based on the survey of the amateur competitions in 13th national games. J. Guangzhou Sport Univ. (2018)
8. Wang, X., Zhang, X., Liu, C., et al.: Music effects on technical training of high-level basketball players. J. North Univ. China (Soc. Sci. Ed.) (2016)
9. Zhao, Y.: Test and simulation of health balance training equipment based on medical multimedia image for exercise balance ability. Multimedia Tools Appl. **79**(15–16), 10639–10654 (2020)
10. Kamal, M., Dlis, F., Hanif, A.S.: Skills of smash backhand on table tennis of 3 dimensional based on multimedia. Indian J. Public Health Res. Dev. **10**(11), 3321 (2019)
11. Wu, G.: Monitoring system of key technical features of male tennis players based on internet of things security technology. Wirel. Commun. Mob. Comput. (2021)
12. Qu, Z.-Y., Qu, Z.-L., et al.: Statistics and analysis of the initiating heavy spins of chinese high level table tennis women's single players. J. Guangzhou Sport Univ. (2017)
13. Wang, J., Zhao, K., Deng, D., et al.: Tac-simur: tactic-based simulative visual analytics of table tennis. IEEE Trans. Visual Comput. Graphics **26**(1), 407–417 (2020)
14. Shen, W.L.: Simulation research on technical standard training of table tennis players. Comput. Simul. **34**(6), 232–235 (2017)

15. Zhang, J.: Automatic detection method of technical and tactical indicators for table tennis based on trajectory prediction using compensation fuzzy neural network. Comput. Intell. Neurosci. (2021)

16. Zhang, S., Mao, H.: Optimization analysis of tennis players' physical fitness index based on data mining and mobile computing. Wirel. Commun. Mob. Comput. Commun. Mob. Comput. **2021**(11), 1–11 (2021)

17. Liu, R., Shi, Z., Ren, J.: Competition momentum analysis model of table tennis based on double moving average. J. Shanghai Univ. Sport (2017)

18. Gong, X., Wang, F.: Classification of tennis video types based on machine learning technology. Wirel. Commun. Mob. Comput.. Commun. Mob. Comput. **2021**(1), 1–11 (2021)

19. Li, Q., Hu, J.-Y., et al.: Ranking model of table tennis players based on ELO-rating. J. Mudanjiang Normal Univ. (Nat. Sci. Ed.) (2017)

On the Design of College Chinese Multimedia Teaching System

FengJiao Shan[✉] and Lingyan Yu

Yanshan College Shandong University of Finance and Economics, Shandong 271199, China
sfjoe2006@163.com

Abstract. Chinese is a language that has been used for thousands of years. It is one of the most spoken languages in the world. Chinese is the official language of China, Taiwan, Singapore, Malaysia and many other countries in the world. At the end of the 19th century and the beginning of the 20th century, immigrants from China first introduced Chinese into the United States. Most of these immigrants are farmers. When they immigrated to the United States, they brought their own agricultural technical knowledge. This has helped to establish a strong agricultural industry in the United States and helped American society develop many different industries (Henderson). Using multimedia to assist college English teaching can improve students' aesthetic level. Literature and art are always inseparable. Turning college Chinese teaching into literature appreciation teaching is an innovation of course teaching.

Keyword: Multimedia teaching · College Chinese · teaching system

1 Introduction

With the rapid development of computer technology and communication technology, human society has entered the information age, and the speed of knowledge updating is getting faster and faster. According to the statistics of UNESCO, the knowledge accumulated by human beings in the past 30 years accounts for 90% of all human knowledge, while the knowledge accumulated previously only accounts for 10%. The rapid development of high-tech has led to the continuous emergence of new industries and the continuous transformation of old industries, which objectively requires people to continuously learn and supplement new knowledge and skills [1]. According to the statistics of foreign scholars, a college student can only obtain about 10% of his required knowledge in school, and the rest 90% is obtained by his continuous learning in future work. Therefore, how to solve the demand for knowledge caused by the rapid increase of knowledge and the frequent renewal of occupation makes it necessary to reform the form and method of focus education. Computer-assisted teaching has changed many disadvantages in the past teaching, such as single form and small amount of information [2]. Multimedia assisted teaching can realize personalized education, give full play to the initiative of the educated, and have good visual and auditory effects, Rich knowledge

Y. Zhang and N. Shah (Eds.): BigIoT-EDU 2023, LNICST 584, pp. 183–189, 2024.
https://doi.org/10.1007/978-3-031-63142-9_18

expression ability and other advantages. With the continuous development of the global informatization process, education informatization is imperative, and network multimedia teaching is gradually becoming the mainstream form of education [3]. Network multimedia teaching has expanded the space-time latitude of teaching, provided more abundant and high-quality learning resources for learners, and will have a positive impact on improving teaching quality, changing teaching concepts and promoting education for all.

In the traditional teaching of college Chinese, teachers should waste a lot of time on the blackboard and constantly wipe the blackboard to change the content. When entering the classroom summary stage, the contents of each link in the classroom process cannot be reorganized, which affects the teaching effect. The teaching capacity of college Chinese is very large. To complete a large number of teaching contents in a limited time, it is necessary to optimize the cumbersome procedures and simplify the work with high repetition rate [4]. The use of multimedia assisted teaching can not only optimize the teaching process, but also reflect the contents that teachers need to write on the blackboard with multimedia pictures, so as to enrich the classroom content while optimizing the teaching process. In addition, while saving a lot of classroom time, it can also extend the classroom teaching content, so that students are no longer bound to the classroom teaching content itself, but expand the amount of data collection and the scope of knowledge according to their own way of thinking. College Chinese textbooks cover a wide range of contents. In addition to literature, human geography, local customs and historical customs will also be involved [5]. Therefore, college Chinese is a subject that covers a wide range, even can be extended to interdisciplinary fields. Creating teaching situations with multimedia courseware is too narrow if it is still based on text content. It guides students to expand their horizons, let students' thinking break the boundaries of time and space, and transform abstract teaching content into seeing, listening and reading through the dynamic pictures displayed by multimedia, thus increasing the knowledge density of Chinese classroom.

2 Related Work

2.1 Current Situation at Home and Abroad

Generally speaking, the network multimedia teaching system can be divided into three categories according to its design principles and implementation methods: pure software implementation, software and hardware combination implementation, and pure hardware implementation. The hardware implementation method was widely used in the early stage, but with the continuous improvement of the networking speed and the continuous enhancement of the processing capacity of the personal computer, the speed advantage of the hardware method in the past is no longer obvious, and its cost is high, maintenance is inconvenient, and upgrading is difficult. The software implementation method can just overcome the shortcomings of the hardware method, and can achieve good performance on the current common configuration of personal computers, Therefore, it has become the mainstream of the market [6]. The following is an introduction to some relevant software products available on the market.

Founder Multimedia Electronic Classroom Founder Multimedia Electronic Classroom software of Founder Group is an advanced multimedia teaching broadcasting system. Through computer network, teachers can conduct computer teaching for hundreds of students at the same time. The teaching and students can use the audio-visual two-way communication function and teaching aids to carry out a variety of multimedia audio-visual interactive teaching [7]. The teachers can also monitor the learning status of all students in real time to help schools or enterprises achieve efficient online teaching objectives.

The Starscream web multimedia teaching system of Chuangxun Software is developed by Guangzhou Chuangxun Software Co., Ltd., referred to as "Starscream Software". This software runs on the WINDOWS98/ME/2000/XP/2003 network loaded with TCP/IP protocol. It mainly realizes the teaching broadcast of multimedia information on the local area network. It is a very good software product to realize the multimedia network teaching in the electronic classroom, multimedia classroom or computer classroom [8]. It integrates the functions of synchronous teaching, control, management, audio and video broadcasting, network examination, etc. in the computer classroom, It can also realize the purpose of network management such as screen monitoring and remote control.

NETOPSCHOOL, the classroom system with the highest sales volume in the world, is a rare world-class teaching software. It is an advanced classroom demonstration and remote control system, which has been widely used in Europe and America. It can run on any LAN and WAN, display the teacher's computer demonstration picture on each student's computer, watch each student's picture on the teacher's computer, or even remotely control any student's big picture, or display any student's picture to other students. The advantage of this system is that it is powerful and easy to operate, without any setting, and the installation of each machine can be started in only one minute.

2.2 Using Multimedia to Assist College English Teaching Can Optimize the Teaching Process

In the traditional teaching of college Chinese, teachers should waste a lot of time on the blackboard, and constantly wipe the blackboard to change content. When entering the classroom summary stage, the contents of each link in the classroom process cannot be reorganized, which affects the teaching effect. The teaching capacity of college Chinese is very large. To complete a large number of teaching contents in a limited time, it is necessary to optimize the cumbersome procedures and simplify the work with high repetition rate. The use of multimedia assisted teaching can not only optimize the teaching process, but also reflect the contents that teachers need to write on the blackboard with multimedia pictures, so as to enrich the classroom content while optimizing the teaching process. In addition, while saving a lot of classroom time, it can also extend the classroom teaching content, so that students are no longer bound to the classroom teaching content itself, but expand the amount of data collection and the scope of knowledge according to their own way of thinking [9]. College Chinese textbooks cover a wide range of contents. In addition to literature, human geography, local customs and historical customs will also be involved. Therefore, college Chinese is a subject that covers a wide range, even can be extended to interdisciplinary fields. Creating teaching situations with multimedia courseware is too narrow if it is still based on text content. It guides students to expand their horizons, let students' thinking break the boundaries of time and space, and transform abstract teaching content into seeing, listening and reading through the dynamic pictures displayed by multimedia, thus increasing the knowledge density of Chinese classroom.

3 Multimedia Teaching Focuses on Creating Situational Classroom Environment

In the context of exam-oriented education, students are very mechanical, rational and utilitarian in the process of learning literary works. They always interpret literary works with abstract thinking. In the long run, they feel rough and insensitive, and cannot integrate their inner feelings into the appreciation of human literary works. Those beautiful literary works are mechanically dismembered into multiple choice questions, blank filling questions and question and answer questions by students. Instead of perceptual appreciation with rational thinking, the utilitarian goal of entering school has replaced delicate emotional experience, resulting in the continuous loss of students' aesthetic outlook and lack of perception of literature and art.

The application of multimedia in college Chinese teaching can create an atmosphere with artistic scenes. Use artistic forms such as voice, image and performance to convey a feeling, stimulate students' emotions, and make them intoxicated and moved. At the same time, the use of synaesthesia between different types of art, through voice, tone and action, makes the text symbols in the static and boring works vivid and vivid, so that students can feel a kind of implicit and implicit meaning [10]. This is an effect that the teacher cannot achieve through mechanical narration or simple blackboard writing. Because voice, tone and action are more specific and vivid than ordinary literary symbols, when literature conveys an image and emotional content through abstract and boring symbolic forms, compared with other artistic forms such as music, art and performance, it is more difficult for literature to convey feelings, and the literal symbols are farther from the image. Through multimedia situational teaching, we can get a general sense of fuzziness. Even though the blackboard writing is simple and clear, the text is only a monotonous silent static symbol, and the monotonous teaching method makes students monotonous from the way of thinking to emotional experience, but the adoption of multimedia teaching methods in college Chinese makes students gain a general sense of fuzziness.

Teachers should not only use music, pictures, operas, paintings and various related video materials to help students understand and understand the emotional connotation of classical works, but also use reading and interpretation of works to deepen their experience of music, pictures and operas, mobilize students' interest in classical literature and art, fully develop students' thinking ability, and cultivate their various interests. For example, in view of the fact that students do not love classical opera, through in-depth interpretation of the thoughts and feelings of the famous literary work "A Dream of Red Mansions", and then using multimedia technology to show the classic "A Dream of Red Mansions" segment of the Vietnamese opera, at this time, students have just finished some other courses (such as mechanical drawing or physics class), the Vietnamese opera segment will become a new look in this special atmosphere, and students are immersed in the euphemistic and beautiful singing, and are completely affected by the charm of classical art. After such a Chinese class, a quiet picture still emerges in front of the students, and an elegant singing still lingers in their ears, achieving the effect of killing two birds with one stone.

4 Design of College Chinese Multimedia Teaching System

In this design, the main line is to reduce the workload of teachers, expand teaching subjects and scope, improve teaching quality, and meet the personalized needs of each student. Based on the idea of CSCW (Computer Supported Cooperative Work), ASP NET, as the main development tool, is designed based on B/S mode. Users can use the most common IE browser for interactive operation, and strive to be convenient and practical.

The design of multimedia teaching system consists of management module, student module and teacher module. The frame is shown in Fig. 1.

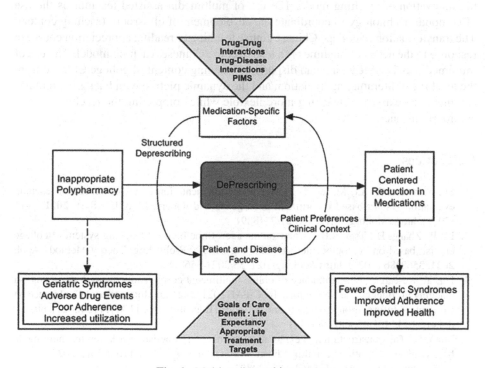

Fig. 1. Multimedia teaching system

Management module: responsible for the management of courses and teachers, the acceptance of students' learning applications, the setting of students' learning qualifications for relevant courses after handling relevant procedures, and the management of students' and teachers' permissions.

Student module: students first apply for, register and go through relevant procedures through the network management system to obtain the qualification of optional courses. Then enter the multimedia teaching system, authenticate the identity, select courses, and choose the way you like to study. After the course is completed, apply for the exam. After the teacher of the selected course agrees, take the online exam to obtain the relevant course results.

Teacher module: enter the multimedia online teaching system, register and verify the identity. Through this system, teachers can upload personal information, submit, modify, add and update teaching materials, read and respond to students' questions, approve students' examination applications, track students' learning progress, and so on.

5 Conclusion

To sum up, with the development of information technology, the establishment of campus network in universities has brought a lot of convenience to teaching, but also promoted the innovation of teaching mode. The use of multimedia assisted teaching is the use of computer technology to coordinate the development of classroom teaching content. The transformation of college Chinese course teaching to reading appreciation course in response to the needs of the times is a leap over the Chinese teaching model. The use of multimedia assisted teaching can display the teaching content of college Chinese from the teaching of literature appreciation, and the dynamic picture with background music can make the classroom teaching more flexible while completing the teaching plan in an orderly manner.

References

1. Su, Y., Chen, G., Li, M., et al.: Design and implementation of web multimedia teaching evaluation system based on artificial intelligence and jQuery. Mob. Inf. Syst. **2021**, 1–11 (2021). https://doi.org/10.1155/2021/7318891
2. Li, P., Zhang, H., Tsai, S.B.: A new online and offline blended teaching system of college english based on computer internet technology. Math. Probl. Eng. Theory Methods Appl. **2021**, 3568386 (2021). https://doi.org/10.1155/2021/3568386
3. Hu, Y.: Research on the influence of online multimedia corpus indexing system on english teaching in colleges and universities. In: CIPAE 2021: 2021 2nd International Conference on Computers, Information Processing and Advanced Education, pp. 1170–1172 (2021). https://doi.org/10.1145/3456887.3457481
4. Yuan, L.: The construction and exploration of university english translation teaching mode based on the integration of multimedia network technology. Math. Probl. Eng. **2022**(3), 1–8 (2022). https://doi.org/10.1155/2023/9820807
5. Ye, L., Su, H., Zhao, J., et al.: The impact of multimedia effect on art learning: eye movement evidence from traditional chinese pattern learning. Int. J. Art Des. Educ. 40(2), 342–358 (2021). https://doi.org/10.1111/jade.12347
6. Liu, C., Hawamdeh, S.: Corpus design of chinese medicine english vocabulary translation teaching system based on python. J. Inf. Knowl. Manag.Knowl. Manag. 21(2), 2240022 (2022). https://www.worldscientific.com/doi/abs/10.1142/s0219649222400226

7. Singh, R., et al.: Prospects of microbial-engineering for the production of graphene and its derivatives: application to design nanosystms for cancer theranostics. Semin. Cancer Biol. **86**, 885–898 (2022). https://doi.org/10.1016/j.semcancer.2021.05.017
8. Li, W., Fan, X.: Construction of network multimedia teaching platform system of college sports. Math. Probl. Eng. (2021). https://doi.org/10.1155/2021/6304703
9. Kai-Tao, H.E., Zhi-Zhong, L.I., Wang, D.M.: Overview on the design of the service and management system for field geological survey based on the remote sensing and beidou satellites. J. Geomech. **18**(3), 203–212 (2022). https://doi.org/10.3969/j.issn.1006-6616.2012.03.001
10. Song, R.: Research on the application of computer multimedia music system in college music teaching. J. Phys. Conf. Ser. **1744**(3), 032214 (2021). https://doi.org/10.1088/1742-6596/1744/3/032214

Application and Method Analysis of Cloud Education Technology in Digital Media Art Design Professional Education

Xu Ya[1,2(✉)], Peijin Chen[1,2], and Jing Guo[1,2]

[1] Modern College of Northwest University, Xi'an 710065, China
873059556@qq.com
[2] East University of Heilongjiang, Heilongjiang 150000, China

Abstract. The role of teaching effect evaluation in art and design professional education is very important, but there is a problem of poor implementation effect. The information management platform cannot solve the unreasonable problems in professional education, and the implementation of teaching effect is low. Therefore, this paper proposes a cloud education technology for digital media analysis. Firstly, the cloud storage theory is used to judge the application effect of professional education, and the application effect is evaluated according to the educational requirements to reduce irrelevant factors in digital media art design. Then, cloud education technology is used to continuously analyze the professional education data and form the final application effect collection. MATLAB simulation shows that under the requirements of architectural education, than those of information management platform.

Keywords: digital media · art design · professional education · Apply · Algorithm

1 Introduction

With the development of cloud computing and network technology, cloud education has become an innovative method in the field of modern education. In digital media art and design education, the application of cloud education technology provides students with more opportunities and resources to create and learn.

Firstly, cloud education technology provides students with a convenient learning environment. Students can access learning resources such as teaching materials, teaching videos, and online cases through cloud platforms, without being limited by time and location. This provides students with greater learning freedom and the ability to independently arrange their learning time and location [1]. At the same time, students can engage in online communication and cooperation with teachers and classmates to jointly solve problems and share creativity, promoting interaction and cooperation in learning. Secondly, cloud education technology provides powerful tools and platform

Y. Zhang and N. Shah (Eds.): BigIoT-EDU 2023, LNICST 584, pp. 190–196, 2024.
https://doi.org/10.1007/978-3-031-63142-9_19

support for students majoring in digital media art and design. Students can use professional design software and tools through cloud platforms to create and practice. The high-performance computing and storage capabilities of cloud platforms enable students to handle and save a large amount of digital media resources, as well as perform complex tasks such as rendering and editing [2]. Intelligent evaluation technology can automatically evaluate students' works and performances, provide accurate and timely feedback and guidance, and help students continuously improve and enhance their design abilities.

In summary, cloud education technology has broad application prospects in digital media art and design education. Through a convenient learning environment, powerful tool platforms, and personalized learning features, cloud education technology can provide richer learning resources and opportunities, promote students' creativity and learning, and improve educational effectiveness and learning experience [3]. At the same time, cloud education technology can also provide teachers with more teaching support and evaluation tools, promoting the interaction and improvement of teaching and learning.

2 Related Concepts

2.1 Mathematical Description of Cloud Education Technology

Cloud education technology is to use cloud storage theory to combine professional content, select teaching judgment indicators [4], and calculate the application effect of art and design majors. Cloud education technology uses the advantages of cloud storage to analyze art design content by practical application and application process, and improves the teaching effect of digital media art design [5].

Hypothesis 1. The educational requirement is x_i, the set of teaching judgments is set_i, the art application effect is y_i, and the teaching judgment result judgment function is $F(x) \neq 1$ as shown in Eq. (1).

$$F(x_i) = \sum (x_i \to y_i) \cdot \overline{\overline{\xi}} \tag{1}$$

2.2 Selection of Application Solutions for Art and Design Majors

Hypothesis 2. The professional education function is $z(d_i)$, the scheme is adjusted is w_i, then, the application scheme is shown in Eq. (2).

$$z(x_i) = \frac{z_i \cdot w_i}{F(x_i, y_i)'} \tag{2}$$

2.3 Application Portfolio of Professional Education

It is necessary to carry out comprehensive teaching judgment, application judgment and effect analysis of content, and standardize professional education to eliminate unreasonable teaching content. First, cloud analysis is carried out on the application effect of art

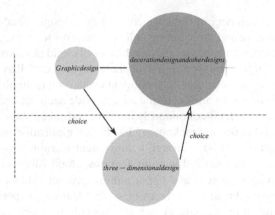

Fig. 1. Results of the selection of professional content in art and design

and design majors, and the weights of cloud analysis the combination. If the results meet the requirements, the design process is reasonable, otherwise, the relevant application scheme is excluded. In of cloud education technology, the art design content, and the specific application effect is shown in Fig. 1.

The survey results show that the application results of art and design majors show a reasonable, indicating that the application analysis of art design majors has strong randomness, which can be used as the research object of this paper. Cloud education technology mainly evaluates professional education content in the cloud, eliminating duplicate and irrelevant factors, so that the entire professional education application is relatively continuous.

3 Portfolio Strategies for Digital Media Art Design

Cloud education technology adopts a random combination strategy for the educational application, and evaluates the application parameters for comprehensive judgment to realize the application's effective combinations. The content mix of cloud education technology application levels, and different application results. In the content of different combinations is completed, the application levels of different combinations are compared to record the best application results.

4 Practical Cases of the Application Effect of Art and Design Majors

4.1 Overview of the Art and Design Major

In order to facilitate the research on the art and design, this paper investigates the effect of professional education and specific parameters with digital media art as the object. This is shown in Table 1.

The assembly process of digital media art design in Table 1 is shown in Fig. 2.

Table 1. Relevant parameters for the application of art and design professions

type	Combination level	Art and design information volume (M)	Dispersion of the application results (%)
Specialized courses	App-level	96.03	85.98
	Method level	75.69	86.57
Art design	App-level	72.95	85.24
	Method level	95.59	85.57
digitization	App-level	77.08	85.03
	Method level	96.07	84.81

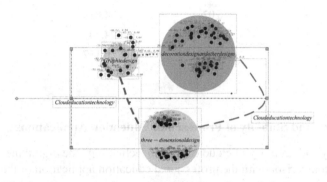

Fig. 2. The process of assembling digital media art design content

Table 2. Application of art and design majors

method	content	rationality	Magnitude of change
Cloud education technology	Art design	75.79	74.54
	Education	73.24	72.17
Information management platform	Art design	74.11	73.10
	Education	72.99	73.06
	X^2	4.117	5.727

As seen in Fig. 2, the combined results of cloud education technologies, and the application results are shown in Table 2.

Compared with the information management platform, cloud education technology is the information management platform application effect. Through the changes in digital media art design content in Fig. 2, it can be seen that the application stability of cloud education technology is better and the combination speed is faster. Therefore, cloud education technology can combine digital media art design faster.

4.2 Application Effect of Art and Design Major

The content of digital media art design includes practical skills, theoretical applications, and practical cases. After the pre-selection of cloud education technology, the preliminary, and the feasibility of digital media. In of cloud education technology, application levels are selected for application, and the shown in Table 3.

Table 3. Overall situation of the application effect of art and design majors

content	Practice rate	Teaching improvement rate
Practical skills	75.59	75.57
Theoretical application	77.08	75.03
Practical examples	76.07	74.81
mean	73.91	74.74
X^2	5.029	6.157

4.3 Accuracy and Stability of Professional Education Applications

In the stability and accuracy of cloud education technology, the digital media art shown in Fig. 3 for comparison with the professional education application of the information management platform.

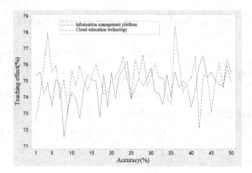

Fig. 3. Educational application results of different algorithms

It from Fig. 4 that the accuracy of cloud education technology is higher the information management platform, but the teaching effect is lower, that the calculation results of cloud education technology are relatively stable. The calculation results of the information management platform are mixed. The average digital media art in Table 4.

It can be seen from Table 4 that the information management platform has in stability, accuracy and teaching effect, and the design and application results have, and the error rate is high. The combined results of cloud education technology have higher accuracy

Table 4. Comparison of teaching accuracy of different methods

algorithm	accuracy	stability	Teaching effectiveness
Cloud education technology	92.88	98.41	82.87
Information management platform	83.31	86.14	85.03
P	6.175	4.377	4.179

than information management platforms. At the same time, the stability of cloud education technology is greater than 80%, and the application results. To further validate the superiority of cloud education technology. In the application of professional education and the result 4 is shown.

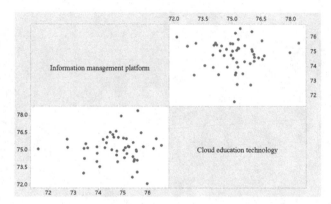

Fig. 4. The comprehensiveness of cloud education technology

As can be seen from Fig. 4, the comprehensiveness of cloud education technology is significantly better than that of information management platform, and the reason is that cloud education technology the of professional education and of digital media to exclude non-compliant analysis data.

5   Conclusion

In view of the inaccurate teaching application effect, this paper proposes a cloud education technology combined with the theory of cloud storage in view of the inaccurate teaching application effect to combine the effects of the call. At the same time, the application level and threshold standards, and the design professional education. The simulation results show that cloud education technology can improve the application and professional education and can improve professional education by making a comprehensive combination. However, in cloud education technology, too much of applications, the unreasonable selection of feasibility for different methods.

References

1. Cheng, L., Hu, L.: Challenges and optimization paths of Guzheng professional education in colleges under big data era. J. Environ. Public Health **2022** (2022)
2. Guo, Y.: Design of financial management talent training model under demand coupling mechanism and IoT applications. Wirel. Commun. Mob. Comput. **2022** (2022)
3. Mathisen, T.F., Sundgot-Borgen, C., Anstensrud, B., Sundgot-Borgen, J.: Intervention in professional dance students to increase mental health- and nutrition literacy: a controlled trial with follow up. Front. Sports Active Living **4** (2022)
4. Qian, C., Ye, J.H., Lee, Y.S.: The effects of art design courses in higher vocational colleges based on C-STEAM. Front. Psychol. **13** (2022)
5. Sun, X.D., Fu, R., Zhang, G.Q., Chen, C.N.: Effects of multimedia integrated fine arts education on students' learning attitude and learning satisfaction. Front. Psychol. **13** (2022)

Application and Practice of Multimedia Technology in Chinese Language Teaching Under the Background of Big Data

Lu Liu[1](✉), Lin Lin[2], Pei Liu[3], and Xiangzhou Liu[4]

[1] College of Ethnic Culture, Yunnan Minzu University, Kunming 650504, China
Liulu006688@126.com
[2] Harbin Normal University, Harbin 150000, China
[3] Shandong Institute of Commerce and Technology, Jinan 250103, Shandong, China
[4] Yunnan College of Business Management, Yunnan 650106, China

Abstract. In recent years, the rapid development and application of multimedia technology has become a trend of modern teaching and plays an increasingly important role in Chinese language teaching. The full and effective use of multimedia technology will help students to carry out independent learning and personalized learning, and improve teaching efficiency. This article aims to comprehensively introduce the application and practice of multimedia technology in Chinese teaching under the background of big data. To achieve this goal, we first introduced the concept of big data, which is defined as "a data set that is too large or complex to be processed by traditional database management systems" (Siekmann et al., 2013). Then, we discussed our research on Chinese learning multimedia resources, such as audio files, video clips and graphics. Finally, through our own work, we use these multimedia resources in classroom activities to support students' listening comprehension and.

Keyword: big data · Chinese language teaching · Multi-Media

1 Introduction

With the gradual maturity of computer network technology and multimedia technology, multimedia has developed rapidly in the education system and is widely used in teaching. Multimedia assisted teaching has many characteristics and functions that are especially valuable for education and teaching process because of its characteristics of pictures, texts, sounds and images. The learning mode of distance education is a new form of education with the development of modern information technology. It is not only an important means for TVU to carry out curriculum teaching, but also the main way for people to carry out lifelong learning in the era of knowledge economy [1]. The development of distance education has gone through three stages: the first stage is based on correspondence education; The second stage is based on radio and television education; The third stage is the teaching activities under the environment of computer network

Y. Zhang and N. Shah (Eds.): BigIoT-EDU 2023, LNICST 584, pp. 197–208, 2024.
https://doi.org/10.1007/978-3-031-63142-9_20

and multimedia technology, known as "modern distance education". Give full play to the advantages of multimedia, which plays an important role in language teaching and remote language teaching.

In a broad sense, textbooks refer to all teaching materials used by teachers and students inside and outside the classroom. All materials that are conducive to learners' knowledge development skills can be called textbooks. In a narrow sense, textbooks refer to textbooks. In this paper, "textbook" is defined in a narrow sense. Chinese textbooks are an important resource for the implementation of language teaching in China. Under the guidance of "one syllabus and many textbooks", various versions of Chinese textbooks are also competing to display different characteristics. However, due to the fact that the Chinese curriculum standard does not make clear provisions on the types of characters, vocabulary, grammar, etc. at each stage, in the actual operation, different editors have different selection concepts, which is likely to make the content of different versions of the Chinese textbooks of the same grade very different. At the same time, in the era when all walks of life are moving towards semi-automation and automation, the selection and compilation of Chinese textbooks is still at the artificial stage, resulting in a huge workload of the selection and compilation of textbooks, and it is difficult to change once it is completed, and the content of Chinese textbooks correspondingly presents the characteristics of lag. Therefore, it is necessary to design an effective method to make full use of the rich resources provided by the Internet, timely recommend high-quality textbook selections for editors, and constantly inject new sources into the textbook.

If Chinese textbooks are the basic tools for learning language knowledge, then reading materials are the best platform for consolidating and improving language knowledge. For learners, the best way to learn a language is to experience the changes of different contexts in the rich and colorful reading materials and acquire the vocabulary and grammar imperceptibly. In the big data environment, there are a lot of reading materials to choose from, but the types of reading materials are too scattered and the quality is uneven. Due to the limited level of understanding of parents and students, they often question the effect of language reading and writing learning methods because they cannot find suitable reading materials. However, relying solely on teachers to find reading materials manually takes time and effort, and the effect is not satisfactory. Therefore, automatic recommendation of reading materials is of great significance to language learners. However, most of the existing book recommendation algorithms focus on the theme book recommendation for online bookstores or personalized book recommendation for digital libraries. For students who mainly focus on language learning, their practicability is low. Therefore, there is a need for a reading material recommendation method that can recommend the required reading materials for readers according to learners' cognitive ability and learning characteristics.

Despite the development of science and technology, Chinese language and culture still play an important role. For a long time, Chinese language and literature is of great significance for improving students' national language and cultural literacy. At the same time, through the teaching of Chinese language and literature, students can understand the splendid culture of the Chinese nation, master the essence of Chinese language and culture, and then establish correct values, outlook on life and world outlook, so as to truly become comprehensive talents who can promote social development [2]. In the context of the current new curriculum, it is more important to innovate the teaching methods of Chinese language and literature in order to fully meet the teaching requirements of Chinese language and literature.

2 Related Work

2.1 Multimedia Technology

Multimedia technology first appeared in the X86 era, but accurately from the hardware point of view, the time when multimedia technology really fully developed was after the first sound card on the PC appeared, which marked that the computer began to have the ability to process audio, and also marked the beginning of the multimedia technology stage.

Since the development of Audio Video Interleaved (AVI), the video technology has begun to develop. During the period of rapid video development, several waves of change were dominated by AVI, Stream and MPEG (Moving Picture Experts Group) [3]. AVI provides a standard for computer video storage mode; MPEG compresses moving images and speech to achieve low bit rate video transmission and accelerate transmission efficiency, as shown in Fig. 1. Nowadays, the video formats for network video transmission are mostly ASF, WMV, RM, RMVB, etc., which generally have the advantages of relatively small file space and convenient transmission.

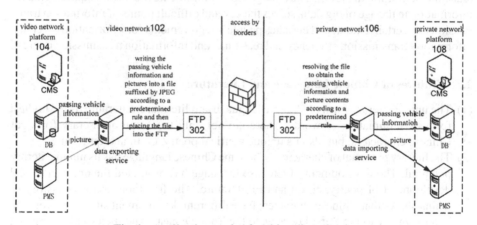

Fig. 1. Application mode of multimedia technology

Besides video technology, audio technology is also indispensable. Its development consists of two stages. One is the sound file format WAV developed by Microsoft and MIDI that connects electroacoustic instruments and communications. WAV has the advantages of high audio quality, simple decoding and universality, but its file size is large. MIDI is a "digital instrument interface". Its files do not contain streaming media information. The file size is small and the sound quality is quite good. However, as an audio control format, it is highly professional and low in popularity; The other is the various audio compression technologies that have emerged since then. In order to adapt to the development of the times and integrate audio into the network information transmission structure, most network audio compresses WAV to form MP3 or WMA format. At present, the audio formats used in multiple networks include MIDI, WAVE (*. WAV), WMA, MP3, RealAudio, OGG, AAC, RMVB, etc. Different audio formats meet the needs of different links and have corresponding format support in hardware, sound quality, performance, and many other aspects [4].

The development of multimedia technology has changed the single way of information transmission in the age of letters. Nowadays, information is transmitted in real time over a long distance and in a wide range through telephone, television and the Internet. The forms of visual and auditory integration include film and television. They use words, images, sounds and special science and technology to transmit information. While providing visual shock, they also meet the needs of auditory senses, thus obtaining an audio-visual feast. Multimedia in various forms also covers a wide range of fields: multimedia teaching courseware in the education industry; Product publicity and enterprise brand establishment in commercial marketing; Introduction to project services and destination scenery in the tourism industry; Video conference for networked office and establishment of resource sharing; Appointment and registration, online diagnosis and remote surgery in the medical industry; As well as multimedia in the booming AI. Multimedia technology is open and almost has no boundary in practical application. It is constantly optimizing our life and environment through the diversification of information media, the diversification of media processing methods, and the interactivity and real-time of multimedia [5, 6]. The emergence of multimedia meets the requirements for information in the age of big data, solves the key and difficult points of information transmission to a certain extent, and enriches people's requirements for information diversity, information transmission efficiency and real-time, and information transmission interest.

2.2 Features of Chinese Language and Literature

(1) The unique literary form of Chinese language and literature. Literature is the highest form of sublimation of words. There are not only the common literary forms of Chinese characters, but also its unique metrical poetry, ci, fu and qu forms.

(2) The literary potential of characters. The same Chinese language has its unique literary potential. The development of Chinese language has promoted the emergence and development of poetry, ci, qu and fu literature. The five thousand year history of China shows that Chinese characters have different development situations from the Tang Dynasty to the Song Dynasty, to the Yuan Dynasty, and then to the Ming and Qing Dynasties. The arrival of each dynasty means the re creation and improvement of the unique literary form of Chinese language and literature. From this process of development, we can find that the development of a certain kind of character depends on the literary potential space of the character [7].

(3) The inheritance and development of the treasure house of chinese language and literature. At this stage, the development of Chinese language and literature has reached a stage of perfection and maturity. Since the emergence of the Internet, people have become increasingly convenient in the exchange of ideas and information, while effectively inheriting and developing the achievements of Chinese language and literature. However, the development of literature has restrained the fast pace of

society to a certain extent. The people's reading time and appreciation enthusiasm for literature gradually declined.

Therefore, setting the order of learning vocabulary according to the size of vocabulary frequency to ensure that high-frequency words are learned first and low-frequency words are learned later is a reflection of students' cognitive law. This paper also believes that in order to select and compile primary school Chinese textbooks more scientifically, it is necessary to develop a "glossary" as the vocabulary outline for the selection of textbooks, and recommend selected articles for editors according to the glossary [8]. The order of the selected words means that certain words in the previous text should appear in the following text in advance, and at the same time, some words that have not been learned in the previous text should be included, so as to achieve the effect of reviewing and learning new words. In order to achieve the order of words, it is necessary to make certain repetition words between the recommended adjacent selections when recommending the selection. The integration of words means that the types of words in the textbooks should be diverse. Chinese textbooks are the tools for students to learn language, and also the basis for learning other subjects. Therefore, the Chinese textbook should not only contain some vocabulary for daily use, but also cover professional vocabulary of many disciplines such as nature, science, culture, history, etc. This requires that our vocabulary syllabus - vocabulary list, should contain as many and diverse vocabulary as possible. Different reading materials have different languages and themes, and a variety of reading materials cover almost all fields of vocabulary [9]. These reading materials are widely collected, and the vocabulary and word frequency are counted, which can be used as the data source of the glossary. In life, the process of students communicating with others is also the process of language learning. In this process, students have used a large number of oral words, but they can only read and use some words, but do not know how to write them. Arrange vocabulary closely related to students' daily communication in the text, which is beneficial to realize the organic combination of inside and outside the classroom and guide students to learn actively.

2.3 Big Data Chinese Language Teaching Text Recommendation Algorithm

The text selection recommendation algorithm is the process of selecting a series of selected articles with the highest matching degree from the high-quality article library to be recommended, based on the required vocabulary of each grade, to form a textbook. Generally speaking, the number of new words contained in a text should be strictly controlled. Therefore, before recommending the selected text, it is necessary to divide the required vocabulary into several ordered vocabulary sets, and the number of vocabulary sets is determined by the number of texts required for the textbook of this grade. It can be seen from the recommendation basis of the selected text in the previous article that there should be certain repetition words between the adjacent selected text to ensure the order of the words in the textbook [10]. The way to solve this problem is to make certain intersection between the vocabulary sets when dividing the vocabulary sets. The process of obtaining the selected text of each textbook is essentially the problem of text classification, that is, the process of classifying the selected text to be recommended into the corresponding vocabulary set. The recommended algorithm for textbook selection is described as follows:

For any two documents a and b, the corresponding matrix representation is:

$$A\left(\mathbf{w}_1^a, ..., \mathbf{w}_i^a, ..., \mathbf{w}_m^a\right) \tag{1}$$

$$B\left(\mathbf{w}_1^b, ..., \mathbf{w}_i^b, ..., \mathbf{w}_n^b\right) \tag{2}$$

where, m and n represent the number of words contained in document a and document b respectively, and w represents the word vector corresponding to the ith word in document a. Here, the subscript of the nearest word of the ith word in document a in document b is defined as:

$$idx_i^a = \min_{s=1,n} \cos\left(\mathbf{w}_i^a, \mathbf{w}_s^b\right) \tag{3}$$

Here, the nearest distance word refers to the word in document b that is closest to the word w in document a, and the distance between the two words can be calculated by $\cos < \mathbf{w}_i^a, \mathbf{w}_s^b >$, that is, the cosine value of the angle between the vector corresponding to the ith word in document u and the s word in document b. Similarly:

$$S_1 = \left\{(s, t) | s \in \{1..n\} \wedge t \in \{1..m\} \wedge \left(idx_i^a = s\right) \wedge \left(idx_s^b = t\right)\right\} \tag{4}$$

In addition to these words, there are the following word sets in documents a and b:

$$S_2 = \{s | s \in \{1..n\}, \forall t \in \{1..m\}, (s, t) \notin S_1\} \tag{5}$$

$$S_3 = \{t | t \in \{1..m\}, \forall s \in \{1..n\}, (s, t) \notin S_1\} \tag{6}$$

Then, the similarity of documents a and b can be defined as:

$$sim^{-1}(\mathbf{A}, \mathbf{B}) = \frac{1}{|S_1| + |S_2| + |S_3|} \sum_{i,j}\left(\left(\cos\left(\mathbf{w}_i^a, \mathbf{w}_j^b\right)\right)_{(i,j \neq S_j)} + \left(\mathbf{w}_i^a \middle| \mathbf{w}_j^b \middle| \mathbf{w}_i^2\right)_{j < S_z}\right) \tag{7}$$

The first item is the distance of matched words, and the last two items reflect the role of unmatched words. The harmony coefficient can be added before each item to coordinate the role of each component [11].

Algorithm analysis: The essence of this algorithm is to divide the required vocabulary into several vocabularies with intersection, and the size of intersection is fixed. Then, the document similarity function is used to match and select articles for each vocabulary set. The specific method of vocabulary set division is to lay the required vocabulary of a learning segment on a line segment, which is divided into length-1 segments, and length represents the length of the vocabulary of the learning segment. As shown in Fig. 2, the number below the line segment represents the position of the word in the vocabulary, and 1 represents the subscript of the first word. Then, set a sliding window w whose width is fixed as width, and move the window backward by width-rep distance in order

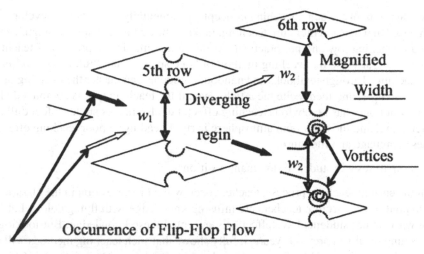

Fig. 2. Schematic diagram of dividing vocabulary set

to form different vocabulary sets, where rep represents the number of repeated words between vocabulary sets.

In each candidate selection set, select the best selection that has the highest matching degree with the vocabulary set and does not conflict with the selection of other vocabulary sets. For some vocabulary collections, due to the limited number of articles in the selected text library, it is possible that the selected text candidate set is empty. When the selected text candidate set of a vocabulary set is empty, this paper selects the two selected text candidates that are closest to it and are not empty, and merges and sorts the elements in them as the selected text candidate set of the vocabulary set [12]. After ensuring that the text selection candidate set of each vocabulary set is not empty, select the article with the greatest similarity to the vocabulary set from the text selection candidate set as the best selection of the vocabulary set. However, for different vocabulary sets, the same best selection may appear [13]. In order to avoid repeated text selection in the textbook, for all the word sets that match the same text selection, the best text selection of the word set with the largest D value remains the same, and the rest of the word sets need to select the unmatched article with the largest D value as the best text selection in their respective text selection candidate sets, and repeatedly compare whether the text selection is repeated until all the word sets have the unique best text selection.

3   Reasons Restricting the Teaching Quality of Chinese Language and Literature

3.1   Chinese Language Teaching Methods

(1) Single teaching method

Influenced by the traditional examination oriented education in China, the ultimate goal of Chinese language and literature teaching is to complete the corresponding teaching tasks, and to meet the needs of students in examinations by mastering the fixed knowledge in books. Such a teaching concept fundamentally restricts the development of Chinese language and literature teaching, making the quality of Chinese language and literature teaching low and not practical. At the same time, in the process of teaching, teachers generally use the teaching method of "one speech" and "full room" to implement teaching. Through textbooks and handouts, students can master the meaning of the article sentences, and then recite the article, even if the teaching task is completed [14]. This way not only has no obvious teaching effect, but also makes students feel dull and uninteresting, and the classroom atmosphere is rigid, leading to poor teaching effect of Chinese language and literature.

(2) Failing to respect students' dominant position

In the current teaching process, teachers occupy the main position in the classroom. Throughout the classroom, teachers are infusing knowledge with flying colors, but it is unknown whether students have effectively accepted these knowledge. But looking at the teaching results in previous years, it fully shows that such teaching methods will not improve the teaching quality. It can only make students more and more tired of Chinese language and literature. At the same time, we will not innovate the teaching methods, let students memorize by rote, and force them to instill corresponding knowledge. In the process of teaching and learning, students are in an absolute passive position [15].

(3) Pay more attention to theory than practice

The teaching of emphasizing theory over practice is almost a common fault of traditional teaching. At present, in the process of Chinese language teaching in many regions, only the theoretical knowledge on books is explained, and there is no too much requirement for students to use these theoretical knowledge in their life. Of course, Chinese language and literature are really theoretical, but in the context of the rapid development of the current knowledge economy, only a few ancient texts can be recited. Memorizing the meaning of the sentences of the articles can not meet the needs of social development, not to mention the needs of students' professional development. Instead, we should encourage students to apply what they have learned [16]. While students master sufficient knowledge reserves, we should pay attention to the cultivation of students' practical ability, enhance their actual expression level, sell themselves to the society, and exercise their language organization ability. However, this is not reflected in the current Chinese language and literature teaching, which is one of the reasons why the quality of Chinese language and literature teaching cannot be improved.

3.2 Application of Multimedia Technology in Chinese Language Teaching in the Context of Big Data

At present, teachers in most colleges and universities will use multimedia teachers to achieve visual beauty in teaching, but students can not directly participate in, separated from multimedia courseware, and the process lacks communication. The teacher can lead and guide students in the theoretical explanation and case demonstration and analysis, and use interactive forms to operate at the same time.

Multimedia courseware is mainly divided into three parts. The first part is the process of appreciation. That is to use excellent works to attract students and lead to the main content of teaching; The second part is mainly about theory, which aims to enable students to master the composition and effect of multimedia courseware. The third part is mainly about the process of students' practice, so that students can freely arrange materials and modify them at any time [7].

Multimedia teaching helps to create teaching situations. In education and teaching, the use of multimedia teaching can make the original abstract and boring learning content become intuitive through graphics, animation, sound and other forms, create vivid and realistic teaching situations, reduce the difficulty of understanding new knowledge, and enhance students' sense of success in learning. By using multimedia teaching, teachers can easily, quickly and fully use modern scientific and technological means, such as PPT, CD, video, projector, electronic whiteboard, etc. to teach, so that the teaching content is more visual and intuitive. At the same time, they can abstract and summarize, and introduce new teaching content without time and space restrictions, as shown in Fig. 3. It can be seen that the use of multimedia teaching can not only save valuable time in the classroom, increase the class capacity, but also activate the classroom teaching atmosphere and improve students' enthusiasm for learning. Psychologists point out that human learning is to transmit external information to the brain through eyes, ears, nose, tongue and other body organs, and to obtain knowledge through comprehensive analysis of the brain nervous system. The experimental data shows that 11% of human learning is achieved through hearing, and 83% is achieved through vision [18]. If vision and hearing are used together, the memory effect will be better. Multimedia classroom teaching fully mobilized the joint participation of students' audio-visual organs, making the teaching situation actively created and the teaching effect very obvious.

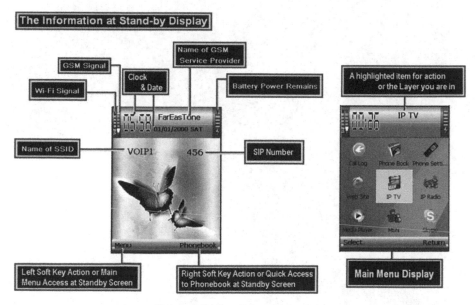

Fig. 3. Multimedia teaching mode

4   Analysis of Experimental Results

This experiment is run on a 64-bit window7 operating system. The experimental equipment uses Intel Core i7 3.4 GHz processor and 4G memory PC. In the experiment, part of the Chinese text in the new curriculum standard, Jiangsu Education Edition, was used as the standard sample set, and a large number of readings were collected as samples to be classified [19]. With the help of Matlab platform, the paper realizes the classification algorithm of scrolling, sets the number of scrolling p of the text, and completes the classification of reading materials. According to the top-N principle, select N readings that are similar to the category standard sample and recommend them to students. According to the results of reading material recommendation, use expert evaluation method to evaluate the rationality of recommendation.

This experiment presupposes that the number of text rotations p = 1 and the recommended number of readings N = 3. The classification algorithm of rotations can be used to determine the category of all candidate readings. When students learn text A; When, between and A; Among the same kind of reading materials, select the 3 closest reading materials as the recommended results [20]. At the same time, 12 backbone Chinese teachers from a primary school in a city were invited as experts to jointly evaluate the recommendation results and test the effectiveness of the recommendation. The test data scatter diagram is shown in Fig. 4 below.

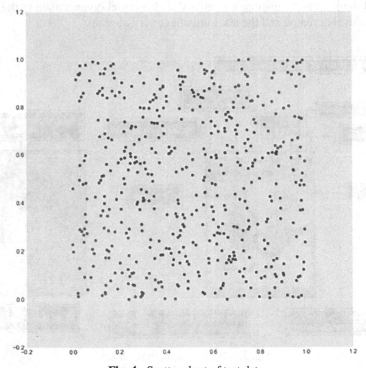

Fig. 4. Scatter chart of test data

Because the experimental data of language exercises is difficult to obtain, and the method in this paper is designed based on the behavior of students, it is only necessary to verify whether the method can mine the potential relationship of the exercises with the help of user's behavior data, without the use of fixed-type exercises, which also shows that the method has strong portability.

5 Conclusion

As a modern teaching method, multimedia plays an important role in Chinese language teaching. It has already been applied to various disciplines, reflecting the progress of education. Only the correct, reasonable and appropriate use of multimedia technology can play the role of multimedia in Chinese teaching, enable students to learn knowledge in a maximum capacity and all-round way, effectively improve the quality of Chinese teaching, and better serve education and teaching.

Acknowledgements. Presided over the Scientific research Fund project of Yunnan Education Department "Research on the Cultivation of Excellent Traditional Cultural Literacy of Private Higher Vocational Students -- Taking Preschool Education Major as an Example";Participated in the Yunnan Province Excellent online open course project of Eloquence and Applied Writing;Participated in the Scientific research Fund project of Yunnan Provincial Education Department "Research on Diversified Education Mode of the Second Chinese Classroom in Higher vocational Colleges".

References

1. Guo, Z.: Discussion on the teaching mode of C language programming under the background of multimedia information technology. J. Henan Mech. Electr. Eng. Coll. (2018)
2. Wang, J.: The application of multimedia technology in technical secondary school language teaching. Teach. For. Reg. (2017)
3. Qian, W.: Development and practice of the course system of embedded technology specialty in the context of "course certificate integration" based on big data analysis. J. Phys. Conf. Ser. **1992**(4), 042009 (6pp) (2021)
4. Yan, D.P.: College english interactive teaching mode under an information technology environment. Agro Food Ind Hi Tech **28**(1), 534–537 (2017)
5. Xiao, X.: Application of digital network resources and multimedia technology in poetry language classroom teaching. In: CIPAE 2020: 2020 International Conference on Computers, Information Processing and Advanced Education (2020)
6. Kjaergaard, H.W.: ICT and feedback practices in the lower-secondary foreign language classroom. J. Educ. Multimedia Hypermedia **26**(2), 161–177 (2016)
7. González-Lloret, M.: A Practical Guide to Integrating Technology into Task-Based Language Teaching. Georgetown University Press (2016)
8. Yuan, Y.: Quantitative analysis of Chinese classroom teaching activity under the background of artificial intelligence. Educ. Inf. Technol. **27**(8), 11161–11177 (2022)
9. Gao, S.: Integrating Multimedia Technology into Teaching Chinese as a Foreign Language: A Field Study on Perspectives of Teachers in Northern California. Academy Publication (6) (2019)

10. Ikyer, A.G., Yusuf, M.M., Ijem, U.B.: Teaching English Language and Literature-in-English Using Multimedia Technology: An Analysis (2017)
11. Trutenko, M.P., Grigorieva, G.F., Трутенко, М.П., et al.: Multimedia technology in university for foreign language teaching (2017)
12. Yin, S.K.: A study of the effects of thematic language teaching on the promotion of multimedia design students' listening and speaking skills (2022)
13. Ying, H.: Innovation in the practice of higher vocational english education in china under the background of big data. J. Jiamusi Vocat. Inst. (2018)
14. Zhang, W.: Innovation and practice of chinese teaching in higher vocational colleges under the background of new media. Educ. Teach. Forum (2018)
15. Beibei, X.U.: The construction and practice of blended teaching evaluation system for japanese under the background of big data. Theory Pract. Innov. Entrep. (2019)
16. Yi, L.: Research and practice of the flipped class in English course under the background of big data. J. Jiamusi Vocat. Inst. (2016)
17. Zhai, W., Xin, L.I., Kong, L.X.: Under the background of big data exploration and practice of college teaching management mode. Educ. Teach. Forum (2018)
18. Wang, Z.: Classroom design & practice of college physics teaching under the age of big data. J. North China Inst. Aerosp. Eng. (2016)
19. Ma, B.: The practice of the multimedia courseware for college foreign language teaching based on the network resources. In: Atiquzzaman, M., Yen, N., Xu, Z. (eds.) BDCPS 2019, pp. 1720–1726. Springer, Singapore (2020). https://doi.org/10.1007/978-981-15-2568-1_242
20. Ma, Q., et al.: Analysis on the teaching model of independent college under the background of MOOC. In: International Conference on Education (2017)

Application of Clustering Algorithm in Intelligent Education Resource Library

Innovation of Entrepreneurship Education in Colleges and Universities Based on K-means Clustering Algorithm

Ling Jin[1,2](✉) and Xiaolei He[1,2]

[1] Yunnan College of Business Management, Yunnan 650106, China
jinling13141030@163.com
[2] School of Music and Dance, Sichuan University of Culture and Arts, Mianyang City 621000, Sichuan Province, China

Abstract. Entrepreneurship education in universities is a hot topic in the current reform of higher education. In order to improve the quality and effectiveness of entrepreneurship education in universities, this article explores innovative approaches to entrepreneurship education in universities based on the K-means clustering algorithm. Firstly, the article analyzes the current situation of entrepreneurship education in universities. At present, the teaching mode of entrepreneurship education in universities mostly combines classroom teaching and practical teaching, but there are problems such as scattered curriculum and insufficient practical teaching. Proposed innovative ideas for entrepreneurship education in universities based on K-means clustering algorithm. This algorithm can cluster students based on different indicators such as entrepreneurial willingness, entrepreneurial background, and entrepreneurial ability, providing personalized entrepreneurial education plans for educators and students. This article proposes an innovative approach to entrepreneurship education in universities based on K-means clustering algorithm and explores its significance. This method can provide strong support for the optimization of entrepreneurship education in universities and make positive contributions to the cultivation of innovative and entrepreneurial talents.

Keywords: K-means clustering algorithm · Innovation and entrepreneurship · Higher education · Teaching resources

1 Introduction

The pointed out that entrepreneurship should drive employment, and employment is the greatest livelihood of the people. Colleges and universities should put employment in an important position, constantly explore active employment policies, further implement the policies of the government to promote employment, the market to regulate employment, workers' independent employment and encourage college students' entrepreneurship, so as to achieve higher quality and fuller employment. We should solve the problem of guiding college students to change their employment concept and encourage college

Y. Zhang and N. Shah (Eds.): BigIoT-EDU 2023, LNICST 584, pp. 211–217, 2024.
https://doi.org/10.1007/978-3-031-63142-9_21

students to obtain employment through multiple channels and forms, so as to stimulate employment by entrepreneurship. College Students' employment is a systematic project, which runs through the whole process of college life. From the current the strategic goal of cultivating high-quality talents in Colleges, it is promote entrepreneurship education and cultivate entrepreneurial talents [1]. The main role of strengthening entrepreneurship lies in cultivating innovative consciousness and practical ability, promoting extensive employment, alleviating social employment pressure and meeting the social demand for talents. On the other hand, through the further study of College Students' entrepreneurship education, innovate the concept and universities, overcome the disadvantages of talent training in higher education, reasonably connect the talent training objectives with social needs, and build a scientific and reasonable talent training model [2]. At China's College Students' started late, and colleges and challenges in carrying out entrepreneurship education. Correctly understanding the connotation, facing the difficulties and exploring the ways of entrepreneurship education have aroused the "resonance" of colleges and universities, society, parents and students, and become the largest livelihood project of colleges and universities.

2   Current Situation of Innovation and Entrepreneurship in Colleges and Universities

The 19th CPC National Congress proposed, take innovation as an important measure to strengthen the country and enrich the people, as a new driving force to promote China's economic development, and as a powerful starting point and important support for economic reform and talent cultivation. Entrepreneurship based on the new concept driving employment and innovation promoting development, focusing on enriching college students' entrepreneurial knowledge, promoting college students' employment and Cultivating College Students' innovative spirit. To actively carry out and universities, we need to explore the development process for college students and deeply understand the rich connotation students, so as to sow the seeds of entrepreneurship among college students and achieve their entrepreneurial goals.

(1) Connotation of entrepreneurship education

An innovation of educational concept and educational model of employment education under the new situation. It is an education aimed at cultivating college students' entrepreneurial consciousness, carrying forward entrepreneurial spirit and improving entrepreneurial ability. P colleges and universities awareness and through theoretical teaching and practical teaching activities, so that they can master entrepreneurial knowledge and skills, improve their management ability, innovation ability and creativity, and strive to cultivate college students' ability to grasp opportunities, optimize and integrate resources, accumulate enterprise management experience and dare to take risks, Theoretical education and methods to make it a potential entrepreneur or an innovator good at business activities [3].

(2) Development students in China

Entrepreneurship Education in foreign countries started relatively early in the United States. The main body in American colleges and universities is business schools. In the 1980s, the United States began to enter the era of knowledge economy.

The entrepreneurship education of American universities and there were more active. After decades of development, entrepreneurship education in the United States covers formal education from middle school, undergraduate and graduate students, and has formed a relatively complete entrepreneurship education system. Affected by it, many countries absorb the experience of the United States into their colleges and universities, infiltrate entrepreneurship education into general, and encourage college graduates to start businesses.

(3) The training objectives and universities in China at the present stage

From the perspective development, the cultivation objectives in different grades are different. It is a process to awaken entrepreneurship awareness, participate in innovation and entrepreneurship activities and practice, and then create entrepreneurial conditions for students, build an entrepreneurial platform, and exercise students' entrepreneurial ability in practice.

3 Clustering Algorithm

3.1 Mathematical Description and Basic Elements of Cluster Analysis

1) Mathematical Description of Cluster Analysis.

The mathematical description of clustering analysis: Let the data set $X = \{x_i | i = 1, 2, 3, \cdots, n\}$ be the initial sample set, and each sample in the sample set contains m sample attributes, that is, each sample can be represented as $x_i = (x_j \mid j = 1, 2, 3, \cdots, m)$. Cluster analysis is the process of dividing a sample set X containing n samples into disjoint k subsets C based on their m attributes, $C_1, C_2...C_k$. And k sets satisfy $C_i \cap C_j = \Phi$, $(i \neq j, i, j = 1, 2 \cdots k)$. And $C_1 \cup C_2 \cdots C_k = X$. Clustering can be divided into hard partitioning and soft partitioning. If the membership function ui is used to represent the degree of membership of the i-th sample point x to the k-th set Ck, then the hard partitioning membership function is represented as follows

$$u_{ij} = \begin{cases} 0, x_i \notin C_k \\ 1, x_i \in C_k \end{cases} \tag{1}$$

That is, if the membership degree of the sample point belongs to a certain class is not 0 or 1, and each sample belongs to and only belongs to one subset, the membership function

$$\sum_{j=1}^{k} u_{ij} = 1, \forall j \tag{2}$$

Soft partition clustering, such as fuzzy clustering, divides the dataset into several fuzzy subsets, with membership values ranging from 0 to 1, i.e.

$$u_{ij} \in [0, 1] \tag{3}$$

And the sum of membership degrees of a certain sample point belonging to each fuzzy subset still satisfies formula (2).

2) Measurement of similarity between samples in cluster analysis.

Cluster analysis relies on the similarity between data as the basis for dividing categories, so how to measure the similarity between data is an important issue. At present, the commonly used similarity measurement methods mainly include distance based measurement, similarity coefficient and correlation coefficient based measurement, information entropy based measurement and other measurement methods for different types of data [4].

Euclidean distance is a very common similarity measure in clustering algorithms, but in reality, there are many data distribution structures that Euclidean distance cannot reflect, such as circular data, as shown in Fig. 1

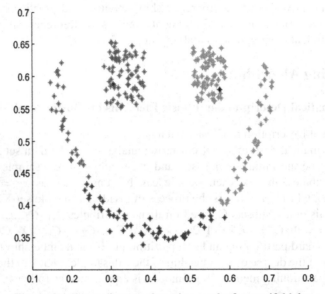

Fig. 1. Euclidean distance clustering results for manifold data

The clustering results in Fig. 1 use Euclidean distance as a similarity measure, indicating that Euclidean distance can only reflect local consistency features of the clustering structure and cannot reflect global consistency features. In order to achieve global consistency, it is necessary to define the length of the line segment on the same manifold where two samples are connected through shorter edges, which is smaller than the length of the path directly connected through low density regions.

3.2   K-means Clustering Algorithm

The k-means clustering algorithm is influenced by the selected similarity measurement method, and commonly used similarity measurement methods use the sum of error squares criterion function to improve clustering performance. Assuming X contains k clustering subsets X1, X2, ... Xk; The number of samples in each cluster subset is $n_1, n_2, ...n_k$; The mean points of each cluster subset are $m_1, m_2, ..., m_k$.

The formula for the sum of squared errors criterion function is:

$$E = \sum_{i=1}^{k} \sum_{p \in X_i} \|p - m_i\|^2 \tag{4}$$

The k-means clustering algorithm process is shown in Fig. 2.

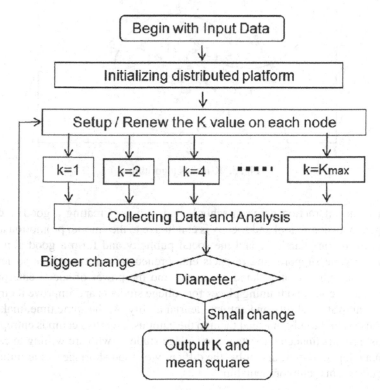

Fig. 2. K-means clustering algorithm process

3.3 Innovation of Entrepreneurship Education in Colleges and Universities Based on K-means Clustering Algorithm

Based on the K-means model in the above paper, this paper disassembles entrepreneurial thinking in multiple dimensions, designs specific topics, obtains data through case investigation, and makes quantitative analysis, so as to obtain relevant information about entrepreneurial thinking of college students in a certain university, objectively, truly and pertinently reflect the actual state, It provides a reference for further exploring problems and putting forward entrepreneurship education reform.

The greater the similarity (as shown in Fig. 3). The compact and independent clusters as the ultimate goal.

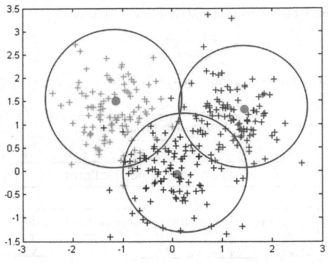

Fig. 3. K-means algorithm

Expand the interaction between schools and society. Creating a good interactive environment between school and society is conducive to the smooth promotion and universities. On the one hand, expand the social publicity and form a good atmosphere in which everyone supports and respects entrepreneurship in the whole society with power of social; On the other hand, we social and the power of social enterprises to provide good practice and training places for college students and improve their practical ability, innovation ability and entrepreneurial ability. At the same time, make every effort to raise social funds and send them to the campus, establish campus entrepreneurship funds, provide financial assistance to college students who are willing to carry out entrepreneurship activities, and solve the difficulty of fund shortage in the initial stage of College Students' entrepreneurship.

4 Conclusion

This article explores the ideas for innovation in entrepreneurship education in universities based on the K-means clustering algorithm. The article analyzes the current situation of entrepreneurship education in universities and proposes that this algorithm can cluster students according to different indicators, providing personalized entrepreneurship education solutions for educators and students. Finally, the article summarizes the significance of this method, which can optimize the teaching mode and content of entrepreneurship education in universities, promote the coordinated development of talent cultivation and socio-economic development in universities. This method provides strong support for the optimization of entrepreneurship education in universities and makes positive contributions to the cultivation of innovative and entrepreneurial talents.

References

1. Zhou, S., Zhou, A., et al.: A fast clustering algorithm based on density. Comput. Res. Dev. (11) (2000)
2. Kebin, J.: Research on cluster analysis method in information system design. J. Beijing Univ. Technol. Third issue (1999)
3. Shi, X.: Path choice of cultivating college students' entrepreneurial risk aversion ability. Career Time Space. (7) (2014)
4. Yu, D.: Analysis of value guidance in classroom teaching. Res. Teach. Theory. (5) (2016)

Construction of College Students' Mental Health Evaluation System Based on Cluster Analysis Algorithm

Xiao Guo[✉] and Sun Hong

Shanghai YZH Education Technology Co., Ltd., Shanghai 201111, China
1220019446@qq.com

Abstract. With the issues such as academic pressure, career prospects, and interpersonal relationships among college students have become one of the main challenges to their mental health. How comprehensive evaluation system of college students' psychological Health assessment has become one of the important topics of education. Based on clustering analysis algorithm, this paper establishes a Health assessment evaluation, in order to provide a more scientific and rigorous health education. The article first discusses the basic principles and application fields of clustering analysis algorithms. Clustering analysis algorithm is a Unsupervised learning method that groups similar data in a dataset. It can divide a set of data into several categories based on similarity, and then analyze and process the grouping results according to specific problem requirements. In the field of mental health, clustering analysis algorithm can be applied to the construction assessment evaluation system.

Then, the paper elaborates on the screening of college students' psychological Health assessment indicators and the construction of the evaluation system. The article selects eight indicators including social ability, psychological regulation, emotional experience, self-awareness, interpersonal relationships, coping ability, achievement experience, self-esteem and confidence, and obtains specific factors under each indicator through actual investigation. Subsequently, cluster analysis algorithm was used to group the obtained factors and ultimately obtain different types models. According to the characteristics of different models, targeted mental health intervention plans and measures can be formulated. Finally, the paper points out the significance and practical significance of applying the psychological Health assessment evaluation system. The e Health assessment constructed in this paper can comprehensively and accurately evaluate college students' psychological health, which provides a useful reference for school psychological health education; At the same time, the adopted in this article also has certain guiding significance for research and application in other related fields.

Keywords: Cluster analysis · Mental health assessment · College student

Y. Zhang and N. Shah (Eds.): BigIoT-EDU 2023, LNICST 584, pp. 218–225, 2024.
https://doi.org/10.1007/978-3-031-63142-9_22

1   Introduction

With the development of society and the improvement of people's living standards, people's attention to mental health is becoming increasingly high. Especially on university campuses, the psychological condition of students has become a hot topic of concern for all parties [1]. The school, teachers, parents, and society all hope to provide better psychological support and services for college students [2]. However, how to scientifically evaluate the mental health level of college students has become an important issue in mental health education. Based on clustering analysis algorithm, this paper constructs a system suitable for college students' mental Health assessment evaluation, hoping to provide a more scientific and rigorous evaluation system for college students' mental health education.

At home and abroad, research on college students' psychological Health assessment has been carried out in an earlier period. However, the practice of college students' psychological Health assessment still faces many challenges and problems, such as different evaluation indicators, the relationship between indicators, and so on. This article selects and constructs evaluation indicators, and ultimately establishes corresponding evaluation models [3]. In today's society, the mental health issues of college students have become an issue that cannot be ignored. The ' mental Health assessment evaluation system can systematically and scientifically evaluate the level, and find problems as early as possible, which is of great significance to the growth of students [4]. However, there are still many problems and challenges in the construction of this evaluation system, such as how to refine the indicator system and its combination, and how to improve the system in practice, which needs further improvement and exploration.

College students are in their prime of life, and their physiology and psychology are becoming more mature. However, due to factors such as poor interpersonal relationships, financial difficulties, breakdowns, and academic setbacks, psychological barriers often arise.

The diversity of college students' behavior is determined by various forms of psychology, not only influenced as their own psychological cognitive level [5].

The idea and method of this paper is based on the Unsupervised learning method of clustering analysis algorithm, which groups different indicators and constructs an evaluation model, which can greatly alleviate the interference of human subjective factors, and greatly improve the scientificity and objectivity of the evaluation system. Meanwhile, based on the establishment of this model, targeted psychological health intervention plans and measures for college students can be formulated to guide them to better adapt to campus life and work [6]. In a word, the research of this paper and method for the evaluation of college students' mental Health assessment, which can play a positive role in evaluating students' mental health, improving the construction of campus spiritual civilization, and promoting the development.

2 Data Analysis of College Students' Mental Health

2.1 Analysis of Psychological Data of College Students

The human brain is a psychological organ in terms of its function. Although it is the center of human behavior and psychological organ, it cannot exist without the whole human body. Besides, people's psychological activities are closely related to people's sensory organs, lower-level centers, peripheral nerves, effector organs and even endocrine system. The human brain is the organ and material base that produces psychology. However, only the human brain can't produce psychology [7]. It can only be said that it has the biological premise and possibility of producing psychology.

Set $|X(t), t = 1, 2, \ldots, n|$ to represent the psychological time series set of college students at different stages. As college students' antagonistic psychology has obvious differences in manifestations, it is necessary to reconstruct the phase space of the psychological formation process to obtain the matrix:

$$
\begin{bmatrix}
x(1) & x(1+\tau)\ldots x(1+(m-1)\tau) \\
x(j) & x(2+\tau)\ldots x(2+(m-1)\tau) \\
 & \cdots \\
x(K) & x(K+\tau)\ldots x(K+(m-1)\tau)
\end{bmatrix} \tag{1}
$$

$$
j = 1, 2, \ldots, K
$$

In the complexity of college students' rebellious psychology, and τ represents the psychological duration, which satisfies:

$$
K = n - (m-1)\tau \tag{2}
$$

Assuming that the probability of k different is $P_1, P_2, \ldots, P_k$, then the inverse mental state sequence probabilities are sorted according to the Shannon entropy form, and the permutation entropy is defined by formula (3):

$$
H_{PE}(m) = -\sum_{j=1}^{k} P_j InP_j \tag{3}
$$

Integrate the state by formula (3), and use formula (4) to express the to the reversal mental state at this stage [8]:

$$
0 \leq H_{PE} = H_{PE}/In(m) \leq 1 \tag{4}
$$

2.2 College Students' Psychological Data Test

All kinds of objective reality have different effects on people's psychological activities, the generation of consciousness tendency and the formation of personality. Among them, human social life is the most important source of people's psychological content, which plays a people's psychological activities and the formation of personality. Students can not only fully understand their own psychological situation, but also relieve themselves of some basic psychological problems, teaching students to face and cope with reality, reasonably constructing correct cognitive behavior patterns, and effectively avoiding many psychological problems [9–11]. The socialization of psychological education makes it very easy, In the process of reflecting the aesthetic reality, people always regulate and control their psychological activities according to the practical standards and feedback, so that it conforms to the laws of objective things. Whether people's psychology can play its active role depends on whether it accurately reflects objective things and their laws.

3 Design of College Students' Mental Health Intelligent Analysis System

When establishing the psychological Health assessment, the key is to select appropriate evaluation indicators and make a reasonable combination. This article selects eight indicators, including social ability, psychological regulation, emotional experience, self-awareness, interpersonal relationships, coping ability, achievement experience, self-esteem and confidence. Firstly, social skills are one of the important aspects in evaluating college students. Social ability includes indicators such as willingness to interact, situational adaptability, and communication ability, which can be used to evaluate students' communication ability and expression level. Secondly, psychological regulation is another important aspect of evaluating the mental health of college students. Psychological regulation includes indicators such as self-monitoring, emotional regulation, and psychological counseling [12], which can evaluate students' ability to regulate emotions and solve problems. Emotional experience is also an important aspect of evaluating the mental health of college students. Emotional experience includes indicators of emotional feelings and emotions such as happiness, anger, sadness, and happiness. Through these indicators, students' emotional and psychological status can be understood, and whether they have psychological problems can be determined. Self understanding is another important aspect of. Self awareness includes indicators such as self positioning, values, and self-awareness. Through these indicators, students' understanding and understanding of their own existence can be understood, and it can also help them establish a more confident and self-esteem mindset. Interpersonal relationships are also an important aspect of evaluating the mental. Interpersonal relationship includes interpersonal communication, interpersonal relationship quality and other indicators, through which students' Interpersonal communication and interpersonal relationship quality can be evaluated [13–15]. Coping ability is also an aspect. Coping ability includes adaptability, crisis response and other indicators. Through these indicators, students' ability to cope with pressure and challenges in life, study and work can be understood.

Achievement experience is also an aspect of evaluating the mental health of college students. Achievement experience mainly refers to the sense of achievement and self actualization that students have achieved in their learning and life. Through these indicators, students' sense of achievement and self actualization can be understood. Finally, self-esteem and confidence are one of the important aspects. Self esteem and confidence include aspects such as self-affirmation, self-expectation, and self-confidence, which can be used to evaluate students' cognition and evaluation of self-worth and abilities. Through the comprehensive consideration and selection of these eight evaluation indicators, this psychological Health assessment evaluation. This evaluation system evaluates and guides the with a scientific and rigorous attitude, providing scientific and effective psychological protection for students, and promoting their comprehensive and healthy development.

Student information should include basic identity information, family and major social relations, psychological evaluation records, psychological consultation records, and periodic evaluation records of mental health, etc.

Through students' identity information and the composition of family of origin, students' potential psychological situation can be found in advance in combination with students' psychological evaluation records, so as to help students find problems in advance.

The psychological crisis graph is shown in Fig. 1.

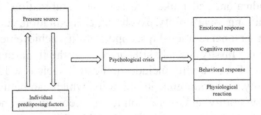

Fig. 1. Psychological Crisis Graph

Psychological problems gradually come into human eyes, which makes student managers realize the importance of paying attention to students' mental health problems, and also realize that an efficient and reasonable mental health information system is also very important. Analysis of students' psychological needs is the core of user research. Understanding students' psychological needs is helpful to improve the management information system and keep their core needs from being replaced at all times. The lack of psychological knowledge will lead to students not knowing how to actively and correctly solve their psychological obstacles when receiving psychological counseling. At this time, university administrators need to use professional psychological knowledge to explain and help them solve and face up to their psychological problems. Everyone is an independent individual, and information and data have their own uniqueness. The information management system of students' mental health should file files for each student independently, which not only prevents the data from being ambiguous, but also protects students' privacy from the perspective of information management workers. Accurately positioning students' psychological needs can not only save time and energy for universities, but also improve their ability to supervise students' psychological health. The difference between psychological problems and physiological problems is that psychological problems are difficult to be discovered by students themselves. At the present stage of development, the protection of college students' psychological problems should focus on the protection of personal privacy.

Set the mixed sample set $X = \{x_1, x_2, x_3, \ldots x_n\}$, based on a certain similarity measure, it is clustered into C separate subsets $X_1, X_2, X_3, \ldots X_c$, each of which is defined as:

$$J_c = \sum_{j=1}^{c} \sum_{k=1}^{n_j} \left\| x_k^{(j)} - m_j \right\|^2 \tag{5}$$

$$m_j = \frac{1}{n_j \left(\sum_{j=1}^{n_j} x_j \right)} \quad j = 1, 2, \ldots, c \tag{6}$$

where m_j represents the jth category, and n_j represents the s in the jth category. The weighted sum criterion is:

$$J_I = \sum_{j=1}^{c} p_j s_j^* \tag{7}$$

$$s_j^* = \frac{2}{n_j(n_j - 1)} \sum_{x \in x_i} \sum_{x' \in x_j} \left\| x - x' \right\|^2 \tag{8}$$

where s_j^* is the average samples within a class. The distance and criteria between classes are:

$$J_b = \sum_{j=1}^{c} (m_j - m)(m_j - m) \tag{9}$$

where m_j is the sample mean vector of type w_j, and m is the samples. is shown in Fig. 2.

Set up an independent account for each student, and one-on-one consultation and counseling is the protection of students' personality and self-esteem when consulting problems occur, so the mental health information management system should take the privacy protection of students as an important concern. In the absence of professional psychological counseling, many people's psychological problems will be ignored at an early stage, and it will be too late to discover that psychological problems have affected their physical health. Therefore, in time before they are serious, and help them get through this period. The database system is the data layer, providing and managing all kinds of databases, including access to all kinds of databases. It mainly stores students' basic information, psychological test papers, students' psychological test files and various intermediate information in statistical analysis. In which the data is constantly changing, and the operation is mainly around it. The construction of university mental health information management system needs a complete technical service team to be responsible for the development, creation, improvement and update of the system. Only when the professionalism of the information system is improved, will more accurate student information be provided to the teachers who participate in psychological counseling, and strive for accurate psychological counseling activities for every student who needs help.

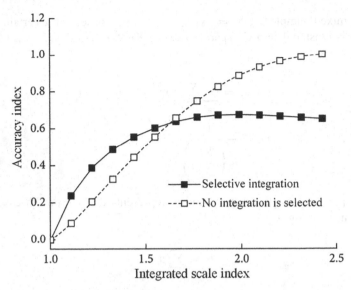

Fig. 2. Simulation result

4   Conclusions

Based on algorithm, this paper constructs a system suitable for psychological Health assessment. Through screening and combining the indicators social ability, psychological adjustment, emotional experience, self-awareness, interpersonal relationship, coping ability, achievement experience, self-esteem and self-confidence, a scientific and complete evaluation system is established. This evaluation system can comprehensively and accurately evaluate the psychological health level of students, providing beneficial reference for schools. This study found that screening and combining college students' psychological Health assessment evaluation indicators through clustering analysis algorithm can remove the interference of subjectivity and human factors, and accurate. At the same time, the establishment of this enable students to better understand their psychological status, formulate targeted mental health intervention plans and measures, and promote students' psychological adjustment and self-development. Of course, there are still shortcomings in the establishing the psychological Health assessment evaluation system, such as the selection of indicators and the optimization of the evaluation system, which need to be further improved and improved in the follow-up research. However, the research ideas and methods of this paper provide new ideas and methods for assessment evaluation, provide useful college students' mental health education, and guiding the application of other related fields.

References

1. Huang, M., Tao, Y., Qiu, S., Chang, Y.: Healthy community assessment model based on the German DGNB system. Sustainability **15**(4), 3167 (2023). https://doi.org/10.3390/su1504 3167

2. Panagiotopoulos, A., et al.: Health-related quality of life in patients with ANCA vasculitides compared to rheumatoid arthritis: a cross-sectional comparative study. Rheumatology **63**(2), 399–406 (2023). https://doi.org/10.1093/rheumatology/kead214

3. Gao, C.Y.: Analysis on the law of differentiating and treating insomnia by physicians based on cluster analysis of drug syndrome. J. Hainan Med. Univ. **28**(1), 56–63 (2022)

4. Wang, Y., Cao, X., Ma, X.: Evaluation of automatic lane-change model based on vehicle cluster generalized dynamic system. Autom. Innov. **5**(1), 91–104 (2022). https://doi.org/10.1007/s42154-021-00171-z

5. Martin, F., et al.: Exploring the extent of mental health practice: content and cluster analysis of techniques used in HIV testing and counselling sessions in Uganda. AIDS Care **35**(2), 191–197 (2022). https://doi.org/10.1080/09540121.2022.2077909

6. Zhou, L.: Applications of deep learning in the evaluation and analysis of college students' mental health. Discr. Dyn. Nat. Soc. **2022**, 1–11 (2022)

7. Liang, F., Li, P., Peng, H., et al.: Evaluation model of college students∈ mental health quality based on computational intelligence. Math. Probl. Eng. **2022**, 1–11 (2022)

8. Crowley, P.: Has the EU become an OCA? Evaluation using model-based cluster analysis (2022)

9. Chu, T.: Research on college students' physique testing platform based on big data analysis. Math. Probl. Eng. **2022**, 1–8 (2022)

10. Han, P.: Multidimensional state data reduction and evaluation of college students' mental health based on SVM. J. Math. **2022**, 1–11 (2022)

11. Liu, X.: Optimization of college students' mental health education based on improved intelligent recognition model. Math. Probl. Eng. **2022**, 1–11 (2022). https://doi.org/10.1155/2022/1573810

12. Haojun, D.: Research on the improvement path of the mental health of the elderly from the perspective of college students'volunteer service activities. Psychol. Res. **12**(9), 730–734 (2022)

13. Vovan, T., Lethithu, T.: A fuzzy time series model based on improved fuzzy function and cluster analysis problem. Commun. Math. Statist. **10**, 51–66 (2022)

14. Sun, X., et al.: Corrigendum to "Trends of college students' mental health from 2005 to 2019 and its rural–urban disparities in China". J. Affect. Disord. **302**, 160–169 (2022)

15. Skehan, B., Chan, V.: Mental health treatment for college students on campus: evolving to meet the growing need. Psych. Ann. **52**(6), 232–237 (2022). https://doi.org/10.3928/00485713-20220523-018

Data Analysis and Predictive Modeling of Teaching Skill Performance of English Normal College Students Based on K-means Clustering Algorithm

Cuiying Wang[1(✉)], Xiaozhe Yu[2], and Kun Tang[3]

[1] Xianyang Normal University, Xianyang 712000, Shaanxi, China
wangcuiying0428@163.com
[2] Middle School of Dalian Economic and Technological Development Zone, Dalian 116000, Liaoning, China
[3] Hohhot Institute for Nationalities, Hohhot 010000, Inner Mongolia, China

Abstract. With the continuous development of basic education and the continuous improvement of educational quality requirements, as a qualified normal school graduate or new teacher, in addition to mastering various educational theoretical knowledge, teaching concepts, and teaching methods, it is also necessary to have excellent teaching skills. Research on Data Analysis and Predictive Modeling of Teaching Skill Performance of English Normal University Students Based on K-means Clustering Algorithm is a research that analyzes and predicts the teaching skill performance of English normal university students based on K-means clustering algorithm. The study was conducted by Dr. Zu Yunfeng, a professor at the Department of Computer Science and Technology, Guangxi University, China. This article will outline this research project, its findings, and conclusions. By analyzing and mining behavioral characteristics data such as students' lives, learning, and activities, an improved K-means clustering algorithm is used to establish a student performance category model, achieving classification of students based on student performance data. Select six attribute data of students' "moral education scores, physical education scores, intellectual education scores, competition grades, poverty student grades, and scholarship grades" as characteristic evaluation indicators. Aiming at problems such as data duplication, deletion, and inconsistent storage types caused by excessive categories in university student management systems, clean, integrate, and transform the data storage format to obtain input data that meets the K-means algorithm.

Keywords: K-means clustering algorithm · English normal students · Teaching skills · Predictive modeling

1 Introduction

In the development of teacher education in China over the past 100 years, teachers' colleges and universities have focused on imparting theoretical knowledge in curriculum design and talent cultivation, while ignoring the cultivation of pre-service teaching

Y. Zhang and N. Shah (Eds.): BigIoT-EDU 2023, LNICST 584, pp. 226–236, 2024.
https://doi.org/10.1007/978-3-031-63142-9_23

skills for normal students [1]. The direct negative impact of this phenomenon of "valuing learning over normal education" and "valuing knowledge over skills" is that normal school students have difficulty entering the job, have a prolonged period of adaptation to the job, and even leave the job. In response to this situation, improving the professional level of teachers and building a high-quality basic education research teacher team have become the focus of attention of scholars in the field of teacher education in China. In 2007, the Teacher Training Department of the Ministry of Education proposed in its key work points that "we should vigorously promote the work of supporting teacher training students in internship, research and promote local experience, and promote the institutionalization of educational practice [2]. In the same year, the Ministry of Education launched the training of free teacher training students, requiring" to strengthen the practical teaching environment, and improve the system of teacher training students' internship in primary and secondary schools for half a year during their school years. ". Six normal universities directly under the Ministry of Education have actively responded to the policy of free normal students, and have successively introduced exemplary new measures on the cultivation of free normal students. "The Outline of the National Medium and Long Term Education Reform and Development Plan (2010–2020) also points out that:" Strengthen teacher education, strengthen internship practice, strengthen teaching ability training, and comprehensively improve the quality of teacher training. "With the deepening of educational reform and the implementation of free education for normal students, the task of higher normal education has gradually shifted from a quantitative satisfaction type to a quality improvement type, and cultivate teachers who meet professional standards" [3].

With the rapid development of knowledge economy and society and the deepening of curriculum reform, higher requirements have been put forward for teachers' educational concepts, teaching skills and thinking modes. As prospective teachers, normal students must have qualified teaching ability. To this end, the state has issued a series of policies one after another. In August 2014, the opinions of the Ministry of education on the implementation of the excellent teacher training plan proposed that through the implementation of the excellent teacher training plan, a group of high-quality professional and innovative primary and secondary school teachers with deep educational feelings, solid professional foundation, courage to innovate teaching, good at comprehensive education and lifelong learning and development ability should be cultivated [4]. In 2018, the Ministry of education and five other departments issued the action plan for the revitalization of Teacher Education (2018–2022), which proposed to comprehensively improve the comprehensive quality and ability of normal students, train teachers at all levels for compulsory education schools, ordinary high schools, secondary vocational schools and kindergartens, and meet the needs of national education and innovative talent training [5]. The successive educational documents issued by the state reflect the great importance attached to the education of normal students, thus requiring colleges and universities to train normal students with advanced teaching concepts and high-quality teaching capabilities.

Teaching skills are the guarantee for English normal students to present a lesson completely. English normal students have a certain understanding of teaching through theoretical knowledge (such as pedagogy, educational psychology, teaching design, etc.), but they are still far from qualified teachers. Before entering primary and secondary schools, English normal students must master teaching skills, so that they can make sufficient preparations before teaching, smoothly carry out teaching Be able to evaluate teaching results after teaching [6]; In order to cultivate the teaching skills of English normal college students, higher normal colleges and educators have always taken it as the focus of research, and the methods of teaching skills training are also gradually developing, of which microteaching is one of the ways to cultivate the teaching skills of English normal college students.

2 Related Work

2.1 Classification of Teaching Skills

Teaching skill is not a separate concept. The research of teaching skill is to decompose the whole complex teaching behavior into a single specific teaching skill. Because of its complexity, teaching skills can be classified from different levels and different standards. Through reading the relevant literature, we can find that there are various classifications of teaching skills at home and abroad.

Sorting out the classification of teaching skills by researchers, the classification basis is not uniform, and the classification of teaching skills is also different. Some researchers, based on teaching elements, such as professor Allen of Stanford University in the United States, divide teaching skills into 11 items; Some scholars, based on teaching behavior, such as British root, divide teaching skills into six categories [7]; Some scholars, based on the teaching process, such as Gao Yan, Zhang Tieniu and the national education "teacher professional skills training program for students in Higher Normal Schools", divide teaching skills into three types: before class, during class and after class; Other scholars divide teaching skills according to the needs of Microteaching. For example, Meng xiankai divides teaching skills into 10 items and Guo you divides teaching skills into 10 items. Hu Shuzhen divided teaching skills into 11 categories [8].

Researchers have classified teaching skills from different angles and levels, but the classification of researchers overlaps with the classification of teaching skills proposed by scholar Meng xiankai. With the development of the new curriculum reform and quality education, some scholars have proposed learning guidance skills to promote students' learning. The introduction of this skill can better reflect the role of teachers as guides and guides for students, and better reflect students' dominant position in teaching.

2.2 Research on Training Methods of Teaching Skills of Normal University Students

At home and abroad, the cultivation of teaching skills of normal students has its own characteristics. The United States attaches great importance to the training of normal students. They believe that only by training a first-class teaching team can we teach high-quality senior talents. At the beginning of the 21st century, the United States launched the reform of the "new era teacher program", which organically combined the pre employment training of teachers with the training of teaching skills and professional learning, and divided the training method into four stages: first, entering the classroom; The second is to start independent teaching; Third, independent teaching; Fourth, pre service education [9].

The model of Teacher Education in Britain is "school-based", which combines with James's three-stage theory – teacher education of training, appointment and training, forming a new teacher education model of teacher education integration. The institutionalized training model of school-based teacher education implemented in Britain, which places the training base in primary and secondary schools, takes partnership as the guarantee and practice as the guide, is an important model of pre service teacher training [10].

Morrison et al. pointed out that teaching skills are a very common and effective way of teaching activities used to achieve certain goals set in teaching. However, this concept ignores the connection between teaching skills and theoretical knowledge, which can easily lead to learners' mechanical imitation and simple repetition; Behavior theory is based on behaviorism, which attributes teaching skills to teachers' teaching behaviors. Most domestic scholars agree with the viewpoint proposed by Li Kedong, who believes that "teaching skills are a series of teaching behaviors in which teachers use professional knowledge and teaching theories to promote students' learning in classroom teaching.". This view also has shortcomings. It ignores the internal psychological factors of human beings and treats teachers' teaching experience as the only factor in teaching skills [11]. The understanding of teaching skills in the structural theory has begun to shift to the combination of observable teachers' explicit behavior and cognitive factors. Teaching skills are seen as a sequence of interaction between teachers' teaching behavior and cognitive activities. R.F. Snow, who holds this view, believes that "teaching skills are composed of a structural sequence of behavioral and cognitive related matters.". Domestic scholar Xu Yuan also pointed out that teachers' teaching skills are a complex psychological process composed of observable, operable, and measurable various explicit behavioral behaviors and cognitive activities such as teachers' original cognitive structure, their understanding of knowledge, their mastery of teaching situations, and their selection of teaching behaviors [12]. The theory of knowledge is based on cognitive psychology and classifies teaching skills into the category of procedural knowledge: teaching skills are a series of operational steps used in specific situations, including teachers' movement skills, intelligent skills, cognitive strategies, and so on.

In China, the training of teaching skills of normal college students is mainly undertaken by normal colleges, normal colleges of comprehensive universities and primary and secondary schools. The training process of normal university students in China can be divided into three stages: in school learning, out of school practice and entry teaching. In the first stage, normal students mainly learn professional knowledge, pedagogy and other relevant teaching theories, so that normal students can accumulate theoretical knowledge. In the second stage, normal students are trained in practice, mainly in Microteaching in school, and normal students are trained in classroom teaching skills. 3. In the third stage, normal students need to carry out off campus practice, which is a period of changing the role of normal students [13]. The duration of practice is 8–10 weeks or even one semester. In this stage, college teachers and primary and secondary school teachers provide common guidance, college teachers teach and train them in professional theory and teaching skill theory, and primary and secondary school teachers guide normal students in practical skills and coping skills in teaching.

Although there are differences in the cultivation and development of the teaching skills of normal students in different countries, all three countries adopt the mode of cooperation between universities and primary and secondary schools to jointly cultivate the teaching skills of normal students. The United States and Britain started earlier. In China, the research on the cultivation of teaching skills of normal university students started relatively late [14]. Many scholars have put forward many views on the cultivation of teaching skills of normal university students. This provides experience and reference for the training of normal college students' teaching skills.

3 K-means Clustering Algorithm

K-means clustering algorithm was first proposed by James Macqueen in 1967. It is simple, fast and suitable for processing large data sets. It is the most widely used and mature clustering analysis method so far. It is applied in scientific research and industrial fields. K-means clustering algorithm compares the similarity between two data objects based on distance to complete clustering of all data objects. However, in the K-means clustering algorithm, the number of clusters K needs to be determined in advance, and the initial cluster center is randomly selected. These two parameters will have a great impact on the clustering results, resulting in instability and uncertainty of clustering.

As an important DM method, clustering measures the similarity between different data objects. On this basis, data objects are divided into multiple clusters, which can mine hidden information in complex data. Clustering algorithm has been studied for a long time. On the basis of predecessors' ideas, academic researchers have made many improvements on clustering algorithm [15]. Everitt once defined clustering analysis as follows in 1974: clustering analysis aims to cluster a sample into several classes according to its own attributes, so as to ensure that the similarity of samples within a class is as high as possible, and the similarity of samples between classes is as low as possible [9]. With the deepening of DM technology research, clustering algorithms based on different ideas have been proposed one after another and have been widely used and studied. Specific problems should be treated in a specific way. According to the basic properties of the data set and the purpose of clustering, the best clustering algorithm can be selected to get better clustering effect.

K-means, as a classical clustering algorithm, mainly achieves different classification of dataset categories through an iterative process. This algorithm has the advantages of simplicity and strong scalability. K-Mcans algorithm first randomly selects K samples from the sample set S as the initial clustering center. Then, according to the rule algorithm, the distance between data objects is calculated iteratively through the obtained data object grouping until the center does not change, and the K clustering results are obtained. The specific implementation process of the algorithm is as follows.

(1) Randomly select K samples from the dataset $D = \{x_1, x_2, \ldots, x_n\}$ as the sub cluster center $\{\mu_1, \mu_2, \ldots, \mu_k\}$.

(2) Calculate the distance between the unclassified samples and the centers of each sub cluster:

$$dist(x_i, \mu_j) = \|x_i - \mu_j\|^2 i = 1, \ldots, n; j = 1, \ldots, k \tag{1}$$

(3) According to the distance obtained in Step 2, the unclassified samples are classified as the nearest sub cluster center, namely:

$$\lambda_j = \mathrm{argmin}_{j \in \{1, \ldots, k\}} dist(x_i, \mu_j) \tag{2}$$

$$C_{\lambda_j} = C_{\lambda_j} \bigcup \{x_j\} \tag{3}$$

(4) Recalculate the sub cluster center, i.e.:

$$u_j^i = \frac{1}{|C_j|} \sum_{x \in |C_j|} x \tag{4}$$

(5) Repeat steps 2, 3, and 4 until the sub cluster center no longer changes or the maximum number of iterations is reached.

The K-means clustering algorithm flow is shown in Fig. 1.

K-means algorithm has many advantages, such as high efficiency, fast convergence, simple mathematical idea, scalability and easy implementation, so it is widely studied and used in processing high-dimensional power data sets. K-means clustering algorithm is an iterative clustering analysis algorithm, which uses the center point of a class to represent a cluster, and then continuously classifies and optimizes the data set, so as to minimize the distance between the centers of two classes. The principle of the algorithm is shown in Fig. 2.

Figure 1 (a) shows the sample points of the original data, which are indicated by green dots. (b) In the figure, two points represented by red and blue are randomly selected as the centroids, and the K value in the k-means algorithm is selected as 2. Then, the Euclidean distance commonly used by people to measure similarity is used to calculate the distance from each sample to the centroid, and a centroid with a small distance is selected as a class of the sample, also known as a cluster, as shown in figure (c). And then calculate the sample center point after classification (the mean value of the data samples in the new cluster). Finally, repeat this process to obtain the effect as shown in Fig. (f).

4   Data Analysis of Teaching Skill Performance of English Normal College Students Based on K-means Clustering Algorithm

4.1   Sample Data Processing

Through the improvement of k-means algorithm, based on the preprocessing of data in the previous section, the data of "poor student grade, scholarship grade, moral education grade, physical education grade, intellectual education grade and competition grade" is selected as the input variable of six-dimensional evaluation, and the maximum number of iterations is set to 10. The data format after preprocessing is shown in Fig. 3.

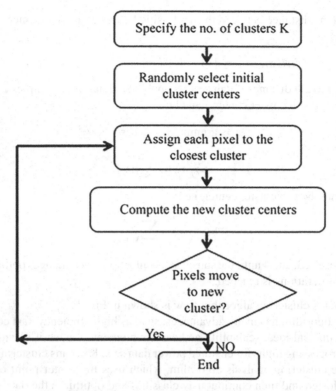

Fig. 1. K-means clustering algorithm flow

The above data is integrated data obtained based on different dimensions. Therefore, it is necessary to unify the dimensions of these different dimensional data. The specific calculation is formula (1).

$$E = \sum_{i=1}^{k} \sum_{p \in X_i} \|p - m_i\|^2 \tag{5}$$

"Statistical analysis of classroom teaching skills evaluation cannot comprehensively evaluate classroom teaching skills of normal students based on a single training session. In the past, microteaching conducted simple evaluations between teachers and groups during each training session, and the evaluation results were stored and statistically analyzed. To demonstrate the teaching skills of normal students, it is necessary to conduct a comprehensive and accurate analysis of their curriculum data,", It is necessary to collect each item of data from normal school students during the microteaching process, conduct statistical analysis with the help of relevant tools, and comprehensively demonstrate the training process of their teaching skills. Based on the above diagnostic concepts, this diagnostic result is divided into two levels: the overall level and the case level. The overall level is mainly targeted at the class. Combining with the online learning platform, the entire class's microteaching course training performance map will be displayed; The case

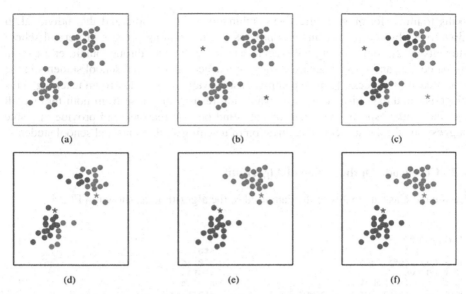

Fig. 2. Principle of K-means algorithm

Out[85]:

	date	high	low	open	close	volume	adjclose
0	2017-12-29	1049.699951	1044.900024	1046.719971	1046.400024	887500	1046.400024
1	2017-12-28	1054.750000	1044.770020	1051.599976	1048.140015	837100	1048.140015
2	2017-12-27	1058.369995	1048.050049	1057.390015	1049.369995	1271900	1049.369995
3	2017-12-26	1060.119995	1050.199951	1058.069946	1056.739990	760600	1056.739990
4	2017-12-22	1064.199951	1059.439941	1061.109985	1060.119995	755100	1060.119995

In [86]: `googDf.describe()`

Out[86]:

	high	low	open	close	volume	adjclose
count	251.000000	251.000000	251.000000	251.000000	2.510000e+02	251.000000
mean	926.898963	915.331412	921.121193	921.780837	1.476208e+06	921.780837
std	78.339844	76.358400	77.250572	77.232561	6.376379e+05	77.232561
min	789.630005	775.799988	778.809998	786.140015	5.370000e+05	786.140015
25%	841.975006	831.254974	835.755005	836.994995	1.089450e+06	836.994995
50%	934.729980	923.619995	929.919983	929.570007	1.287600e+06	929.570007
75%	979.365021	965.515015	972.969971	972.759979	1.639000e+06	972.759979
max	1078.489990	1063.550049	1075.199951	1077.140015	5.167700e+06	1077.140015

Fig. 3. Collated data of English Normal Students

study aims to provide a comprehensive statistical display of each training performance and teaching reflection of normal school students, showing their individual teaching skills training, forming an effective combination of the whole and the individual. It aims to establish a mature analysis process for the training process of normal school students' classroom teaching skills, achieve training statistics throughout the entire stage of the course, and provide data statistics for teachers and normal school students in the microteaching process, Realize comprehensive evaluation of classroom teaching skills diagnosis and data visualization of evaluation results, diagnose from both the overall and individual aspects, analyze problems, find out the reasons, and provide operable suggestions for the subsequent cultivation of teaching skills of normal school students.

4.2 Core Code Optimization of Algorithm

Define the class attributes of the data used in the algorithm, as shown in Fig. 4.

```
UNIT FILE                                    STATE
proc-sys-fs-binfmt_misc.automount            static
dev-hugepages.mount                          static
dev-mqueue.mount                             static
proc-fs-nfsd.mount                           static
proc-sys-fs-binfmt_misc.mount                static
sys-fs-fuse-connections.mount                static
sys-kernel-config.mount                      static
sys-kernel-debug.mount                       static
tmp.mount                                    masked
var-lib-nfs-rpc_pipefs.mount                 static
brandbot.path                                disabled
cups.path                                    enabled
systemd-ask-password-console.path            static
systemd-ask-password-plymouth.path           static
systemd-ask-password-wall.path               static
session-1.scope                              static
session-4.scope                              static
```

Fig. 4. Initialization function running code

Where k is the number of clusters; Logo is the classification identifier; Center refers to the old data center; centernew refers to the new data center; Train is the input data sample; Dimension is the data dimension. The algorithm data is initialized, and the initialization function is executed every time the optimization algorithm is performed. Figure 3 shows the running code of the function. Where, it means that there are 30 groups of test data, one group of 6 dimensions, and the size of the initialization data center and the K value are determined.

5 Conclusion

In this paper, the campus performance of English normal students is selected for research. Through the analysis and mining of the behavior characteristics of English normal students such as life, learning and activities, a clustering algorithm is used to establish a classification model of English Normal Students' life performance, so as to realize the classification of English Normal students based on their life performance data. Based on the data of the Campus All-in-one Card system, the educational administration management system and the English normal student management system, this paper pre-processes the "dirty data" in the data system, and obtains dimensional input data that meets the k-means algorithm through data cleaning, integration and transformation of data storage format. In view of the fact that the selection of the clustering number k and the center point of the traditional K-means algorithm can easily lead to the deviation of the algorithm results, the range of clustering is limited according to the actual situation, the best clustering K value and the center point are obtained, and the dimensional matrix coefficient is added to cluster the performance of English normal students. Finally, the performance model of English normal students is established by writing the core code of the algorithm in the English normal student management system, This paper analyzes the behavior characteristics of different types of English normal students, and guides the management of English normal students.

References

1. Lazareva, A.V., Karnaukhova, A.A.: Research on the Students' Perception and Evaluation of Task-Based Language Teaching Approach at the University English Classes (2021)
2. Yao, D.: Research on the application analysis of four-dimensional teaching method in higher vocational English teaching based on big data analysis. J. Phys: Conf. Ser. **1744**(3), 032059 (2021)
3. Li, X.: Research on English teaching ability evaluation algorithm based on big data fuzzy k-means clustering. In: Jan, M.A., Khan, F. (eds.) Application of Big Data, Blockchain, and Internet of Things for Education Informatization BigIoT-EDU 2022. LNICSSITE, vol. 467, pp. 36–46. Springer, Cham (2023). https://doi.org/10.1007/978-3-031-23944-1_5
4. Liu, Y., Bai, H.: Teaching research on college English translation in the era of big data. Int. J. Elect. Eng. Educ. **60**, 3923–3943 (2021)
5. Wang, Q.: Research on teaching quality evaluation of college English based on the CODAS method under interval-valued intuitionistic fuzzy information. J. Intell. Fuzzy Syst. App. Eng. Technol. **1**, 41 (2021)
6. Wu, X.: Research on the reform of ideological and political teaching evaluation method of college English course based on "Online and Offline" teaching. J. High. Educ. Res. **3**(1), 87–90 (2022)
7. Asegid, A., Assefa, N.: Effect of simulation-based teaching on nursing skill performance: a systematic review and meta-analysis. Front. Nurs. **8**(3), 193–208 (2021)
8. Wang, F.: Artificial intelligence-based simulation research on the flipped classroom mode of listening and speaking teaching for English majors. Mob. Inf. Syst. **2021**, 1–14 (2021)
9. Zhao, Y.: Research on the blended teaching model of university English based on artificial intelligence. Tobacco Regul. Sci. **7**, 1107–1112 (2021)
10. Xu, J., Feng, L.: Research on the Application of "Production-Oriented Approach" Based on Blended Teaching in College English Writing Teaching in Private Undergraduate Colleges. Destech Publications Inc., Lancaster (2021)
11. Xu, W., Meng, J., Raja, S.K.S., et al.: Artificial intelligence in constructing personalized and accurate feedback systems for students. Int. J. Model. Simul. Sci. Comput. **14**(01), 2341001 (2023)
12. Doe, P.F., Berchie, G.O., Addo, S.A., et al.: Explorative–descriptive study on the effects of COVID-19 on access to antiretroviral therapy services: the case of a teaching hospital in Ghana. BMJ Open **12**(5), e1-2 (2022)

13. Van, E.T., Hens, N., White, L.J., et al.: Modeling respiratory syncytial virus adult vaccination in the United States with a dynamic transmission model. Clin. Infect. Dis. **77**, 480–489 (2023)
14. Jia, Y.: Research on the practice of college English classroom teaching based on Internet and artificial intelligence. J. Intell. Fuzzy Syst. **1**, 1–10 (2021)
15. Qiang, Y.: Application of genetic algorithm in exergy and sustainability: a case of aero-gas turbine engine at cruise phase. In: Wang, T., Patnaik, S., Ip, A.W., Tavana, M. (eds.) Advances in Decision Science and Management ICDSM 2021. AISC, vol. 1391, pp. 627–632. Springer, Singapore (2022). https://doi.org/10.1007/978-981-16-2502-2_65

Application of Parallel H-mine Algorithm in Smart Campus Students

Sha Li[1,2]([⊠]), Jing Shen[1,2], and Jingyu Sun[1,2]

[1] Wuxi Vocational Institute of Commerce, Wuxi 214153, Jiangsu, China
wxlisha@163.com
[2] Yunnan College of Business Managemen, Yunnan 650106, China

Abstract. The continuous development and application of big data information technology provides more effective support and guidance for students' social practice and behavior analysis in smart campus to a large extent, thus providing guidance for the effective promotion of Internet information technology in the real sense. Especially under the effective promotion of parallel H-mine algorithm, H-mine algorithm is a parallel algorithm for intelligent campus students. It is a very effective and efficient algorithm, which can be used to solve many types of problems. The main purpose of this paper is to outline the application of H-mine algorithm in intelligent campus students, and explain how to apply it to solve various types of problems. Introduction to H-Mine algorithm In this section, we will discuss the introduction of H-Mine algorithm and its application. This paper studies and analyzes the parallel H-mine algorithm in the application design of intelligent campus, the parallel H-mine algorithm in the social practice effect analysis of intelligent campus students, and the parallel H-mine algorithm in the social practice behavior analysis strategy of intelligent students, which lays a relatively perfect foundation for the effective realization of students' practice behavior. Applying parallel big data technology to the growing campus big data can not only quickly analyze the behavior characteristics of students, and then provide auxiliary decision-making for colleges and universities and student management, but also take corresponding measures to adapt to the teaching mode according to the behavior rules of students, and realize personalized and high-quality teaching.

Keywords: Parallel H-mine algorithm · Smart campus · Social practice behavior · Students

1 Introduction

With the advent of the Internet era, the continuous development of information technology, the continuous construction of smart campus in colleges and universities, and the continuous improvement of the campus all-in-one card service platform, the accumulated data on campus has also continued to grow, and has initially formed a campus big data environment. The traditional serial algorithms and data statistics methods have been difficult to efficiently handle the growing data. How to efficiently process the growing

© ICST Institute for Computer Sciences, Social Informatics and Telecommunications Engineering 2024
Published by Springer Nature Switzerland AG 2024. All Rights Reserved
Y. Zhang and N. Shah (Eds.): BigIoT-EDU 2023, LNICST 584, pp. 237–247, 2024.
https://doi.org/10.1007/978-3-031-63142-9_24

campus data, analyze the characteristics of students' behavior using big data analysis methods, and serve the analysis results in student management and provide auxiliary decision-making is one of the problems faced by the construction of smart campus service system [1].

Traditional student behavior analysis is often based on experience and passive analysis. With the application of big data technology in student education data, it can actively analyze the characteristics and laws of student campus behavior, and then make auxiliary decisions for university management. Therefore, mining educational data has great significance in teaching management. Education data mining is a research field that uses statistics, machine learning and data mining algorithms to analyze student education data on different types of student education data to analyze student behavior characteristics. Student education data has fixed semantic information, which has many kinds, such as course data, online data, course selection data and grade data. Student education data has some special characteristics. Different data need to be processed with different mining methods. Specific data mining techniques can be used for specific problems. In a broad sense, data mining refers to applying machine learning algorithms to different types of data to mine useful information [2]. There are many algorithms for machine learning, and the commonly used algorithms are classified into four categories, namely, classification, regression, clustering and association algorithms. These algorithms provide technical support for studying student behavior.

There are two ways to generate campus big data. One is generated during the use of campus all-in-one card. Common data include consumption data, library data and access control data. The other is generated through campus application system, including student course selection data, course data, score data, attendance data and network access data. These data are stored in the campus information system in corresponding forms. They provide data support for studying students' behavior rules and analyzing students' behavior characteristics.

With the development of parallelization technology, big data technology has been combined with parallelization technology, which makes it possible to process big data in parallel, thus enabling rapid processing of growing data. Applying campus big data to parallel big data technology can not only analyze students' behavior characteristics, and then provide auxiliary decision-making for student management, but also take corresponding measures according to students' behavior rules to adapt to the teaching mode and realize personalized and high-quality teaching [3].

2 Related Work

2.1 Research Status of Campus Data Mining

In recent years, many colleges and universities have used campus big data to carry out a lot of research on student management and teacher and student services. Relying on big data mining methods to support campus management and decision-making in the field of education, as well as the analysis of student behavior rules, has received widespread attention.

Rodrigues et al. used cluster analysis to help researchers identify the way students choose English courses or online courses to participate in the interaction, and used the interaction mode discussed in the Openredu platform to improve students' participation in online learning. Research shows that this research can increase students' participation in online learning and enable students to gain better learning experience. In order to study the problem of students failing or dropping out of class, Elbadray et al. used multiple regression and matrix decomposition methods to predict students' future course performance and classroom performance, and achieved good results. Grivokostopoulu et al. used the decision tree method to analyze students' learning and extract semantic rules, and used the rule and decision tree method to predict students' final performance in the course. They have integrated the results into the education system to analyze students' performance and learning. Hasbun et al. studied the impact of extracurricular activities on students' dropout, and used the control variable method to train and verify the model. The results show that extracurricular activities are very important indicators of dropout. Sweeney et al. predicted students' grades in the next semester based on the factorization algorithm, and the results showed that the algorithm could achieve the lowest prediction error [4]. These studies combine the data generated by the campus application system with the big data technology, analyze the characteristics of students' behavior, and have achieved good results. Some of the results have been integrated with the system, providing convenience for student management.

Campus all-in-one card (hereinafter referred to as all-in-one card) is a powerful guarantee for the construction of digital campus. The all-in-one card has the functions of identity recognition, data management, financial services, etc. It integrates the university's student information system and combines with many student management systems. At this stage, major universities in the West have established a comprehensive all-in-one card system, which takes the perfect all-in-one card information as the basis of all-in-one card data analysis and management, and has produced an all-in-one card data analysis system based on service and management. They take whether to provide data for the senior management of the school as the analysis index, and use data warehouse and data mining methods with high accuracy and efficiency to analyze the all-in-one card data of all departments, businesses and systems of the school. This data analysis method based on the one-card data can discover the deep rules in school management, correctly guide the senior management personnel of the school to optimize and adjust the school management strategy for various departments and departments, and has achieved good results. Anapol State University of India has effectively analyzed and applied the life behavior of students in school through the "hot map" application product developed by the one-card big data. In this study, through the study of the one-card data, the students' various school behaviors are detected, the students' personality trends are analyzed, the students' abnormal behaviors are predicted, and human intervention is timely carried out to solve the students' various life problems. With the popularity of digital campus, more and more one-card cards are used. At the same time, the research on one-card data has also been concerned by many people. In recent years, many scholars in China have analyzed the data of all-in-one card [5]. Among them, Xu Jian and others put forward a research on the correlation between the one-card data and the students' grades, and analyzed the consumption habits of college students from the perspective of early rising. Secondly, the research object will be transferred to the achievement, and the students' academic achievements will be studied. Fan et al. proposed an analysis of student behavior based on campus all-in-one card. By defining a structural entropy to quantify the diversity of social circles in the student learning partner network, they studied the relationship between book borrowing behavior and academic performance in two different departments of a university in China, as well as the distribution of students' consumption ability and the track of campus movement [6]. The research results show that the learning partners of top students are more diversified in academic performance, Students are more willing to become learning partners with students with good academic achievements. Based on the mature analysis of all-in-one card data, student behavior is closely related to all-in-one card data, so combining all-in-one card data with student behavior can mine more information.

2.2 H-mine Algorithm

From the above analysis, we can see that the two main problems of FPGrowth algorithm are: first, when mining frequent items, the memory required by the algorithm is unpredictable, and when the data size increases, the memory required will also increase sharply; Second, when the data volume is large and sparse, FPTree will be large, which may lead to memory overflow. H-mine algorithm solves these two problems to a certain extent. It uses a new data structure (HStruct) to store data, which can be used to traverse data faster. HStruct has three attributes (item frequent items, support number, and link pointer list). In theory, H-mine has a polynomial space complexity. In terms of generating frequent items, it saves more space than generating candidate items and increasing frequent patterns. The algorithm partitions the data, only mining the data of one partition at a time, and finally merging the results of each partition. Therefore, in the process of mining frequent items, the algorithm greatly saves memory and can process more large-scale data. Experiments show that H-mine is a high-performance, scalable, limited and predictable algorithm, and its comprehensive performance is better than Apriori and FPGrowth algorithms in any scenario [7]. The steps of H-mine mining frequent items are as follows:

Step 1: traverse the data set and count the frequent 1-item set (F-list);
Step 2: Take each row of data as the unit, select the items with support not less than the minimum support, and then sort the items in each row in ascending order to generate frequent item projection;
Step 3: The F-list is represented by HStruct (FlistHStruct for short), and the frequent items in the FlistHStruct are sorted in ascending order. Traverse the frequent items in the FlistHStruct in turn, then traverse each row, connect the same frequent items of the first data item in each row in turn, until all the frequent items in the FlistHStruct are traversed, and partition the data set according to the first data item;
Step 4: traverse the partition. If the partition has been traversed, it is over. Otherwise, go to step 5;
Step 5: traverse the dataset in the partition to count the frequent items in the partition, and partition the partition dataset according to the frequent items in the partition;
Step 6: traverse the partition. If the partition has been traversed, judge whether the number of cycles is greater than 1. If it is greater than 1, return to the upper loop. Otherwise, the data set of the partition will be re-partitioned after the loop is completed, and go to step

4; If the partition has not been traversed, partition the data set of the previous partition again, and go to step 5.

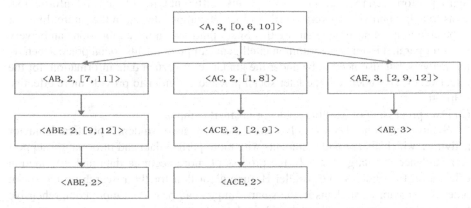

Fig. 1. H-mine algorithm flow

It can be seen from the above that the H-mine algorithm only mines data sets of one partition at a time. On a single machine, it reduces the single memory usage, so it can process larger data sets. So, how large data sets can H-mine algorithm handle? If the data set size is S, the memory size is M, and the number of frequent itemsets is L, the memory required for mining a partition is at least:

$$S \times \frac{1}{L} \tag{1}$$

It can be seen from the formula that the memory required for H-mine will increase linearly with the increase of data set S under the premise that 1/L changes very little. When the dataset S > ML, it will cause memory overflow and make the algorithm unable to run normally in memory. With the development of distributed technology, some scholars have proposed the MRH-mine algorithm, which uses MapReduce as the technical support to realize the efficient parallel mining of the H-mine algorithm, and each node is independent of each other. The experimental results show that the MRH-mine algorithm is superior to the H-mine algorithm and the MRApriori algorithm on the premise of large data sets, but the disadvantage is that it will store a large number of intermediate results on the disk [8].

3 Application Design of Parallel H-mine Algorithm in Smart Campus

(1) Parallel H-mine algorithm based on the Spark platform.

Under the effective promotion of the smart campus, the Internet information application platform has gradually been effectively reflected. In particular, Spark, as a feasible and extended predictive algorithm with relatively high performance, can provide effective guidance for the improvement of accuracy in data and information computing.

Through the effective application of modern Internet information technology, we can further understand that the parallel H-mine algorithm has its unique application value and advantages in the social practice behavior analysis. In the actual display process, Spark platform can more accurately distinguish different types of data and information, so as to help improve the overall quality of smart campus design in the future. In order to be able to more accurately ensure that Spark platform in the application can be very good for parallel H-mine algorithm in intelligent campus students social practice behavior analysis, but also need to be under the guidance of perfect data information, for the effectiveness of students in the later social practice activities to provide more effective help [9].

(2) Data processing of learning behavior in smart campus.

Smart campus has been widely used in the analysis of students' practical behavior activities, which also provides students with more perfect data and information support and guidance at a large level. In the process of more accurate data and information calculation for students, the parallel H-mine algorithm for the research on the social practice behavior of students in the smart campus can provide a more comprehensive help for different types of model analysis later. In order to more accurately combine students' personal information with behavior characteristics, it is also necessary to show the specific application of parallel H-mine algorithm in the analysis of social practice behavior of students in smart campus. For more details, you can also refer to the table below and Table 1.

Table 1. Students' personal information and behavioral characteristics indicators

Student behavior characteristics	feature	weight	data type	span
Student gender	C2	W2	Enumeration type	Male / female
Attendance indicators	C3	W3	numeric type	0–1
Regular diet indicators	C4	W4	numeric type	0–30
Book borrowing indicators	C5	W5	numeric type	0–60
Study length index	C6	W6	numeric type	1–240
Physical exercise indicators	C7	W7	numeric type	0–30

In the analysis and research of students' later academic performance, we can also well understand the powerful value and advantages of parallel H-mine algorithm in the analysis of social practice behavior of students in smart campus. It is also precisely because, in the specific digital applications, there are relatively obvious differences in different location information, which also has a very direct impact on the effective promotion of your work efficiency in various families later.

(3) An Analysis of the Performance Test Results.

Specific parallel H-mine algorithm, in the wisdom of campus students social practice behavior analysis has a very powerful application value, in order to be able to better guarantee the effectiveness of the performance test results analysis, the staff should further strengthen the further study and analysis of different types of performance, for the long social practice behavior and stable development, also has a great level of help. Through the specific data information calculation, we can also show the validity of the numbers through Table 2 below. Especially under the effective guidance of the following support degrees, a number of data can be well tested, which provides an effective impetus for the parallel H-mine algorithm in the analysis of students' social practice behavior in smart campus[10].

Table 2. Multiple time comparison of the algorithm

Algorithm / Support	0.1	0.2	0.3	0.4	0.5
Parallel H-mine algorithm	6 s	5.4 s	5.5 s	5.5 s	5.5 s
MRH-mine algorithm	7 s	7 s	6.9 s	7.1 s	6.8 s

For a distributed system, fault tolerance is very important. Spark uses the lineage mechanism to ensure the fault tolerance of RDD and recover the lost partition. The lineage mechanism is based on the dependency between RDDs, and then recalculate and recover the lost partitions. If a node fails, it will first check the lineage record. If it is a narrow dependency, it is only necessary to recalculate the parent RDD. If it is a wide dependency, it is necessary to calculate all the parent RDDs of the child RDDs. The fault tolerance cost is too high. Therefore, Spark can use the checkpoint mechanism to restore the parent RDD partition in the wide dependency and reduce the cost. Checkpoint mechanism refers to persisting the RDD state in memory to disk in a certain calculation step. When a failure occurs and the data being calculated is lost, the state in disk will be deserialized to memory and the operation will be restarted from the checkpoint.

In Spark, a job is divided into multiple groups of tasks, each of which corresponds to a stage. Task types are divided into ShuffleMapTask and ResultTask. Spark will first build a directed acyclic graph (DAG) based on the application, and then divide the DAG into multiple stages according to the RDD dependency. When it is a narrow dependency, the partition conversion process will be handed over to a thread for execution, and the narrow dependency will be divided into the same thread by Spark for execution; When it is a wide dependency, the child stage can start the operation only after the parent RDD shuffle is completed. Spark's idea of dividing stages is to adopt a bottom-up strategy. When encountering a wide dependency, it will be disconnected, and the wide dependency will be divided into a stage. When encountering a narrow dependency, it will add this RDD to the stage, and then continue to execute upwards. The specific process is shown in Fig. 2.

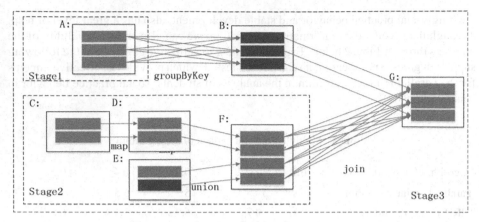

Fig. 2. Spark processing

4 Application Strategy of Parallel H-mine Algorithm in Smart Campus Student Social Practice Behavior Analysis

4.1 Flow Chart of Data Processing

In the context of the continuous development and progress of the society, the people have begun to pay more and more attention to the modern new scientific and technological means. In order to be able to more comprehensively to ensure the quality of students 'daily life and value, under the effective guidance of parallel H-mine algorithm, the data information processing, also can very good students nature behavior characteristics, so also can in the real sense for the wisdom of campus students' social practice behavior show to provide more good guidance. After the more perfect data introduction, guidance and analysis is completed, the relevant technical personnel also need to conduct more deeply dynamic processing of the data. It is precisely because the data information has a very strong timeliness, the data information processing work can immediately improve through the sliding window in the subsequent dynamic management work. And, in this process, the staff should also further strengthen the effective control of the window length, so also can further ensure the effectiveness of data information analysis and management, in the true sense of parallel H-mine algorithm in wisdom campus students social practice behavior analysis in the embodiment of the overall value to provide more effective guidance and help.

The system workflow is also working under the support of more perfect data and information. This paper is also a detailed study of the parallel H-mine algorithm in the analysis of smart campus students' social practice and behavior, more accurately integrating different types of data and information, so that it can provide strong support and guidance for the improvement of the system workflow efficiency in a real sense. For students, various data and information resources can provide good help for them to obtain more knowledge and content, so that they can also guide and effectively promote the intelligent campus practice activities in a real sense.

4.2 Data Preprocessing

Through the detailed analysis and processing of the specific resources in the data information, it can provide help to improve the rationality of the parallel H-mine algorithm application under the effective guidance of different types of formats. It is precisely because the parallel H-mine algorithm can well input the data and information in the social practice behavior analysis of students in smart campus students, so as to ensure the reasonable transformation of discrete data. It can be seen that in the specific data pretreatment work, the staff should first accurately transform different types of data to ensure the scientificity and rationality of the discrete data. In the specific transformation steps, the values of different positions can be also more accurately positioned through the continuous sorting method, so that the effectiveness of the data pretreatment model can be guaranteed under the effective regulation of different intervals later.

In order to ensure the comprehensive progress of data pre-processing work to the maximum extent, we should also provide the most basic technical guidance for the improvement of the quality of data discretization work. It is in the specific discrete data method application process, for the requirements of category information is relatively high, which makes after the work of various methods need to be more accurately reflected quality, and should also be in bins, histogram analysis, cluster analysis, custom discrete and other effective help, further provide support for the data information preprocessing work efficiency promotion. Consumption processing and the selection of course content can provide good help for the effective promotion of data pre-processing work, and ensure that the parallel H-mine algorithm can be more fully reflected in the analysis of social practice behavior of students in smart campus.

4.3 Student Behavior is Frequent Item Set Mining

After completing the above data information preprocessing work, the relevant staff can also conduct a detailed research and analysis of different types of numerical information, so that the accuracy and effectiveness of each group of data information processing work can be guaranteed in the subsequent algorithm output data preprocessing work. According to the application of parallel H-mine algorithm in the analysis of social practice behavior in smart campus, we can also further understand the final result of frequent students' behavior. Especially in the more sparse data information support and guidance, a large number of spare numbers can be good for parallel H-mine algorithm in the intelligent campus students social practice behavior analysis effective help, to avoid after the wisdom of the campus social analysis activities, some more serious security problems. Thus, with the development and progress of all kinds of modern information technology of means, teachers also began to actively use modern science and technology to guide students' social practice, so also can be very good for the process of social development, parallel comprehensive application of H-mine algorithm has brought effective help, promote the development of the socialist market economy.

4.4 Analysis of Student Behavior

In the specific learning process, students are also often affected by external factors, which also has a very direct and in-depth impact on students' learning efficiency and quality. In the specific behavior analysis process, association analysis is a comparative fundamental and critical existence. It mainly refers to a unique potential connection of data and information separated in the centralized management of big data and information, which can lay a perfect foundation for the effective embodiment of parallel H-mine algorithm in the analysis of social practice and behavior of students in smart campus. The mining of frequent item set and the generation of corresponding rules on the basic level of frequent item set are both the main methods and means of analyzing students' basic behavior nowadays. This correlation analysis way, in the process of specific student behavior research and analysis, can be good through parallel H-mine algorithm in wisdom campus students social practice work, so as to maximize the maximum in the perfect data information guidance, for the wisdom of campus students social practice efficiency to help。

In addition, the correlation analysis is also an important kind of the parallel H-mine algorithm in the social practice behavior analysis of the students in the smart campus. Mainly through support, confidence and more perfect correlation principle of work, although in the process of such work, often exist certain problems, but after the analysis of different numerical work, also often because of the lack of digital specificity, and lead to the final correlation efficiency is difficult to get the real embodiment. In the process of analyzing the average score of students, the overall value of data and information calculation can also be reflected under the guidance of specific formula calculation.

Conclusion: To sum up, with the continuous development and progress of The Times, the people's production and life style have also been effectively improved. In order to be able to more comprehensively enhance our new era youth comprehensive quality ability, we should also actively through parallel H-mine algorithm in the wisdom of campus students social practice behavior analysis of effective management, so also can fundamentally for students in the specific social practice activities, the overall ability to provide help. In the above discussion in this paper, the specific numerical values in the parallel H-mine algorithm are studied, which well improves the adverse factors in the students' learning process.

5 Conclusion

The traditional data statistics method is difficult to deal with the increasing amount of data efficiently. The continuous development of parallelization technology and big data technology makes it possible to deal with big data in parallel, making it better serve the construction of today's smart campus service system. By combining campus big data with parallel H-mine algorithm and Spark platform, the algorithm is used to mine frequent itemsets, and then the frequent itemsets are used to analyze student behavior. According to the performance test and experimental results, the H-mine algorithm has excellent scalability and relatively good comprehensive performance, can further improve the mining efficiency, greatly save memory and can process larger data sets, thus providing auxiliary decision-making for campus management. Although the integration method of the parallel H-mine big data mining algorithm has achieved some results, there are still some shortcomings. The parallelism of the parallel H-mine algorithm needs to be improved. The parallelism is parallel between two partitions in the H-mine algorithm, but there is obvious serial phenomenon in the partition. Improving the parallelism in the partition will be a direction of subsequent research.

References

1. Li, B., Tuo, A., Kong, H., Liu, S., Chen, J.: Application of multilayer perceptron genetic algorithm neural network in chinese-english parallel corpus noise processing. Comput. Intell. Neurosci. **2021**, 1–12 (2021). https://doi.org/10.1155/2021/7144635
2. Liu, S., Gai, D., Lu, Q., et al.: Application of CT image based on three-dimensional image segmentation algorithm in diagnosis of osteoarthritis. J. Med. Imaging Health Inform. **11**(1), 230–234 (2021)
3. Huang, H., Tan, X.: Application of reinforcement learning algorithm in delivery order system under supply chain environment. Mob. Inf. Syst. **2021**, 1–11 (2021). https://doi.org/10.1155/2021/5880795
4. Zhang, R., et al.: Visually meaningful image encryption algorithm based on parallel compressive sensing and cellular neural network. In: Wu, T.-Y., Ni, S., Chu, S.-C., Chen, C.-H., Favorskaya, Ma. (eds.) Advances in Smart Vehicular Technology, Transportation, Communication and Applications: Proceedings of VTCA 2021, pp. 351–360. Springer, Singapore (2022). https://doi.org/10.1007/978-981-16-4039-1_35
5. Aygun, H., Turan, O.: Application of genetic algorithm in exergy and sustainability: a case of aero-gas turbine engine at cruise phase. Energy **238**, 121644 (2022). https://doi.org/10.1016/j.energy.2021.121644
6. Zheng, X., Wu, H., Ye, Q.: A cloud fog intelligent approach based on modified algorithm in application of reinforced smart microgrid management. Sustain. Cities Soc. **76**, 103455 (2022). https://doi.org/10.1016/j.scs.2021.103455
7. Maria, C.: Discussion of: "experimental evaluation of algorithm-assisted human decision-making: application to pretrial public safety assessment. J. R. Statist. Soc. Ser. A. Statist. Soc. (2023)
8. Wang, Y., Li, H., Tian, J., et al.: The application of machine learning algorithm in relative permeability upscaling for oil-water system. In: International Petroleum Technology Conference (2021)
9. Zeng, W., Wang, Q., Xia, Z., Li, Z., Han, Q.: Application of XGBoost algorithm in the detection of SARS-CoV-2 using Raman spectroscopy. J. Phys. Conf. Ser. **1775**(1), 012007 (2021). https://doi.org/10.1088/1742-6596/1775/1/012007
10. Shi, J., Yan, H., Wei, Y.: Application of the denoising technique based on improved FastICA algorithm in cross-correlation time delay estimation. J. Phys. Conf. Ser. **1754**(1), 012196 (2021). https://doi.org/10.1088/1742-6596/1754/1/012196

Design and Implementation of Music Education and Teaching Management System in Colleges and Universities

Qi Hongda(✉), Ying Sun, and Li Miao

Nanchang Vocational University, Nanchang 330500, Jiangxi Province, China
qi18720900791@163.com

Abstract. The teaching work in colleges and universities is mainly composed of teaching conditions, teachers and students. If these three conditions are met, education and training can be carried out well. However, for some large training institutions, they have a large number of teaching resources and student groups, which is why they need a good educational administration management system to carry out teaching work better. The design and implementation of music education and teaching management system in colleges and universities is a process involving system design, development, implementation, testing, evaluation and maintenance. The main purpose of this process is to ensure that faculty members can effectively perform their duties without any hindrance. The design of this system should be completed with the help of experts who have sufficient knowledge of the subject, so as to develop a perfect system for this purpose.

Keywords: Teaching management · System design · Music teaching

1 Introduction

The music course assistant teaching system provides multiple functions for online learning of music knowledge, real-time appreciation of music works, online homework management of music, network user management of music assistant teaching system, music creation and other activities [1]. The system makes use of the advantages of rapid network information transmission, rich resources, and interaction free from geographical restrictions to help music learners learn effectively and quickly, expand music knowledge, and meet the personalized requirements of different users.

A set of management system for music education and teaching in colleges and universities will be designed and implemented to simplify a lot of calculation and statistics in the process of score summary, and ensure that the score information obtained is objective and fair according to unified accounting standards. And through the college music education and teaching management system to achieve the comprehensive management of student file information, to provide a convenient tool for college music education and teaching management, improve management efficiency. Through the design and implementation of this system, the practice of network distance education is realized in the field of music teaching.

Y. Zhang and N. Shah (Eds.): BigIoT-EDU 2023, LNICST 584, pp. 248–258, 2024.
https://doi.org/10.1007/978-3-031-63142-9_25

In the actual construction process, how to integrate new development concepts and make the construction of music education in colleges and universities to a higher level is currently the primary issue facing colleges and universities. As we all know, the music education and teaching management system in colleges and universities is an important component of music teaching in colleges and universities, which is conducive to the rational allocation of music teaching resources in colleges and universities, and fully realizing the construction goal of scientific, standardized, and comprehensive management of music education and teaching in colleges and universities. Based on this realistic development background, studying the teaching management system of music education in universities has important practical significance for improving the overall quality of music education in universities.

Research has found that music plays a very important role in students' intellectual development, aesthetic ability, and appreciation ability. Learning music can effectively enhance their artistic temperament, while mastering certain music skills can also have a relatively positive effect on cultivating their own musical literacy. However, due to the impact of the exam-oriented education system at this stage, Most schools and families completely ignore the cultivation of students' music literacy. This article mainly analyzes the current situation of music teaching management, and proposes relevant solutions.

Due to the impact of the exam-oriented education system, music education has been affected, and the awareness of education managers is relatively backward. There is no professional team of music education teachers, no professional theoretical level, and the teaching equipment provided for music teaching is relatively simple, making music teaching encounter greater difficulties and challenges. The current situation of music teaching management mainly includes the following aspects:

The professional quality of the teaching staff has a very important impact on music education. However, according to the survey, there is a severe shortage of music teachers at the current stage, and each school only has a few or even one music teacher, and the music teachers provided by each school do not have professional teaching ability [2].

In order to better solve the problem of a small number of teachers in many schools, most of the music teachers equipped in schools are appointed in the face of crisis, and they have not conducted professional music teaching, not overly solid professional theory, and there are also problems with comprehensive skills. Due to the low professional quality of the teacher team, some schools believe that music lessons are about teaching students to sing without involving music knowledge, which seriously hinders the development of music education in schools.

The relevant education departments have not put forward clear requirements for music teaching, nor have they clearly proposed teaching objectives. Schools and families do not attach much importance to music education. They believe that the most important thing is the study of cultural courses. It does not matter whether music education is accepted or not. Moreover, schools do not provide preferential treatment to music teachers. When assessing professional titles, they always scrutinize cultural teachers first, greatly reducing the enthusiasm of music teachers in their work, and seriously hindering the development of music education. Although some schools have offered music courses, they have not taken music courses in the actual teaching process. The new curriculum standards point out that cultivating all-round development talents enables students to develop morally, intellectually, physically, aesthetically, and industrially in an all-round manner, including music education. It also emphasizes that music education is an essential discipline in the educational process, because relaxed and pleasant music melodies play a very important role in regulating the atmosphere, stimulating students' interest in learning, and making them happy to learn music.

According to the characteristics of music education in ordinary colleges and universities, a successful music education requires coordination and cooperation in many aspects. Only by working together to study the teaching mode of music education in ordinary colleges and universities in line with China's national conditions can we promote the continuous improvement of teaching quality [3]. According to the current situation of music education in colleges and universities, the main content of the curriculum should include two types: basic courses and practical courses. Based on this, this paper studies the design and implementation of music education and teaching management system in colleges and universities.

2 Related Work

2.1 Functions of Teaching Management System

According to the current survey of the setting of music education and teaching management institutions in ordinary colleges and universities in China and the relevant documents and development plans of the Ministry of Education, it is an inevitable trend and requirement for the development of music education in ordinary colleges and universities in China to establish a unified and independent teaching management institution. In this way, music education and teaching activities in colleges and universities will be carried out more smoothly and orderly [4], which is more conducive to the improvement of teaching level and quality and the effective realization of teaching tasks.

1. Organize teaching work

    The educational administration management staff can use the educational administration management system to implement their work, such as preparing lessons, preparing schedule, live teaching, online examination, coordinating teaching equipment, supervisor punching, after class testing, statistics of student scores, question bank, etc. [5].

2. Coordination

    The educational administration staff can know the teaching situation of students and teachers in time through the educational administration background, and adjust and coordinate in time according to the problems. To ensure that the teaching work goes on naturally and orderly.

3. Teaching supervision

    The essence of the educational administration manager is to monitor and evaluate the quality of teaching [6]. With the educational administration management system, the manager can combine the previous data in the evaluation process to formulate the corresponding rules and regulations, and regulate and guide the teaching work of teachers [4].

4. Give play to the role of bridge

The educational administration management system mainly relates teachers, students and other departments to ensure the smooth completion of teaching tasks. The educational administration administrator can analyze the relationship between the three through the data fed back by the educational administration management system, screen and summarize the teaching situation, so as to provide a reliable basis for the successful completion of teaching [7].

2.2 Architecture Mode

At present, the main contradiction of the school system is to gradually increase information. The school system can not meet the requirements and will be stable soon. The number of such information will be processed. At present, the campus system adopts a relatively single platform mode, basically using the B/S structure of the Web form. In this structure, due to the server, network speed, number of nodes and other factors, the server will be under great pressure to handle large-scale information. Under long-term pressure, the system will collapse, causing losses to both schools and students. Now the solution to this problem is to use a hybrid structural model. In the school, the main administrator is the teacher, and the students are just a simple query and modification operation [8]. According to this situation, the system can be developed according to these two aspects. The teacher side uses the C/S mode, and the student uses the BS mode. Because the teacher basically uses the same computer in the office, and the student is uncertain about the time and place in the operating system, the browser mode is more convenient. Therefore, this system adopts the method of C/S mode and B/S mixed mode.

In B/S architecture, the browser acts as a distributed communication server on the client and network. The user sends a request to the server through the browser, and the server parses and processes the requested browser, and then returns the required information to the user browser. With B/S architecture, the work of the client has been simplified [9]. In this mode, you can develop and maintain the required application software by installing the client operating system and browser. On the server, the efficiency of system development and maintenance has been greatly improved. On the contrary, you need to complete a lot of database access and application execution on the server, which is a relatively difficult task. The training process of B/S architecture is shown in Fig. 1 below.

The music teaching system adopts B/S (browser/server) structure, namely browser and server structure. Web browser is the most important application client software of the network architecture model after the rise of B/S based WEB. Use this mode to develop the music education system, because this mode unifies the core of the centralized server of the client and system functions, and simplifies the development, maintenance and use of the system [10–12]. As long as the installation of the browser on the client can access the server, students can learn at school or at home.

2.3 Web Service Related Technologies

There are three roles in the Web Service architecture, including service provider, service registry, and service requester. Service providers openly publish their services and provide a standardized description of their services. The service registry obtains the service

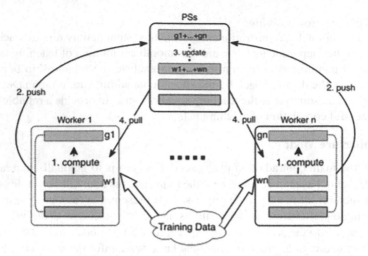

Fig. 1. B/S architecture training process

description of the service publisher, classifies the service, and provides external service search functions. The service requester searches for and obtains services (Note: The "service" obtained here includes business operations and data information) [13].

WSDL is the Web Services Description Language. In the Web Service architecture, it is a set of XML language specifications used to describe Web Service services. WSDL defines a series of service types, port numbers, service addresses, and message types that can describe the service situation among Web service providers. WSDL will be used by the service registry to describe the service situation of the service provider to the service requester, who then requests the services provided by the service provider based on the description of the WSDL service situation.

UDDI is Universal Description, Discovery and Integration. A set of protocols that a service registry provides external registration specifications. The service provider registers its own services with the service registry through WSDL according to the UDDI protocol of the service registry [14, 15]. After searching the WSDL in the service registry according to the UDDI specification, the service requester can communicate with the service provider.

CXF is an important open source project in the APACHE open source community. It is a very useful technology implementation framework in the implementation of the Web Service architecture. It integrates the advantages of the two major Web Service technology implementation frameworks, Celtix and Xfire, and eliminates the cumbersome and insufficient programming implementation process of Celtix and Xfire through interface encapsulation [16]. The database management system is shown in Fig. 2 below.

The CXF technical implementation framework includes technical implementation rules such as service publishing for Web Service service providers, service description registration for service registration centers, and so on. Therefore, when Java developers develop Web services, the preferred technology is CXF.

Oracle is a database management system of Oracle, and to date, the database management system still occupies a major market share [17–20].

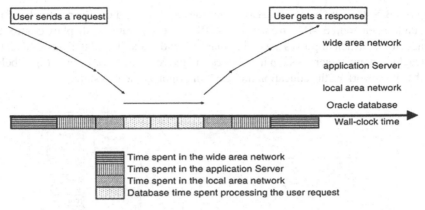

Fig. 2. Database Management System

The database describes data through tables, indexes, synonyms, directories, sequences, and database chains, and provides SQL query language to add, delete, modify, and query data. The database has the following characteristics:

(1) Complete data management functions;
(2) Having complete data relationships;
(3) With distributed processing function;
(4) Data warehouse operations can be easily implemented.

In addition, compared to other database management systems, Oracle databases also have the characteristics of scalability and high availability.

3 Design and Implementation of College Music Education and Teaching Management System

As this system is a comprehensive system of music education and teaching management in colleges and universities, the design goal of this music education and teaching management system in colleges and universities will ultimately be positioned on the basic model of completing the main business of colleges and universities. The music education and teaching management system of our university is a comprehensive system for the management of college students. The system aims at the educational administration management of colleges and universities.

The management objects of the music education and teaching management system in our university are single, all of them are students and teachers at school. According to the characteristics of users of the system and the design of the music education and teaching management system in universities, JSP technology, B/S and CS combined architecture development mode, JDBC connection database, and Struts technology are selected for implementation. The C/S architecture is adopted for the course arrangement management part of the music education and teaching management system in colleges and universities, which has centralized management and complex interaction; Other parts of the music education and teaching management system in colleges and universities adopt the B/S structure based on J2EE technology system, and use the relatively mature and stable open source MVC framework STRUTS to separate the display, control and business logic, which improves the maintainability and scalability of the music education and teaching management system in colleges and universities. As shown in Fig. 3 below, it is the framework of the education and teaching management system.

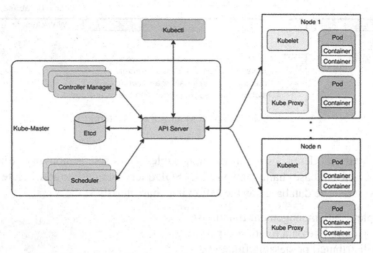

Fig. 3. Framework of education and teaching management system

Based on the establishment of a standard music curriculum evaluation system, evaluation and implementation are the values, basic concepts, objectives and conditions of the curriculum. The goal and specific content of music teaching are mainly realized by analyzing the results of teaching conditions and teaching. The music teaching method is based on the changes of teaching conditions, teaching methods, teaching development achievements and teaching diversity.

Due to the limitation of various music and sounds, it is impossible to achieve four harmonies in the final result. In addition, teachers' teaching level is limited, which not only affects the actual voice but also affects students' understanding. If audio software is used, it can not only solve the problems in classroom teaching, but also make the teacher system of computer multimedia teaching music teaching simple and clear. The student segmentation layer of the music teaching system is shown in Fig. 4 below.

For example, we can save time when we want to copy. You can write it directly on the media. As long as you click in the process of clicking the teaching mouse, you can also see the music score and hear the sound, and you can freely choose to listen to any clip or part. It not only saves writing time in the classroom, but also greatly reduces the recognition difficulty score, thus stimulating students to learn music and doubling the learning efficiency.

The database is mainly responsible for accessing and maintaining the basic data of the system. At the data layer, it is mainly responsible for receiving instructions related to data maintenance (adding, modifying, deleting, and querying) from the data access layer, without caring about the business logic and data encapsulation issues of the system.

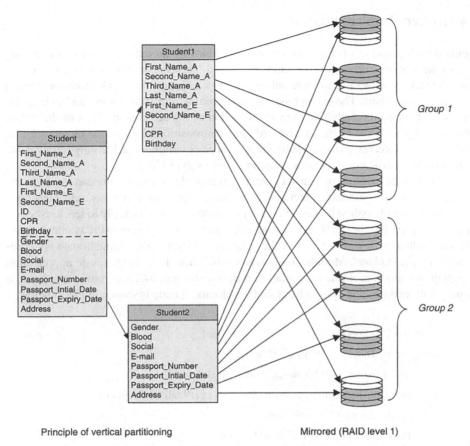

Fig. 4. Student segmentation layer of music teaching system

The data layer is mainly responsible for initializing data objects, initializing data models managed by relational databases into data objects, thereby accepting access from the business logic layer.

The application service layer includes all the business logic of the system and is responsible for communication between the presentation layer and the data access layer. This layer first receives the relevant data or instructions transmitted from the presentation layer, and then executes the corresponding business logic. After completion, the results are transmitted back to the presentation layer. During the execution of business logic at this layer, if access to data is involved, the data is accessed through the data access layer interface.

The user layer is mainly responsible for interacting with the end user. This layer generally receives data and instructions from the user, and then transfers these information to the underlying business logic layer. After processing the information, it retrieves the data from the business logic layer and displays it on the interface.

We can also use the MW3 music score editing function to demonstrate in class, analyze and explain in work, and this function can achieve unexpected results.

4 System Implementation

Function description of music common sense learning module: student users can log in to the system to enter this module, select and learn music common sense courses, select teachers, select to complete online homework, query homework scores or reply to teachers' comments. The teacher user or the system administrator user can log in to the system to enter this module to view the situation of the selected students or the online homework completed by the students. Module composition: this module includes music common sense learning display sub module, music common sense learning retrieval sub module, and music common sense learning query sub module.

Function description of music appreciation module: student users can log in to the system to enter this module, select and learn music appreciation courses, select teachers, select to complete online homework, query homework scores or reply to teachers' comments. The teacher user or the system administrator user can log in to the system to enter this module to view the situation of the selected students or the online homework completed by the students. Module composition: This module includes music appreciation display sub module, music appreciation retrieval sub module, and music appreciation query sub module. The system front-end development code is shown in Fig. 5 below.

```
java.text.SimpleDateFormat          sdf          =          new
java.text.SimpleDateFormat("yyyyMMdd");
        String fname = sdf.format(new java.util.Date());
        String upath = config.getServletContext().getRealPath("/upload/");
        upath = upath + "\\" + fname;
        FolderMaker fm = new FolderMaker();
        boolean bmk = fm.CreateFolder(upath);
        String a = request.getServletPath();
        upath = upath.replaceAll("\\\\","\\\\\\\\");
        upath = upath.replaceAll("/","//");
            if(upath.indexOf("/")>-1){
        upath = upath + "//";
    }else{
        upath = upath + "\\\\";
    }
```

Fig. 5. System front-end development code

Through the process of function improvement, sub modules are constructed in each module according to various functions. On the basis of defining each detailed function, we can further design and implement the music course auxiliary teaching system and the music basic theory knowledge learning module, the music common sense learning module, the music appreciation module, the assignment management module, and the user management module.

The performance test of the system includes the response speed of various operations, the maximum number of concurrent users, and the maximum data capacity of the test data. Its goal is (1) the correctness of multiple system data acquisition; (2) Real-time performance of system data acquisition between multiple systems; (3) The robustness of the system when multiple users access it simultaneously. After tests such as multiple person access, administrator addition and modification of query data, there were no system crashes and access errors, ensuring the correctness and timeliness of data acquisition in the music teaching information management system, as well as the robustness of the system.

The overall test is a test conducted after software integration to check whether the calls between various modules are normal. In the overall test, multiple people and multiple locations are directly used to log in and receive or send documents at the same time. Check whether the system can operate normally.

Through testing, it is found that there are indeed some shortcomings and areas for improvement in the system, as follows:

1. The reliability and stability of the system need further verification.

In terms of system calls, it is possible that the called program does not exist or is abnormal;

2. The prompt function of the system needs further improvement.

Through the above relevant system testing, the developed music teaching information management system meets the actual operation requirements of our department.

5   Conclusion

The progress of science and technology, the change of teaching mode, music teaching mode has also undergone tremendous changes. The traditional single teaching mode has been changed, and the multimedia technology has pushed music teaching to a new height. The teaching stage of integrating various technologies is also the embodiment of the era of education. As a modern teaching, the support of multimedia technology and the establishment of Internet platform provide a new and broader world for music teaching. Today, with rapid changes, more and more people have a deeper understanding of multimedia technology and network technology, and have gradually joined the modern music appreciation education.

References

1. Ouyang, Z.: Design and implementation of the digital resource library for music education in colleges and universities. Basic Clin. Pharmacol. Toxicol. **S1**, 124 (2019)
2. Wen, Y.: Design and implementation of safety hidden trouble shooting management system based on cloud computing in university experimental training sites. In: 2019 International Conference on Robots & Intelligent System (ICRIS) (2019)
3. Ai, Y.: Study on teaching quality evaluation criteria of general music education course in colleges and universities. In: 2nd International Conference on Arts, Design and Contemporary Education (2016)

4. Leser, J.: Performance and intimacy: understanding economies of recognition for women professors in universities of the arts, music, and theatre. In: Gender, Work & Organization (GWO) 10th Biennial International Interdisciplinary Conference (2018)
5. Wang, C., Ma, X., Zhong, S.: Design and implementation of music distance education learning system (2021)
6. Ferm, C., Zandén, O.: Implementation of a new assessment system: consequences for teaching and learning of music in Swedish schools year 5–7 (2016)
7. Lu, N.: Design and implementation of fetal education music management system. In: 2016 International Conference on Intelligent Transportation, Big Data & Smart City (ICITBS). IEEE Computer Society (2016)
8. Hallam, S., Creech, A., Mcqueen, H.: The perceptions of non music staff and senior management of the impact of the implementation of the musical futures approach on the whole school. Br. J. Music Educ. **33**(02), 133–157 (2016)
9. Armawati, A., Syamwil, R., Florentinus, T.S.: Implementation of quality management system ISO 9001:2015 integrated with accreditation standards in SMK 1 Sragi. J. Voc. Career Educ. **3**(2), 16179 (2018)
10. Li, J.: Design and implementation of the management system of music education teaching materials in colleges and universities. Wireless Internet Technology (2018)
11. Guang-Yu, Z.: Colleges and universities music education teaching management system design and implementation. Educ. Teach. Forum (2018)
12. Huali, H., Music, D.O.: On the significance and implementation strategies of music practice in art education teaching in colleges and universities. J. Guilin Normal College (2018)
13. Shi, C.: On the optimization design and implementation of personnel information management system in Colleges and Universities. Electronic Test (2017)
14. Cao, J., Chen, W., Zhang, Q.: Challenges and countermeasures for the implementation of credit system in colleges and universities: take guangdong university of foreign studies. J. Guangdong Univ. Foreign Stud. (2017)
15. Zhu, J.F., University, G.M.: Research and practice of "student-centered" internal teaching quality assurance system in colleges and universities. Heilongjiang Res. High. Educ. (2019)
16. Cai, F.S., Wang, C.G.: Research on the integrated educational system of tourism management specialty in colleges and universities. J. Heilongjiang College of Educ. (2017)
17. Zhang, L., Cao, H., Management, S.O.: A survey of research teaching in chinese colleges and universities in recent ten years. J. Wuyi Univ. (2017)
18. Li, P., Wei, Y., Zhang, R., et al.: Design and implementation of employment management system in colleges and universities. Electronic Test (2019)
19. Liu, S., Xiao, C., Chen, Z.: Design and implementation of laboratory management system in colleges and universities. J. Heilongjiang Bayi Agric. Univ. (2019)
20. Yang, S.X.: Research on the application of teaching mode based on inquiry and practice idea to teaching introduction to folk music in colleges and universities. Tribune Educ. Cult. (2018)

Analysis of Educational Resource Allocation Scheme Based on Differential Evolution Algorithm

Shiyu Wu[✉]

Ningbo University of Finance and Economics, Ningbo 315000, Zhejiang, China
a22092100012@cityu.mo

Abstract. The allocation of educational resources is closely related to the efficiency, quality and development of educational work, so in order to help find the best resource allocation scheme, this paper will carry out relevant research. The research mainly focuses on differential evolution algorithm, introduces the basic concept, application advantages and process of the algorithm, and then relies on the algorithm to optimize the education resource allocation scheme, and the final result is the best scheme. Through research, differential evolution algorithm can continuously optimize the education resource allocation scheme and help people find the best resource allocation scheme.

Keywords: Differential evolution algorithm · Educational resources · The allocation of resources

1 Introduction

The research on the efficiency of basic education services by domestic scholars is increasingly increasing in methods and content. "Some scholars analyze the content of educational resource flow from the perspective of resource flow," while others evaluate the regional inequality of compulsory education supply through the establishment of a Taylor index evaluation system framework, and then analyze the allocation efficiency of educational resources. "2; Some scholars have also studied the impact of fiscal gaps on the equalization of basic public services in urban and rural areas from the perspective of uneven distribution of central and local finance under China's tax sharing system.

Through relevant research by some scholars, it can be found that empirical research on the efficiency of basic education services mostly focuses on the evaluation of indicator systems, and there is less research on the "input output" aspect. Based on existing research, this article conducts a systematic analysis of 2019 data from 16 cities in Anhui Province, and uses the DEA model to study the supply efficiency of corresponding equalization of basic education services.

Education resources in China in the past simple structure, a single project, so it is not difficult to do fair distribution, leading to our country for a long time always thinking

Y. Zhang and N. Shah (Eds.): BigIoT-EDU 2023, LNICST 584, pp. 259–269, 2024.
https://doi.org/10.1007/978-3-031-63142-9_26

on education resource allocation scheme design based on the experience of its core idea is to statistical information education main body the next stage work, we analyzed the education subject to which resources, demand for all kinds of resources, then the relevant resources are sorted out from the total resources and distributed after combination, so that the final results of distribution can meet the basic principle of equal supply and demand.

The reform of the tax sharing system implemented in China in the 1990s has played an important guiding role in China's development. While establishing a local transfer payment system, the goal of equalization of basic public services was also proposed under the impetus of the tax sharing system, and the policy of equalization of basic public services was officially included in the policy agenda in 2002. In 2005, the "Proposal of the Central Committee of the Communist Party of China on Formulating the Eleventh Five Year Plan for National Economic and Social Development" adopted at the Fifth Plenary Session of the 16th Central Committee of the Communist Party of China believed that the living conditions of residents in terms of residence, transportation, education, and culture have greatly improved, but still need to adhere to development, and proposed for the first time the proposal of "improving the public financial system and gradually realizing the equalization of basic public services"; In 2006, "improving the basic public service system and improving government management and service levels" became one of the goals of a socialist harmonious society; At the 17th National Congress of the Communist Party of China in 2007, it was emphasized that "promoting the equalization of basic public services and improving the public finance system" was crucial to narrow the development gap between regions and achieve the equalization of basic public services, and the public finance system should be promoted and improved around the construction of the equalization of basic public services; The Decision of the Central Committee of the Communist Party of China on Several Major Issues Concerning Promoting Rural Reform and Development, adopted in 2008, also emphasizes the importance of promoting the equalization of basic public services in urban and rural areas; In 2012, the 12th Five Year Plan for the National Basic Public Service System proposed the requirements for improving the regional basic public service equalization system and mechanism; In 2016, the 13th Five Year Plan for National Economic and Social Development of the People's Republic of China further proposed the importance of improving basic public service systems such as education, sports, culture, housing, and medical care; Basic public education is the most urgent part of this policy that needs to be realized and improved. Achieving the equalization of basic public education resources is not only conducive to narrowing the gap between urban and rural areas, but also can promote the improvement of education equity and education allocation efficiency.

But with the domestic education career in scale, the internal development of educational administration, academic departments, etc., of our country's education resources demand structure becomes more complex, more resources project requirements, so the education resource allocation difficulty rising sharply, and the traditional way doesn't guarantee equivalence between supply and demand, so related fields in order to improve the education resource allocation, differential evolution algorithm is proposed, the algorithm can assist human to find the best resource allocation scheme and guarantee the supply and demand equivalence. But to play the role of differential evolution algorithm in education resource allocation, we must first understand differential evolution algorithm, so it is necessary to carry out relevant research.

Differential Evolution (DE) is a novel random parallel direct search algorithm proposed in 1995 to solve Chebyshev polynomials. It can minimize nonlinear, non differentiable, and continuous spatial functions by introducing a special differential mutation pattern for iteration. Due to its simple structure, robustness, and strong global search ability, DE has been applied in multiple fields. DE initializes the population randomly, using the fitness value of individuals in the population as a criterion. The main process includes three steps: differential variation, crossover/recombination, and selection. Compared to genetic algorithm (GA), his key idea is to use the information in vector populations to change the search space, using two randomly selected different population vectors to perturb the existing vector, that is, the mutation vector is generated by the parent difference vector, and intersects with the parent individual vector to generate a new individual vector for direct selection with the parent individual. In the optimization process, if the termination conditions are not met, the three steps of mutation, crossover, and selection are repeated in sequence. The flow chart of the standard DE is shown in Fig. 1.

2   Basic Concept, Application Advantages and Process of Differential Evolution Algorithm

2.1   Basic Concepts

Differential evolutionary algorithm is a kind of similar to the mathematical method of genetic algorithm, the main functions are based on global optimization, the only difference is that two kinds of algorithms for different steps in the process of definition, in generating of initial population steps, for example, the definition of differential evolution algorithm to the initial population is generated after the "all conform to the requirements of the individual integration, untreated group", and the definition of genetic algorithm is "original, whether meet the requirements of the population after the integration of individuals". This difference makes the operation mechanism of the two algorithm also has had the difference, namely the operation mechanism of differential evolution algorithm is mainly from the initial population, combined with environmental flaws which initial population, and then is optimized, and the genetic algorithm from the initial population, combined with the environment to find out the population after the current defects, put forward a number of possible genetic direction, then the combination in each direction is put into the environment for comparison to naturally generate the optimal genetic results in the environment [1–3]. Figures 1 and 2 show the operation topology of the two algorithms.

Combined with Figs. 1 and Fig. 2 can see, the differential evolution algorithm is the output of the results for the local optimal solution, starting from the existing environmental conditions, the solution is no optimize space, genetic algorithm and the output is the global optimal solution, is the existing environment conditions in both the possibility of the best solution, but this does not mean that the best solution is no optimize space [4].

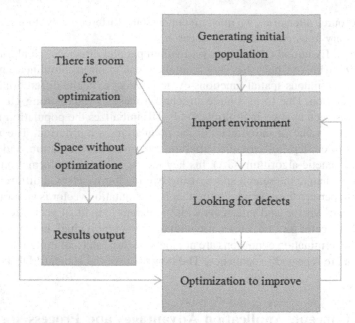

Fig. 1. Operation topology of differential evolution algorithm

In addition, although differential evolution algorithm and genetic algorithm have some differences, but they have the same basic principle. Differential evolutionary algorithm of the whole operation process is referred to as "evolution", it is derived from the biological evolution mechanism, namely the differential evolution algorithm, initial population of each individual as a creature, and environmental parameters is given, the population of import, population within different individuals will react with the environment parameter, appear the difference on the fitness, then find the highest fitness individuals, if the fitness of the individual to achieve the highest level, can be directly output as the final result, but did not reach the highest level, just as the next generation of population evolution of the template, aiming at its defect is improved, before its environmental fitness wasn't up to the highest level, the process will continue to cycle, during this period, the individual will evolve according to the mutation vector V [5–7]. Equation (1) is the expression of mutation vector V in differential evolution algorithm.

$$V(i) = x(r0) + F(x(r1) - (x(r2)) \tag{1}$$

where, V (i) is the ith solution of mutation vector V, x is the parameter vector initializing the population number in a certain dimension, F is the mutation operator, and r0, r1 and r2 and r3 random numbers respectively, which are used to ensure the randomness of mutation.

2.2 Application Process

The application process of differential evolution algorithm is highly similar to that of genetic algorithm. See Table 1 for details.

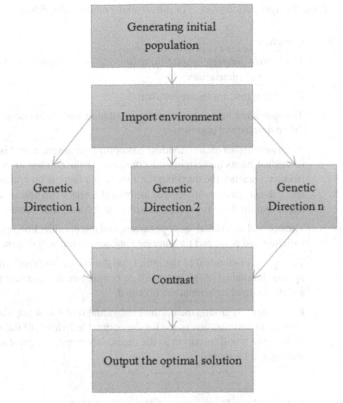

Fig. 2. Operation topology of genetic algorithm

2.3   Application Advantages

Compared with genetic algorithm, differential evolution algorithm's advantage lies in two aspects: first, the differential evolution algorithm is more efficient, the reason is that the algorithm is directly based on the initial population is optimized to improve, but the genetic algorithm requires the initial population can be divided into a number of possible genetic populations, then contrast, optimization, so the efficiency of natural lower than that of differential evolution algorithm; Second, the differential evolution algorithm gives the result of higher quality, that is the result of differential evolution algorithm is given there is no any optimization space, represents the results under fixed environment parameter must be the optimal solution, even may be the only optimal solution, and the result of the genetic algorithm for the global optimal solution, big probability there is a certain optimization space [8–10].

Table 1. Application process of differential evolution algorithm

The serial number	Content
1	The control parameters and fitness function of differential evolution algorithm are determined
2	Generate a random initial population
3	The individual fitness of the initial population was evaluated according to the environmental parameters
4	Analyze whether each individual has optimization space, that is, if the individual meets the termination condition, or the number of evolutionary iterations reaches the maximum, it means that there is no optimization space, and then find the optimal individual. Otherwise, optimize and improve until there is no optimization space for all individuals
5	The optimal individual was optimized, and the optimization operation was variation and poor, and the intermediate population was obtained
6	The optimal individual of the initial population is connected with the optimal individual of the intermediate population, and the new population and the optimal individual are obtained
7	Repeat step (3) around the optimal individual of the new population. If there is no optimization space for the optimal individual of the new population, it will be output as the result; otherwise, the cycle steps (5) and (6) will be started

3   Optimizing Education Resource Allocation Schemes

3.1   Basic Information

Assuming that the educational resources to be allocated include three types of resources, namely teachers, teaching equipment, and counselors, the three types of resources need to be allocated to the two educational subjects, L and M, and the resources obtained by the two subjects are required to be consistent with their actual needs. The maximum error interval is 3%.

The requirements of L and M are as follows: First, L has 101 teachers, 13 sets of teaching equipment for teachers to use in turn, and 12 counselors, each of whom is responsible for the guidance of all students of a grade. Recently L education body in response to the call of modern education, in the internal actively carried out a variety of reform work, mainly opened three new professional education curriculum system, and expanded the scope of enrollment, according to the statistics, the number of students in each grade last year on average increased by 1.6%. Therefore, the existing resources of teachers and counselors in the educational subject of L cannot meet the needs of teaching and student counseling of all subjects, so the quantity of the two resources needs to be increased, and the improvement of the quantity of the two resources indirectly increases the demand of teachers for the quantity of teaching equipment, so the quantity of teaching equipment should also be increased. Secondly, M Education now has 122 teachers, 19 sets of teaching equipment, which can be used by teachers in turn, and 9 counselors, who are responsible for the guidance work of all students of different grades. Recently, M education body has also actively carried out various internal reforms, mainly opening two new professional education curriculum system, and expanding the scope of enrollment. According to statistics, the number of students in each grade increased by 3.8% on average last year. Therefore, the existing three resources of M education subject are also insufficient and need to be supplied through distribution.

3.2   Design and Optimization of Educational Resource Allocation Scheme

With the demand of L, M two education main body, to the traditional method to formulate an initial resource allocation scheme, namely data according to the demand, is expected to name of l1 and l2 teachers tutor, l3 set of teaching equipment allocated to L education main body, the teacher m1, m2, a counselor, m3 teaching equipment allocated to M education main body. Theoretically, as long as the demand meets the actual demand and the error does not exceed the maximum range, the program can be directly implemented. However, the allocation of educational resources in practice also needs to consider the total amount of educational resources. Only when the total amount is greater than the sum of all the needs of the two educational subjects, L and M, can the program be implemented smoothly. Instead when amount is less than L, M two education main body the sum total of all requirements, will be considered in the allocation of resources to maximize meet the demand of both sides of the issue, consider the problem is not in order to fully meet the demand of the two education main body, but under the condition of limited and insufficient resources to find can let the two education main body the highest satisfaction with the result of the allocation of resources allocation, This becomes a complicated problem [11].

Aiming at this problem, differential evolution algorithm is adopted to improve the operation and process the two L, M after the reform of education main body education work on the demand for resources as environment parameters, structures, environment model, then the education resources in each component as a control parameter, according to the formula (1) set the variation vector V, after using the differential evolution algorithm to analyze the initial plan, In this way, the initial scheme will form an initial population. During the operation, the component of each resource can be compared with the resource demands of the two educational subjects, L and M, and then the initial result can be obtained. Through comparison, the difference between the component of each resource and the relevant demands of the educational subject, L, is 0.3%, 1.2% and 0.05% respectively. The relative demand difference with M education subject is 1.1%, 1.1% and 0.1%, respectively.

According to this result, the initial plan does not meet the needs of L and M education subjects in terms of various resources [12]. Although the difference is small, it will still affect the demand of education work after the reform. Therefore, it is necessary to optimize this plan. Need for resources from the economic point of component in optimization of adjustment, the assumption of existing education resources of the communist party of China has 10 teachers, but it doesn't meet the demand of L, M two education main body, then consider economic costs, cut the other two resources will be more economic cost for expansion of teacher resources, makes the increase in the number of teacher resources, this way leads to two other resources and demand gap is bigger, but it can make teachers resources and demand the gap between the smaller, which is the key to avoid the gap between two other resources and the demand is too big, allow teacher resources and the demand, there is a certain gap between do this scheme, the optimal means education resources [13].

Combined with this idea, differential evolution algorithm is used to optimize the scheme cycle, and the final results are shown in Table 2.

Table 2. Education resource allocation scheme optimized by differential evolution algorithm

Project	Proportion of total economic cost of resources
Teachers'	67%
Teaching equipment	13%
The counselor	30%

According to the scheme in Table 3, the allocation of educational resources is carried out. The results show that in the education subject of L, the teacher resources are fully met, and the supply and demand are equal, while the demand for teaching equipment and counselors is not improved, with the difference of 2.7% and 0.4%. In M education subject, the teacher resources have not been fully met, the difference is 0.3%, and the demand for teaching equipment and counselors has not been improved, the difference is 1.3% and 1.9%., by contrast, the optimized education resource allocation scheme meets the requirements of L education subject teacher resources, don't meet the demand of teacher resources M education subject, but the difference is not big, combines the condition of two education main body, you can see that because [14] L education subject opened three new professional education curriculum system, so the highest demand for teachers, counselors original resources more so have cut space, teaching equipment increases with the increase of the number of teachers, and is the second highest demand. In the scheme, the teacher resources of L education subject are satisfied. The second highest teaching equipment has a small difference, and the third highest counselor has a large difference in resource demand, but its quantity is relatively sufficient, indicating that the scheme maximally meets the needs of L education subject. M various resources to compare the average education subject itself, and after the reform demand gap is not big, but because of reform to pursue all-round development, so the demand for all resources have same level, and the optimized method does not meet any needs, but close the gap between the actual resources and demand, so as to maximize meet the demand of M education main body [15].

After distribution, the average number of books per student in six universities is not very balanced. The main reason for this situation may be that the total number of books in the six universities before allocation was several million, with a relatively large number. Therefore, the number of books assumed to be allocated in the model is still too small compared to the number of books owned by previous universities. It is still difficult to significantly improve the imbalance in the number of books per student by allocating these 100000 new books. This also indicates that in order to fundamentally improve the imbalance in educational resources caused by a large base, it is necessary to anticipate whether the distribution of educational resources is balanced in advance, rather than making up for the shortcomings.

Using the method of systematic genetics, this paper analyzes the occurrence mechanism of educational inequality in China, and concludes that its process can be composed of dynamic mechanism, intermediary mechanism, process mechanism, and integration mechanism, and ultimately be explained in depth in the context of resources. From the perspective of the reaction chain of the occurrence mechanism, the initial motivation was the contradiction between the development theme of efficiency and the educational laws themselves, the conflict between individual educational expectations and resource acquisition capabilities, and the inducement that early education had presented implicit differentiation, which formed the logical endpoint and dynamic mechanism for the unequal development of the entire education; The implicit differentiation mediated by educational quality gradually moves towards explicit differentiation, resulting in the accumulation of high-quality resources and the deprivation of inferior resources. That is, the intermediary mechanism of inequality. The completion of the intermediary function can be specifically decomposed into two intermediary variables, namely, the class composition of schools and students' academic achievements. These two variables respectively connect schools and families, educational opportunities, and educational quality to complete the intermediary transformation; Reducing these different variables to a generic form that takes resources as its ontology, namely, the process mechanism for achieving the generation of educational inequality, is essentially a reinterpretation based on the resource perspective. Through the introduction of the nature of resources and the supporting analysis of relevant theories of economic resources, the essential attribute of resource production efficiency determines that it has an inevitable realistic representation of optimal matching [16]. It is necessary to break the single role of the market and achieve the overall efficiency optimization of resources, It requires macro policies to regulate and control in different directions; This is also reflected in the synergy of macro system and market forces, which constitute external participation in the generation of educational inequality and ultimately form an integration mechanism that connects and integrates inequality with practice.

Overall, the allocation of educational resources is a very complex and tedious task. With the expansion of the scope of allocation, the allocation of educational resources in the entire school, the entire city, the entire province, and even the entire country requires a set of intelligent technologies to support. Because even small areas of artificial allocation can have errors or errors, let alone the scope of allocation is slowly expanding, so in the process of allocating educational resources, To improve the issue of differentiated allocation of educational resources, it is necessary to rely on the support of big data technology. Through the allocation model based on the Zuanhai Sheath algorithm, the intelligent optimization allocation of educational resources is carried out, and the current situation of resources in various universities can be calculated in a decision-making allocation that does not add human factors [17–20]. The optimal allocation result of educational resources is achieved, thereby improving the imbalance of educational resources. Optimizing intelligent allocation algorithms provides scientific support for resource allocation decision-making departments, making allocation strategies balanced.

4 Conclusion

In conclusion, differential evolution algorithm is highly similar to genetic algorithm in functions, application scenarios and other aspects. In comparison, differential evolution algorithm has its own unique advantages and has good application value in the process of optimizing education resource allocation scheme. Using this algorithm, the initial scheme can be optimized, and the optimized scheme can meet the comprehensive situation and maximize the demand of the main body.

References

1. Li B., Zhang, H., Hong, J., et al.: Energy-aware resource allocation scheme for device-to-device communication based on NOMA underlaying cellular networks. In: 2017 IEEE 17th International Conference on Communication Technology (ICCT). IEEE (2017)
2. Liu, P., Cao, H., Feng, S., et al.: Study on the application scheme of aerodynamic coefficient identification based on the differential evolution algorithm. Math. Probl. Eng. **2020**, 1–10 (2020)
3. Li, J., Zhang, R.B.: Multi-auv distributed task allocation based on the differential evolution quantum bee colony optimization algorithm. Polish Maritime Res. **24**(s1), 65–71 (2017)
4. Hadi, M.K.: Special protection and control scheme based on generation rescheduling using differential evolution and electromagnetism-like algorithm (2016)
5. Zhang, X., Tan, Y., Yang, Z.: Resource allocation optimization of equipment development task based on MOPSO algorithm. JSEE **30**(6), 1132–1143 (2019)
6. Zhang, X., Tan, Y., Yang, Z.: Resource allocation optimization of equipment development task based on MOPSO algorithm. JSEE **30**(6), 1132–1143 (2019)
7. Pal, M., Bandyopadhyay, S.: Differential evolution for multi-modal multi-objective problems. In: The Genetic and Evolutionary Computation Conference Companion (2019)
8. Ding, F., Gao, P., Zhang, X., et al.: Thrust allocation of dynamic positioning based on improved differential evolution algorithm. In: 2020 39th Chinese Control Conference (CCC) (2020)
9. Kumar, S.: A novel based resource allocation method on cloud computing environment using hybrid differential evolution algorithm. J. Comput. Theoret. Nanosci. **14**(11), 5322–5326 (2017)
10. Zhang, S., Zhao, X.: Power allocation for sensing-based spectrum sharing cognitive radio system with primary quantized side information. China Commun. **13**(9), 33–43 (2016)
11. LuyuQian, X.: On the optimal allocation of earthwork in railway subgrade based on green construction. J. Eng. Stud. **11**(01), 64–74 (2019)
12. Jing-Wei, L.I., Sun, B.: A task scheduling optimization algorithm based on fusion of IDEA and Taguchi in cloud computing. Control Eng. China (2017)
13. Jin, M., Chen, P., Malaikah, H., et al.: Research on fuzzy scheduling of cloud computing tasks based on hybrid search algorithms and differential evolution. Fract. Interdiscipl. J. Complex Geom. Nat. **30**, 2248003 (2022)
14. Qiu, B.: Resource allocation optimization strategy using improved differential evolution algorithm in multi-radio multi-channel WSNS. Int. J. Innov. Comput. Inf. Control 3, 16 (2020)

15. Wang, Y., Chen, C.R., Huang, P.Q., et al.: A new differential evolution algorithm for joint mining decision and resource allocation in a MEC-enabled wireless blockchain network. Comput. Ind. Eng. **155**, 107186 (2021)
16. Sheng, X.Z., Li, M.Z., Tang, K.S., et al.: Multi-layer competitive-cooperative framework for performance enhancement of differential evolution. Inf. Sci. **480**, 86–104 (2018)
17. Wang, H., Liu, C., Shen, L., et al.: Delay-aware resource allocation scheme for heterogeneous multi-radio access system based on Lyapunov optimization. In: International Conference on Communications & Networking in China. IEEE (2016)
18. Ge, J., He, Q., et al.: Cloud computing task scheduling strategy based on improved differential evolution algorithm. AIP Conf. Proc. **1834**(1), 1–7 (2017)
19. Mousavirad, S.J., Rahnamayan, S.: Differential evolution algorithm based on a competition scheme. In: 2019 14th International Conference on Computer Science & Education (ICCSE) (2019)
20. Jiang, C., Li, Y., Su, R., et al.: A load balancing based resource allocation algorithm in UAV-aided MEC systems. In: 2020 IEEE 6th International Conference on Computer and Communications (ICCC). IEEE (2020)

Construction of a Hierarchical Mathematical Model of Junior High School Mathematics Based on Two-Step Clustering Algorithm

Yuxiao Jing[1]([✉]), Yuan Deng[2], and Songli Jin[2]

[1] Liaocheng Wenxuan Middle School, Liaocheng 252000, Shandong, China
515528588@qq.com

[2] Institute of Educational Innovation, Chongqing University of Arts and Sciences, Chongqing 402160, China

Abstract. The traditional classification method of mathematics teaching resources is inefficient. Therefore, a two-step clustering algorithm is proposed to merge and classify mathematics teaching resources. The mathematical foundation and thinking ability of junior high school students are very different. In the teaching process, the individual differences between students should be fully respected. However, junior high school students come from different primary schools, and the education they receive and the habits they develop are different. Same. If our junior high school math teachers use traditional teaching methods to teach junior high school students, it is difficult for each of them to master math knowledge and complete our teaching tasks. In the teaching process, teachers and students should work together, give full play to their residual heat, put forward constructive opinions, and contribute to the construction of an efficient classroom. The primary purpose of mathematics teaching in junior high school is how to use the limited classroom teaching time to improve teaching efficiency and teaching quality faster. That is to say, the traditional unified teaching should be transformed into different levels of teaching content. This article mainly expounds the superiority of the layered teaching mode and how to integrate the layered progressive method into the mathematics teaching of junior high school.

Keywords: Two-step clustering algorithm · junior high school mathematics · hierarchical mathematics · model construction

1 Introduction

In the process of mathematics teaching, there are many factors that make students' mathematics level uneven. According to the traditional unified teaching method, it will inevitably affect the initiative of students to learn, making them lose their enthusiasm for learning. The older teacher said that based on years of teaching experience, in order to promote the teaching effect, he has been practicing the teaching organization form of layered teaching and the concept of teaching students according to their aptitude,

Y. Zhang and N. Shah (Eds.): BigIoT-EDU 2023, LNICST 584, pp. 270–277, 2024.
https://doi.org/10.1007/978-3-031-63142-9_27

but they do not know that this method has a professional term called Layered teaching [1]. It not only contradicts the teaching concept of the new curriculum standard, but also restricts the growth and development of students. Therefore, it is urgent to build an efficient junior high school mathematics classroom teaching. This strategy of grouping students according to their knowledge and ability can make students' development and potential more fully improved. Teachers can also use this layered model to teach the actual ability levels of different classes. In the process of teaching as a junior high school teacher, we should adopt a new teaching method, which can achieve the teaching task and allow every student to gain something [2]. The layered teaching can well meet this requirement. Mathematical thinking will not be effectively improved. For some students with poor learning ability, they may not be able to grasp even the most basic mathematical concepts and properties of mathematics, nor can they keep up with the teacher's teaching progress, thus failing to achieve the goal of improving the quality of all students. Make full use of digital teaching resources to improve the intuitiveness of courses in the course of teaching, which has the advantages of broadening horizons and enhancing students' thinking ability. Digital mathematics teaching resources refer to the digital resources formulated for mathematics courses, and students need to have high learning interest when learning mathematics courses. It is imperative to carry out classroom teaching reform and build an efficient classroom; to solve these problems, teachers need to take appropriate measures for different students. We must let junior high school students become interested in mathematical knowledge in the process of learning, and let their interest guide their continuous learning, so as to cultivate their mathematical literacy [3].

2 Merging and Classification of Digitized Mathematics Teaching Resources Based on Two-Step Clustering Algorithm

2.1 Feature Extraction of Digital Mathematics Teaching Resources

In the application process of digital mathematics teaching resources, with the increase of teaching course hours, the resource data shows an incremental development trend. In the process of extracting the characteristics of digital mathematics teaching resources, new data and historical data should be considered at the same time, and feature extraction should be realized based on a global perspective to avoid ignoring the hidden information contained in the resources [4]. Let every student discover their own interests, learn happily, find a learning method that suits them, so that every student can experience the joy of learning, and ultimately improve the classroom atmosphere and mobilize the subjective initiative of learning. The stratification should be continuously adjusted and dynamically managed according to the students' learning situation during this period. Only in this way can we continuously stimulate students' interest in learning in every period of time [5]. For stratified teaching, it emphasizes the following three points: the first is students' existing knowledge and ability level; the second is stratification; the third is that the ability level of all students should be improved. Figure 1 shows the comparison results of the three methods for merging and classifying digital mathematics teaching resources when counting different window sizes.

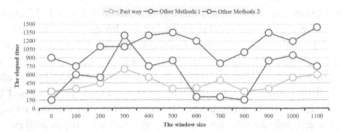

Fig. 1. The effect of window size on the efficiency of merge classification

In the mathematics teaching of junior high school, teachers should pay attention to the introduction of the classroom, so that students will have greater interest in the new knowledge to be learned at the beginning of the classroom, and lay the foundation for the construction of an efficient classroom. However, with the development of the times, the individual differences between students are becoming more and more significant. The teaching mode of unified standards, unified requirements and unified evaluation in the past is less and less suitable for today's students and does not meet the requirements of the new national curriculum standards. The adaptive sliding window mutual information method is used to process the historical data and incremental data of digital mathematics teaching resources, and realize the feature extraction of digital mathematics teaching resources. According to the definition of mutual information, the expression of mutual information matrix can be obtained as follows:

$$Z = \frac{1}{m+r}(Z_1 + Z_2) \tag{1}$$

Students' learning ability is stratified, evaluation methods are stratified, and homework assignments are stratified. Through stratification, each student can actively and autonomously participate in the classroom. The goal of layer A focuses on the improvement of ability and the cultivation of mathematical thinking; layer B focuses on consolidation and improvement on the basis of basic knowledge; layer C focuses on the most basic concepts and knowledge points. These three levels correspond to students at different levels of good, medium and poor. The diagonalization process uses the unit matrix to represent the eigendecomposition formula of Z as follows:

$$I = G_1^T Z_2 G_1 \tag{2}$$

According to the eigenvectors and eigenvalues, the eigenvalue formula of all samples of digital mathematics teaching resources is obtained as follows:

$$\Lambda = \frac{1}{m+r}(I + \mu_i) \tag{3}$$

This kind of stratified teaching is selective and non-eliminating teaching, and it is a beneficial supplement to the traditional class teaching system. The core content of layered teaching is to face all students, face up to the individual differences of students, it can make each student make the greatest progress, so that all students can actively and actively participate in mathematics learning. Everyone can get a good mathematics education, and different people have different development in mathematics. In order to achieve the above goals, teachers have adopted the strategy of preparing lessons in different layers [6]. Each class has some high-level questions specially prepared for students with higher grades, which are very helpful for their further improvement. In this way, it can obviously better promote the common development of all students.

2.2 Tiered Measures

The students in the class are divided into three groups: A, B, and C. The level of group B is equivalent to the average level of the school, then the level of group A is higher than the average level, and the level of group C is lower than the average level. The layered teaching mode creates a relaxed environment for students at different levels or categories to stretch their hands and feet, so that they can develop freely, freely and fully. The stratification of lesson preparation requires a lot of time and energy of the teachers, which virtually increases the workload [7]. Doing what you say is not an easy, simple thing. It can make students' body and mind relax, and reduce students' dislike of mathematics learning, which is deeply loved by teachers and students. Applying it to junior high school mathematics teaching, teachers did not notice this difference between students, and adopted the same teaching standards for students at different levels, so that in the previous junior high school mathematics teaching, students' knowledge and ability levels were presented. A state of severe polarization. When we explain the content of the chapter "One-dimensional linear equations" to students, we can divide the establishment of abstract mathematical models of one-dimensional linear equations and the problem-solving thinking of one-dimensional linear equations into A in the process of preparing lessons. Floor. The B layer focuses on the solution of the one-dimensional linear equation and how the one-dimensional linear equation is applied in real life, and what problems can be solved for us. For group C students, the central idea of pulling and encouraging more is to cultivate students' good study habits and correct study attitude, which is the most basic learning goal; cultivate students' good logical thinking ability and abstract thinking ability., spatial imagination ability, etc. [8]. In the process of solving practical problems in mathematics, we should apply what we have learned and draw inferences from other facts, improve teaching efficiency, improve learning efficiency, and jointly build an efficient classroom. Using the obtained eigenvectors to establish a principal component decision matrix, and mapping digital mathematics teaching resources to the established principal component decision matrix, data dimension reduction can be achieved. Subsequent windows repeat the above process to achieve feature extraction of all digital mathematics teaching resource samples. Classroom teaching in the new era must be multi-polar, multi-directional and multi-objective hierarchical and classified teaching. The basic requirements of classroom teaching can be summarized as "integration and division, full participation, and layer-by-layer advancement". The researchers investigated teachers' feelings of students during the implementation of layered teaching to verify teachers' implementation of layered teaching strategies, and to explore The difficulties and existing problems faced in the implementation process, the chi-square test of teaching methods and classes are shown in Table 1.

Table 1. Chi-square test of teaching methods and classes

Table 1. Chi-square test of teaching methods and classes

	Value	DF	Gradual Sig
Pearson chi-square	13.548	5	.021
Likelihood ratio	13.465	5	.031
Linear and linear combinations	.124	2	.624
N in a valid case	247		

3 The Construction of the Stratified Teaching Mode of Mathematics in Junior Middle Schools

3.1 Student Stratification

The substantive significance of stratification lies in: revealing the hidden diversity among students in the class with several "layers", so that teachers can use corresponding measures to "prescribe the right medicine" in each link of teaching. In this way, students are leading their learning, and they can easily acquire knowledge through analysis and research on problems. This kind of teaching completely changes the traditional mode of comprehensive teaching by teachers, and turns it into active and active learning for students. Therefore, the school requires teachers to try to return the classroom to students in the process of stratified teaching, and organize students' discussion and independent practice appropriately. The survey statistics of students' willingness to teach are shown in Table 2.

Table 2. Survey statistics of students' willingness to attend classes

		Frequency	Percentage	Effective percentage	Cumulative percentage
Effective	Very want to go to	91	31.7	31.7	31.7
	Compared to the	124	55.2	55.5	66.8
	Don't want to go up to also don't hate	58	21.0	23.4	88.4
	Very hate	1	.6	.6	99.1

I used multimedia to play the video of the sunrise at sea for the students, so that the students could feel the three positional relationships of the straight line and the circle, and combined the practical problems with the mathematical theory knowledge to help the students understand the knowledge of the textbook. Only in this way can students of different ability levels get better development. In this process, teachers' teaching objectives are also easier to achieve. Therefore, for junior high school mathematics teaching, the application of hierarchical teaching mode is very necessary. We want to set up different coaching programs based on their foundation. For students with a good foundation, they mainly cultivate their rigorous mathematical thinking, for students with an average foundation, they focus on strengthening the extension of basic knowledge, and for students with a poor foundation, they focus on stimulating their interest in learning and cultivating their mathematics. Self-confidence, guide them to continue to learn. Cultivate their interest in learning mathematics, improve their basic mathematical operation skills, encourage them to answer more questions in class, and usually encourage them, ask more questions, and provide more guidance, so that they can gradually develop a good habit of self-study, and guide these students from the B level to the C-layer transformation [9]. Compare existing nodes and subsequent observations by similarity measure. When the comparison result is similar, add similar observation samples to the existing nodes; when the comparison result is dissimilar, create a new node in the feature tree until all digital mathematics teaching is completed. The resource data comparison is completed, and the feature tree construction is realized. In the stratified practice, each student and teacher must establish a student view and teaching view that conforms to the characteristics of the times, love each student, and move their hearts with love. Only with sincere love and equal respect for each student, as a student, the basic learning goals must be achieved, the improving learning goals are to complete the teaching requirements, and the final developmental goals are beyond the outline requirements. For students with spare capacity to choose. However, in the implementation of stratified teaching, teachers will still prefer eugenics and focus on middle-class students. This is an area for improvement in the implementation of tiered teaching. Teachers should not label students and should treat them equally.

3.2   The Teaching Process is Layered, and Classroom Guidance is Done Well

Classify teaching objectives. Teaching goals refer to the direction of the implementation of teaching activities and the expected results, and are the starting point and final destination of all teaching activities. The three-dimensional teaching goals are knowledge and skills goals, process and method goals, emotional attitudes and values goals. The processing of continuous variables as well as categorical variables is implemented using the likelihood log distance, which is a probability value obtained based on the distance. The log-likelihood decreases when different classes are merged into the same class, and the distance between different classes changes. In the teaching process, teachers should understand the relationship between the front and back of the teaching materials, grasp the specific status of each knowledge point, some should be properly analyzed, and some should be extended and foreshadowed so that students can better absorb; Affirm the little progress of each student. The advantages and potentials of students are discovered through evaluation, which provides a basis for the promotion of stratification, so as to overcome the tendency problems in the group, correct and adjust the teaching design, and achieve the purpose of treating both the symptoms and the root causes. Hierarchical exploration is to enable students to have an active and active learning attitude, so there should still be a problem of hierarchical evaluation for them. As long as they achieve the predetermined effect of the hierarchical target, they should be affirmed. Teachers should consider whether the homework is not. Investigate the learning content of the day, and examine the students' mastery. It should not be too simple, and students need to think about it during the homework process. The assigned homework content is challenging for students, and it does not deviate from the teaching theme or the students' mathematical knowledge mastery. In this way, it can not only improve the comprehensive quality of students, but also create favorable conditions for the construction of efficient classroom teaching. And this is exactly what the principle of feeling success is about. Improving this worrying distribution of mathematics achievement is a challenging problem faced by junior middle school mathematics teachers in rural schools like researchers. Therefore, the implementation of tiered mathematics teaching is particularly necessary. The cross-statistics between mathematics classroom gains and achievement is shown in Fig. 2.

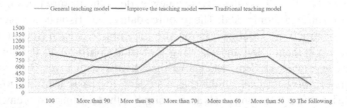

Fig. 2. Cross-statistics between mathematics classroom gains and grades

Therefore, in the layered teaching mode, teachers should adhere to the principle of feeling success, so as to fully maintain students' enthusiasm for learning. During the inspection, our junior high school mathematics teachers are required to design different inspection contents according to the learning level of different students, so that every student can find their own shortcomings through the inspection, and at the same time, their self-confidence will not be hit, and they will be led to continuous improvement. Growing up. Teachers can better mobilize the learning enthusiasm and initiative of students at different levels by designing individualized teaching methods for students at different learning levels, truly give full play to the subjective initiative of students' learning, and promote the efficient operation of the classroom.

4 Conclusion

The two-step clustering algorithm is applied to the merging and classification of digital mathematics teaching resources, and the massive sample clustering performance of the two-step clustering algorithm is used to improve the effectiveness of the merging and classification of digital mathematics teaching resources. It has excellent operation of continuous variables and discrete variables. It has the advantages of strict classification and easy operation. The implementation of stratified teaching is also a comprehensive and holistic educational reform, which requires our front-line teachers to further strengthen theoretical study and practical exploration in teaching, so that the operation of stratified teaching becomes more scientific and rational. Every student has their own shining point. Hierarchical teaching requires us to seize these shining points of students, adopt different teaching methods, and continuously motivate them to learn better. It is hoped that the research on the strategies of creating effective problem situations in primary school mathematics teaching can give readers some help in theory and practice. And continue to explore effective strategies that can promote the construction of an efficient mathematics classroom in junior high schools, so that the traditional mathematics classroom teaching can be changed, and the classroom teaching of mathematics in junior high schools will be continuously optimized to improve the efficiency of mathematics teaching in junior high schools.

References

1. Wen, Y.: On the advantages and measures of stratified mathematics in junior high school mathematics. Wen Yuan (Primary School Edition) **20**(5), 6 (2020)
2. Bin, Z.: Effective application of stratified teaching in junior high school mathematics classroom. Western Qual. Educ. **4**(32), 2 (2018)
3. Fan, J.: Talking about the stratified teaching of mathematics in junior high schools. Modern. Educ. **39**(48), 12 (2017)
4. Fan, L.: On the stratified teaching in junior high school mathematics teaching. Chin. Sci. Technol. Periodical Database (Citation Edn.) Educ. Sci. **2**(89), 48 (2017)
5. Zhang, J.: Attempts on middle-level teaching in mathematics teaching in junior high schools. Xue Weekly **13**(2), 3 (2018)
6. Fei, H.: Talking about the strategy of stratified teaching of mathematics in junior high school. Future Talents **21**(89), 87 (2021)
7. Chen, G.: A preliminary exploration on the stratified teaching of mathematics in junior middle schools. Teach. Ref. Middle Sch. **8**(2), 19 (2018)
8. Zeng, K.: Talking about the application of grouping and hierarchical teaching in junior high school mathematics classroom teaching. Sci. Weekly **18**(2), 31 (2017)
9. Xuan, Y.: How to implement hierarchical teaching in junior high school mathematics teaching. Xueyuan Educ. **47**(56), 84 (2017)
10. Yu, L.: On the understanding and perception of stratified teaching of mathematics in rural junior high schools. Read. World Compr. **32**(4), 7 (2020)

Construction of Chinese International Education Corpus Based on Fuzzy Clustering Algorithm

Lu Chen[1(✉)], Lingya Ma[2], and Xiao Guo[2]

[1] Shaanxi Normal University, Xi'an 710062, Shaanxi, China
578127346@qq.com
[2] Shanghai YZH Education Technology Co., Ltd, Shanghai 201111, China

Abstract. The construction and development of the corpus plays an important role in improving the teaching efficiency and teaching quality of Chinese International Education. The existing Chinese International Education Corpus includes Beijing Language and Culture University HSK Dynamic Composition Corpus, Chinese Learner Spoken Corpus, Sun Yat-sen University Chinese Character Error Continuity Sexual interlanguage corpus, Jinan University written language corpus for international students, etc. Compared with the Chinese ontology corpus, the construction of these corpora is not perfect, and there are still many problems. There are only a handful of corpora known to be available for international education in Chinese. Compared with the Chinese ontology corpus, the number of the corpus is relatively small, and the content of the corpus is relatively simple. The standards for building databases are not unified, and unified standards can help us determine the size of the corpus and how to mark the corpus. Existing corpora have not been well unified either in scale or in the way of corpus labeling. This research believes that the use of collaborative innovation can improve the current problems. The specific methods are as follows: ① Collaborative innovation between teachers and students, the collection or uploading of corpus can not only be done by professional research teachers, but also by ordinary teachers. or collect data. At the same time, students can also assist teachers in collecting corpus or upload their own corpus to the corpus. The participation of students and teachers of other majors in the construction of the corpus is not only conducive to the collection of a large amount of corpus, but also can increase the number of countries of the corpus. ② Collaboration and cooperation between universities. The mutual cooperation between universities can be reflected in the joint undertaking of the task of building a database or the sharing of corpus resources. ③ Collaborative cooperation between the government and universities. It is mainly the cooperation between universities. The government provides policy and material support for the construction of the corpus, and the universities provide professional research results for the construction of the corpus. The collaborative innovation cooperation between the government and universities has a positive role in promoting the construction and development of the Chinese International Corpus.

Keywords: Fuzzy algorithm · Chinese international education · corpus construction

Y. Zhang and N. Shah (Eds.): BigIoT-EDU 2023, LNICST 584, pp. 278–286, 2024.
https://doi.org/10.1007/978-3-031-63142-9_28

1 Introduction

As the name suggests, corpus is the language data repository [1]. There are a large number of language materials in the corpus, and these language materials are language materials that have actually appeared in practical use. These real corpora are of great significance for language teaching and textbook compilation [2]. The corpus in the Chinese International Education corpus records some problems in the use of language and characters by foreign students in the process of learning Chinese [3]. These corpora can help us adjust the key and difficult points of the teaching content and focus on the language points that are easy to make mistakes. At the same time, the basic training designed according to these corpora is closer to the actual application environment of Chinese and can help students learn more authentic, practical and authentic Chinese [4]. In addition to improving the teaching process and teaching efficiency, the corpus also has positive guiding significance for the formulation of the International Chinese Teaching Syllabus. The real corpus in the Chinese corpus provides a scientific reference for the study of vocabulary, grammar syllabus and Chinese character syllabus. [5]. At the same time, by analyzing the corpus in the corpus to adjust the imperfect parts of the teaching syllabus in time, the Chinese teaching syllabus can better serve the Chinese teaching, which is beneficial to improve the teaching quality [6]. Due to the influence of the language environment and language usage, the teaching materials for teaching Chinese as a foreign language cannot be equivalent to those used by students whose native language is Chinese [7]. Therefore, adjusting the Chinese teaching content according to the language situation of Chinese learners can make the teaching content more practical. After all, the fundamental purpose of Chinese as a foreign language is to cultivate students' ability to communicate in Chinese [8]. The huge amount of real Chinese actual usage information stored in the Chinese corpus also provides more practical language reference materials for the compilation of Chinese as a foreign language textbook [9]. This shows the importance of corpus for international Chinese education, and the construction and development of corpus provides a strong theoretical guarantee for international Chinese education [10]. This is also the reason why this paper studies the construction of the corpus [11].

2 Research Significance and Construction Status of Chinese International Education Corpus

2.1 Research on the Significance of Chinese International Education Corpus

At present, the domestic research on Teaching Chinese as a foreign language corpus mostly focuses on the construction, current situation and development of Chinese International Education corpus, while the research on the solutions to the problems existing in the construction, application and development of corpus is relatively few. There are many urgent problems to be solved in the existing Chinese International Education Corpora: first, the types and quantity of the existing Chinese International Education corpora are few, the quantity is limited, the rules are small, and the corpus is not comprehensive enough; Second, there is no unified and reasonable standard for the establishment of

Chinese International Education corpus; Third, the use of the resources of the existing corpus. Although some of the existing corpora have been built, they are not used by learners, so the value of the corpus has not been fully reflected. The problems of Chinese International Education corpus are not only these three points, but as a user, these three problems are the most urgent to be solved. As for solving these problems, it is not enough to rely only on individual or individual strength. Universities and colleges need cooperation and government support, which precisely reflects the concept of collaborative innovation.

The main research purpose of this paper is to study the problems existing in the existing corpus for international Chinese education and propose suggestions for solving these problems. Consent and corpus resources cannot be fully shared. Analyzing and researching these problems and finding out the corresponding solutions can further promote the construction of the corpus for international Chinese education, and at the same time, it can continuously update and improve the existing corpus. The use of corpus is helpful for the formulation of the syllabus of Chinese international education, the compilation of teaching materials and the improvement of classroom teaching efficiency. The rich corpus in the Chinese International Education Corpus can also provide a large number of real language learning and basic practice materials for Chinese International Teaching. The construction and further improvement of the corpus for international Chinese education is conducive to deepening the theoretical foundation of international Chinese education, and at the same time has a positive effect and significance in improving the teaching effect of international Chinese education. The overall process of corpus construction is shown in Fig. 1.

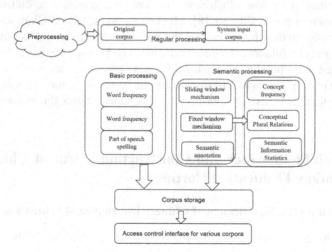

Fig. 1. Overall process of corpus construction

2.2 Construction Status of Chinese International Education Corpus

Compared with Chinese ontology corpus, the author believes that Chinese International Education corpus has the professional characteristics of "specialized in technology".

Although the analysis of the corpus in the Chinese International Education corpus needs to be judged and modified according to the language knowledge of words, words, sentences and grammar in modern Chinese, the Chinese International Education corpus does not involve multi-disciplinary content like the Chinese monolingual corpus, For example, the national large-scale balanced Chinese corpus established by the national language and writing working committee includes multi-disciplinary corpus such as economy, history, chemistry, astronomy and geography, etiquette and rhetoric and so on. The corpus of Chinese international education mainly includes Chinese teaching materials, wrong words, typos or grammatical errors in students' Chinese learning process or examination. Comparing the similarities and differences between the two, the author believes that the main purpose of Chinese International Education corpus is similar to that of Chinese monolingual corpus. General Chinese monolingual corpora are mainly used for academic research, formulation of language norms and standards, or language education. The purpose of Chinese International Education corpus is to give a scientific reference basis for the formulation of syllabus, clarify the key and difficult points of teaching, or assist in the compilation of teaching materials. As for the differences between the two, this paper believes that the differences between the two are mainly reflected in the source of corpus. The sources of modern Chinese corpus are mainly books, newspapers, teaching materials, commentary of TV and film, translation works and so on. The connection between Chinese corpus construction and internet corpus is shown in Fig. 2.

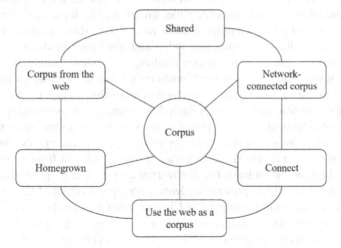

Fig. 2. The way of connecting Chinese corpus construction with Internet corpus

The development and construction of Chinese corpus is much higher than the development of Chinese International Education corpus. Not only Chinese domestic professional scholars have conducted hard research and active construction, but also a few foreign scholars have also established some Chinese corpora, which has contributed to the construction and improvement of Chinese corpus. Chinese International Education corpus not only develops slowly in quantity, but also is not as perfect as Chinese ontology corpus in terms of corpus update, corpus use and corpus construction standards. In the above survey design, we can see that there are various construction problems in the existing Chinese International Education corpus, which need to be improved and improved. At the same time, the maintenance and updating of the corpus after completion is also an urgent problem to be solved.

3 Design and Application of Corpus of Chinese International Education and Teaching Resources

3.1 Overall Design

Based on the above analysis, we believe that the construction of a corpus of teaching resources for international Chinese education is of positive significance and practical for transforming the classroom teaching mode and training mode and improving the professional ability of students. Considering that this corpus is aimed at students of Chinese international education, and the purpose of construction is to improve students' teaching practice ability, the teaching resource corpus we designed includes Chinese teaching material library, classroom teaching corpus, learner corpus and resource expansion library, etc. Four sub-corpora, the specific composition is as follows: (1) Chinese teaching material library. The main purpose of this sub-corpus is to provide students with abundant Chinese teaching materials. According to the content and characteristics of Chinese teaching, it mainly includes Chinese character table, vocabulary table, grammar point table, example sentence table, situation table, topic table, text table, etc. Text material, including stroke order demonstration animation, vocabulary and grammar point pictures, dialogue audio, text video and other multimedia materials. These corpora are mainly derived from various teaching syllabuses, examination syllabuses and Chinese textbooks commonly used in teaching Chinese as a foreign language. (2) Classroom teaching corpus. The main purpose of this sub-corpus is to provide students with real classroom teaching examples, including teaching videos, teaching courseware and teaching plan texts of various types of courses such as listening, speaking, reading and writing, and various language elements such as pronunciation, vocabulary, grammar, and Chinese characters. These corpora are mainly derived from coursework and homework submitted by students. (3) The learner corpus. The purpose of constructing this sub-corpus is mainly to provide students with typical errors of Chinese learners, including written and spoken corpora of Chinese learners with different Chinese proficiency and different native language backgrounds. These corpora are mainly derived from the written and oral assignments of Chinese learners collected by the students during the practice. (4) Resource extension library. The purpose of the corpus is to provide students with multi-channel learning resources, including official account related to Chinese teaching and research, overseas Chinese teaching, useful teaching tools, websites and WeChat public numbers. These materials are mainly derived from the collection and arrangement of teachers and students, especially the sharing of students who are sent to Chinese volunteers. The WeChat official account "Central China Normal University International Chinese" has also played an important role. The above four sub corpora are not isolated, but cooperate with each other. The Chinese teaching material database and learner corpus show the content of Chinese teaching, the classroom teaching corpus shows the process of Chinese teaching, and the resource expansion database shows the resources available outside class. From the teaching content to the teaching process, and then to the expansion of resources, these four sub corpora connect knowledge, skills and resources, thus forming a multi-type, multi-level and unified whole. The process of dynamic clustering algorithm is the fuzzy set in the Cartesian product set $Y \times V$ of fuzzy relation R, so the definition and properties of fuzzy set operation are also fully applicable to fuzzy relation. Let R, S be the fuzzy relation from set Y to V, then for any $(x, y) \in Y \times V$, there are the following operations:

The "union operation" of R and S is recorded as RUS, and the membership function is defined as:

$$\mu_{RYS}(x, y) = \mu_R(x, y) \vee \mu_s(x, y) \tag{1}$$

The "intersection operation" of R and S is recorded as RIS, and the membership function is defined as:

$$\mu_{RIS}(x, y) = \mu_R(x, y) \wedge \mu_s(x, y) \tag{2}$$

The "complement operation" of R and S is recorded as $\sim R$, and the membership function is defined as:

$$\mu_{\sim R}(x, y) = 1 - \mu_R(x, y) \tag{3}$$

In this way, a one-to-one correspondence is established between the general relation and the Boolean matrix, and a one-to-one correspondence is established between the fuzzy relation and the fuzzy matrix. Therefore, in the future, the corresponding fuzzy relationship and fuzzy matrix are always regarded as the same, and because the fuzzy matrix is more intuitive and convenient for operation, the fuzzy relationship is always transformed into fuzzy matrix.

After the completion of this teaching resource corpus, it will have the following characteristics: ① authenticity. The teaching resource corpus can present real language examples and vivid classroom teaching situations including native speakers and non-native speakers, which makes the teaching resource corpus authentic. ② Dynamic. Many corpora of the teaching resource corpus are not only derived from the teaching classroom, but also applied to students' teaching. They are both results and materials and can be used repeatedly, which makes the teaching resource corpus dynamic. Not only the content can be updated dynamically, but also the retrieval results can be presented dynamically. ③ It realizes the four changes in teaching. In terms of teaching methods, from theoretical teaching to teaching in practice and practice in teaching; The teaching process is from teacher teaching to task-based teaching; Students' role from passive learning to active practice and reflection; The role of teachers is from main speaker to leading.

3.2 Application Ideas

Finally, the design and construction of teaching resource corpus should be applied, that is, it should be applied to the teaching of Chinese international education. The application idea of teaching resource corpus is to carefully distinguish the differences in the content setting of various professional courses before application, and realize the application of teaching resource corpus in batches. According to the nature of each professional course, we can take the lead in using the teaching resource corpus in the courses with high practical requirements, further expand it to the courses combining theory and practice, and finally extend it to the courses with strong theoretical requirements, so as to realize the full coverage of the teaching resource corpus in the whole undergraduate professional courses of Chinese international education. The design idea of Chinese semantic tendency corpus follows the "language subjective multi-dimensional description system" constructed by us. The multi-dimensional description system of language subjectivity is an intermediate "interface" guided by the theory of language subjectivity and oriented to the application of text subjectivity analysis, cohesion theory and application. It is connected with various linguistic theories and various subjective analysis. It aims to provide a unified framework for subjective analysis at different language levels, different granularity and different application purposes Cross language description standards. The system is represented by six dimensions: category, degree, form, component, relevance and model. Each dimension reflects an attribute of language subjectivity and also represents a kind of research perspective, covering various sub tasks that are being solved by the current academic circles and may be carried out in the future. The relationship between the main annotation elements of the semantic tendency of Chinese corpus is shown in Fig. 3.

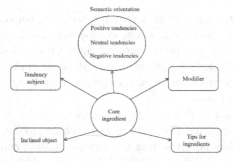

Fig. 3. Relationship between main annotation elements of semantic tendency in Chinese Corpus

In the application, the four sub-corpora should be focused on each other, and practical and effective application should be carried out in the corresponding links of each professional course. For example, using the Chinese teaching material library can consolidate and practice the knowledge of Chinese ontology, and help students design the content details of teaching plans and courseware; using the classroom teaching corpus can carry out observation, discussion and comparison of different teaching contents and teaching methods, and help students understand when they will teach in the future. Possible situations and difficulties; the use of the learner corpus can be used to analyze Chinese learner biases and help students determine the key and difficult points of teaching; use the Chinese teaching material library, learner corpus and resource expansion library to carry out group discussions and task-driven, so that Students "do it by hand, really practice", design, discuss, speak, comment and give feedback on a certain teaching topic step by step and plan, and the formed courseware, lesson plans and videos can be used as the corpus of the new classroom teaching corpus. After the application, it is necessary to understand the feedback of students in time and improve it accordingly. Let students learn and use the corpus of teaching resources in different professional courses, and even participate in the construction of the corpus, and accumulate some opinions and suggestions in the process. Correspondingly expand and adjust the teaching resource corpus.

4 Conclusions

The practical significance of Chinese international education is self-evident, which should be paid attention to. In the actual work, we need to clarify the existing deficiencies, take perfect countermeasures in combination with specific needs, better promote the international education of Chinese, improve the work level, and enhance the degree and influence of opening to the outside world. At present, all parties need to make efforts to cultivate Chinese talents who can adapt to the difficulties of international cooperation and realize the sustainable development of Chinese education. From the perspective of curriculum construction and teaching, this paper attempts to build a teaching resource corpus including four sub Corpora: Chinese teaching material database, classroom teaching corpus, learner corpus and resource expansion database Through a series of measures and adjustments during and after application, this teaching resource corpus is applied to the teaching of Chinese international education courses, so as to improve students' professional ability, especially Chinese teaching practice ability. It is hoped that our idea can provide new ideas and means for the in-depth development of the undergraduate major of Chinese international education.

References

1. McCrohon, M., Nyland, B.: The perceptions of commoditisation and internationalisation of higher education in Australia: an interview study of Chinese international students and their lecturers. Asia Pac. Educ. Rev. **19**(1), 17–26 (2018). https://doi.org/10.1007/s12564-018-9515-z
2. Lee, W.S.: Circulating east to east: understanding the push–pull factors of Chinese students studying in Korea. J. Stud. Int. Educ. **21**(2), 102831531769754 (2017)
3. Liu, W., Lin, X.: Meeting the needs of Chinese international students: is there anything we can learn from their home system? J. Stud. Int. Educ. **20**(4), 357–370 (2016)
4. Zhou, J., Zhou, S., Huang, C., et al.: Effectiveness of problem-based learning in Chinese pharmacy education: a meta-analysis. BMC Med. Educ. **16**(1), 23 (2016)
5. Chunming, W.M., Harrison, R., Macintyre, R., et al.: Burnout in medical students: a systematic review of experiences in Chinese medical schools. BMC Med. Educ. **17**(1), 217 (2017)
6. Howard, C., Eugenio, B.D., Jordan, P., et al.: Exploring initiative as a signal of knowledge co-construction during collaborative problem solving. Cogn. Sci. **41**(6), 1422 (2017)
7. Harmsen, R., Braband, G.: The OECD and higher education policy: agenda-setting, organizational dynamics and the construction of convening authority. High Educ. Pol. **34**(3), 582–602 (2021)

8. Liu, Z., Ting, K.F.: Deconstruction and reconstruction of legal education in China: legitimacy and diffusion of an academic discipline from 1949 to 2012. Comp. Educ. Rev. **61**(3), 000 (2017)
9. Wei, Y., Miraglia, S.: Organizational culture and knowledge transfer in project-based organizations: theoretical insights from a Chinese construction firm. Int. J. Project Manage. **35**(4), 71–585 (2017)
10. Liu, Q., Wang, S., Zhang, W., et al.: China's municipal public infrastructure: estimating construction levels and investment efficiency using the entropy method and a DEA model. Habitat Int. **64**, 59–70 (2017)
11. Li, C.-T., Ran, Y.-P.: Self-professional identity construction through other-identity deconstruction in Chinese televised debating discourse. J. Pragm. **94**, 47–63 (2016)

Construction of English Word Collocation Error Analysis System Based on Fuzzy Clustering Algorithm

Wenjia Ma[1]([✉]), Zhang Xiaoying[2], and Jian Xi[2]

[1] Sichuan University Jinjiang College, Meishan 620860, Sichuan, China
18273449@qq.com
[2] Zibo Normal College, Zibo 255130, Shandong, China

Abstract. Collocation is a central aspect of vocabulary learning. Collocation can broaden and deepen the understanding of vocabulary. In English learning, learners should pay attention to the characteristics of words in different contexts that are arranged and combined in different forms, their co-occurrence relationship and the fixed semantic relationship formed. This paper proposes an optimization design scheme of English word collocation error analysis system based on FCM (Fuzzy c-means) arithmetic. The English word collocation system is constructed by using classification analysis. The simulation results show that the arithmetic has a certain accuracy, which is 7.34% higher than the traditional arithmetic. Vocabulary plays an important role in language teaching and word collocation plays an important role in vocabulary teaching, which is the most difficult to master. Core vocabulary is the focus of English teaching. Students should not only master the basic usage of core vocabulary, but also master the collocation habits of these words. Effective teaching of vocabulary collocation can not only improve pupils' English level, but also improve the quality of English teaching.

Keywords: Fuzzy c-means algorithm · English words · Mismatching

1 Introduction

With the development of corpus linguistics, more new approaches to the study of collocation have been opened up, and a set of research ways and means have been formed, which will greatly enrich the theory of collocation [1]. The collocation of words can be divided into different types according to different principles. According to the nature of collocation, it can be divided into grammatical collocation and lexical collocation; According to the part of speech of the dominant words in collocation, it can be divided into noun collocation, verb collocation, adjective collocation, etc.; According to the number of collocation components, it can be divided into simple collocation and consistent collocation; According to the necessity of collocation, it can be divided into necessary collocation and unnecessary collocation; According to the restrictions on the choice of lexical collocation, it can be divided into free collocation, restrictive collocation, fixed

© ICST Institute for Computer Sciences, Social Informatics and Telecommunications Engineering 2024
Published by Springer Nature Switzerland AG 2024. All Rights Reserved
Y. Zhang and N. Shah (Eds.): BigIoT-EDU 2023, LNICST 584, pp. 287–296, 2024.
https://doi.org/10.1007/978-3-031-63142-9_29

collocation, etc. [2]. English collocation is an important part of English vocabulary learning [3]. The real definition of a word's meaning should be the combination of its referential meaning and collocation scope [4]. Learning a word without knowing its collocation range is not really the word "know" or "master" [5]. Therefore, the mastery of collocation knowledge directly affects the quality of English vocabulary learning and the improvement of English vocabulary ability.

Collocation is a phenomenon that is "ready-made, observable, some words and other words frequently appear together in the natural language environment". It is not logic and any rules that determine collocation, but language habits [6]. These characteristics of word collocation create insurmountable obstacles for second language learners: the key is not which words can replace which words, but which words usually appear in front of or behind which words [7]. Collocation is habit, and it is an unconscious habit of native speakers. Cluster analysis is a clear way to divide the characteristic attributes of objects. It strictly divides each object to be identified into a certain class, which has the property of either or. Therefore, the category boundaries of this classification are clear [8]. Fuzzy clustering analysis expands the value of membership relationship from $\{0,1\}$ binary logic to $[0,1]$ interval, so as to more reasonably represent the intermediary between things [9]. Because FCM obtains the uncertainty degree of the sample belonging to each category, it expresses the "this and that" nature of the sample category, that is, the fuzziness of the sample to the subordination relationship different from that of the same category, and the description and expression of the real world are more reasonable, which has been greatly developed in the theory of cluster analysis. In view of the advantages of FCM, this paper adopts the way of individual analysis function in FCM in order to reduce the execution cost of the arithmetic.

There may be many reasons that affect the collocation of English words, but it can be said that the iconicity of prophecy, conceptual categorization and conceptual metaphor are absolutely the ways, means and mechanisms of different English word collocation [10]. Therefore, English as a foreign language teaching starts from the pupils' cognition and concepts, to grasp how English gives concepts to things, how to use image language to reproduce life, and how to express oneself through metaphor. In a sense, learning a language is learning to use the language to recognize the world from a new perspective. When English cognitive ability is improved and English is learned well, the problem of collocation is naturally solved. Vocabulary learning should not be isolated. Vocabulary learning should combine cognitive process, concept composition and concept decomposition process, understand the composition and structure of concepts, and master the collocation knowledge of words. In this paper, a feature reconstruction model of English collocation error analysis and optimization design system is established. Its innovation lies in:

(1) In this paper, the way of individual analysis function in FCM is used to reduce the execution cost of the arithmetic.
(2) This paper constructs the key features of the English collocation error analysis and optimization design system, and uses the analysis way to realize the optimization design and identification of English collocation error analysis.

The research framework of this paper is as follows:

The first section is the beginning. It mainly describes the research background and value of the subject, and puts forward the research purpose, way and innovation of this paper. The second section describes the subject literature, summarizes it and puts forward research ideas. The third section is the research way, which mainly combines the analysis way and FCM way to optimize the design of the project. The fourth section is the experimental part. This part has carried on the experimental verification in the data set, and analyzed the performance of the model. Section V, conclusion and outlook. This part mainly reviews the main contents and results of this study, summarizes the research conclusions and points out the direction of further research.

2 Methodology

2.1 The Basic Framework of English Collocation Analysis

In order to obtain large-scale collocations and their real linguistic environment information, we must obtain collocations from large-scale corpora. In order to improve the accuracy of obtaining collocations, it is also necessary to find ways on the corpus itself. Generally speaking, the deeper the corpus is processed, the deeper and more accurate the relevant research based on the corpus will be. The segmentation or part of speech tagging of the corpus is only a shallow processing way of the corpus. In order to improve the accuracy of collocation acquisition, we should consider using the corpus that has been deeply processed. The use of syntactic analysis corpus to obtain collocations has theoretical basis. When using word segmentation or part of speech tagging corpus to obtain collocations, only the co-occurrence information of words is often considered, and the available corpus knowledge can only be limited to the word level. In the syntactic analysis corpus, there is not only knowledge at the word level, but also knowledge at the grammatical level, that is, at the syntactic level. As long as this knowledge can be used properly, the accuracy and efficiency of collocation acquisition will be greatly improved. The results of syntactic analysis cannot be 100% correct, but the same parts of multiple syntactic analysis results are often correct analysis results, or at least highly reliable analysis results. With this idea, you can first adjust the results of different versions of syntactic analysis to make them uniform in format for mutual comparison; Then compare with each other and keep the same analysis results; Finally, in the syntactic analysis results with high reliability obtained after comparison, according to certain acquisition ways and acquisition principles, we can get the word collocation. The specific acquisition process is shown in Fig. 1.

Generally speaking, English syntactic analysis can be divided into two ways: one is phrase structure analysis, that is, sentence is divided into phrases to analyze the hierarchical relationship between sentence phrases. The other is dependency structure analysis, that is, to analyze the dependency relationship between sentences and words. Phrase structure analysis and dependency structure analysis are the two most widely studied grammar systems in the field of syntactic analysis. Dependency grammar reveals its syntactic structure by analyzing the dependency relationship between the components in a language unit. It claims that the core verb in a sentence is the central component that dominates other components, but it is not dominated by any other component itself. All the dominated components are subordinate to the dominator in a certain dependency

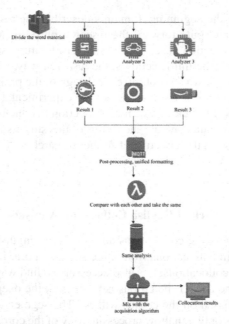

Fig. 1. Acquisition process of large-scale collocations

relationship. The basic unit of the dependency tree is the binary dependency relationship. The dependency relationship is a directional or asymmetric relationship, that is, one of the two words is the dominant word, and the arrow on the arc indicates this directivity. Compared with phrase structure parsing, dependency relation can clearly indicate the dominant relationship between words, and can easily develop into semantic dependency description. In recent years, researchers at home and abroad have completed the corresponding English tree bank for phrase structure analysis and dependency structure analysis. Different analysis systems have different tree base annotation ways. Tree base can be roughly divided into two categories according to the analysis system: phrase structure tree base and dependency structure tree base. The English tree library of commonly used phrase structures is the Pennsylvania tree library. The structure is shown in Fig. 2.

2.2 Translation Correction and Optimization of English Word Collocation Errors Based on Fuzzy Clustering

Due to the lack of relevant nonverbal information for language structure learning, the limited exposure to foreign languages, and the strong tendency of the brain to use previous language learning experience. Therefore, the mother tongue knowledge, including the non linguistic information matching with the mother tongue, will inevitably be transferred to fill the gap, which is the main reason for mother tongue interference and the main obstacle to foreign language learning. When pupils are at the primary stage of English learning, they will rely more on the mother tongue model to think and express.

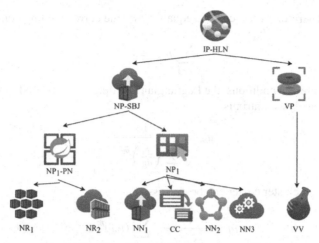

Fig. 2. Marking form of Pennsylvania tree library

Chinese pupils are prone to make Chinglish mistakes because of the influence of Chinese expression habits. For example, the problem of adjective collocation is mainly due to the interference of mother tongue. According to the collocation of Chinese, go to English to find the words that seem to correspond.

In the process of analysis and clustering, its essential meaning is data mining of cache package. Clustering arithmetic is an important part of data mining. In the traditional system, when faced with a large number of word translation cache packets, the clustering arithmetic has a large resource overhead, resulting in low efficiency of the clustering arithmetic. The system in this paper adopts the FCM arithmetic. Each translation cache sample $x_k(k = 1, 2, ..., n)$ in the set X has a number of characteristics, and the characteristic set is represented as $x_k(x_{k1}, x_{k2}, ..., x_{ks})$. The word translation cache sample object dataset X to be clustered is divided into c clusters. In order to describe the situation of FCM, it is necessary to introduce a fuzzy classification matrix $U = [\mu_{ik}]_{c \cdot n}, \mu_{ik} \in [0, 1], \mu_{ik}$ to indicate that the sample object x_k belongs to the i cluster classification membership function. Suppose $X = \{x_i, i = 1, 2, ..., n\}$ represents the data set composed of the word translation cache sample objects to be clustered.

Based on the above analysis, it is necessary to find more reasonable clustering division results from many possible clusters, so it is necessary to establish isolated FCM objective criteria and correlation functions:

$$\min J_m(U, P) = \sum_{k=2}^{n} \sum_{i=1}^{c} (\mu_{ik})^m (d_{ik})^2 \tag{1}$$

In formula (1), P represents the representative vector of each cluster class, and $P = [p_i]$ is the cluster center; m represents the weighted number, which is generally 2; d_{ik} represents the Euclidean distance between sample object x_k and cluster center p_i in each cluster. Therefore, for the above equation, set the corresponding constraints:

$$\sum_{i=1}^{c} \mu_{ik} = 1 \qquad (2)$$

Under the above conditions, the Lagrangian multiplier way is used to solve, and the optimal FCM analysis matrix is:

$$u_{ik} = \frac{1}{\sum_{j=1}^{c} \left(\frac{d_{ik}}{d_{jk}}\right)^{\frac{2}{m-1}}} \qquad (3)$$

The obtained cluster center can be expressed as:

$$p_i = \frac{1}{\sum_{k=1}^{c} (u_{ik})^m} \sum_{k-1}^{n} (u_{ik})^m x_k \qquad (4)$$

In the formula, m represents the weight. It can be seen from the above two formulas that FCM is mainly solved by iteration. The flow of FCM analysis is shown in Fig. 3.

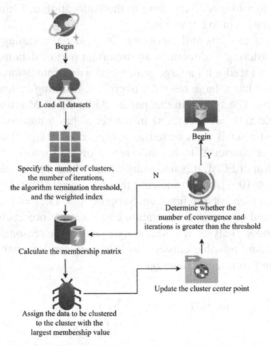

Fig. 3. Flow of FCM arithmetic

In the process of Fig. 3, set the corresponding parameters from all the loaded datasets to be clustered, calculate the center distance and membership degree and assign them to the corresponding clusters to complete the optimization of FCM.

3   Result Analysis and Discussion

The analysis and discussion of collocation errors show that vocabulary collocation learning is very important. Learners should not only master the correct usage of these words, but also master the collocation habit of words in the target language. The focus of English vocabulary learning is the core vocabulary, and the collocation teaching of English words should also focus on the collocation of the core vocabulary. Corpus index can provide authentic and reliable contextual information, so that teachers and pupils can verify whether the collocations used in translation practice are authentic in real language applications. The establishment of the corpus provides an environment for the realization of student-centered teaching. Teachers should mobilize the pupils' subjective initiative to enable pupils to search, analyze and summarize the relevant collocations of the learned phrases in the corpus outside class, so that they can understand and master the knowledge they want to acquire in an exploratory way, thus deepening the impression of the knowledge they have learned.

There are multiple data items in the collocation database. If you focus on the association between any two items, the number is too large, and every two data items are associated and compared, which is a combination problem in probability statistics. Secondly, the association between some data items is actually a reflection of the association between other data items, which will repeat statistics. Sometimes there is no association between two data items, such as "part of speech distribution" and collocation distance ". Based on these two considerations, two data items that are the most important and directly related to collocation in the collocation database are selected: collocation frequency and collocation type. Focusing on these two data items, we focus on the correlation between these two data items and other data items. Through the association analysis between the data items of the collocation library, we hope to achieve the goal of more comprehensive description of the appearance of the collocation library and more accurate analysis of the characteristics of the collocation library.

Association analysis of collocation frequency and word frequency: as in individual analysis, the number of collocations is divided into 15 intervals, and the frequency of collocations in each interval is counted according to the location. Figure 4 is to more intuitively reflect the relationship between collocation times and word frequency. The abscissa is the interval of collocation times. The two curves in the figure represent the trend of word frequency at two positions of collocation.

It can be clearly seen in Fig. 4 that the frequency of words in the two positions is also increasing with the increasing number of collocations, and by comparing the two trend curves, it can be seen that the change trend of the frequency of words in the two positions is similar. This shows that in the collocation library, collocations composed of high-frequency words often occur many times, and occasionally occur collocations are often composed of low-frequency words. This rule applies to both the first word and the second word of the collocation.

Correlation analysis of collocation times and collocation distance: the collocation times are divided into 15 intervals, and the collocation distance is averaged. In addition, the proportion of adjacent collocations is calculated, that is, the number of adjacent collocations is divided by the number of all collocations. In Fig. 5, the abscissa is the

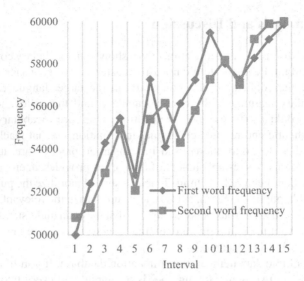

Fig. 4. Trend of word frequency

collocation degree interval, and the two curves represent the change trend of collocation distance and adjacent collocation proportion respectively.

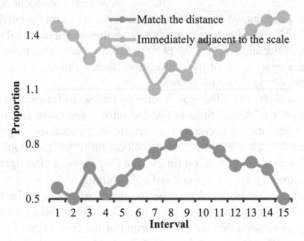

Fig. 5. Change trend of adjacent proportion

In the 15 collocation frequency intervals, the average value of collocation distance does not exceed, which also shows that the number of adjacent collocations in the collocation library is absolutely superior, which is consistent with the analysis of collocation distance in individual analysis. The two curves in Fig. 5 tend to be flat with little fluctuation, which indicates that with the increase of collocation times, collocation distance and proportion of adjacent collocation have not changed significantly. The collocation distance and the proportion of adjacent collocations are not affected by the number of collocations; It is not that the more collocation times, the greater or smaller the collocation distance.

4 Conclusions

This paper proposes an optimization design scheme of English word collocation error analysis system based on FCM arithmetic. The English word collocation system is constructed by using classification analysis way. The simulation results show that the arithmetic has a certain accuracy, which is 7.34% higher than the traditional arithmetic. This result fully shows that the way is effective in the analysis, recognition and processing of collocation errors. English word collocation is actually a habitual word formation between the two poles of idiom and free vocabulary combination, which also explains why English second language learners will never catch up with English native speakers unless they have the opportunity to live in an English environment. The analysis and discussion of collocation errors show that the impact of Chinese on learning English collocation is disastrous. At the same time, educational institutions should re-examine the use of bilingual dictionaries and textbook models. The mutual conversion arithmetic between dependency analysis and phrase analysis is not accurate enough, which affects the alignment of syntactic analysis results. The comparison arithmetic of multiple parsing results is not perfect, so the similarity comparison mechanism of parsing results needs to be added to filter out incorrect parsing results.

References

1. Pustokhina, I.V., Pustokhin, D.A., Lydia, E.L.: Energy efficient neuro-fuzzy cluster based topology construction with metaheuristic route planning algorithm for unmanned aerial vehicles. Comput. Netw. **2021**(4), 196 (2021)
2. Xiangping, Z., Liu, J., Xiao, Q.: Web services clustering with multi-functionality based on LDA and fuzzy C-means arithmetic. J. Central South Univ. **2018**(5), 78 (2018)
3. Gao, W., Zhang, Q., Lu, Z.: Modelling and application of fuzzy adaptive minimum spanning tree in tourism agglomeration area division. Knowl.-Based Syst. **143**(1), 317 (2018)
4. Esmaeilzadeh, A., Shahriar, K.: Optimized fuzzy cmeans - fuzzy covariance - fuzzy maximum likelihood estimation clustering method based on deferential evolutionary optimization algorithm for identification of rock mass discontinuities sets. J. Neurosurg. Sci. **2019**(2), 63 (2019)
5. Huang, W.: Fuzzy clustering-based neural networks modelling reinforced with the aid of support vectors-based clustering and regularization technique. Neurocomputing **2022**(14), 482 (2022)
6. Sartajvir, S., Rajneesh, T., Engineering, E.C.: Response of FCM on different threshold determination arithmetics in spectral change vector analysis over Western Himalaya, India. J. Mountain Sci. **2017**(4), 53 (2017)
7. Surono, S., Putri, R.D.A.: Optimization of fuzzy c-means clustering algorithm with combination of Minkowski and Chebyshev distance using principal component analysis. Int. J. Fuzzy Syst. **2021**(1), 23 (2021)

8. Chan, C.-C., Lin, C.C.K., Ju, M.S.: Neuro-fuzzy system combined with clustering algorithm for continuous ankle angle estimation from Tibial and peroneal electroneurograms in functional electrical stimulation. J. Chin. Soc. Mech. Eng. Ser. C Trans. Chin. Soc. Mech. Eng. **38**(1), 13 (2017)
9. Aissa, M., Bouhdid, B., Mnaouer, A.B.: SOFCluster: safety-oriented, fuzzy logic-based clustering scheme for vehicular ad hoc networks. Trans. Emerg. Telecommun. Technol. **2022**(3), 33 (2022)
10. Hao, Z., Liu, X.: Mechanical properties of loess in mountainous area based on FCM and construction of basketball venues. Arab. J. Geosci. **2021**(24), 14 (2021)

Early Warning Mechanism of College Students' Psychological Crisis Based on Clustering Extraction Algorithm

Hailan Lu[✉] and Wang Mingjian

Nanning University, Nanning 530200, Guangxi, China
1797850452@qq.com

Abstract. This article proposes a psychological crisis warning mechanism for college students based on clustering extraction algorithm. This mechanism monitors and analyzes the psychological state of college students, and uses clustering algorithms to classify students according to their psychological state, thereby achieving early warning of psychological crises. The specific implementation process includes three steps: first, collect students' psychological state data; Then, use clustering algorithms to divide students into different groups; Finally, evaluate the psychological crisis risk of students based on the characteristic values of each group, and provide timely intervention for high-risk students. The experimental results indicate that this mechanism can effectively improve the accuracy of early warning for college students' psychological crisis, and provide timely help and support for students' psychological problems. This study has certain reference value for improving the mental health level of college students.

Keywords: Clustering algorithm · College students · Psychological crisis · early warning mechanism

1 Introduction

Psychological crisis is becoming increasingly common among college students, which may be caused by factors such as academic pressure, interpersonal problems, and career development anxiety. If not intervened in a timely manner, these crises may lead to mental illness, suicide, and other negative consequences. Therefore, establishing an effective psychological crisis warning mechanism is very important.

Now, with the advancement of technology and the application of intelligent algorithms, it is possible to use machine learning methods to achieve psychological crisis warning. Among them, the psychological crisis warning model based on clustering extraction algorithm has been widely applied in the college student population. This algorithm can divide individuals into different clusters based on the similarity in the dataset, thereby identifying students with potential psychological problems [1]. Psychological crisis is becoming increasingly common among college students, especially in

© ICST Institute for Computer Sciences, Social Informatics and Telecommunications Engineering 2024
Published by Springer Nature Switzerland AG 2024. All Rights Reserved
Y. Zhang and N. Shah (Eds.): BigIoT-EDU 2023, LNICST 584, pp. 297–304, 2024.
https://doi.org/10.1007/978-3-031-63142-9_30

the current context of the epidemic. In order to timely detect and intervene in these psychological problems, it is necessary to establish an efficient psychological crisis warning mechanism. The method based on clustering extraction algorithm can analyze and classify a large amount of psychological data, thereby helping schools or social institutions discover psychological problems more quickly and take targeted measures.

This article aims to explore the concepts, background, and related work involved in the clustering extraction algorithm based psychological crisis warning mechanism for college students. Firstly, we will introduce the current situation of psychological crisis among college students, including its causes and impacts. Then, we will explain the core concepts and applications of clustering extraction algorithms. Next, we will discuss the application of this algorithm in college students' psychological crisis warning and introduce existing empirical research. Finally, we will briefly summarize the advantages and disadvantages of this algorithm, as well as future development directions and challenges.

Through reading this article, readers will understand the basic principles and applications of clustering extraction algorithm, as well as how to use this algorithm to assist in psychological crisis warning and intervention for college students. In addition, it will also recognize some possible limitations and limitations of this algorithm, in order to provide inspiration and guidance for future research in this field.

2 Related Work

2.1 The Concept of College Students' Psychological Crisis

The psychological crisis centered around college students refers to the difficulties and pressures they encounter in learning, life, emotions, interpersonal communication, and other aspects, which cannot be resolved, leading to serious abnormalities in their psychological state and affecting their physical health and normal learning, work, and other aspects. These difficulties and pressures include but are not limited to the following aspects [2]:

1. Learning pressure. The content of college students' learning is relatively specialized and difficult, with many requirements and tasks to complete, making them prone to stress, especially during exams.
2. Life pressure. The living conditions of college students may not be as comfortable and convenient as living at home. In addition, factors such as heavy workload, accumulated negative emotions, and communication difficulties can easily form various life pressures, leading to the occurrence of psychological crises.
3. Emotional distress. The emotional aspect is quite complex, including psychological emotional distress and external emotional pressure. For example, issues with love, breakups or breakdowns, difficulties making friends, etc.
4. Tight interpersonal relationships. College students come into contact with various groups of people in the new environment, and their interpersonal relationships are relatively complex, including those with family, classmates, teachers, etc. These aspects are prone to various conflicts and contradictions. If not handled properly, it can easily lead to psychological crisis.

In short, the psychological crisis of college students is a complex of multifaceted difficulties and pressures, which can be resolved through appropriate psychological counseling and assistance, helping college students maintain mental health and enhance their ability to cope with stress.

2.2 The Characteristics of College Students' Psychological Crisis

The psychological crisis of college students has the following main characteristics:

1. Age characteristics. The occurrence of psychological crisis among college students has age characteristics. In this important stage of human life development, college students are more likely to experience psychological crisis when facing various contradictions and challenges in work, life, and interpersonal relationships.
2. The influence of multiple factors. The psychological crisis of college students is a composite effect of multiple factors, caused by the interaction of multiple factors, including family environment, social culture, etc. Among them, factors such as learning, life, emotions, and interpersonal relationships have a greater impact.
3. Polymorphic manifestations. There are various manifestations of psychological crisis among college students, including anxiety, depression, insomnia, stress, inferiority complex, loneliness, autism, and other different types of psychological problems, which also pose challenges for psychological intervention [3].
4. Hidden characteristics. College students often hide their emotions in their hearts during psychological crises, unwilling to reveal them. Faced with emotions such as depression and frustration, most people tend to choose introversion, which also increases the difficulty of intervention.
5. Concentration during high incidence period. The high incidence period of psychological crisis among college students is generally at the nodes of enrollment, facing college exams, and finding a job. At this time, college students are prone to emotional fluctuations, which is particularly important for psychological crisis prevention and intervention.

In summary, the psychological crisis of college students has obvious characteristics such as age characteristics, multifactorial influences, polymorphic manifestations, hidden characteristics, and concentration during the high incidence period, which increases the necessity of paying attention to and paying attention to the psychological health of college students. The basic student information management process is shown in Fig. 1.

The focus is mainly distributed in: (1) Internet addiction student group; (2) Study-weary student group; (3) Group with poor interpersonal relationship; (4) Group with confused career planning; (5) Family background Poverty, heavy financial burden, and deep feeling of inferiority; (6) Students who are not suitable for their majors; (7) Those who demand too much of themselves; (8) Students who have difficulty in learning, are warned of their studies, or even change grades; (9) Groups with a history of mental health diseases; (10) Groups of students suffering from serious physical illnesses, personal suffering, and long treatment cycles; (11) Groups of students who are too introverted, withdrawn, and lack social support; (12) Groups of students whose families undergo major changes, encounter crises, are stimulated by natural or social accidents, etc. Particular attention should be paid to students whose multiple characteristics coexist [4].

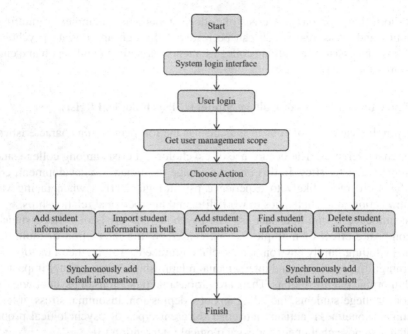

Fig. 1. Flow chart of student basic information management

Students with poor tolerance for setbacks and cognitive biases are at greater risk, and teachers should treat them as key targets for intervention.

3   Construction of Psychological Crisis Early Warning System Based on Big Data Technology

3.1   Collection of Psychological Early Warning Data

The collection of psychological warning data can be done through the following channels:

Survey questionnaire: The survey questionnaire can be distributed face-to-face and online to collect the psychological status and problems faced by college students, including anxiety, depression, stress, inferiority, and other aspects, providing objective data support for psychological warning. Psychological assessment: Psychological assessment can be conducted by professionals or by selecting some online psychological testing websites for reasonable psychological assessment, which can provide scientific, timely and convenient records for collecting psychological warning data. Monitoring and observation: Psychological warning data can also be collected through real-time monitoring and observation. For example, monitoring and observation can be conducted through aspects such as college student attendance, homework submission, and interpersonal communication. Frequent and abnormal psychological events and behaviors should be collected and analyzed. Social media: Nowadays, many college students like to use various social media tools, and these platforms can become important sources of collecting psychological warning data. Negative emotions such as self neglect and complaints may appear in college students' social media or recent updates, and integrating these data can also help improve the warning effect. Psychological counseling: Psychological counseling for college students is an important way to deal with various psychological problems. By recording the content and situation of college student counseling, effective psychological warning data can be obtained. Collecting and analyzing psychological warning data through the above channels can provide important support for psychological intervention, timely processing, and prevention of psychological problems. The data mining process is shown in Fig. 2.

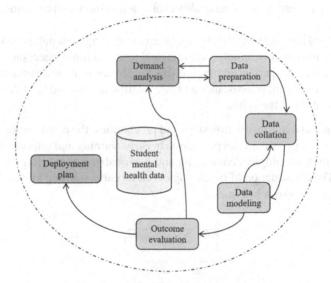

Fig. 2. Data mining process diagram

The reflection of the psychological committee members of the class. As a class psychological Committee member, you should know the students in the class better and care about their psychological status. Take Changsha University as an example, the psychological Committee member requires that the mood barometer of the students be handed in every week, and the information provided by the psychological Committee member is also a very important indicator. Investigation on mental health status of schools.

3.2 Construction of Psychological Crisis Early Warning System

System development: Develop, test, and accumulate experience based on system planning and design. This stage is actually to integrate the contents involved in the above stages and transform them into a usable psychological early warning system. For the technical development team, it is necessary to consider user interface, Data and information visualization display, alarm mechanism design and other aspects. System implementation: Conduct system implementation, user training, and dispatch of administrators and maintenance personnel. At the same time, continuous monitoring and adjustment are carried out as needed to continuously optimize the system.

During the system implementation process, the following key points need to be noted:

1. Protection of privacy: Psychological warning data involves user privacy, so when collecting and processing data, it is necessary to comply with relevant regulations and standards to protect user privacy from infringement.
2. Data quality: The accuracy, completeness, reliability, and other quality characteristics of data are closely related to the effectiveness of early warning. In order to ensure the quality characteristics of data, it is necessary to strengthen the review, screening, and filtering of data, establish a data quality evaluation system, and continuously improve data quality.
3. Psychological intervention: Psychological crisis warning does not mean solving problems. More importantly, timely psychological intervention is necessary. For students who have already experienced psychological problems or have entered a state of psychological crisis, timely assistance and intervention are needed to effectively prevent the deterioration of the crisis.

Through the above construction steps and precautions, the construction of a psychological crisis warning system can play a role in early warning and intervention, adapting to the needs of psychological counseling and personalized counseling services within universities.The construction of psychological crisis early warning system based on big data technology is shown in Fig. 3.

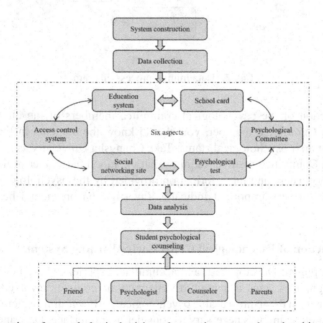

Fig. 3. Construction of a psychological crisis early warning system based on big data technology

Based on the collected data, use data mining techniques to analyze and model to predict the probability of students' psychological crisis. Usually, methods such as classification analysis are used to establish classification models through machine learning to predict whether students are in a state of psychological crisis.

Absolute distance:

$$D(X,Y) = \left\{ \sum_{i=1}^{k} |X_i - Y_i| \right\} \tag{1}$$

Xi, Yi represents the i attribute of sample X and the i attribute of sample Y respectively, K represents the number of attributes of the sample, and $D(X,Y)$ represents the distance between samples.

European distance:

$$D(X,Y) = \left\{ \sum_{i=1}^{k} |X_i - Y_i|^2 \right\}^{\frac{1}{2}} \tag{2}$$

Chebyshev distance:

$$D(X,Y) = \left\{ \sum_{i=1}^{k} |X_i - Y_i|^\infty \right\}^{\frac{1}{\infty}} \tag{3}$$

Mahalanobis distance:

$$D(X_i, X_j) = (X_i - X_j)\prime * S^{-1} * (X_i - X_j) \tag{4}$$

X_i and Y_j are vectors composed of M indexes of the i and j samples respectively, and S is the covariance of the sample matrix.

For the system after establishing warning rules, conducting actual effect testing and experimental verification is an important means to test the reliability, effectiveness, and accuracy of the warning system. When the warning results obtained by the system match the actual situation, the warning rules can be further optimized to increase the accuracy and timeliness of the warning.

4 Conclusion

The data fields that need to be processed for psychological crisis warning are very extensive, including students' learning, life, interpersonal relationships, and other aspects. Based on these data, data mining techniques can be used to establish a psychological crisis warning system. These data can come from personal information provided by students, as well as from staff such as teachers, counselors, and student service centers. Clean collected data, eliminate duplicate data, handle abnormal and missing data, and unify data formats. This ensures that the generated data is accurate and consistent, facilitating the use of data mining techniques for analysis and modeling.

Based on the collected data, use data mining techniques to analyze and model to predict the probability of students' psychological crisis. Usually, methods such as classification analysis are used to establish classification models through machine learning to predict whether students are in a state of psychological crisis. In summary, data mining technology can provide effective support for psychological crisis warning. A warning system is established based on students' learning, life, social and other aspects of data, providing real-time data for accurate warning and effective intervention based on data analysis.

References

1. Qudah, M.A., et al.: Psychological security, psychological loneliness, and age as the predictors of cyber-bullying among university students. Community Ment. Health J. **56**(3), 393–403 (2020)
2. Lannoy, S., et al.: Distinct psychological profiles among college students with substance use: a cluster analytic approach. Addict. Behav. **109**, 106477 (2020)
3. Kilgo, C.A., Mollet, A.L., Pascarella, E.T.: The estimated effects of college student involvement on psychological well-being. J. Coll. Stud. Dev. **57**(8), 1043–1049 (2016)
4. Wolff, J.M., Rospenda, K.M., Colaneri, A.S.: Sexual harassment, psychological distress, and problematic drinking behavior among college students: an examination of reciprocal causal relations. J. Sex Res. **54**(3), 1–12 (2017)

Design and Implementation of Multi-modal Teaching Resources Retrieval Algorithm Model Based on Random Forest

Yang Zhang[✉] and Xiuyan Song

Lanzhou Resources & Environment Voc-Tech University, Gansu, Lanzhou 730020, China
49361786@qq.com

Abstract. This article introduces the design and implementation of a multimodal teaching resource retrieval algorithm model based on random forests. With the continuous development of educational technology, the quantity and diversity of teaching resources are constantly increasing. How to efficiently retrieve and match resources that are suitable for teaching needs has become an important issue. This study proposes a multimodal teaching resource retrieval algorithm model based on random forests, aiming to provide accurate and personalized teaching resource recommendations. The algorithm model consists of the following main steps. Firstly, collect and organize characteristic data of teaching resources, such as keywords, themes, difficulty, etc. Then, based on the user's query conditions and needs, multiple feature vectors of different patterns are constructed and trained using the random forest algorithm. Random forest is an ensemble learning method that can effectively process data with multimodal features and generate accurate classification and recommendation results. During the training process, techniques such as cross validation and feature importance assessment are utilized to optimize and select models. The experimental results show that the multi-mode teaching resource retrieval algorithm model based on random forest has good performance in terms of accuracy and personalization.

Keywords: Random forest algorithm · Multimodal teaching · Teaching resource retrieval

1 Introduction

With the advent of the online learning era, utilizing online teaching resources on the Internet for learning has become a common trend [1]. These online teaching resource databases provide rich and diverse learning materials, but they also face the problem of information overload. In this case, machine learning algorithms have become an effective tool for providing personalized teaching resource recommendations. Supervised learning is a commonly used method in machine learning algorithms for solving classification and regression problems. In classification problems, we hope to predict the category of new samples based on existing training data; In regression problems, we

Y. Zhang and N. Shah (Eds.): BigIoT-EDU 2023, LNICST 584, pp. 305–314, 2024.
https://doi.org/10.1007/978-3-031-63142-9_31

hope to predict the values of new samples based on existing training data [2]. Classical algorithms such as support vector machine algorithms and decision tree algorithms are widely used in solving classification problems. However, these algorithms are usually single classifiers, prone to overfitting, and have certain limitations in improving performance. In order to solve these problems, ensemble learning algorithms have emerged [3]. The ensemble learning algorithm combines multiple base classifiers together to form a powerful ensemble classifier. This can compensate for the shortcomings of a single classifier, improve classification performance and generalization ability. Common ensemble learning algorithms include random forests, AdaBoost, and Bagging [4]. The random forest algorithm is based on decision trees and can effectively reduce overfitting risks by randomly selecting features and samples for modeling. The AdaBoost algorithm assigns a weight to each sample through iterative training and attempts to construct multiple weak classifiers to continuously improve overall classification performance [5]. The Bagging algorithm creates multiple training sets through self-service sampling and random feature selection, and votes or averages the results for final classification.

With the continuous development of educational resource bank, there is a lot of valuable educational information in it. However, these educational resources are in a scattered distribution state with different forms and contents [6]. Although it can point to the target through the search engine, it is not conducive to users' direct retrieval and use. At present, there are two types of online search: simple key field search and complex full-text search, both of which are logical operations based on keywords [7]. The quality of a search engine depends not only on its search speed, the quality of the information searched, but also on its user interface. The development of retrieval technology has gone through generations. It is generally believed in the world that the first generation of search engines mainly solve the problem of "searching all", while the second generation of search engines basically solve the problem of "searching all" and consider how to "searching accurately". However, the study requires the individual requirements of users as the evaluation standard, and the search engines are more intelligent and personalized [8]. It can automatically identify users' interests, and automatically correct and improve users' interests according to their usage habits, that is, it has self-learning function, which makes the search results more accurate and flexible [9]. This kind of search precision will inevitably lead to many high-quality resources being hidden in the database and unknown because of the lack of good information retrieval methods. As a classical ensemble learning algorithm, random forest used in various fields because of its easy understanding, strong adaptability and difficult over-fitting.

2 Method

2.1 Random Forest Algorithm

Traditional classification algorithms include multiple methods, among which decision tree and random forest algorithms are one of the most common and effective methods. Decision tree is a classification method based on a tree structure, which gradually divides the dataset into different features and ultimately assigns each leaf node to the corresponding category [10]. The process of establishing a decision tree is recursive, starting from the root node and dividing the dataset into smaller subsets, until the prede-termined termination conditions are reached (for example, the remaining samples belong to the same category or reach a certain depth limit). The pruning process of the decision tree is to prevent overfitting and optimize the structure and complexity of the decision tree through pruning operations.

The random forest algorithm is an ensemble learning method based on decision trees, which constructs multiple decision trees through random sampling and random feature selection, and combines them for classification [11]. In a random forest, each decision tree is constructed based on a subset of data obtained through bootstrap sampling, which means that there will be a small number of duplicate and absent samples in the training set of each decision tree. In the process of constructing a decision tree, random forest also introduces random feature selection, which means that each partitioning node only considers partial features, thereby increasing the diversity of the decision tree [12].

By combining the classification results of multiple decision trees, random forests can reduce the overfitting risk of a single decision tree, improve classification accuracy and stability. In a random forest, each decision tree can vote or average to make the final classification decision, thus obtaining a more reliable overall classification result. Ensemble learning methods for single classifier, serialization method are the two most common methods. Given the training data set $D = \{(x_1, y_1), (x_2, y_2), ..., (x_k, y_k),\}$ and a group of weak learning algorithms $H = \{h_1, h_2, ..., h_m\}$, The formula is as follows:

Majority voting principle:

$$H(x) = majority\{h_1(x) \mid i = 1, 2, ..., m\} \tag{1}$$

Average method:

$$H(x) = \frac{1}{m} \sum_{i-1}^{m} h_1(x) \tag{2}$$

AdaBoost is an ensemble learning algorithm used to solve classification problems. It iteratively trains multiple weak learners (classifiers) and weights them based on their performance to obtain a powerful ensemble model. The final prediction result is obtained by weighting and averaging the prediction results of each weak learner. These weights are usually determined based on the performance of weak learners (such as error rate), and better performing weak learners have larger weights [13]. By repeatedly adjusting sample weights and training weak learners, the AdaBoost algorithm can gradually improve the overall model performance and combine the weak learners into a strong learning model. It has good generalization ability and robustness when dealing with complex classification problems.

The formula describes the process of weighting and averaging the final results using the AdaBoost ensemble model. The prediction results of different weak learners are weighted based on their weights, and then summed to obtain the final result.

Weighted average method:

$$H(x) = \frac{1}{m} \sum_{i-1}^{m} w_1 h_1(x) \tag{3}$$

The uses majority voting principle to obtain the final result. RE construction process is shown in Fig. 1.

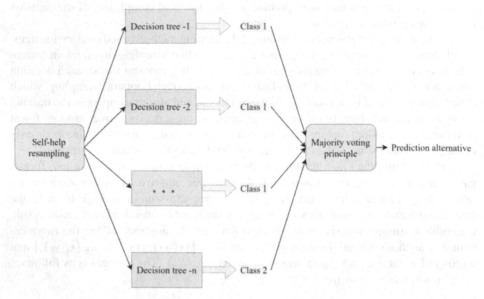

Fig. 1. Construction process of RF algorithm

As a single classifier decision model, decision trees do have some problems, including local optimal solutions, complex classification rules, and possible overfitting problems. The Random Forest algorithm, as a combination classifier, can effectively solve these problems. The random forest algorithm constructs a classification model by integrating multiple decision trees. To construct a random forest model, first generate, that is, each decision set [14]. The process of generating training sets is based on statistical sampling techniques, mainly including non reverse sampling and reverse. The random forest algorithm uses the Bagging method to generate a training set for each decision tree. The Bagging method is a sampling technique with put back sampling, which generates multiple training subsets from the original dataset. The number of generated training subsets decision trees in the random forest model, and the subset is approximately set size. By using the Bagging method to generate training subsets, the random forest model are independent and have low with each other, thus overfitting in the model.

The random forest model consists of multiple decision trees, each of which classifies the samples. The result is determined by voting based. After a majority vote, the classification result with the highest number of votes is obtained as the algorithm.

By integrating multiple decision trees and adopting voting decision rules, the random forest algorithm can overcome some problems of decision tree single classifier, such as local optimal solutions and complex classification rules. Moreover, since the tree is generated through the Bagging method and is independent of each other, it can reduce the risk of model overfitting. The of RF algorithm is shown in Fig. 2.

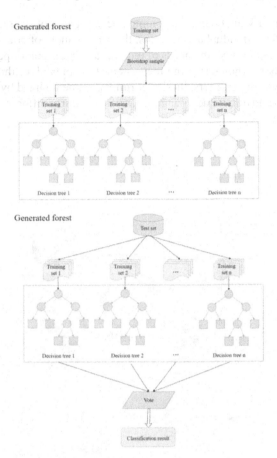

Fig. 2. RF algorithm

2.2   Multi-modal Teaching Resource Retrieval Algorithm Model

Every user has his own specific information needs when using the resource information base. The high matching degree is closer to learners' interest than the low matching degree. The application of personalized recommendation in the online learning environment is helpful to track the behaviors occurring in online learning sites, and to prompt learners to make improvements, put forward correct learning patterns and behaviors, or make them more suitable for the course content. For example, you can identify frequent access paths, never access paths, or a group of learners who follow these access paths. Using personalized recommendation in online learning environment is helpful to receive tips from online learning system, which may be due to similar behaviors of other "successful" learners. For example, the system may recommend some shortcuts derived from previous users' frequent visits to pages, or recommend some behaviors that can make similar learners more "successful". It is also very helpful if the system adapts the logical structure of course content to learners' learning pace, interests, or previous behaviors. In addition, the course content based on is not always presented and organized in an intuitive way. By analyzing the common access paths of course content pages or frequent changes of individual access paths, the arrangement of courses should be able to be identified or better meet the needs of individuals or a group of people. This should be taken into account when designing the system. Complex algorithms are transparent to users, but for system designers, these algorithms can be realized by pattern discovery with simple filters and direct query language, so as to control different levels of systems, as shown in Fig. 3.

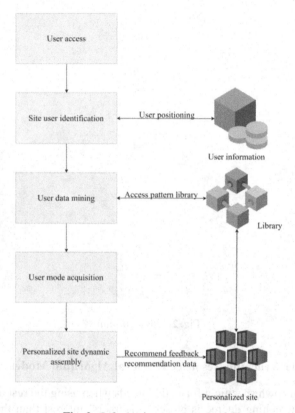

Fig. 3. Information resource model

Knowledge maps are generally and domain knowledge maps, while educational knowledge maps belong to the latter. There are many general knowledge maps, such as DBpedia, YAGO, Word Net, etc. in scientific research fields, Baidu's Intimate, etc. in engineering fields. Many domain knowledge maps have also been constructed, such as Geonames for geographical areas, and enterprise domain knowledge maps of "Tianyancha". Therefore, to a great extent, the traditional knowledge map only completes the collection and integration of written knowledge. For students, without the cooperation of multimedia resources such as pictures, audio and video, boring knowledge of words. However, multimedia information, such as pictures, audio and video, is of great help to students in understanding boring knowledge points.

Users, such as instructors, are allowed to simply express their requirements by specifying constraints and filters in the preprocessing stage, pattern discovery stage, or pattern evaluation stage. Defining filters in the pre-processing stage will definitely reduce the search space, and adding constraints in mining can not only speed up the process, but also control the discovered patterns. Adding constraints in the evaluation stage helps to select the required patterns from a large number of extracted patterns. In the whole data mining stage, restrictions and controls are added to allow interaction between data mining and restriction specifications, which restrict that the discovered patterns must be related to the current recommended task.

This paper attempts to apply multimodal knowledge map to teaching. Specifically, the application of multimodal knowledge map to teaching has at least the following three advantages: (1) By showing the hierarchical relationship and connection concise and clear knowledge network map can be formed. This kind of graph structure can help students quickly sort out the relationships and differences among various knowledge points, and it is very helpful to master the overall structure of the course. (2) Learning from the implementation principle of personalized recommendation, by modeling learners' interest and resource information respectively, then matching them, an accurate retrieval algorithm of educational resources based on learners' interest model matching is realized.

Pattern discovery algorithm is used to discover trends and relationships in usage data. These constraints are used to guide the process of knowledge discovery and limit the search space. Statement constraints are the only interaction between users and data mining models, so users don't need to master complex knowledge of data mining algorithms.

3 Reference Text and Citations

The results of feature selection analysis show that in the random forest model, student behavior characteristics have a significant impact on the prediction results. Especially, features such as "student classroom activities" and "small class test results" have a high weight on the predicted results. This indicates that teachers can stimulate students' enthusiasm and promote classroom interaction to stimulate their interest in the course. In addition, strengthening regular course exams can also encourage students to study harder. These findings provide guidance for teachers to improve students' learning experience and performance.

In addition to random forests, other machine learning algorithms such as support vector machines, logistic regression, etc. can also be tried. Different models may have different evaluation methods for the importance of features, providing more comprehensive feature selection results. Based on the understanding of the problem and domain knowledge, feature engineering can be carried out to create more meaningful and useful features. This helps to improve the predictive performance of the model and the effectiveness of feature selection. By comprehensively analyzing the results of feature selection and combining actual situations and domain knowledge, teachers can develop targeted teaching strategies and measures to further improve students' learning level and grades (Fig. 4).

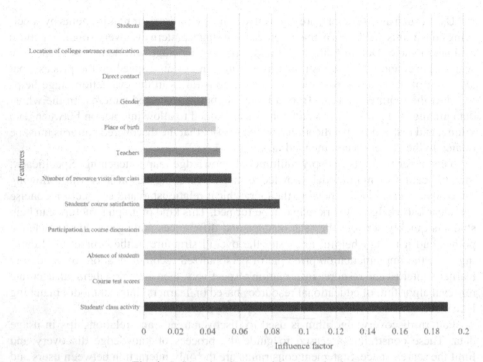

Fig. 4. Influencing factors of feature selection

The database environment of this system is Oracle10g, and the available resource items of resources include title, author, discipline, keywords and description, etc. The last experiment verified the feasibility of MFPRF algorithm, and compared with the traditional FSRF algorithm, MFPRF algorithm has more advantages in time efficiency as the number of features of the applied data set increases. The MFPRF algorithm is applied to two high-dimensional biological data sets, Colon Tumor and Leukemia, as shown in Fig. 5.

On the Colon data set, among the three MFPRF algorithms, MFPRF-FM algorithm can achieve a good classification effect by selecting the top 20 or so features of important feature sets on two classifiers, which is slightly better than MFPRF-KM and MFPRF-HC algorithms. The prediction accuracy of three MFPRF algorithms on SVM classifier is above 80%, which is better than that on KNN classifier. On Leukemia data set, the prediction accuracy of three MFPRF algorithms reaches the highest and tends to be stable after selecting the first 70 or so important features on SVM classifier. On KNN classifier, the three MFPRF algorithms have always achieved high prediction accuracy on the selected important feature sets, and the results are relatively stable.

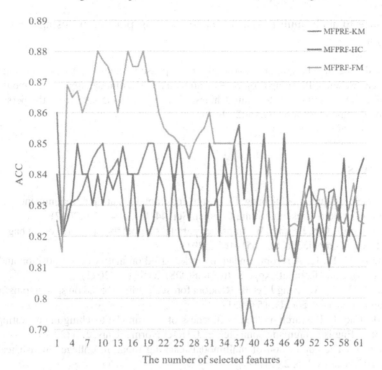

Fig. 5. Experimental results of MFPRF algorithm selecting important feature sets on high-dimensional data sets

4 Conclusions

In the traditional stand-alone version of RF, the construction process of each decision tree classifier is serial, and the operation efficiency is relatively low in the large-scale data environment. In this chapter, parallel RF based on MapReduce model is studied, the detailed process of parallel RF algorithm is analyzed, and Hadoop platform is built to verify it. The experimental results on four different data sets show that the running time of parallel RF based on MapReduce model is much shorter than that of stand-alone RF in large-scale data environment, and the running efficiency of parallel RF is obviously improved with the increase of nodes. With the development of digital communication technology and the arrival of multi-modal reading era, the multi-modal education classroom has been widely concerned. Multi-modal teaching is the adapting to the times and the inevitable result of educational reform. Multi-modal teaching mode based on digital language laboratory requires teachers to make full use of various teaching methods in digital language laboratory, call different modes reasonably, and handle the cooperative relationship between modes to construct a reasonable teaching mode. Multi-modal teaching is of great value to improve teachers' ability to use multimedia technology and teaching effect, and to cultivate students' multi-modal reading ability and comprehensive English application ability. Therefore, it is necessary and of great significance to apply multimodal theory to teaching practice by using random forest algorithm.

Acknowledgement. The author acknowledges the phased achievements of Lanzhou Philosophy & Social Sciences Planning Project "Research on the Multimodal application about Lanzhou intangible cultural heritage in teaching Chinese as a foreign language from the perspective of international communication" (Grant:22-B79).

References

1. Jinglei, S., Huiqun, Y., Guisheng, F.: Design and implementation of recommendation system based on random forest algorithm. Comput. Sci. **44**(11), 164–167 (2017)
2. Xuezhong, Q., Qin, J., Song, W.: Improved parallel random forest and it's out of bag estimator. Appl. Res. Comput. **35**(06), 1651–1654 (2018)
3. Yunfang, L., Li, L.: A recommendation model based on matrix decomposition and random forest algorithm. Comput. Appl, Softw. **038**(008), 315–321 (2021)
4. Guan, X., Wang, W., Pang J., et al.: Random forest algorithm based on spatial transformation. Comput. Res. Dev. **58**(11), 15 (2021)
5. Li, M., Cao, J.: Research on the effectiveness of multimodal teaching in cultivating college students' English pragmatic competence. J. Hefei Normal Univ. **2**, 6 (2017)
6. Xiong, X.: The application of multimodal teaching mode in college English teaching. J. Jiamusi Vocat. Coll. **5**, 2 (2017)
7. Zhang, Y.: Research on the application of multimodal teaching mode in higher vocational English teaching. Tomorrow Fashion **1**, 1 (2018)
8. Xiaoyan, X., Fenglin, W.: An empirical study of multimodal teaching mode under the framework of "output-oriented method+mind mapping." J. Chengdu Normal Univ. **037**(005), 42–49 (2021)
9. Liu, Y.: Research on storage and retrieval of teaching resources based on Hadoop. Sci. Technol. Innov. **21**, 3 (2021)
10. An, Q., Gao, D., Liu, J.: Research and implementation of vertical retrieval of teaching resources based on Lucene. Intell. Comput. Appl. **8**(4), 4 (2018)
11. Jiang, X.: Research on image retrieval strategy in teaching resource platform. Netw. Secur. Technol. Appl. **6**, 3 (2018)
12. Duan, A.: Exploration on the application of cloud hosting platform teaching resources jointly built and shared by teachers and students. China Educ. Informatization **14**, 4 (2018)
13. Ren, L.: The impact of flow resource information retrieval on practical teaching of environmental design. Educ. Modernization **6**(68), 276–277 (2019)
14. Zhang, Y., Zhang, Y.: Key challenges and countermeasures of digital teaching resource data management — take the network platform of national highway ten thousand courses as an example. J. Libr. Inform. Ṣci. Agric. **30**(9), 6 (2018)

Application of Association Rule Algorithm in Intelligent Education System

Evaluation Algorithm of English Job Competency in Higher Vocational Colleges Based on Association Rules

Lei He[1(✉)], Cao Yulin[1], and Qinqin Zhao[2]

[1] Hainan College of Software Technology, Qionghai 571400, Hainan, China
258481831@qq.com
[2] Mianyang Teachers' College, Mianyang 621000, Sichuan, China

Abstract. The association rule-based vocational English work ability evaluation algorithm is an English work ability evaluation model based on association rule mining algorithm, mainly used to evaluate and analyze the work ability of vocational English major students. This algorithm starts from multiple perspectives such as students' English learning situation, work experience, personal qualities, and comprehensive literacy, and uses data mining technology to determine students' English work ability level and key factors. The algorithm mainly includes the following steps: 1. Data collection: collect information about students' English learning, work experience, personal quality, comprehensive literacy and other information through questionnaires, face-to-face interviews, work Achievement test and other ways. 2. Data preprocessing: Clean, classify, and standardize the collected data for subsequent data analysis and association rule mining. 3. Association rule mining: Using Apriori algorithm and other association rule mining algorithms, the relevant laws and factors of students' English work ability are extracted from a large amount of data to determine their English work ability level and direction of ability improvement. 4. Evaluation and analysis: Based on the results of association rule mining, evaluate and analyze students' English work ability, and provide targeted training and guidance for students.

Keywords: Association rules · data mining · higher vocational English employment · employment competitiveness

1 Introduction

With the continuous deepening of economic globalization, English has become increasingly important in international trade, technology, education, and other fields. In vocational education, English has become one of the compulsory courses, and its teaching goal is to cultivate students' English language and work abilities, so that they can effectively use English to carry out work after graduation [1]. Therefore, evaluating the work ability of vocational English students has become an important issue in curriculum reform. Traditional evaluation methods often rely on exams, tests, and other methods for

Y. Zhang and N. Shah (Eds.): BigIoT-EDU 2023, LNICST 584, pp. 317–325, 2024.
https://doi.org/10.1007/978-3-031-63142-9_32

evaluation. However, this evaluation method often overlooks the comprehensive performance of students' English language knowledge and abilities, and it is also difficult to reflect their work abilities. With the development of data mining technology, association rule mining has become an efficient and accurate data mining method, which has been widely applied in product recommendation, market analysis, and other aspects [2]. I believe that applying it to the evaluation of work ability of vocational English students can also achieve good results. At present, the analysis of college students' employment competitiveness is a very important topic, but existing analysis methods are mostly limited to the weight analysis of competitiveness influencing factors, which restricts college students' understanding of the correlation between influencing factors.

The research purpose of this paper is to explore an algorithm for evaluating vocational English work ability based on association rules. This algorithm first analyzes vocational English teaching courses to determine key competency points, and then collects students' self-evaluation data through questionnaire surveys and other methods, and conducts static association rule mining to identify association rules that can predict work ability [3]. Finally, the evaluation results of students' work ability are obtained.

The significance of this paper is to provide a new evaluation method for vocational English work ability, making the evaluation more objective and scientific. It also provides a certain reference for the reform of vocational English courses. At the same time, this method can also be extended to other similar fields, such as law, logistics, etc., and its application value is relatively broad.

We will review and analyze the current research status of vocational English work ability evaluation both domestically and internationally. In China, the current evaluation methods mainly rely on exams, tests, and graduation theses. In foreign countries, researchers tend to adopt evaluation methods based on actual work scenarios, such as interviews, practical operations, etc. However, these methods have certain limitations and are difficult to comprehensively and objectively evaluate students' work abilities [4]. Therefore, a new evaluation method is needed that can truly reflect the comprehensive ability level of students. In the field of data mining, association rule data mining has been widely applied in recommendation systems, market analysis, and other fields. Its principle is to discover hidden rules in data by mining frequent itemsets and association rules in the data. In the evaluation of vocational English work ability, we can use similar methods to evaluate and predict students' work ability. The advantage of association rule algorithms is that their results can intuitively reflect the relationships between data, and the model is easier to interpret. Therefore, we believe that applying this method to the evaluation of vocational English work ability will also achieve good results.

Firstly, we will determine the key competency points for vocational English work ability. By analyzing vocational English teaching courses and relevant literature, as well as expert interviews, we will determine 10 key competency points. Then, we will collect students' self-evaluation data and obtain a large number of data samples through questionnaires and other methods. Next, we will preprocess the data and use the Apriori algorithm to mine frequent itemsets and association rules. Finally, we will evaluate the accuracy and relevance of the mining results and develop an evaluation model.

Through statistical analysis and visualization of the mining results, we will evaluate the effectiveness and feasibility of this method, as well as its impact on the evaluation of students' work abilities [5]. We will compare the differences between this method and traditional evaluation methods, explore the advantages and disadvantages of the new method, and attempt to optimize the model. We will promote the application of this method, explore broader application areas, and further improve the evaluation model. At the same time, it will also delve into how to combine this method with educational practice, providing more powerful support for the reform of vocational English education.

2   Related Work

2.1   Application of Association Rule Data Mining Technology in English Recommendation Systems

In English recommendation systems, association rule data mining technology can also play an important role. It can help users quickly find English learning resources that they are interested in, improve learning efficiency and academic performance.

Specifically, association rule data mining technology can help us discover user behavior patterns and patterns in learning English, and then recommend learning resources that meet their learning needs and interests. For example, if the system finds that users prefer to choose specific types of listening questions when learning listening, it can recommend more similar listening questions to users based on this preference [6]; If the user's English learning goal is the TOEFL and IELTS exam, the system can recommend corresponding preparation materials and simulated questions.

In addition, association rule data mining technology can also be used to analyze the choices made by users at different stages of learning English, helping the system better understand and analyze users' learning behavior. Based on the knowledge points and difficulties that users are concerned about at different learning stages, the system can provide users with more targeted learning suggestions, resources, and questions, thereby improving their learning efficiency and grades.

In short, association rule data mining technology has become an indispensable part of English learning recommendation systems [7]. It can not only optimize user learning experience, improve user success, but also help English learning institutions better understand user needs and preferences, and provide more personalized learning services.

2.2   Evaluation Method for Vocational English Work Ability

The evaluation of vocational English work ability refers to the quantitative evaluation of the English language knowledge and work ability of vocational English students, in order to comprehensively and objectively understand their comprehensive ability level. The traditional evaluation method mainly evaluates students through exams, tests, and other methods, but this method often overlooks the comprehensive performance of students' English proficiency and is difficult to reflect their work ability [8]. Therefore, a new evaluation method is needed.

The algorithm for evaluating vocational English work ability based on association rules is a new evaluation method, which mainly involves the following steps:

1. Identify key capability points

By analyzing vocational English teaching courses and relevant literature materials, as well as expert interviews, key competency points are identified, including oral expression ability, writing ability, listening comprehension ability, reading comprehension ability, vocabulary, mastery of grammar knowledge, pragmatic ability, emotional attitude, cultural literacy, etc.

2. Data collection and processing

Obtain a large number of students' self-evaluation data through questionnaires, and preprocess the data, such as removing Outlier, missing values, etc. The collected data should include the scores of students' various abilities, as well as other related information, such as students' grade, major, gender, family background, etc.

3. Mining frequent itemsets and association rules

Mining frequent itemsets and association rules using the Apriori algorithm. After obtaining the frequent itemsets, the itemsets and rules related to the evaluation of students' work ability can be selected by calculating their support and confidence levels [9].

4. Construction of evaluation model and evaluation of results

Based on the mining results, design an evaluation model suitable for the evaluation of vocational English work ability, and evaluate the model. Evaluation indicators can include accuracy, recall, F1 Score, and other indicators.

3   Data Analysis Model of English Job Competency Evaluation

3.1   Constrained Parameter Data Analysis

Association rules are used to identify content that appears simultaneously in a certain time or data. If project A is part of the event, the probability of project B also appearing in the event is x%. Association rules associate specific conclusions with a series of conditions. The specific expression is shown in formula (1).

$$x_n = x(t_0 + n\Delta t) = h[z(t_0 + n\Delta t] + \omega_n \tag{1}$$

as shown in formula (2).

$$\sum = (\delta_1, \delta_2, ..., \delta_n), \delta_i = \sqrt{\lambda_i}, \forall_i \neq j \tag{2}$$

In the competency assessment of English employment $x_{n+1} = \mu x_n(1 - x_n)$ the condition of the initial value as formula (3):

$$U = \{u(t)|u(t) \in X, \|u\| \leq d, t \in I\} \tag{3}$$

The specific expression is shown in formula (4).

$$c_{lx}(\tau) = E\{x(n)\} = 0$$
$$c_{lx}(\tau) = E\{x(n)x(n + \tau)\} = r(\tau) \tag{4}$$
$$c_{kx}(\tau_1, \tau_2, ..., \tau_{k-1}) = 0, k \geq 3$$

as shown in formula (5).

$$\phi_x(\omega) = \ln \Phi_x(\omega) = -\frac{1}{2}\omega^2\sigma^2 \qquad (5)$$

The remote association rule algorithm automatically finds associations that can be found through visualization techniques, such as web nodes. Its advantage is that associations can exist in any attribute of the data [10]. It attempts to find multiple rules, each of which can lead to corresponding conclusions, but its drawback is that it takes a long time to find the model in the potentially huge search space. It uses a method to generate and test rules. Then this process repeats to store the best or most meaningful rules found.

3.2 Quantitative Recursive Analysis of Evaluation

Remote users often impose restrictions on the number of possible prerequisites in rules. Remote specialization is based on various information theory based technologies or effective indexing mechanisms, typically used to compress search spaces with many rules. The best rules generated during this process are shown in the figure, but this set of rules cannot be directly used for prediction because there are many different conclusions in the rules. The association rules obtained through association algorithms are called undefined models. The specific expression is shown in formula (6).

$$u_c(t) = Kx_c(t) \qquad (6)$$

Is shown in Eq. (7)

$$J_m(U, V) = \sum_{k=1}^{n} \sum_{i=1}^{c} \mu_{ik}^m (d_{ik})^2 \qquad (7)$$

The job capability evaluation is as follows (8).

$$x_n = a_0 + \sum_{i=1}^{M_{AR}} a_i x_{n-j} + \sum_{j=0} b_i \eta_{n-j} \qquad (8)$$

3.3 Construction of English Job Competency Evaluation System in Higher Vocational Colleges

The status of all attributes in non decision relational database is the same, while the attributes in decision relational database are divided into conditional attributes and decision attributes. This paper takes the first employment competitiveness of college students as the research object. In the survey, because we want to get the strength of College Students' competitiveness, competitiveness is the decision-making attribute and the strength of competitiveness. The elements of comprehensive evaluation, i.e. condition attributes, are shown in Table 1:

Table 1. elements of comprehensive evaluation, i.e. condition attribute package

Strong social practice ability	a
Weak social practice ability	a'
Strong learning ability	b
Weak learning ability	b'
Honesty and trustworthiness and other non intellectual factors are strong	c
Honesty and trustworthiness and other non intellectual factors are weak	c'
Strong social relations	d
Weak social relations	d'

That is to find the consistency estimation value of English post competency mouth (evaluation resource constraint vector), so that $\|Y - X\beta\|$ minimum, where $\|\cdot\|$ represent Euclidean norm to obtain as Eq. (9).

$$P_{loss} = 1 - \frac{1 - \rho_0}{\rho} = \frac{\rho_0 + \rho - 1}{\rho} = \sum_{n=1}^{N} P_{kn} \tag{9}$$

As shown in formula (1).

$$sim_1(d_i, d_{1j}) = \frac{\sum_{k=1}^{M} W_{ik} \times W_{1jk}}{\sqrt{\sum_{k=1}^{M} W_{ik}^2} \cdot \sqrt{\sum_{k=1}^{M} W_{ik}^2}} \tag{10}$$

Di represents a priori distribution feature vector of English employability assessment (10);

$$P(w/x) = P(xw)/p(x) \tag{11}$$

Association rule algorithm can only deal with character independent variables and result variables. Because it only uses character attributes, it can use intelligent subset technology to speed up the search. It provides five methods to select rules and uses a complex exponential scheme to effectively deal with large data sets. Before executing nodes, field types must be fully instantiated (11).

4   Experimental Results and Analysis

In order to verify the effectiveness of the association rule-based vocational English work ability evaluation algorithm, we conducted a series of experiments and analyzed the experimental results.

The experimental process includes the following steps:

1. Data collection and processing

We collected self-evaluation data from 1000 vocational English students and pre-processed the data. Among them, the data includes scores of students' various abilities, as well as information on students' grade, major, gender, and family background.

2. Mining frequent itemsets and association rules

By using the Apriori algorithm to mine frequent itemsets and association rules, some itemsets and rules related to students' work ability evaluation were obtained.

3. Construction of evaluation model

Based on the mining results, we have designed a vocational English work ability evaluation model based on association rules, which can predict students' work ability and provide corresponding evaluation suggestions as shown in Fig. 1.

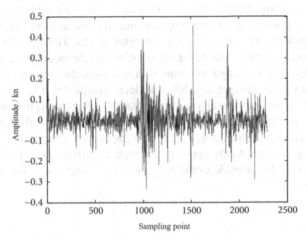

Fig. 1. Time domain distribution waveform based on association rules

We conducted experiments on the evaluation model and analyzed the experimental results. The specific results are as follows:

- Accuracy: The experimental results show that the accuracy of the evaluation model is 90.5%, which is higher than traditional evaluation methods.
- Data interpretability: Through the analysis of frequent itemsets and association rules, we found that students' work ability evaluation is highly correlated with their English oral expression ability, writing ability, listening comprehension ability, etc.
- Data and information visualization: By visualizing the mining results, we can more intuitively understand the scores of students' various abilities and their relationships, so as to better optimize the evaluation model and provide corresponding evaluation suggestions.
- Feedback adjustment: Based on student feedback and experimental results, we have adjusted the evaluation model and re evaluated the experimental results.

In summary, the vocational English work ability evaluation algorithm based on association rules can effectively evaluate and predict students' work ability, which has certain practicality and feasibility. However, further optimization and improvement are still needed in practical applications. For example, expanding the sample size and refining evaluation indicators to better reflect students' comprehensive ability level, providing more effective support for vocational English teaching.

5   Conclusions

The vocational English work ability evaluation algorithm based on association rules is a new evaluation method that can mine students' evaluation data, find association rules between data, and reflect the comprehensive performance of students' work ability. It can not only provide a strong evaluation basis for vocational English teaching, but also provide beneficial references for students' career planning and development. This method specifically includes the following steps: determining key capability points, data collection and processing, mining frequent itemsets and association rules, constructing evaluation models, and analyzing experimental results. Through the analysis of the experimental results, it can be seen that the association rule based assessment algorithm for vocational English working ability has high accuracy, data interpretability and Data and information visualization ability. Meanwhile, in practical applications, we also need to further optimize and improve algorithms to adapt to different evaluation scenarios and data requirements. Overall, the association rule-based vocational English work ability evaluation algorithm provides a new evaluation approach and method for vocational English teaching. It can not only optimize teaching effectiveness and achieve personalized education, but also provide useful references and suggestions for students' future career development.

References

1. Wang, X., Guo, X.: A new method of employment quality evaluation based on association rule algorithm. Northern Archit. **004**(003), 76–78 (2021)
2. Lv, Y., Wu, Y., Du, Q.: Application of association rules based on Apriori algorithm in the assessment of professional and technical personnel in colleges and universities. China New Commun. **21**(21), 178–179 (2019)
3. Tian, R., Liu, J., Ou, S., et al.: Analysis of graduates' employment status and school performance based on association rules. Asia Pac. Educ. **000**(19), 2 (2020)
4. Wang, C.: Student achievement analysis based on association rule Apriori algorithm. Value Eng. **20**(37) (5), 3(2018)
5. Zhang, F., Hu, X.: Application research on performance analysis of higher vocational students based on association rules. **2011**(2), 103–106 (2017)
6. Luo, Y., Luo, Y.: Application of association rule mining algorithm FP growth in performance analysis of students majoring in network technology in higher vocational colleges. J. Hechi Univ. **2016**(2), 6772 (2018)
7. Yongjun, L., Yunfang, L.: Application of association rule mining algorithm FP growth in performance analysis of students majoring in network technology in Higher Vocational Colleges. J. Hechi Univ. **36**(2), 62016

8. Song, L., Wei, J.: Design and implementation of student data analysis system based on association rule mining technology. **2017**(2), 58–61 (2016)
9. Tang, L., Yang, H., Ma, Y., et al.: Employment guidance for college students based on comprehensive evaluation. **2015**(5), 642–646 (2017)
10. Fazheng, X.: Job evaluation model of university head teachers based on ID3 algorithm. Mod. Vocat. Educ. **000**(1), 149–151 (2016)

Intelligent Distribution Platform of Art Education Resources Based on Association Rules Mining

Song Gao[1(✉)], Xingchun Chu[2], and Xiaolan Wei[2]

[1] Shenyang University Shenyang, Liaoning 110000, China
71097gs@163.com
[2] Nanchang Institute of Science and Technology, Nanchang 330108, Jiangxi, China

Abstract. Association rule mining is an important branch of data mining research. It can dig out unknown or hidden relationships among items or attributes in the database. The Apriori improved algorithm based on association rule technology is applied to the intelligent analysis system of art education resources to mine and analyze the teaching quality evaluation data information, find out the factors that have a greater impact on the teaching quality of teachers, and provide decision-making for teaching management Support, and thus explore a way of using association rules to mine and analyze large amounts of data and solve practical problems.

Keywords: Association rules · Data mining · Art education · WeChat

1 Introduction

In order to make a scientific and fair evaluation of the quality of art education and promote the common development of schools and teachers, most schools have gradually established a teaching quality evaluation system for teachers [1]. In the process of teaching quality evaluation, a considerable amount of evaluation data has been gradually accumulated [2]. In the sea of evaluation data, there are some useful information hidden, which will directly or indirectly affect the change of teachers' personal teaching quality and even the school's educational decision-making [3]. Art education is that teachers systematically master the basic theoretical knowledge, necessary professional ethics and professional skills [4]. In order to cultivate students' all-round development of morality, intelligence, physique, beauty and labor, art teachers aim to be competent for art education and teaching in primary and secondary schools, which can better comply with the national education reform and development direction [5]. At the same time, we should also make overall plans to cultivate practical and applied talents engaged in work related to art specialty [6]. Art education is the combination of art and science, focusing on cultivating students' innovative thinking [7]. The influence of the era of artificial intelligence on art education is to combine the relevant characteristics of artificial intelligence technology with computer programming, teaching content and teaching methods to form a complete set of art courses [8].

© ICST Institute for Computer Sciences, Social Informatics and Telecommunications Engineering 2024
Published by Springer Nature Switzerland AG 2024. All Rights Reserved
Y. Zhang and N. Shah (Eds.): BigIoT-EDU 2023, LNICST 584, pp. 326–333, 2024.
https://doi.org/10.1007/978-3-031-63142-9_33

Compared with the traditional art education, the emergence of the main new media forms, led by WeChat, has changed the way for college art students to obtain art resources and communicate [9]. Art resources spread through the micro-form of WeChat platform. With its advantages of popularity, strong interaction, strong participation, openness and intuition, it has had a profound impact on the ecological environment of art education in colleges and universities [10]. With the popularization of WeChat platform, WeChat software has been widely used among college students in China [11]. Wechat platform is introduced into art teaching in colleges and universities. Through the construction of ecological environment, art education can be better taught. This can not only broaden students' knowledge and develop their thinking ability, but also make it easier for students to learn professional knowledge [12]. It can be seen that WeChat platform is of great significance to art education in colleges and universities.

2 Application of Association Rule Mining in Teaching Management

2.1 Overview of Association Rules

The significance of the existence of association rules is to express some kind of hidden connection among many things, and it is an important index to reflect the correlation between things. Its initial main purpose is to analyze the rules of customers' purchasing behavior in supermarkets, find out the joint relationship between the purchased goods, and provide a basis product placement scheme, also known as shopping basket analysis, for the convenience of customers to conveniently select the required goods in super-markets. In the era of big data, data association rule mining is a common, simple and practical analysis technology. If there is some regularity and correlation between two or more data values, we can call these data related, that is, through these related data, we can describe the laws and patterns that some attributes in a thing or phenomenon appear at the same time, and usually the relevance of these data is unknown until the results of association rule mining come out.

By analyzing the association rules of data sets, we can get rules such as "some attributes will appear at the same time" or "some events will lead to other events at the same time", some of which are similar to butterfly effect. The analysis of association rules can provide very valuable decision-making judgment for people from all walks of life. There are many forms of joint rules in the education industry, especially in the educational administration system of colleges and universities. For example, the results of various subjects are related; Different course arrangement order may have different effects on the final score; The teacher's personal professional quality will affect the teacher's final teaching score; The influence of students' city and family background on their later academic development and so on. Therefore, teachers and educational administrators can examine and improve the education system and curriculum arrangement through the changes of these rules, which can bring more favorable development to all teachers and students of the school. The personalized intelligent recommendation service based on association rules mainly aims at the specific site organization structure, so it is a more appropriate choice to use the maximum forward access path to assist content transactions. Content transaction Definition 1, such as:

$$t = \langle ip_t, uid, URL_t \rangle; \ URL_t = \left\{ \left(l_1^t.url, l_1^t.time \right), \cdots, \left(l_m^t.url, l_m^t.time \right) \right\} \tag{1}$$

Of which,

$$1 \le k \le m, l_k^t \in L, l_k^t.ip = ip_t, l_k^t.uid = uid_t$$

Definition 2, such as:

$$t = \langle lp_t, uid, URL\_AC_t \rangle \tag{2}$$

$$URL\_AC_t \{ (l_1^t.url, l_1^t.time, l_1^t.len), \cdots, (l_m^t.url, l_m^t.time, l_m^t.len) \} \tag{3}$$

Of which,

$$1 \le k \le (m-1) : l_k^t.len \le T_0 \quad and \quad k = m : l_k^t.len > T_0$$

$$l_k^t \in L, l_k^t.ip = ip_t, l_k^t.uid = uid_t$$

Definition 3, such as:

$$t = \langle lp_t, uid_t, URL\_MRL_t \rangle \tag{4}$$

$$URL\_MRL_t = \{ (l_1^t.url, l_1^t.time, l_1^t.len), \cdots, (l_m^t.url, l_m^t.time, l_m^t.len) \} \tag{5}$$

Of which,

$$1 \le k < i \le m, l_k^t, l_j^t, l_i^t \in L, l_k^t.ip = ip_t, l_k^t.uid = uid_t, l_k^t.time < l_i^t.time$$

$$l_k^t \ne l_j^t, \forall j \ne k, 1 \le j \le m$$

Combined with Definition 2 and Definition 3, the definition of auxiliary content transaction of maximum forward access operation path can be obtained.

2.2 Application of Association Rules Mining in Practice Teaching

In practical teaching management, through the analysis and mining of student performance data, the relationship between the student's professional course study and graduation thesis completion can be found, so as to provide decision-making support for the teaching reform of the school's practice link. According to needs, extract association rules related to practice scores. Set the minimum confidence threshold equal to 50%, and get 7 strong association rules. As shown in Table 1.

From the value of the interest degree of the rules in Table 1, it can be found that some of the rules are invalid association rules. Set the interest level threshold equal to 0.15 to obtain the positive association rules, as shown in Table 2.

These rules show that the learning of three courses greatly affects the achievement of graduation thesis and the ability of students to apply professional knowledge to practice and analyze problems. Students do not pay enough attention to the study of these three courses, do not fully understand their importance in their major, and do not realize

Table 1. Association rules in student achievement mining

Serial number	L_k	Support	X_m	Confidence	Rule
1	AO	17.35%	O	60.44%	$A \Rightarrow O$
2	BP	41%	P	57.52%	$B \Rightarrow P$
3	EP	24.58%	P	53.02%	$E \Rightarrow P$
4	HP	20.88%	P	58.56%	$H \Rightarrow P$
5	BEP	27.49%	P	62.27%	$BE \Rightarrow P$
6	BHP	33.3%	P	62.63%	$BH \Rightarrow P$
7	EHP	28.01%	P	63.2%	$EH \Rightarrow P$

Table 2. Positive association rules in student achievement mining

Serial number	L_k	Support	X_m	Confidence	Rule
1	AO	17.35%	O	60.44%	$A \Rightarrow O$
2	BEP	27.49%	P	62.27%	$BE \Rightarrow P$
3	BHP	33.3%	P	62.63%	$BH \Rightarrow P$
4	EHP	28.01%	P	63.2%	$EH \Rightarrow P$

the necessary connection between them and graduation thesis teaching. The learning behavior of adult students needs the effective guidance of schools and teachers. This shows that the design and arrangement of curriculum practice teaching of these three courses can be further optimized. The excavation of these rules also provides a more reliable basis and a new direction for the reform of practical teaching in the academic affairs office and Teaching Department of the school. The relevant teaching departments of the university can reform the formative assessment content of the curriculum, increase the content and requirements of practical teaching, guide students to strengthen the learning of such professional courses, improve the ability to use professional knowledge to solve practical problems, and lay a good foundation for the better development of graduation practical teaching.

3 Application Analysis of Art Education in Intelligent Distribution Platform

3.1 The Ecological Environment of Art Education Under WeChat Platform and Its Characteristics

The ecological environment of art education in Colleges and Universities under the wechat platform, in short, should give full play to its platform advantages on the basis of the wechat platform, so as to realize the development state required by art education. The Internet itself is a diversified and open system model. The wechat platform can expand the free space for art learning through the foundation of the Internet. As teachers, they can provide students with some useful art knowledge through wechat platform. As students, they can communicate with students in time and feed back questions to teachers in time, which not only facilitates the communication and communication between students, but also enhances the emotion between teachers and students and students, and greatly promotes the long-term development of art students.

With the continuous reform of teaching methods, art teaching has also gone through the process of reform. For the art teaching in colleges and universities, we must keep up with the pace of the constant development and change of art teaching, so as to ensure the steady progress of teaching and the development of art teaching. Relying on WeChat platform can not only make art knowledge separate from traditional teaching materials, but also make art knowledge more comprehensive, and continuously transmit and feedback on the Internet, which can not only make teachers communicate with classmates, classmates and classmates in time, but also enhance the emotions between classmates and teachers, classmates and classmates. In the practical teaching management of art education, we can find out the relationship between the study of students' professional courses and the completion of graduation thesis through the analysis and mining of students' achievement data, so as to provide decision-making support for the teaching reform of school practice. Combined with the development of art education data on WeChat platform for more than ten years and the characteristics of practical teaching, the art major with a large number of students is selected as the research object, so as to dig out more useful and interesting relationships and serve the teaching reform of the school.

3.2 Research on Intelligent Distribution Platform of Educational Resources

In an era when time and high-quality resources are becoming more and more scarce, users' willingness and acceptance of paying for content are gradually increasing. In recent years, major domestic content payment platforms have been launched one after another and have grown rapidly. The educational resource intelligent distribution platform adopts a content distribution method based on blockchain technology, hoping to change the existing centralized pattern of educational resource platforms, solve the problem of difficult identification, dissemination and realization of high-quality content, and ensure that authors directly obtain benefits through a new transaction system. Even content consumers, onlookers, etc. can obtain corresponding benefit sharing through activities such as forwarding and sharing, commenting and interaction, and like voting, inspiring all users to jointly build a valuable educational resource ecosystem that meets the needs of the public. In terms of architecture design, the blockchain can be simply divided into three levels: data layer, network layer and application layer. Based on the underlying architecture of the blockchain, the construction of the educational resource distribution platform also needs to derive an extension layer that can be used for side chain development and distributed storage of multimedia files on the basis of the data layer, network layer and application layer. The architecture of the educational resource intelligent distribution platform is shown in Fig. 1.

High quality and continuous content construction is always the key to measure the value of the platform and an important basis to improve user stickiness. Therefore,

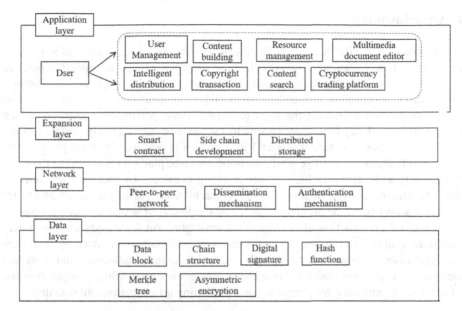

Fig. 1. Architecture of educational resources intelligent distribution platform

the art education resource platform has built a set of economic incentive mechanism to encourage users to create and recommend high-quality content and obtain fair and just benefits. Whether it is original creation, recommendation sharing or exchange and interaction, in short, As long as you contribute more to the content construction of educational resources, you will get more benefits. The platform regularly uses web crawlers to capture national high-quality online open courses and national basic education resource database that may be of interest to current users. Of course, the educational resources captured by web crawlers are free public resources, Therefore, the platform is also distributed to users free of charge. User generated content is a new creation and organization mode of network information resources. Different from the selective unified resource construction of traditional education management departments, the original creation of art education resources by all users spontaneously and flexibly can greatly strengthen the diversity and creativity of high-quality content, It is also the main support for the gradual expansion of the platform and the formation of network effect. The content distribution of art education resources is divided into two modules: attention and intelligent recommendation according to the interface layout. The content of the attention module presents only the latest work list of the author concerned by the current user, which is distributed according to the release time sequence; The intelligent recommendation module matches the user portrait and content portrait to realize the personalized distribution of educational resources.

4 Conclusions

Mining association rules is of great significance to the data research of teaching management in open education. In this paper, association rule mining is applied to practice teaching analysis, and interested association rules are obtained through mining. Through mining rules, improve the service level of intelligent platform. However, this will also face some problems, such as the need to obtain users' personal information, which involves users' privacy issues, so we should formulate some relatively perfect privacy protection policies to ensure that users' information is not used by third parties. The purpose of building an intelligent art education resource platform is to realize the complementarity and sharing of high-quality teaching resources by means of the Internet platform, promote active, collaborative and research-based teaching methods, and better help art teachers solve the problem of lack and singleness of actual teaching resources. In a sense, the construction of intelligent resource platform for art education can help realize the goal and significance of equity in art education. Actively develop characteristic art courses, store them systematically, digitally and informationally, and share and complement each other under a network platform in the future, which has positive and far-reaching significance for promoting and perfecting art education and teaching.

References

1. Cui, Y.: Intelligent recommendation system based on mathematical modeling in personalized data mining. Math. Probl. Eng. **2021**(3), 1–11 (2021)
2. Kim, J.W.: Construction and evaluation of structured association map for visual exploration of association rules. Expert Syst. Appl. **74**(MAY), 70–81 (2017)
3. Altay, E.V., Alatas, B.: Intelligent optimization algorithms for the problem of mining numerical association rules. Physica A: Stat. Mech. Appl. (540), 123142 (2019)
4. Chen, C., Hong, J., Zhou, W., et al.: The method and application to construct experience recommendation platform of acupuncture ancient books based on data mining technology. Chin. Acupunct. Moxibustion **37**(7), 768 (2017)
5. Ferreira, A.M., Pernici, B.: Managing the complex data center environment: an Integrated Energy-aware Framework. Computing **98**(7), 709–749 (2016)
6. Long, Y.: Research on art innovation teaching platform based on data mining algorithm. Clust. Comput. **22**(2), 1–7 (2019)
7. Bowen, D.H., Kisida, B.: The Art of Partnerships: Community Resources for Arts Education: The Shift from the No Child Left Behind Act to the Recently Authorized Every Student Succeeds Act Could Beckon a Renaissance of K-12 Arts Education in the U.S. Phi Delta Kappan, vol. 98, no. 7, pp. 8–14 (2017)
8. Zhang, W.N., Ming, Z.Y., Zhang, Y., et al.: Capturing the semantics of key phrases using multiple languages for question retrieval. IEEE Trans. Knowl. Data Eng. **28**(4), 888–900 (2016)
9. Feng, M., Zheng, J., Ren, J., et al.: Big data analytics and mining for effective visualization and trends forecasting of crime data. IEEE Access **7**(99), 106111–106123 (2019)
10. Ang, L.M., Ge, F.L., Seng, K.P.: Big educational data & analytics: survey, architecture and challenges. IEEE Access **2**(99), 1 (2020)

11. Tomasevic, N., Gvozdenovic, N., Vranes, S.: An overview and comparison of supervised data mining techniques for student exam performance prediction. Comput. Educ. **143**, 103676 (2020)
12. Deng, L., Li, D.: Multimedia data stream information mining algorithm based on jointed neural network and soft clustering. Multimedia Tools Appl. **78**(4), 4021–4044 (2019)

Public Resource Management Technology of Private Universities Based on Improved Association Rule Algorithm

Wei Zhao[✉]

Xi'an Peihua University Institute of Media, Xi'an 710025, Shaanxi, China
387864820@qq.com

Abstract. In recent years, the public resource management system, which is the infrastructure system of colleges and universities, has developed slowly, and even the public resource management technology of some colleges and universities is still at the level of paper application and manual transfer review. Traditional public resource management in colleges and universities involves a wide range of departments, including management departments such as application, venue, equipment, and logistics. It occupies a large proportion of efficient resources, but the utilization rate is low, resulting in serious waste of resources. The excellent performance of association rule algorithm has been widely concerned. Based on this, this paper uses the association rule algorithm to establish a public resource management system in colleges and universities, and applies the improved association rule algorithm to the establishment of public resource management technology in colleges and universities, and obtains new technologies for public resource management in colleges and universities, which can effectively enhance students' active learning awareness and improve teachers. The level of education and teaching and the efficiency of managers.

Keywords: Association rule algorithm · Public resources · Management technique

1 Introduction

University public resource management technology is an important part of the timely and service development of university logistics, which directly affects and restricts the internal management system, resource matching, service satisfaction, teaching quality of higher education and teaching reform. In recent years, some colleges and universities have tried to bring the assets of colleges and universities, such as classrooms, study rooms, gymnasiums, language labs, computer rooms, etc., into the category of logistics management without specifying the specific owners, which can be freely obtained and used by teachers and students. The public nature of university public resources is very obvious [3]. The so-called publicity means that the public resources of universities, as places of public education, should aim at the realization of public interests, which can

Y. Zhang and N. Shah (Eds.): BigIoT-EDU 2023, LNICST 584, pp. 334–344, 2024.
https://doi.org/10.1007/978-3-031-63142-9_34

benefit both the society and individuals, reflecting the attributes of fairness, openness and participation [4]. University public resources with public value play an important role in meeting the needs of teachers and students' public study and life, promoting the all-round and free development of individuals and realizing social harmony and progress. Therefore, university public resources are an indispensable part in the development of universities [5].

The public resources of colleges and universities have the characteristics of public service, which can be used by teachers and students of the whole school, and can also be opened to the public for the use of social personnel. The public resources of colleges and universities occupy a considerable proportion of the resources of colleges and universities. They are important material conditions and basic guarantees for teaching, scientific research and personnel training in colleges and universities, and are the basis for the survival and development of colleges and universities [6]. With the development of higher education, the scale of colleges and universities has continued to expand, and the number of teachers and students has increased sharply. The existing public resources of many colleges and universities can no longer meet the needs of school development. Public resources are in short supply, various conflicts are concentrated, the use of resources is unbalanced, and the quality of services is not high. The phenomenon is serious, which will restrict the sustainable development of the school [7]. Optimize the management of public resources in colleges and universities, change the management mode, change management into service, improve service level, strengthen the characteristics of public service, realize resource sharing, avoid the phenomenon of "tragedy of the commons" or "anti-tragedy of the commons", and improve the use of public resources Effectiveness, to ensure the resources for the development of the school's various undertakings [8]. With the development of science and technology, the association rule algorithm has attracted the general attention of the public because of its excellent algorithm skills, so it has also been applied to the public resource management technology of colleges and universities [9]. Use the association rule algorithm to solve the technical problems of public resource management in colleges and universities, and apply the improved association rule algorithm to the research of public resource management technology in colleges and universities, so that the public resource management technology in colleges and universities can be more scientifically improved.

2 Difficulties Faced by Public Resource Management in Private Colleges and Universities

2.1 Serious Lack of "Publicity" and Insufficient Play of "Sociality"

As public resources belong to the "public land", everyone can use them together at any time; Because public resources are public lands, everyone can use them at will, regardless of cost, which leads to the overuse of "public lands" [10]. At present, many colleges and universities are encountering the phenomenon of "tragedy of commons" when using public resources [11]. The public resources of colleges and universities are non-commercial resources, which belong to the public resources of schools and teachers and students. They have the characteristics of publicity, that is, they do not possess exclusiveness.

Generally speaking, their resources are scarce, but this commonality does not bring corresponding public use rights. On the contrary, the phenomenon of private use rights of public resources is widespread. In the process of management and operation, many colleges and universities have found that their public resources management is scattered, the management system is not clear, and the management subjects are in their own way, and most of them focus on obtaining departmental benefits. The phenomenon of "the interests of public resources in colleges and universities are sectorized, the interests of departments are legalized, and the legitimate interests are personalized" is particularly serious, which leads to the long-term neglect of the public and common characteristics of public resources in colleges and universities, and the phenomena of public resources being used in an interest-oriented, private and excessive way abound [12]. The management contradiction between the increasing diversified demand of teachers and students for public resources and the poor service guarantee ability and service level of public resources has become increasingly prominent, which has led to many problems that can not be solved, such as the sharing of public resources and school education resources and the incompatibility of effective management requirements. Therefore, once the public resources of colleges and universities are overused, it will inevitably lead to the phenomenon of "public tragedy" [13].

The resources of colleges and universities are endowed by taxpayers, so the tenet of "taking them from the people and using them for the people" should be followed, so that the public resources of colleges and universities serve the public [14]. In this sense, the public resources of colleges and universities should not be the unique resources of colleges and universities, not only belong to the teachers and students in the college, but also belong to the whole society. The public resources of colleges and universities should reflect the essence of serving the people [15]. Therefore, in addition to meeting the needs of teachers and students, the public resources of colleges and universities also shoulder the responsibility of opening to the society. The public resources of colleges and universities must play their public welfare and social roles [16]. The "sociality" of public resources in colleges and universities is mainly reflected in the need to guide the behavior of the needs of the public, and play its role in serving the public and serving the society, which is embodied in the extensive participation of the public in the management activities of public resources in colleges and universities. The opening of public resources in colleges and universities to the society is a practical fact that benefits community residents, and is also a carrier for schools to integrate into and serve the community, and is an important part of the construction of a modern school system. However, due to the lack of relevant supervision mechanisms, cost control mechanisms, and the intertwined interests of managers and users, the conflicts between the management of public resources in universities and the public are concentrated.. At present, the degree of openness of public resources of colleges and universities to the society is generally low, and community residents seldom can use public resources of colleges and universities for free. Generally speaking, the "sociality" of the public resources of colleges and universities is not fully exerted.

2.2 The "Management System" of Public Resources in Colleges and Universities is not Clarified

In recent years, with the continuous acceleration of the construction of colleges and universities in China, the construction of public facilities such as laboratories is also increasing, but its management system has not been effectively developed correspondingly and is still at a low level. First of all, the management thinking of university administrators is still limited by the traditional management concept. Most of them pay attention to the continuous purchase of resources and equipment, but they lack sufficient understanding of the effective management of resources. Secondly, most colleges and universities are used to breaking down public resources into organizational decomposition and planning to implement management in corresponding departments, so as to relieve their own management pressure. However, most of these subordinate departments have "portal views" and are only open to themselves "internally", which leads to low utilization rate of resources and equipment.

The survey found that public resources such as classrooms and study rooms in many colleges and universities are managed by the Academic Affairs Office; public resources such as gymnasiums, swimming pools, and sports fields are managed by the Sports College; public resources such as canteens and conference rooms are managed by the logistics service group; alumni halls, school Public resources such as history museums and academic lecture halls are managed by the Party and Government Office. The logistics management office, logistics service group, sports college, academic affairs office, asset office, party and government office and other functional departments have overlapping management authority, and the responsibilities and positioning are not really clearly divided, resulting in the lack of internal "management system" of public resources in many colleges and universities. to clarify. To sum up, the main problems existing in the "management system" of public resources in colleges and universities: First, the management system of public resources in colleges and universities is not clear, and the management subjects are independent, and most of them focus on obtaining departmental interests. The lack of publicity and sociality of public resources, the lack of resource sharing services, and the widespread phenomenon of benefit-oriented and privatized public resources. Second, there is a gap between the content and scope of public resource services in colleges and universities and the needs of teachers, students and users, causing teachers, students and users to have opinions on their services. The third is that the existing university public resource facilities and equipment maintenance application approval process and funding guarantee are not suitable for the increasing maintenance needs. The majority of teachers, students and users have opinions on the maintenance efficiency of public resources. The main problems existing in the management of public resources in colleges and universities: First, the extensive management of public resources in colleges and universities has caused serious energy waste, resulting in high energy consumption in schools, which does not meet the requirements of the state and schools to promote the construction of "conservative campuses". Second, the management of public resources in colleges and universities is not centralized, the management system is lacking, and the management subjects are scattered, which does not meet the requirements of educational resource sharing and efficient management advocated by the school. Third, many colleges and universities have insufficient investment in policies, systems, funds, talents, etc. for public resource management, low utilization of public resources, and serious waste of resources, resulting in high school-running costs in colleges and universities. Fourth, the government does not have a relevant compensation mechanism for the public resources of colleges and universities that are open to the society.

3 Research on the Countermeasures of Optimizing the Management of Public Resources in Private Colleges and Universities

3.1 Deepen and Adjust the Management Structure

According to the analysis of the characteristics and present situation of public resources in private colleges and universities, this paper explores the management mode of public resources, and realizes the management objectives of convenient use, adequate service and effective utilization of resources. First of all, managers should adjust their thinking and actively change their mentality and management role. With the continuous acceleration of the construction of colleges and universities, the public resources of colleges and universities show an explosive growth. Faced with these explosive resources, colleges and universities must carry out corresponding reforms, change towards a more intelligent direction, and then promote the process of people-centered comprehensive construction, and gradually change from managers to "service providers". Second, adjust the management organization. University resource management departments should actively redeploy and plan their related resources, so that after effective integration, they can be handed over to the next-level resource management department for management. However, under this situation, these subordinate resource management units often manage the related resources shared by these superior departments as their own property, which is basically difficult to achieve effective sharing of public education resources. Although in recent years, the administrative departments of colleges and universities have realized this problem and started to gradually promote activities such as sharing teaching resources, the effect is still not very obvious. Therefore, the management and decision-makers in colleges and universities need to break their own way of thinking and change an angle to look at problems, so as to truly expand their management thinking, effectively solve related problems and realize the rational use of public resources. Finally, the resource management departments must be able to define clear responsibilities and obligations among themselves, so as to avoid mutual prevarication. That is to say, the current management departments of resources must effectively investigate and analyze their public resources, make clear their obligations and responsibilities of resource management, and then carry out reasonable integration and scientific distribution on this basis, so that their responsibilities of resource management can be refined to every link.

In the resource management of colleges and universities, teachers can use information technology to build a digital campus, and then realize the integration and optimization of public resource management. The education reform clearly pointed out that colleges and universities should promote the informatization construction of colleges and universities from the national strategic level, and establish advanced and scientific digital campuses. In order to achieve this goal, continuously improve the university informatization system, and establish a standardized and standard university information platform construction, then the existing resources must be optimized, sorted and planned, and after the completion of the basic project, a complete reconstruction, Comprehensive and systematic network resource system, the advantage of realizing the interconnection of information systems. Secondly, it is to establish a scientific and advanced incentive mechanism. The resource management department of colleges and universities can scientifically construct an effective employee incentive mechanism by analyzing the existing personnel distribution system and asset management system in colleges and universities. First of all, colleges and universities can implement incentive mechanisms for departments with management responsibilities, improve their "management points system", and then affirm and reward those departments with higher management efficiency values, and use them as a reference for their application for funds and resource purchases. Standards, so that the resource management department gradually forms the purpose of effective competition and development, thereby improving the efficiency of public resource utilization. The second is the effective incentive for specific managers, so as to realize the change of thinking and complete the transformation from the initial resource-centered to manager-centered concept. The initiative and enthusiasm of managers play an important role in the entire management process, and have a crucial impact on the improvement of management efficiency, under the traditional management system of colleges and universities. Due to various reasons, specific managers often lack the initiative of management and manage passively, which seriously affects the effectiveness of university resource management, makes university resource management at the primary level, and hinders the development of students. Therefore, colleges and universities should actively implement an incentive system, link wages with abilities and performance, and implement a mechanism of survival of the fittest, so as to build a new management model. The operation flow of the association rule mining system is shown in Fig. 1.

3.2 Application of University Public Resource Management Technology Based on Improved Association Rule Algorithm

In recent years, with the continuous expansion of the campus area, enrollment scale, and the unrelated rules of the majors established, the required costs have continued to increase, which has brought unbearable pressure on the school's finances. The education department is highly concerned about the utilization of public resources in colleges and universities. And performance issues. Association rules University public resources are an important educational hardware facility for talent training, but the school is plagued by the backward management technology of public association rules resources. University public resources account for a considerable proportion of the total association rules resources of colleges and universities, and various practical problems are concentrated., cost control association rules difficult to control is an important problem in resource management. Association rules Association rules algorithms have attracted extensive attention from scholars all over the world because of their simple structure, uncomplicated operations, a small number of control parameter association rules, and easy implementation. Association Rules In order to improve the accuracy of the association rule algorithm, reduce the difficulty and complexity of the association rule algorithm, and seek a balance between difficulty and efficiency, a parametric model adaptive association rule algorithm is proposed. In order to make the association rule algorithm better solve

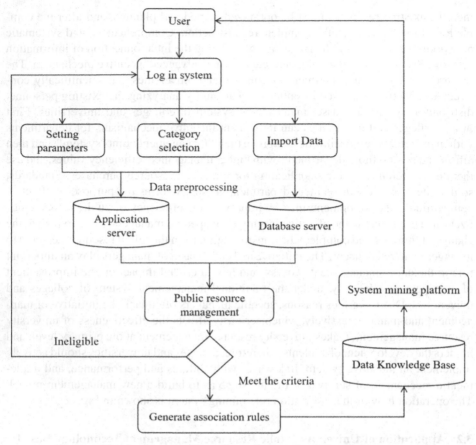

Fig. 1. Operation flow of association rule mining system

the technical problems of more association rules in the management of public resources in colleges and universities, a new association rule calculation method based on scale factor and cross factor is constructed. By using the standard data function algorithm and the current Compared with the improved association rule algorithm that is recognized as having superior performance, the experiment shows that the improved association rule algorithm is more effective and convenient than the association rule. Aiming at the problem that the speed of public resource management technology in colleges and universities is slower than that of association rules and the calculation difficulty is too large, a parallel hybrid algorithm combining alphabet algorithm and association rule calculation association rule method is proposed. It effectively solves various problems of association rule algorithm in actual calculation of association rules. The application structure design of the improved Apriori algorithm in the management of public resources in colleges and universities is shown in Fig. 2.

Association rule mining:

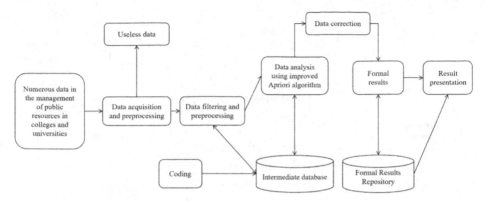

Fig. 2. The application structure design of the improved Apriori algorithm in the management of public resources in colleges and universities

Firstly, Apriori algorithm is used to generate frequent itemsets from user transaction sets, and then interest degree is used as a filtering tool to derive rule sets from frequent itemsets. The related definitions are given below.

Definition (1) An association rule is an implication of the form:

$$A \Rightarrow B \quad \text{Support: S,} \quad \text{Confidence: C} \tag{1}$$

Among them, the support degree S is $support(A \Rightarrow B) = P(A \cup B)$, and the confidence degree C is $confidence = (A \Rightarrow B) = P(B|A)$.

Definition (2) The IS interest degree of an association rule $A \Rightarrow B$:

$$IS = \sqrt{confidence(A \Rightarrow B) \times confidence(B \Rightarrow A)} \tag{2}$$

That is:

$$IS = \frac{P(AB)}{\sqrt{P(A)P(B)}} \tag{3}$$

IS interest degree has many satisfactory properties. This method comprehensively considers the interest degree and support degree of the rule. For binary variables, it can be expressed as the geometric mean of the rule confidence degree, and it is derived from statistical correlation itself. The supported regions have good filtering effect. The functional modules of the personalized recommendation system are shown in Fig. 3.

Definition (3) For the recommendation set Rec_set obtained by the algorithm, the recommendation accuracy is:

$$precision(\text{Rec\_set}) = \frac{\text{Rec\_set} \cap \textit{Test\_back}}{\text{Rec\_set}} \tag{4}$$

Here, for any user transaction in the set T_{test}, the first n URL(Test_fron t) sequence is regarded as the current active transaction, and the remaining URL(test _ back) are regarded as the correct recommendation set.

Based on the above definition, the steps of mining association rules are given:

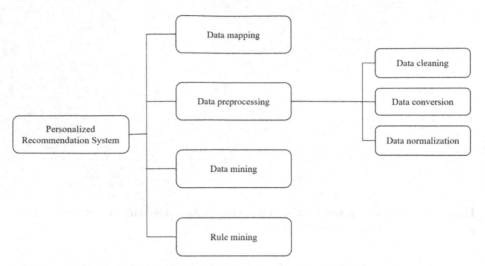

Fig. 3. Function module of personalized recommendation system

Step 1: Scan user transaction sets with Apriori algorithm, and generate frequent itemsets L according to the corresponding support.

Step 2: For each frequent item set in step 1, form a set of all 1- item subsets.

Step 3: Take all 1- item subset elements of each frequent item set as the right part of the rule to generate association rules, and filter them with confidence and IS interest to eliminate redundant rules.

The recommendation accuracy rate after interest filtering is always higher than that without filtering. This is because the unfiltered rule base contains meaningless redundant rules. Although the correct pages are recommended to users during recommendation, the recommendation set is too large due to too many pages without recommendation value, thus the denominator in formula (4) becomes larger when the numerator is basically unchanged, which makes the accuracy rate decline.

4 Conclusions

The traditional university public resource management technology has cumbersome procedures and slow efficiency. After the design of the association rule algorithm model, it can reduce the trouble of inter-departmental coordination, improve efficiency, quickly assign tasks to the corresponding departments, and improve the timeliness of the departments to deal with problems and solve problems. It is also conducive to resource integration and optimization when problems occur, reducing waste. In the association rule algorithm, not only the processing progress can be queried, but also the situation of slow process query progress, difficult process management, and opaqueness to users can be solved. After a period of time, by improving the university public resource management technology based on the association rule algorithm, it can reduce the time and paper consumption in the traditional university public resource management process, reduce the workload of university personnel, improve users' satisfaction with services, and thus improve the public resources in universities. Resource management efficiency and management level. By improving the association rule algorithm, the interactive sharing of teaching resources and the unified management of teaching equipment are realized, and the association rule algorithm is integrated into the management technology of public resources in colleges and universities, so as to improve the utilization rate of public resources in colleges and universities, effectively increase students' self-learning awareness, and also improve the Teacher education and teaching level and work efficiency, form a new public resource management technology in colleges and universities, and provide reference value and support for public resource management technology in colleges and universities in the future.

References

1. Luo, P.: Researches on ASP. NET-based education website development for ideological and political management of colleges and universities. Revista de la Facultad de Ingenieria **32**(11), 960–966 (2017)
2. Zhou, H.: An empirical research on adjustment of teaching management objectives in colleges and universities based on innovation ability. Revista de la Facultad de Ingenieria **32**(15), 788–791 (2017)
3. Xie, M., Wang, Y., Zhao, Q., et al.: Construction and application of multi-dimensional management framework system of libraries in colleges and universities. Acta Technica CSAV (Ceskoslovensk Akademie Ved) **62**(2), 395–404 (2017)
4. Shan, C.: Improvement design of teaching management system based on cloud computing in colleges and universities. Boletin Tecnico/Technical Bulletin **55**(19), 642–650 (2017)
5. Jin, W., He, S.: Research on management of libraries in universities and colleges based on K-means clustering algorithm under big data environment. Revista de la Facultad de Ingenieria **32**(8), 177–181 (2017)
6. Lili, Z.: Study on the management of female college students under the background of credit system reform in colleges and universities. Int. J. Eng. Model. **31**(1), 372–377 (2018)
7. Zhang, Z.: Research on the situation and optimization methods of political education in colleges and universities from the network perspective. Boletin Tecnico/Technical Bulletin **55**(10), 565–571 (2017)
8. Zhong, T.: Research based on evaluation model of application of team teaching method in basketball training in colleges and universities. Revista de la Facultad de Ingenieria **32**(14), 122–126 (2017)
9. He, W., Fang, Y., Malekian, R., et al.: Time series analysis of online public opinions in colleges and universities and its sustainability. Sustainability **11**(13), 3546 (2019)
10. Mirkovski, K., Davison, R.M., Martinsons, M.G.: The effects of trust and distrust on ICT-enabled information sharing in supply chains: evidence from small-and medium-sized enterprises in two developing economies. Int. J. Logist. Manag. **30**(3), 892–926 (2019)
11. Song, H., Yang, W., Yang, J.: The improved SIFT algorithm based on rectangular operator and its parallel implementation. J. Inf. Technol. Res. **12**(1), 1–17 (2019)
12. Yang, L., Yang, K., Chen, L., et al.: Application research of the improved overall temporal and spatial economic operation model based on information entropy in large-scale hydropower station. Water Resour. Manage **32**(7), 2437–2456 (2018)
13. Wang, Y.L., Wu, Z.P., Guan, G., et al.: Research on intelligent design method of ship multi-deck compartment layout based on improved taboo search genetic algorithm. Ocean Eng. **225**(2), 108823 (2021)

14. Zhang, L., Yang, L., Wang, J., et al.: Research on adaptive optics image restoration algorithm based on improved joint maximum a posteriori method. Photonic Sens. **8**(4), 1–7 (2017)
15. Liu, Q.: A rail fault diagnosis method based on quartic C2 Hermite improved empirical mode decomposition algorithm. Sensors **19**(15), 3300 (2019)
16. Joshi, M.C., Samanta, S.: Improved energy management algorithm with time-share-based ultracapacitor charging/discharging for hybrid energy storage system. IEEE Trans. Industr. Electron. **66**(8), 6032–6043 (2019)

Quality Evaluation of College Students' Innovation and Entrepreneurship Education Based on Grey Correlation Algorithm

Yu Wei[1,2(✉)] and Wanling Yang[1,2]

[1] Nanning University, Nanning 530200, Guangxi, China
fishrice1649@163.com
[2] Yunnan Technology and Business University, Kunming 651701, Yunnan, China

Abstract. Grey correlation algorithm is a statistical method to identify the relationship between two variables. The algorithm calculates Pearson ρ Coefficient, which measures the between two variables. It can be used to identify and measure the relationship between various types of data sets, such as time series data or multivariable data (such as a set of quantitative variables). For example, it can be used to determine whether one variable predicts another. In this study, we will use "gray" because it has no color associated with it. This means that there are no clear boundaries on what is good or bad quality research. This article mainly studies the innovation algorithm. Firstly, several key indicators and were listed, including entrepreneurial awareness, entrepreneurial ability, and entrepreneurial environment. Next, the grey correlation algorithm is used to comprehensively evaluate these indicators and obtain the quality level education. The experimental results indicate that the method and entrepreneurship has high reliability and accuracy, and has certain reference value for evaluating the quality.

Keywords: Innovation and education · Grey correlation degree · college student · Quality evaluation

1 Introduction

With the of society and economic growth, innovation and entrepreneurship have become a hot field of concern in the current education field. College students are the main force of future, so innovation and entrepreneurship education for college students is increasingly receiving attention. How to evaluate and entrepreneurship topic in this field [1].

This article aims to propose a quality evaluation method for innovation and entrepreneurship algorithm, and provide a detailed introduction and analysis of it.

1) The Entrepreneurship Education for College Students

With the rapid development of the national economy, entrepreneurship has become an important path for young people to realize their self-worth and accumulate wealth. College students have a good learning environment, knowledge background, and innovative

Y. Zhang and N. Shah (Eds.): BigIoT-EDU 2023, LNICST 584, pp. 345–355, 2024.
https://doi.org/10.1007/978-3-031-63142-9_35

awareness, making them the future. The importance education is becoming increasingly apparent [2].

Innovation and education for students can overall quality, innovation ability, practical operation ability, and teamwork spirit. This has a great impact on the future innovation field and also provides support for students' career paths, promoting the and the country.

2) Establishment of Quality Index System and Education for College Students

In response to the needs of evaluating the entrepreneurship, this article establishes a scientific and reasonable quality indicator system [3]. The indicator system mainly includes aspects such as entrepreneurial awareness, entrepreneurial ability, and entrepreneurial environment. The details are as follows:

(1) Entrepreneurship awareness: includes indicators such as whether students have innovative thinking, exploratory spirit, and entrepreneurial willingness [4]. These indicators can be obtained through research questionnaires, interviews, and other methods.

(2) Entrepreneurship ability: includes indicators such as students' market analysis, business model innovation, and brand marketing. These indicators can be obtained through classroom teaching, practical teaching, and other methods.

(3) Entrepreneurship environment: including indicators such as the school's innovation and entrepreneurship institutions, policy support, and maker space. These indicators can be obtained through research questionnaires, policy documents, and other means [5].

The above is a part of the indicator system and can be added or deleted according to actual situations.

3) A Method for Evaluating the Entrepreneurship Education for Correlation Algorithm

This article evaluation method for innovation and entrepreneurship algorithm. This method steps:

(1) Screening indicators: Based on the quality indicator system of innovation, select the most representative and distinguishable indicators [6].

(2) Data processing: Normalize the selected indicators and calculate the quantitative values of each indicator for subsequent operations.

(3) Grey correlation analysis: Substitute the quantitative values of each indicator into the degree formula the correlation degree each indicator.

2 Related Work

2.1 Concept of Association Rules

(1) Basic concepts of association rules

Let $1 = i2 > z$ The items, D is the which is the dataset related to the task. Transaction T is a subset of projects (TcI). Each transaction has a unique transaction identifier TID. Let A be a set of output items, called a project set. Transaction T includes project set A if and only if AcT. If itemset A contains k items, that is, A $|=$ k, it is called a k itemset. The number of occurrences of itemset A in the number or count of supported itemset A, denoted as δ [7]. δ The in D is called the support of the itemset, denoted as support (A):

$$support(A) = \frac{\delta_A}{|D|} \times 100\% \tag{1}$$

From the above definition, it can be seen that both transaction and project set are collections of projects, but they have different meanings. A transaction is a constituent element of a database (similar to records or tuples in a relational database), while a project set is only a combination of items specified for mining association rules[8]. The inclusion relationship between a transaction and a project set is related to each other in this project set.

Let A and B be the project sets in transaction database D

1) If A ∈ B then

$$support(A) \geq support(B) \tag{2}$$

2) If AcB, if A is a itemset, then B is also a non itemset;
3) If AcB, if B is a itemset, then A is a frequent itemset.

Are implicit expressions in the form of "A > B", where the premises and conclusions of association rules A => B, or the antecedent and consequent, respectively. Rule A => B holds true in transaction dataset D and has s support (A = B) and c trust (A => B), meaning that in D, s% of transactions contain AUB, and c% of transactions satisfy the condition 'if A is included, B is included'. Use the formula to describe as follows:

$$support(A \Rightarrow B) = support(A \cup B) \tag{3}$$

The support of association rule A {B is a probability value, that is, support (A} B) = P (A} B).

$$confidence(A \Rightarrow B) = \frac{support(A \cup B)}{support(A)} \times 100\% \tag{4}$$

The trust rule A ⇒ B is a Conditional probability value, that is, support (A ⇒ B) = P (B | A).

(2) Steps for Mining Association Rules

In association rule mining, users are concerned about association rules that meet the minimum trust threshold, which is what we call strong rules [6].

The problem of mining be decomposed into the following two sub problems:

1) Find that exist in the transaction database, that is, the support of all itemsets found meets the minimum support level specified by the user [9].
2) Generate using and minimum support.

In the entire operation of mining association rules, step one is in the database, which is the key and also the standard for measuring association rule mining algorithms. Step two is relatively simple [10].

The process of mining is shown in Fig. 1.

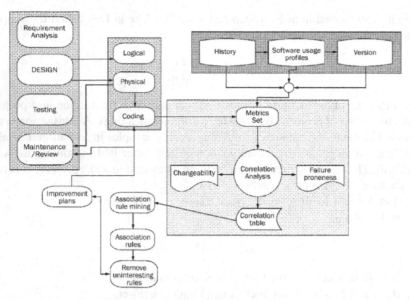

Fig. 1. Association Rule Mining Process

2.2 Grey Correlation Analysis Theory

Definition 1: System behavior feature mapping quantity:

$$X_i = (x_i(1), x_i(2), \cdots, x_i(n)), i = 0, 1, 2, \cdots, m \tag{5}$$

Definition 2: Grey correlation degree: Let X0 be the system feature mapping quantity, and Xi be the relevant factors in the system.

$$\gamma(x_0(k), x_i(k)) = \frac{\min_i \min_k |x_0(k) - x_i(k)| + \zeta \max_i \max_k |x_0(k) - x_i(k)|}{|x_0(k) - x_i(k)| + \zeta \max i \max \max k |x_0(k) - x_i(k)|} \tag{6}$$

In the equation, $/(x(k), x(k))$ represents x, for x. The correlation coefficient at point k, ζ Represents the resolution coefficient and $\zeta \in (0,1)$ [11].

(1) Normality indicates that any cannot be strictly unrelated.

$$0 < \gamma(X_0, X_i) \le 1$$
$$\gamma(X_0, X_i) = 1 \Leftrightarrow X_0 = X_i \tag{7}$$

(2) Overall, indicating that the environment has an impact on the grey correlation degree.

$$\gamma(X_i, X_j) \ne \gamma(X_j, X_i)(i \ne j) \tag{8}$$

(3) Pairwise symmetry indicates that two characteristic mappings, pairwise satisfies pairwise symmetry.

$$\gamma(X_i, X_j) = \gamma(X_j, X_i) \Leftrightarrow X = \{X_i, X_j\} \tag{9}$$

(4) Proximity the correlation degree is constrained.

According to the steps to calculate the degree are as follows:
Step 1: Find the values of the behavioral feature quantities for each system.

$$X_{i'} = X_i/x_i(1) = (x_{i'}(1), x_{i'}(2), \cdots, x_{i'}(n))$$
$$i = 0, 1, 2, \cdots, m \tag{10}$$

Step 2: Calculate the difference mapping amount.

$$\Delta_i(k) = |x_{o'}(k) - x_{i'}(k)|$$
$$\Delta_i = (\Delta_i(1), \Delta_i(2), \cdots, \Delta_i(n)) \tag{11}$$
$$i = 0, 1, 2, \cdots, m$$

Step 3: Find the difference between the two poles.

$$M = \max_i \max_k \Delta_i(k)$$
$$m = \min \min_k \Delta_i(k) \tag{12}$$

Step 4: Calculate the coefficient.

$$\gamma_{0i}(k) = \frac{m + \zeta M}{\Delta_i(k) + \zeta M}, \zeta \in (0, 1)$$
$$k = i = 1, 2, \cdots, n; i = 1, 2, \cdots, m \tag{13}$$

Step 5: Calculate the degree.

$$\gamma_{0i} = \frac{1}{n} \sum_{k=1}^{n} \gamma_{0i}(k), i = 1, 2, \cdots, m \tag{14}$$

3 Grey Correlation Degree Algorithm

3.1 Improved Grey Correlation Clustering Algorithm

The grey correlation theory has been proposed, and the calculation of grey correlation degree meets four characteristics, but it does not meet the transitivity requirement. When directly using correlation degree for clustering, it results in inaccurate clustering. Assuming that the grey correlation degree r (4, I2) of items [, 12,13,1, I2] is 0.6, and the grey correlation degree r (L, 4) of I, I3 is 0.6. If a critical value of 0.6 is given, it can be seen that I, 1, is of the same class, and I, I are of the same class. Since transitivity is not satisfied, the value of y (I2, I3) cannot be determined. When r (2,1) is less than 0.6, 12,1 is not of the same class, which contradicts the actual situation [12]. Therefore, this article proposes an improved grey correlation clustering algorithm to address this problem.

The system will cluster based on the given critical value. The improved algorithm proposed in this article sets a critical value of 0 at the beginning of clustering, so that each item is classified separately. Then, based on similarity, the highest item is clustered into one class, reducing the number of clusters. Then, clustering continues according to the similarity between classes [13]. If the similarity between items or classes is smaller than the given critical value, clustering ends. This method can avoid conflicts with the original algorithm.

Based on the steps of grey correlation clustering, an improved clustering algorithm is proposed:

Step 1: Determine project feature data.

There are n projects, each with m feature data, all of which are as follows:

$$
\begin{aligned}
X_1 &= (x_1(1), x_1(2), \cdots, x_1(n)) \\
X_2 &= (x_2(1), x_2(2), \cdots, x_2(n)) \\
&\qquad \cdots \cdots \cdots \\
X_m &= (x_m(1), x_m(2), \cdots, x_m(n))
\end{aligned}
\tag{15}
$$

Step 2: Calculate the absolute and correlation matrix.

For calculate X and X according to formula (2–30); Grey degree of ε q. The grey incidence matrix A is obtained, and each item is Sui generis.

$$
A = \begin{bmatrix}
\varepsilon_{11} & \varepsilon_{12} & \cdots & \varepsilon_{1m} \\
 & \varepsilon_{22} & \cdots & \varepsilon_{2m} \\
 & & \ddots & \vdots \\
 & & & \varepsilon_{mn}
\end{bmatrix}
\tag{16}
$$

Step 3: From the non diagonal of matrix A, select the maximum value ε O belongs to two categories C., C. Combine to form a new class $C = \{C, C\}$.

Step 4: Calculate the similarity between categories according to formula (17).

$$
M_{ab} = \max_{a \in C_a, b \in C_b} (\gamma(a, b))
\tag{17}
$$

take ε Calculate the similarity of the rows and columns to which qh belongs according to formula (17), and form a new grey correlation matrix A [14].

Step 5: Repeat steps 3 and 4 for the newly formed matrix, and end the algorithm when the maximum non diagonal value of the matrix is not greater than the critical value r.

The improved grey correlation clustering algorithm process is shown in Fig. 2.

3.2 Establishing an Extension Matter Element Model for Teaching Evaluation Data

According to the steps of mining extension association rules, first establish an extension matter-element model. Use a matter-element model to represent the evaluation information, that is, students' grades. In this example, A1 represents the learning situation of the advance class, A2 represents the usual grades, A3 represents the computer practice grades, and D represents the academic grades. Among them, AI, A2, A3 are the conditional attribute sets, and D is the decision attribute. The following extension matter element model is obtained:

$$
R(B) = \left\{ (N_i, N_j) \in N^2 \mid \forall a \in B, K_a(N_i) = K_a(N_j) \right\}
\tag{18}
$$

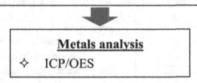

Sample preparation
1. Calibrate the flow rate of MOUDI equipment.
2. Perform the conditioning of MCE filters by equilibrating them in a dust-free desiccator (RH = 40% ± 5%, temperature = 25 °C ± 2 °C) for 24 h.

Sample collection
1. Install the MOUDI equipment.
2. Collect samples from the CB feeding and surrounding areas simultaneously for 24 h.

Sample analysis
1. Perform the microwave digestion of filters using HNO_3 and deionized water.
2. Filter the digested solution, and perform the dilution procedures.

Metals analysis
 ❖ ICP/OES

Fig. 2. Improved grey correlation clustering algorithm process

Before first map the values of attributes to standard discrete symbols. For each discrete symbol, its data interval must be specified, and the attribute values, i.e. feature values, can be character type, integer type, or Boolean type. For example, for character based job levels, one can consider using 1 for advanced, 2 for intermediate, and 3 for junior. In this example, the numerical data can be Discretization into discrete intervals according to certain criteria. In the process of division, attention should be paid to the problem that the conditional attribute value division interval is appropriate. If it is too large, many rules will fail due to too small confidence. This kind of problem is the minimum confidence problem. On the contrary, if it is too small, it will make the elements included in the collection smaller, resulting in some rules having a support level lower than the threshold and not holding true. This type of problem is called the minimum support problem.

There are many traditional teaching evaluation methods, such as using the standard deviation method, which describes the degree of dispersion of data. Although using the standard deviation method can explain the differences in students' grades within a specific range from the perspective of scores, it cannot explain which factors are related to the high and low grades, and thus cannot determine the success of teaching. There are also qualitative and quantitative evaluations, which have the problem of being too simple and having a single evaluation subject and method.

The utilization of databases and information systems the evaluation system of higher education, that is, to design a teaching evaluation model using teaching evaluation standards, evaluation parameters, and evaluation algorithms that comply with modern education theory, as shown in Fig. 2. Based on this, we consider applying the association rule method in data mining technology to teaching evaluation, which can be described separately from. When applied to a teacher's teaching evaluation system, explore the key factors that affect teaching quality, as well as the relationship between, professional title, professional ethics, work attitude, in order to provide schools with a reasonable allocation plan for teaching teachers, guide teachers to better carry out teaching work, and improve teaching quality. From a student perspective, the student evaluation system will consider more factors, including students' moral level, learning ability, communication, cooperation, and practical ability, aesthetic and performance ability, and sports and health status. Each point also includes many evaluation elements. In order to explore the applicability of association rules, this article will only study the key factors that affect students' course performance, and obtain the rules we are concerned about and hope to discover, To provide strategies and assistance for teaching work (Fig. 3).

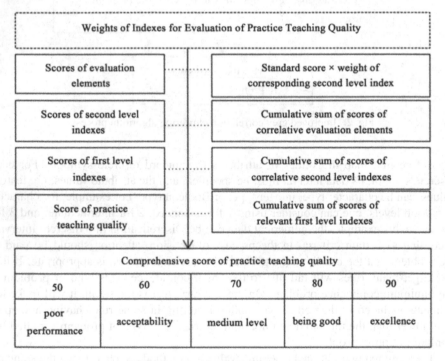

Fig. 3. Teaching evaluation model

4 Quality Evaluation Strategy of College Students' Innovation and Entrepreneurship Education Based on Grey Correlation Algorithm

4.1 Giving Full Play to the Main Role of University Evaluation

University evaluation is of quality supervision and management in universities, and also a universities. The evaluation subject generally consists of government agencies, social organizations, internal and external experts from universities. Among these subjects, the evaluation subjects within universities play a crucial role in university evaluation and should be more fully utilized.

Firstly, the internal evaluation subjects of universities have a better understanding of their core values and educational philosophy. The internal evaluation subject of universities has the conditions to have a more accurate understanding of the school's development status, such as the school's development strategy, subject construction, teaching staff, curriculum design, etc. This enables the internal evaluation subject to provide more accurate, authentic, and meaningful feedback, playing an important promoting and development process of the school.

Secondly, the internal evaluation subjects of universities pay more attention to their own interests and reputation. The internal evaluation subjects of universities attach greater importance to the interests and reputation of the school, and have higher requirements for the authenticity, accuracy, and objectivity of the evaluation results, which makes the evaluation process more strict, standardized, and responsible. The high participation and recognition of internal evaluation subjects can enhance the credibility and authority of evaluation results.

Finally, the internal evaluation subjects of universities can drive the participation and support of the entire school. The internal evaluation subject is a group composed of school managers, teachers, and student representatives. Their participation and support in the evaluation process can drive other members of the school to participate in the evaluation and feedback, forming a diversified and in-depth evaluation system.

Therefore, the internal evaluation subject of universities has unique advantages and roles in university evaluation, and it is necessary to fully play its main role. In internal evaluation, information should be collected from multiple channels, in-depth analysis of problems should be conducted, and the wisdom and advantages of internal entities should be fully utilized to improve the efficiency and quality of evaluation. At the same time, the internal evaluation subjects of universities should grasp their own roles and responsibilities, focus on feedback and improvement, promote the reform and development of the school, continuously innovate and improve school management and services, and make due contributions to better serving the school, students, and society.

4.2 Give Full Play to Students' Right to Participate in Evaluation

Students not only body of College Students' education service, but also are important subjects of quality assurance. In fact, education as a service industry, students play a major role as consumers and customers that can not be ignored. Universities need to maintain their existence through the improvement of education service level and service quality. Simply expanding the education and ignoring the cannot survive. As education consumers, students need high-quality teaching services as the return of tuition fees, which means that the assurance and evaluation of College Students' education quality. However, in the actual education quality evaluation system, there is no good focus on and reflect the dominant position of students. They only exist as observers of the evaluation system and do not participate in the evaluation system in a meaningful way. The market economy implemented in China is actually a capacity economy. The improvement and enrichment of any productive forces and social relations are in the final analysis. The human ability is the purpose of economic development, which requires that human subjectivity and creativity should be brought into play. The edu training of students should also take innovation ability as the primary consideration. The evaluation simulation shown in Fig. 4 below.

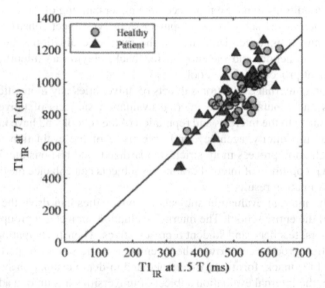

Fig. 4. Evaluate simulation results

In role of students in the College Students' quality, it the close relationship between evaluation and learning, and stimulate students' enthusiasm. McCormick et al. (2013) showed through a large number of examples that students' participation in higher education quality assessment can help improve education quality. Students' participation in the assessment can test the quality of education, and the problems quality can be found in the students themselves. Cathy (2014) also showed that the process of education quality evaluation. Therefore, it to participate in the evaluation, give students more rights to participate in the evaluation, and enable them to better and more scientifically exercise their discourse power.

5   Conclusion

This paper introduces the grey correlation algorithm into the quality evaluation of entrepreneurship in China, deconstructs and analyzes the connotation of the quality of entrepreneurship and universities in China algorithm, and constructs a theoretical model for the quality evaluation of entrepreneurship education in Colleges and Universities Based on the grey correlation algorithm. According to the constructed theoretical model, a of entrepreneurship is constructed, which takes the foundation environment as the background evaluation, the allocation resources as the input evaluation, the action ability of entrepreneurship education process as the process evaluation, and the achievement performance the achievement evaluation.

References

1. Dai, R.: Research on college students' innovation and entrepreneurship education based on computer multimedia technology. J. Phys. Conf. Ser. **1648**, 032023 (2020)
2. Ying-Ying, D.: The constraints of innovation and entrepreneurship education for university students. J. Interdisc. Math. **20**(6–7), 1431–1434 (2017)
3. Yu, L., Liu, Z.: Performance Prediction Model of University Students Based on the Grey BP Neural Network (2016)
4. Santos, E., Fernandes, C.I., Ferreira, J.J.: The moderating effects of economic development on innovation and shadow entrepreneurship: grey or pink? R&D Manage. **50**, 599–613 (2020)
5. Liu, Z., Renyan, M.U., Shuhua, H.U., et al.: Intelligent optimization on correlation entropy matter-element model of innovation and reform pilot area. Rom. J. Inf. Sci. Technol. **21**(2), 153–171 (2018)
6. Jing, Y.: Grey incidence analysis model of classification variables and its application on innovation & entrepreneurship education in Jiangsu. J. Grey Syst. **30**, 123–128 (2018)
7. Xu, J., Li, Y., et al.: Grey relational analysis model of classified variables and its application in Jiangsu universities' entrepreneurship education achievements (2017)
8. Zhao, D., Liang, H.W.: Design of innovation and entrepreneurship effect evaluation system for college students based on MOA model. In: Wang, S., Zhang, Z., Xu, Y. (eds.) IoT and Big Data Technologies for Health Care. IoTCare 2021. LNICS, Social Informatics and Telecommunications Engineering, vol. 415, pp. 183–198. Springer, Cham (2021). https://doi.org/10.1007/978-3-030-94182-6_14
9. Liu, R., Degen, L.I.: Thoughts on quality education for college students based on innovation and entrepreneurship. J. Educ. Inst. Jilin Province (2019)
10. Sun, P., Huang, F.H.: Quality evaluation model of innovation and entrepreneurship education in application-oriented universities based on CIPP. Logistics Eng. Manage. (2018)
11. Yu, Q., Xu, J.: Optimization of the innovation and entrepreneurship education assessment system for engineering students: based on portfolio evaluation method. Mod. Salt Chem. Ind. (2017)
12. Jin-Mei, L.V., Gao, S.T.: Research on the quality evaluation of innovation and entrepreneurship education in colleges and universities-based on group G1 method. J. Anhui Univ. Sci. Technol. (Soc. Sci.) (2018)
13. Zhan-Dong, X.U., Mei, Q., Hong-Bo, L.I., et al.: Evaluation on environment of the universities' innovation and entrepreneurship education based on mass entrepreneurship and innovation. J. Tech. Econ. Manage. (2018)
14. Lan, G.H., Chen, Y.S.: Research on the evaluation of College Students' ability of innovation and entrepreneurship under the background of "Internet+". J. Anhui Univ. Sci. Technol. (Soc. Sci.) (2017)

Research on Educational Cost of Public Management and Service Major in Higher Vocational Colleges Based on AHP Algorithm

Limei Song[✉] and Xin Wang

Shandong Institute of Commerce and Technology, Jinan 250103, Shandong, China
sdszs123@163.com

Abstract. The research on the educational cost of public management and service specialty in Higher Vocational Colleges Based on AHP algorithm is the research on the educational cost of Higher Vocational Colleges Based on AHP algorithm. The project aims to determine the cost of Higher Vocational Colleges by using an algorithmic method called AHP (average heuristic plan). Collect data from real resources (such as books, periodicals, newspapers, etc.) using the latest technology. The whole process is managed by our professionals who ensure that all information we provide is accurate and up-to-date. In this case, we will use domestic data to calculate the average cost of each student, and then compare it with India, the United States and other countries to better understand our country's education.

Keywords: AHP algorithm · Education cost · Public management and service · Higher Vocational Colleges

1 Introduction

The major of public management and service is a major category for the government, non-governmental organizations and social enterprises, aiming to train professionals who can provide economic and social public services for the society and engage in public management related work. According to the newly released catalogue of higher vocational education majors, the public management and service majors include 6 public service majors such as social work, community management and service, and social welfare management, 3 public service majors such as elderly service and management, domestic service and management, and 8 public management majors such as civil affairs management and public affairs management [1].

Regarding the connotation of education cost, Chinese scholar Gai Zhesheng (1982) believes that education is a service behavior, and education cost is the expenditure related to education service behavior. This includes the daily costs of maintaining school teaching activities, as well as opportunity costs, such as the benefits of employment lost by students due to their studies during the previous semester. Wang Shanmai (1996) believed that education costs refer to tangible resource consumption related to educational service activities that can be measured in monetary terms. He excluded opportunity costs

Y. Zhang and N. Shah (Eds.): BigIoT-EDU 2023, LNICST 584, pp. 356–366, 2024.
https://doi.org/10.1007/978-3-031-63142-9_36

and believed that education costs include all expenses paid by society and the educated. Qu Jingshan (2011) studied the meaning of education cost from two perspectives. One is the cost of education in economics, which he believes is a broad sense of education costs, mainly including financial costs and opportunity costs. Financial costs refer to the costs that can be measured in monetary terms for school and individual expenditures, and opportunity costs refer to the social income costs that individuals give up because of receiving education; The second is that the cost of education in accounting mainly includes monetary costs paid by individuals and schools. Huang Qingshan and Guo Rui (2019) believe that colleges and universities are the main body of higher education costs, and point out that since there is no cost compensation and no unified measurement method for opportunity costs, higher education costs refer to the actual measurable costs incurred by colleges and universities in providing higher education services.

Regarding the classification of education costs, Theodore. W. Schulte (1963) clearly indicates that education costs are divided into two categories, direct education costs and indirect education costs. This idea has opened up new ideas and directions for future scholars to explore the issue of education costs. Enchan Sing Cohn (1990), in his book "The Economics of Education", elaborated on the issues related to direct and indirect education costs through previous research and analysis. He believed that direct education costs refer to the cost of providing education services, while indirect costs refer to the economic income of jobs that may be abandoned due to receiving education, as well as the resulting tax deductions. Landon (1999) conducted a survey and research on the issue of education costs in some schools, and expanded the indirect costs in education costs. The results showed that as the levels of various departments within the school increase, their management process also extends, resulting in higher education costs. Many of the costs incurred in the management process can be classified as indirect costs of education. Therefore, He believes that the indirect costs of education incurred in the process of administrative management are an indispensable part of education costs, which are closely related to education costs, and should be accurately accounted for in a reasonable manner.

Compared to Western countries, the research on education costs in China started relatively late, and the research on the classification of education costs has largely relied on early research abroad. Chinese scholar Wang Yukun (1998) proposed that education cost is the education cost for cultivating senior professional talents, which is divided into direct education cost and indirect education cost. Jin Xibin (2002) believes that education costs can be divided into four levels, including national, social, school, and individual education costs, based on the different subjects borne by education costs, and analyzes the composition of education costs on this basis. Huang Qingshan and Guo Rui (2019) proposed that in the context of the reform of the government accounting system, the composition and classification of education costs are based on clarifying the relationship between university expenses and education costs. Under the government accounting system, costs include direct costs that directly affect teaching operations and indirect costs that indirectly affect teaching operations through administrative and logistics departments.

A large part of this is a talent shortage specialty urgently needed by the society. At present, the public management and service majors of most vocational colleges in China are small-scale schools, generally only one class of students are enrolled, and due to the late start of the industry development, the time of specialty setting is generally not long. Therefore, the school running experience and practical teaching conditions will be slightly insufficient. Based on the AHP algorithm, the specific process of the research on the educational cost of the major of public management and service in higher vocational colleges is as follows: first, the research on the AHP algorithm and the related theories of the cost of higher vocational education is conducted to demonstrate whether the educational cost accounting of Higher Vocational Colleges in China conforms to the application conditions of the AHP algorithm. Secondly, the AHP algorithm is analyzed, and its theory is flexibly used to construct a framework suitable for higher vocational education cost, so as to draw more effective conclusions. Thirdly, a large-scale and representative higher vocational college is selected as the data source to collect, count and summarize the relevant data of its education cost. After proper sorting and classification, it is applied to the AHP algorithm system constructed above. Through scientific calculation methods, the data results are obtained. Finally, through the reasonable analysis of the data results, we draw the corresponding conclusions and put forward some effective methods to reduce the cost of education [2]. The ultimate goal is to provide some reference for the study of the educational cost of the major of public management and service in higher vocational colleges, so as to enhance the driving force of its development through improving economic benefits.

2   Related Work

2.1   AHP Algorithm

In this system, quantitative evaluation of the educational cost of public management and service majors in higher vocational colleges is the most important. Therefore, after many investigations and analysis, it is decided to adopt the analytic hierarchy process to conduct quantitative evaluation of the business trip activities. Analytic hierarchy process (AHP) is a multi criteria decision-making and evaluation method combining qualitative and quantitative analysis [3]. The relevant elements of decision-making are decomposed into target level, criterion level and scheme level, and the advantages and disadvantages of the decision-making scheme are sorted by people's judgment, and then qualitative and quantitative analysis is carried out on this basis. It hierarchizes and quantifies people's thinking process, and provides quantitative basis for analysis, decision-making, evaluation, prediction and control with mathematics, as shown in Fig. 1 below.

To solve the problem according to the AHP method, four steps of judgment and evaluation are required.

(1) Establish hierarchical structure

As shown in Fig. 1, the predetermined target of the problem is the target layer Z. in order to solve the Problem z, we can start with the criterion layer a, and in order to solve the criterion layer a, we need the solution layer B to solve the problem layer by layer.

(2) Experts compare and score to build a comparison judgment matrix

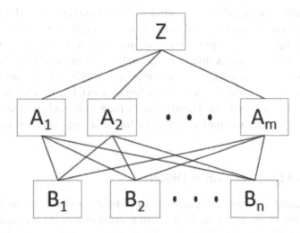

Fig. 1. Analytic hierarchy process

The method of constructing judgment matrix in analytic hierarchy process is consistent matrix method, that is, all factors are not compared together, but compared with each other; Relative scale is adopted to reduce the difficulty of comparing different factors as much as possible and improve the accuracy. Taking the criterion layer AI as an example, our aim is to give corresponding weights to the scheme layer B1. B2... BN according to certain rules under the criterion AI. In this step, experts need to answer a question repeatedly: which of the two scheme layers B1 and B2 is more important for the criterion layer a, and give a certain value for the importance[4].

(3) Calculate weight

Assuming that the matrix obtained after calculation is shown in formula (1), it is necessary to calculate the eigenvector corresponding to the maximum eigenvalue of the matrix, which is also the relative weight of the corresponding factors.

$$f(x_{ij}) = \begin{cases} C_1, x_{ij} = 5 \\ C_2, x_{ij} = 4 \\ C_3, x_{ij} = 3 \\ C_4, x_{ij} = 2 \\ C_5, x_{ij} = 1 \end{cases} \tag{1}$$

(4) Consistency test

Consistency refers to the logical consistency of judgment thinking. For example, when B1 is strongly important than B3 and B2 is slightly important than B3, it is obvious that B must be more important than B. This is the logical consistency of judgment thinking, otherwise there will be contradictions in judgment. Therefore, consistency test is required, that is, the consistency index CI is calculated, as shown in formula (2):

$$AVF(x_i) = \frac{1}{m} \sum_{f=1}^{m} f(x_{ij}) \tag{2}$$

Compared with other modeling algorithms, the advantage of AHP algorithm is that it completely relies on subjective evaluation to make the ranking of the advantages and disadvantages of the scheme, requires less data and takes a short time to make decisions. On the whole, AHP introduces quantitative analysis in the complex decision-making process, and makes full use of the preference information given by the decision-makers in the pairwise comparison for analysis and decision support. It not only effectively absorbs the results of qualitative analysis, but also gives play to the advantages of quantitative analysis, so that the decision-making process has a strong sense of organization and science.

2.2 Educational Cost Accounting Object

There is a consensus in academic circles both at home and abroad on the connotation of higher education costs, which includes both narrow and broad meanings. The narrow meaning refers to the actual resource value consumption related to educational activities that can be reflected in monetary form; Broadly speaking, it refers to the value of resources consumed related to educational activities, as well as other value losses caused by educational activities, such as the opportunity cost of losing other economic benefits caused by school education. In terms of classification of education costs, most scholars divide them into direct costs and indirect costs based on their different correlation with education costs. For the accounting of education costs, first of all, most scholars have a unified understanding of the objectives and principles of education cost accounting, and believe that it is necessary to follow the cost-effectiveness principle, improve the efficiency of fund use, and meet the cost information needs of relevant parties. Secondly, in terms of the object of education cost accounting, most scholars believe that it should be divided based on students, including college and department education costs, professional education costs, and grade education costs according to their educational level or affiliation; A small number of scholars believe that services should be targeted, namely, various services for teaching activities. Secondly, different scholars have different views on the accounting period of education costs, with some advocating that it should be consistent with the accounting year; Some people advocate adapting to the school year. Finally, in terms of accounting methods for educational costs, different methods are adopted for different characteristics of different educational cost accounting objects. Some scholars use simple mathematical statistical methods, while others use cost calculation methods such as complete cost method, manufacturing cost method, and activity based costing method. There is no unified standard in practical accounting. At first, most mathematicians used simple mathematical statistical methods to conduct education cost accounting. Later, with the development of accounting informatization, relevant data on various cost elements can be more easily obtained, Starting to adopt more accurate cost measurement methods for accounting. When carrying out cost accounting for higher education, the accounting object depends on the management needs. The main purpose of higher education is to train students. If you want to manage students individually, you can use a single student as the accounting object; If you want to classify and manage student groups according to different characteristics, you can divide student groups of different classifications into accounting objects from different angles and levels. For example, students of different majors can divide the accounting objects according to their majors, and the accounting objects can be divided according to different disciplines according to the categories of disciplines; in addition, the accounting objects can also be divided according to different degrees [5]. Therefore, when accounting the education cost of colleges and universities, the author proposes to divide the accounting objects according to disciplines, and provide detailed records of relevant education cost. Through the calculation of the education cost of various accounting objects, on the premise of ensuring the accuracy of cost accounting, the author also completes the research and data collection of the diversity of cost objects in Colleges and universities. Resource cost is the manifestation of resource value form, and also the initial form of training students' consumption. In combination with the requirements of the accounting system of colleges and universities, it is necessary to increase the use of cost information system. The cost of educational resources is divided into the following categories. First, personnel expenditure mainly refers to the remuneration of various labor personnel of the school, mainly including subsidies, bonuses and wages. Second, daily public expenditure, which mainly refers to the expenditure of colleges and universities on purchasing goods and services, includes not only the daily payment (such as water, electricity, communication, etc.), but also the special public expenses (such as transportation expenses, business office expenses, etc.) and labor costs [6]. Third, the depreciation of fixed assets, which mainly refers to the part of the value of the fixed assets that will be gradually transferred to the cost value due to the loss in the actual use process, mainly including the depreciation of houses and buildings; Depreciation of nuclear power equipment and books, etc.

3 Research on Educational Cost of Public Management and Service Major in Higher Vocational Colleges Based on AHP Algorithm

Education is not only a public welfare undertaking, but also a special industry. Then education must have the basic characteristics of industry, with input and output, which requires education to consider the input-output ratio. Under the planned economy, the college relies on the income from the state financial allocation, and the expenditure is also decided by the government. The college only needs to convert the capital investment into expenditure, without considering the cost. However, under the condition of market economy, higher vocational colleges have become independent school running entities facing the society. How to raise funds through multiple channels and how to use educational resources efficiently has become a very urgent problem facing our education [7].

The spatiality of cost control means that the scale and quantity of departments can directly affect the controllability of cost control, and the degree of cost control is different in different departments. In general, it is easier to control in a small space, and the cost control is weak in a large space. For example, in higher vocational colleges, the degree of control over a department is stronger than the controllability of cost control over the whole college. Therefore, in the actual implementation process, reduce the space scope of cost control as much as possible, decompose the cost control indicators, implement them to each department and each post, and finally assign the responsibility to the person, so as to improve the cost control intensity. In general, the cost control of higher vocational colleges is divided into three levels, namely, task control at the grass-roots level, management control at the middle level and decision control at the top level. Three levels, each performing his duties. However, the cost control must be carried out under certain conditions. For example, the cost control must be limited by personnel. The middle-level management control of the college requires the middle-level management of the college to have certain management ability and quality. In addition, there are also requirements for the number of people to carry out management control, which should not be too many. Another example: cost control must also cooperate with institutional constraints [8]. Without a complete control system, it is difficult to carry out cost control reasonably and effectively. It should be noted that the controllability and uncontrollability of costs are not absolute. Some costs are uncontrollable under existing conditions and can be controlled when certain conditions are met. There are also some costs that are uncontrollable in the near future, but become controllable from the long-term perspective of the development of the college. Therefore, higher vocational colleges should, from a long-term perspective, create conditions to make the cost with weak control become the cost with strong control, and make the originally uncontrollable cost become the controllable cost, so as to enhance the cost control ability of the college.

The research foundation of AHP algorithm is the cost driver. Its theme is that products consume activities, activities consume resources, and cost drivers cause costs. The cost drivers of various costs are uncertain. Some are related to production activities and some are related to operation management [9]. Each cost has its exact cost driver. In the implementation process, due to different work items and tasks of enterprises, the cost drivers of each cost are different. In the traditional cost control methods, only the cost drivers related to the quantity are usually considered, and most indirect costs are ignored. In the actual work, some indirect costs are not directly related to the quantity. The AHP algorithm analysis is based on the cost drivers, and the indirect costs are allocated to the relevant activities and activity centers. According to the procedure of AHP algorithm, cost drivers can be divided into resource drivers and AHP algorithm [10–12].

The AHP algorithm is the motivation that can cause related activities. It is the standard and basis for allocating the cost in the activity-based cost database to the cost object, and also establishes an organic relationship between the product and the related resources it consumes. Then, in the same place as the resource driver, the cost in the activity-based cost database can be allocated to the relevant cost objects according to the actual situation through the specific analysis of the AHP algorithm.

4 Construction of Cost Accounting for Public Management Education

Different cost accounting objects can meet different cost accounting objectives. The public management and service majors can determine education cost accounting objects based on the needs of different cost objectives for different levels of cost information [13]. There are different departments under the public management and service majors, and different departments have different professional levels that are closely related, so education cost accounting objects can be divided by level.

For the first target cost control, it is necessary to control the overall education cost of the college. Users of cost information need to obtain the overall education cost accounting data of the public management and service majors, so the overall education cost of the public management and service majors can be one of the cost accounting objects [14].

For the second objective performance evaluation, the main core business activities of the public management and service specialty are professional teaching activities for students. Professional teaching activities are undertaken by different departments of the public management and service specialty, and cost data can be provided to reflect the implementation effect of the main core business teaching activities of the public management and service specialty by calculating the education costs of eight departments of the public management and service specialty.

For the third goal of establishing cost sharing standards, professional education costs can be used as a cost object. If you want to provide cost data for students' tuition standards, students' tuition fees are divided by majors, and the charging standards for different majors are different [15].

In summary, the educational cost accounting objects of the public management and service specialty are divided into the total educational cost of the public management and service specialty, the educational cost of the public management and service specialty departments, and the educational cost of the public management and service specialty. The analysis of education costs is shown in Fig. 2 below.

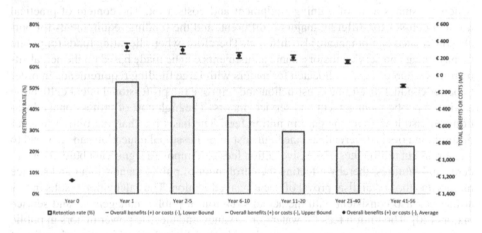

Fig. 2. Education cost analysis

The education cost of the public management and service major is attributable to its main educational function and service object, that is, the resource consumption of students' educational activities. The current expenses incurred in the cost center are classified into specific expense items of the cost project. The specific expense items are divided according to direct expenses and indirect expenses, and calculated according to different proportions to obtain the total education cost of the public management and service major [16]. Using the complete cost method to collect the total cost of public management and service professional education, and then using the parameter allocation method, we can obtain the education costs of public management and service professional departments and professional education costs.

When collecting education costs for the public management and service majors, the first step is to divide the various expenses incurred by the cost center of the public management and service majors into direct expenses, indirect expenses, and unrelated expenses based on the actual situation according to the principle of relevance, based on whether they are related to teaching [17]. For the education costs of the public management and service specialty, the accounting scope includes expenses related to educational activities. Some expenses are indirectly affected by educational auxiliary and administrative logistics departments. Based on the principle of whether they are related to the main business activities of the public management and service specialty, namely, student education activities, various expenses incurred by the cost center of the public management and service specialty are divided into direct, indirect, and unrelated expenses according to the actual situation [18]. The total education cost for public management and service majors can be obtained by adding up various expenses based on the proportion.

From the perspective of education costs for various majors in public management and service, the majors with higher education costs include A6, A11, A3, A4, B6, B7, D4, G2, and A12. Among them, the majority of majors are offered by Department A, which also corresponds to the previous analysis of the education cost of public management and service majors. The higher cost of professional education is also for hydropower majors [19]. The major of public management and service is an engineering college, which consumes a lot of training equipment and costs a lot. The content of practical training courses for different majors is different, and the funding requirements for purchasing related equipment are also different. Therefore, when allocating funds for public management and service majors, some adjustments can be made based on the actual situation. Resources can be allocated for majors with large funding requirements, in order to better conduct discipline construction and improve the professional talent cultivation ability of public management and service majors. The high cost of professional education can also lead to an increase in tuition fees. The basis for charging tuition fees for different majors is different, and the high cost of professional education can also lead to an increase in tuition fees. Excessive tuition fees can impose a significant burden on students and families, thereby affecting the enrollment of public management and service majors and the social disapproval of vocational education. The calculation results in this article are also consistent with the actual situation of public management and service majors [20]. The tuition fees for water conservancy and electric power majors in public management and service majors are relatively high, which also verifies the rationality of the application of the cost accounting system for public management and service majors.

5 Conclusion

AHP algorithm is a method to estimate the education cost of public management and service specialty in Higher Vocational Colleges Based on the following factors: the average salary of graduates. Number of graduates per academic year. Duration required to complete the plan (years). By calculating the actual education costs of different public management and service majors, it is conducive to the management of the college to allocate resources more rationally, effectively improve the utilization rate of resources, and also provide a reliable basis for the formulation of student tuition fees. Through the calculation of break even point, we can get the reasonable number of students to reach the balance point, which is conducive to formulating the enrollment plan for the next year. Moreover, by analyzing the actual cost of each major, we can further determine the best number of students for different majors, expand enrollment on the basis of ensuring the scale of the college, reduce the unit change cost, and effectively use resources. Since higher vocational colleges have changed from full allocation in the past to partial financial allocation, college leaders can compare the annual costs of different students through financial analysis, provide reference standards for formulating new plans, reduce non value-added activities, increase value-added activities, improve the input of educational resources according to the cost difference of different majors, reduce educational resources through various channels, and control educational costs, Finally, improve the efficiency of running a school.

Acknowledgements. Research results of 2021 annual planning project of Higher Vocational College Branch of China Educational Accounting Society (No. YKJ2021-089MS) "Research on the cost of public management and service major in Vocational Higher Education"; Research results of school level project of Shandong Institute of Commerce and Technology (No. C126) "Research on average education cost of students majoring in public management and service".

References

1. Hu, S., Huang, M.: Teaching reform of practical training course for financial management major in higher vocational colleges based on skills. In: IPEC 2021: 2021 2nd Asia-Pacific Conference on Image Processing, Electronics and Computers (2021)
2. Song, S.: Research on the training and teaching model framework of tourism management major in higher vocational colleges based on social market demand. Basic Clin. Pharmacol. Toxicol. **S1**, 127 (2020)
3. Chen, L.: Discussion on the construction status and teaching program reform of industrial robot technology major in higher vocational colleges from the micro level. In: 2020 International Conference on Big Data & Artificial Intelligence & Software Engineering (ICBASE) (2020)
4. Wang, X.F.: Construction of curriculum system for automobile marketing and service major in higher vocational colleges based on modern apprenticeship——taking liaoning mechatronics college as an example. J. Yueyang Vocat. Tech. Coll. (2019)
5. Xiaowen, L.I.: Research and practice on the educational reform of the logistics management major in higher vocational colleges based on the British Modern Apprenticeship. Logistics Sci-Tech (2018)
6. Chen, J.H.: Research on the curriculum reform of logistics cost management in higher vocational colleges based on the cultivation of sustainable competitiveness. Logistics Eng. Manage. (2018)
7. Liu, Q.: Construction of the curriculum system of household service and management specialty in higher vocational colleges based on AHP. High. Vocational Educ. (J. Tianjin Vocational Inst.) (2018)
8. Wei, S.U., Kuang, J.Q.: Research and development of teaching standards for hotel management major in higher vocational colleges based on professional standards. Commun. Vocational Educ. (2019)

9. Song-Hua, W.U.: Construction and practice of teaching model of accounting major in higher vocational colleges based on the integration of schools and enterprises. J. Hub Open Vocational Coll. (2019)
10. Shi, S.: Analysis of library management and service innovation in higher vocational colleges. The Science Education Article Collects (2018)
11. Yuan, X.: Reform and practice of management curricula in higher vocational colleges based on PDCA cycle theory. J. Liaoning Provincial Coll. Commun. (2019)
12. Yang, Q.: Innovative research on the education and management of party members in higher vocational colleges based on the new media era. J. Hubei Open Vocational Coll. (2019)
13. Tao, G.: Discussion on the hierarchical teaching mode of accounting major in higher vocational colleges——based on multiple intelligence perspectives. Vocational Technol. (2018)
14. Haitao, X.U.: Research on evaluation of innovation and entrepreneurship education in higher vocational colleges based on AHP. J. Changzhou Coll. Inf. Technol. (2018)
15. Zhang, R.: Exploration on smart logistic in higher vocational colleges based on perspective of service and education. J. Changzhou Coll. Inf. Technol. (2019)
16. Zhang, D., Amp, J.F.: Practical exploration of curriculum construction and management in higher vocational colleges based on SPOC platform: taking Jiangsu Food & Pharmaceutical Science College as an example. Wirel. Internet Technol. (2018)
17. Zhao, X.H.: Research and implementation of vocational skills appraisal management system in higher vocational colleges based on bi-ternary system. Comput. Knowl. Technol. (2019)
18. Dang, C.L., Cao, T.S.: Research on the construction of social service system of management and service-related higher vocational colleges. J. Yangling Vocat. Tech. Coll. (2018)
19. Chen, W.X.: Research on the ways of innovation and entrepreneurship education in higher vocational colleges based on the all-round development of human beings. Educ. Teach. Forum (2019)
20. Huang, C., Cao, Y.Y.: Innovative education in higher vocational colleges under CDIO mode—taking engineering cost major as an example. Educ. Teach. Forum (2019)

Application of Intelligent Multi-level Teaching Method in Ancient Literature

Yuan Zhang[✉] and Yang Rong

Hohhot Vocational College, Hohhot 010051, China
beibeijia@188.com

Abstract. Ancient literature is the most important part of Chinese students' study. It is the basis for understanding and mastering all other subjects. Hierarchical teaching method is an important teaching method, which is particularly important in the process of ancient literature teaching. This paper aims to explore the application of intelligent multi-level teaching method in ancient literature teaching. The research question is: how to apply the intelligent multi-level teaching method in ancient literature? In order to answer this question, a practical experiment was conducted. This experiment is based on the following assumptions: teachers can teach students at two levels; I.e. basic level and advanced level. When teachers use different methods to teach students at these two levels, they will have different effects on students' learning results.

Keywords: intelligence · Multi-level teaching · Ancient literature

1 Introduction

Since the 21st century, the number of Chinese language learners in China has been increasing, and the demand for language and culture is increasing. Culture teaching can meet the needs of students. In order to enhance cultural soft power, we have actively engaged in economic and cultural exchanges with countries around the world, and foreign friends have gradually increased their interest in the Chinese language and culture. The teaching of ancient literature for students has effectively improved their language and cultural abilities. Teaching mainly focuses on the language aspect, teaching students the language skills of listening, speaking, reading, and writing, with the aim of being used in daily oral communication. However, the learning of language knowledge cannot meet the needs of learners, and more and more students are inclined to learn the knowledge of ancient Chinese literature. Language and culture are a whole and cannot be separated. Language teaching serves cultural teaching, while cultural teaching is applied to language teaching. For learners at the primary stage, more emphasis is placed on language teaching, while learners at the advanced stage prefer cultural teaching. In recent years, China has been committed to research in the teaching of ancient literature for students, enabling more and more students to improve their language and cultural abilities. Ancient Chinese literature contains rich cultural connotations, laying a solid

Y. Zhang and N. Shah (Eds.): BigIoT-EDU 2023, LNICST 584, pp. 367–377, 2024.
https://doi.org/10.1007/978-3-031-63142-9_37

foundation for the development of modern literature. By studying ancient Chinese literature, students can learn about China's unique culture and the outstanding ideas contained
therein, and improve their own literary literacy. The following is a related study on the
importance of ancient Chinese literature in teaching Chinese as a foreign language.

The discussion method can improve students' ability to cooperate in groups, enable
them to obtain more perspectives and opinions during discussions, broaden their thinking, and also enhance student friendship. However, in the classroom, teachers should
play a leading role in controlling classroom discipline and progress. The whole body
response method uses various body languages for teaching, which can stimulate students' enthusiasm, make the classroom full of vitality, and stimulate students' interest
in ancient literature courses. Multimedia teaching methods can intuitively display some
pictures and videos, making teaching more vivid and vivid, but this does not mean that
teachers need to rely on multimedia. Teachers should interact more with students and
engage in emotional communication. In the classroom of teaching Chinese as a foreign
language, students come from different countries, which requires teachers to respect and
accommodate the cultures of other countries in the teaching process, and seek common
ground while reserving differences in treating foreign cultures.

Tolstoy said: "what successful teaching needs is not compulsion, but to stimulate
the desire of students." Teaching is to make students love to learn through teachers'
work, and students' enthusiasm for learning is very important. Learning enthusiasm is a
strong thirst for knowledge, which is the need for learning. If a teacher is eager to spread
knowledge and does not try to stimulate the students' inner state, this kind of teaching
will easily lead to apathy and learning will become a burden for students. Therefore, in
teaching, we should strive to create a good atmosphere of inquiry, so that students can
be placed in a situation of inquiry, so as to stimulate students' learning desire and make
them happy to learn. Heuristic teaching method is an effective teaching method to stimulate students' learning desire [1]. Heuristic teaching is based on the teaching purpose
and content, students' knowledge level and knowledge law, and adopts the method of
heuristic induction to impart knowledge and cultivate ability, so as to promote students
to learn actively. Through teaching practice in recent years, the author has realized the
key points of implementing the "inspiration" method: teachers should aim at students'
knowledge, thinking and psychological barriers; Grasp the key points, difficulties and
doubtful points of the teaching materials, from three aspects, i.e. knowledge content,
learning methods and learning practice, through three ways, i.e. mastering the essentials of knowledge, realizing the transfer of ability, and achieving the mutual benefit of
teaching and learning, so as to achieve the goal of mastering knowledge, developing
ability and forming habits, and finally come down to the comprehensive improvement
of students' ability to learn ancient literature [2]. The author gives a few examples for
reference.

In the teaching of ancient literary works, the focus is on the appreciation and interpretation of works. The teaching practice that often occurs is that teachers are fond of talking
about the knowledge they know at a glance, repeatedly fighting guerrillas outside the
text, and repeatedly nagging the well-known, ready-made and lifeless knowledge [3].
However, in the places that need to be explained most, they evade the important and
neglect the important, or even avoid talking about it, which leads to a great discount in

the effectiveness of teaching, and also fails to stimulate students' aesthetic perception and understanding, and makes teaching in a predicament. Therefore, this paper is based on the application of intelligent multi-level teaching method in ancient literature.

2 Related Work

2.1 Research on the Connotation of Domestic Hierarchical Teaching Method

In China, different scholars, professors and senior teachers have defined the hierarchical teaching method. The research background of this paper refers to the definition of hierarchical teaching method by Ren Zhenhai, and there are many other definitions. Among them, Mr. Wang panfang believes that "the so-called hierarchical teaching is a teaching organization form that designs multi-level teaching objectives and uses different teaching methods according to the requirements of the syllabus and teaching materials and the different knowledge bases and acceptance abilities of students, so that all students can learn on the original basis and make the most of their potential in learning mathematics." Teacher Xin Yan thinks that "Layered teaching is an important means of teaching according to the actual level of students at all levels under the class teaching system according to the individual differences of students [4]. It is targeted to carry out layered lesson preparation, layered teaching, layered training, layered guidance and layered evaluation on the basis of students' stratification, so as to achieve targeted teaching and differentiated treatment, maximize the enthusiasm of students at all levels, and enable each student to obtain Respect and development."

Through the above three definitions, we can clearly see that hierarchical teaching is aimed at the objective conditions with different students' foundations and abilities. Then, students are divided into groups to provide different lesson preparation, teaching and guidance for different groups of students, so as to maximize the development of each student [5].

Although the earliest theoretical thought of the hierarchical teaching method in China can be traced back to the spring and Autumn period, and foreign countries are more than a thousand years later than us, the application of this thought was introduced into China from abroad. It can be seen that in the early days, we emphasized theory rather than practice. However, since the 1980s, China's hierarchical teaching method has started a cycle process from theory to practice and then to theory, which not only attaches importance to the guiding role of theory, It also follows the law that theory comes from practice, and now the research on the hierarchical education method in China's educational circles has embarked on a scientific road. Looking at the research status at home and abroad, the hierarchical teaching method has a deep theoretical and practical origin. In different teaching research and experiments, it has also made fruitful research results, which provides a good theoretical basis for our teaching research, especially the teaching practice of ancient literature teachers [6–8]. The suggested research model for hierarchical teaching is shown in Fig. 1 below.

The hierarchical teaching method always adheres to the educational concept of taking students as the main body and teaching students according to their aptitude. The hierarchical teaching method sets different course content, teaching tasks, and course objectives for students at various stages regarding their knowledge level and learning

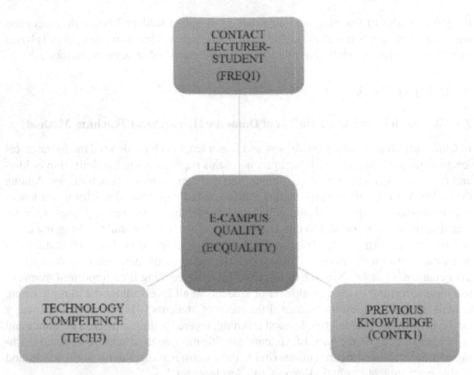

Fig. 1. I Research model of hierarchical teaching suggestions

acceptance. In short, it uses different teaching methods and means [9]. Teaching students in accordance with their aptitude means being able to better accept the teaching content in accordance with the development requirements of each student, so that each student can obtain better development in their own "recent development zone" [10].

The traditional teaching method arranges all students' ancient literature scores in order from high to low, often placing great pressure on students' psychological development. The hierarchical teaching method can adopt different educational evaluations for each student at various stages, such as relative process evaluations for each student at lower levels, so that students can more clearly understand their own progress in the learning process, and thereby mobilize their learning motivation, allowing them to obtain the joy of success, and achieving success in the teaching process, So that students have a good emotional feeling [11]. Alternatively, a relatively individual education evaluation can be conducted for each student at each stage to evaluate whether they have made progress or regressed, which can better improve their learning efficiency.

2.2 Composition of Multi-level Structure of Ancient Literary Texts

Ancient literature has an indelible historical position in the history of Chinese literature. It plays a role in inheriting excellent Chinese culture and communicating ancient and modern times [12]. Ancient Chinese literature records the excellent culture of our country for thousands of years, providing a source of life for the development of Chinese literature, allowing our literature to lead the forefront of the era and move forward.

The brilliant achievements of ancient Chinese literature are the source of the development of modern literature. It has rich historical achievements and cultural connotations. Ancient Chinese literary works generally include the Book of Songs, Ci Fu, prose, poetry, drama, novels, and other content. In the process of the development of ancient Chinese literature, a large number of famous scholars and literary works have emerged, embodying the rich wisdom and ideas of previous generations, most of which reflect the practical problems of Chinese society [13]. The diverse forms of works have made great contributions to the development of modern literary forms in future generations, guiding our progress. By studying ancient Chinese literary works, foreign students can draw on the excellent ideas of their predecessors and apply them to daily life, helping them solve some of the difficulties in life, and also enriching their own literary knowledge and enhancing their spiritual realm [14].

In short, ancient Chinese literature has promoted the development of modern literature in terms of content, form, and ideological level. It has a lofty position in history and laid the foundation for the development of modern literature.

(1) Text composition

The text composition of a text refers to the words, words, sentences, sentence groups, paragraphs, etc. that constitute the text. It is they who build a text world with rich meaning and infinite charm. The accurate and in place understanding of these words, words, sentences, sentence groups, paragraphs, etc. is the key to correctly understand the essence of the text. The primary task of high school Chinese literature text teaching is to guide students to remove the obstacles on the text, and then to deeply understand the artistic charm of the text. Yu Guangzhong once wrote: "every word is a bottomless abyss" [15–18]. Every Chinese character has its unique meaning in different contexts. In high school Chinese teaching, students need to be guided to gradually grasp the connotation of the text through continuous reading. The text based hierarchical teaching decision tree is shown in Fig. 2 below.

(2) Construction order of text

The construction order of the text refers to the combination of various elements of the text. Fang Bao of the Qing Dynasty once pointed out when expounding the relationship between "things" and "order": "meaning means the so-called" words and things "in the book of changes; law means the so-called" words and order "in the book of changes, meaning means the classics and the law, and then becomes a text." It can be seen that the ancient literary theory has long realized that the text must have a certain construction order, which is an important part of the "stylistic form" of the text [19]. The construction order of the text is often a new order that the author breaks the normal natural order, transcends the original time and space order, and reconstructs the text according to the needs of his expression [20]. And this order is often hidden in the text, without trace. In high school Chinese teaching, if we want to guide students to understand the text, we must guide students to grasp the multi-level and multi-dimensional order that the author deliberately creates to break the natural convention because of the creation needs through layers of fog.

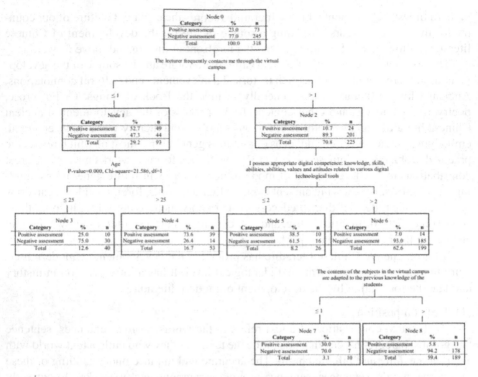

Fig. 2. Text-based Hierarchical Teaching Decision Tree

3   Application of Intelligent Multi-level Teaching Method in Ancient Literature

3.1   Application of Intelligent Multi-level Teaching Method in Hierarchical Positioning

Hierarchical positioning is the key first step of the intelligent multi-level teaching method. Scientific stratification can make full preparations for the gradually unfolding teaching work. Practice has proved that stratification after the first month of school is more scientific and effective. During this period, students have a certain understanding and grasp of this course, and gradually understand their interests and development direction. Students with clear employment orientation pay more attention to the study of professional basic knowledge; Students who like literary creation hope to improve their writing skills and appreciation ability; Students who take the postgraduate entrance examination are more willing to improve their thinking ability, as shown in Fig. 3. At the same time that the students have a clear self direction, the teachers also have a comprehensive understanding of the students' abilities and interests, and can guide the follow-up work more accurately. Then, the students fill in the self-test form and report their interests and specialties. On the premise of respecting the students' wishes, the teachers finally divide the students into three groups according to the professional nature and stratification conditions: (1) teaching ability training group; (2) Creative writing group; (3) Academic exchange group. Each group can also be subdivided into two to three groups to facilitate intra group competition. During the study period, students can apply for transfer to a more suitable group according to their own conditions.

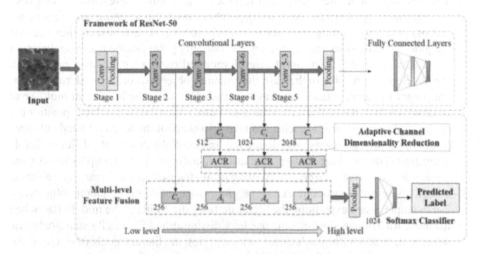

Fig. 3. Intelligent multi-level teaching method

There are individual differences between people, and the impact of individual differences in the process of human development is also very complex. Therefore, their understanding of things and their perspective on observing things will also vary, as well as their ability to accept knowledge and physical fitness. Therefore, schools should adopt the educational principle of teaching students in accordance with their aptitude and treating them differently. They have adopted a hierarchical teaching approach to schools, creating a very harmonious learning atmosphere for students during their learning process, and conducting the most efficient learning under conditions acceptable to them. Emphasize the ability differences between each learner to cultivate their self-confidence, personally experience the joy and success of sports during practice, and cultivate their learning habits to enable them to practice better. American educational psychologist Bloom advocated "mastery learning theory". His remarks made it clear that students have the ability to fully master and understand all content. In order to achieve a complete mastery level, as long as better teaching conditions are created, the group differences in abilities, speed, and motivation among most students will disappear, and these students will also achieve better grades.

3.2 Application of Intelligent Multi-level Teaching Method in Classroom Teaching

The hierarchical positioning of intelligent multi-level teaching method provides a hierarchical teaching environment for classroom teaching and is conducive to the orderly development of classroom teaching activities. Based on the rigorous and complex characteristics of classroom teaching, it is necessary to divide the intelligent multi-level teaching method into specific steps and integrate them into each link.

(1) The embodiment of intelligent multi-level teaching method in teaching objectives

Teaching objectives are the starting point of classroom teaching and the primary link of classroom teaching. Once the teaching objectives are established, they become the guide of classroom teaching. They can not only point out the teaching direction for teachers, but also point out the development direction for students and predict the development results. In the past, the teaching objectives of the modern and contemporary literature course were vague and single, while the intelligent multi-level teaching method has a clearer teaching objective after the hierarchical positioning of the students. It requires teachers to take into account the teaching needs of three levels in preparing lessons, and divide the teaching objectives into different levels according to the teaching contents: the teaching ability training group focuses on the knowledge objectives, the creative writing group focuses on the literary appreciation objectives, and the academic exchange group focuses on the academic objectives. For example, when explaining the literature from the 1950s to the mid-1970s, when teaching Ru Zhijuan's novels, the teachers distinguished the intellectual goals (the development of Ru Zhijuan's novel writing style), the literary goals (the role of the detailed description in Lily in shaping heroes) and the academic goals (the relationship between Lily and Seventeen Year Literature) according to different levels. The teaching goal is the navigation mark of the classroom teaching work. The teaching goal set by the intelligent multi-level teaching method can not only overcome the randomness, blindness and singleness of the classroom teaching, but also help to broaden the students' knowledge vision and enable them to complete their learning tasks with high quality and efficiency.

(2) The embodiment of intelligent multi-level teaching method in teaching interaction

In addition to the teaching objectives, the intelligent multi-level teaching method is also reflected in the interaction between teachers and students in classroom teaching. In the past, the classroom interaction was basically limited to two modes: the communication and discussion class with the participation of all students or the classroom demonstration class with the lecture of a certain student. In this kind of interaction, students lack initiative and participation rate is low, so it is difficult to obtain satisfactory classroom effect. The interactive link of the intelligent multi-level teaching method guides each student to participate in the field of interest according to different levels, highlights the main position of students, and more effectively mobilizes the enthusiasm of students. The interactive link of the intelligent multi-level teaching method is embodied in the form of interactive lessons. The teacher takes four teaching weeks as a teaching section, the first three weeks are taught by the teacher, and the fourth week is a teaching interactive lesson. In the interactive class, three groups of students will display, 30 min for each group, 20 min for students to display, and 10 min for teachers to comment. Based on the consideration of the teaching content from simple to deep and from layer to layer, the teaching interactive course should be displayed by the teaching ability training group first.

In order to promote the use of cutting-edge teaching methods by this group of students, the teacher needs to change the previous method of requiring students to give lectures on the spot, and instead require students to refer to the demonstration video provided by the teacher and play the "micro class" video produced by the group in the classroom. In the production of micro class hours, the students collectively decide on the content of lesson preparation, teaching methods, blackboard writing design, and complete the recording. After the basic knowledge is explained by the teaching ability training group, the creative writing group will analyze and appreciate the works more deeply and display the excellent original works of the group. Finally, the academic exchange group will raise the teaching content to the level of theoretical research, and use PPT to explain the latest research trends of relevant content.

4 Establishment of Curriculum System

The learning process of ancient literature includes: learning, practice, discussion, examination, and other links. OJ, who adapts to multi-level ancient literature teaching, should play a good auxiliary role in these links, allowing students at different levels to adapt to their own ability development, and monitoring the growth trajectory of students, accumulating relevant data for later level transfer, ultimately reducing the teaching burden of teachers, The goal of improving student performance.

As mentioned earlier, students' learning is conducted in an information based environment, where they receive a lot of information. On the one hand, they receive relevant information through teacher explanations in class, and on the other hand, they absorb other auxiliary information during the practice process. Some of these information comes from teachers, some come from the Internet, and some come from senior students.

In general, the resources are very rich, but it also means that there is some clutter. If OJ can integrate the information content that students need, then students do not need to search for needles in a haystack in the ocean of information, and learning can be more efficient.

Reasonably adjusting the curriculum of ancient literature in teaching Chinese as a foreign language mainly refers to offering optional and compulsory courses of ancient literature for students, with a reasonable allocation of majors and grades. Reasonably allocating courses can improve students' classroom effectiveness and enhance their interest in learning. The recommendations in this article are as follows:

First of all, students should have a reasonable distribution of elective and compulsory courses in ancient literature and the majors offered. Students' ancient literature courses are only required for undergraduate students majoring in Chinese language, while optional courses are offered for other majors. Undergraduate students majoring in Chinese language have a higher learning level and a strong purpose than other majors. Therefore, in order to meet their needs, ancient literature courses for Chinese language majors should be taken as compulsory courses. Secondly, the distribution of elective and compulsory courses in ancient literature among students is reasonable, mainly reflected in the provision of elective courses for junior students and compulsory courses for middle and senior students. Middle and senior level students have a higher level of Chinese than junior learners, and have a strong ability to learn ancient literary works. The characteristics of ancient literature also require students to have a higher level of Chinese language.

Reasonably adjusting the course of ancient literature in teaching Chinese as a foreign language plays a significant role in the teaching of students. The allocation of courses affects students' interest, thereby affecting their learning efficiency.

The content of ancient Chinese literature is very rich, and many of the contents in the textbooks are also very difficult to understand. The use of supporting textbooks can help students reduce the difficulty of ancient literature, such as the background knowledge of the author of poetry in ancient literature, the interpretation of rare words in classical Chinese, the expansion of extracurricular knowledge, the author's thoughts and feelings, and after-school exercises. These contents can be written into supporting textbooks, Helping students understand the knowledge in textbooks can quickly improve their learning efficiency, thereby increasing their interest in learning ancient literature. However, supporting textbooks for ancient literature need to have the following points: 1. Authoritative 2. Practical 3. Knowledgeable.

Firstly, the compilation of supporting textbooks for ancient Chinese literature needs to be authoritative. Authoritative teaching materials are reflected in the following: the author who compiled the teaching materials is a very influential figure in the ancient Chinese literature industry, and the teaching materials are uniformly distributed by the country. Students have great confidence in authoritative textbooks. Secondly, supporting textbooks for ancient Chinese literature must be practical. Supporting textbooks are intended to assist textbooks and help students more easily understand the content of textbooks. Their content must be practical, closely related to the knowledge in the textbooks, and be able to integrate the knowledge learned into practical life. Finally, there is no doubt that ancient Chinese literature textbooks must be knowledgeable. Ancient Chinese literature is inherently a highly knowledgeable discipline, and the compilation of its supporting textbook knowledge must be accurate, scientific, and within the acceptance range of students. These three points are necessary for the teaching materials of ancient Chinese literature for students.

5 Conclusion

Practice has proved that the application of the multi-level teaching method in modern and contemporary literature is effective. It makes students develop in a diversified way and is no longer a mechanical product carved out of the same mold. It also strengthens students' learning ability and self-confidence through steady teaching practice, and students truly accept this new teaching method from the depths of their hearts. As a new teaching method, although it has its shortcomings and needs to be improved and perfected, as long as teachers use it flexibly and give full play to its advantages, I believe that the multi-level teaching method can help teachers better complete the teaching tasks of modern and contemporary literature and cultivate more high-quality compound talents for the society.

Acknowledgements. Inner Mongolia Fifteen planning issues: Research on the cultivation mode of emotional quotient of higher vocational college students integrated with Chinese traditional culture, Project number: NZJGH2019124.

References

1. Hoganson, K., Brown, J.: Intelligent mitigation in multilevel feedback queues. In: Southeast Conference. ACM (2017)
2. Huan, M.A.: Research on the multi-interactive intelligent teaching model of college English in the information technology environment **2019**(3), 3 (2019)
3. Taras, T., Ivan, T., Vasyl, T., et al.: Intelligent components of multilevel system for energy efficiency management in regional economy. In: 2017 14th International Conference The Experience of Designing and Application of CAD Systems in Microelectronics (CADSM). IEEE (2017)
4. Li, H.: Intelligent restoration of ancient murals based on discrete differential algorithm. J. Comput. Methods Sci. Eng. **3**, 21 (2021)
5. Yang, C.: Application of mixed multiple teaching method in classroom teaching of ancient literature course. Educ. Teach. Forum (2018)
6. Multi-level semantic feature extraction method for behavior data of intelligent wearable equipment (2017)
7. Jiang, Z., Chaole, G.E., University S: Discussion on Chinese ancient literature teaching methods——take Shangluo University as an example. Guide Sci. Educ. (2016)
8. Zhang, L., Cai, C., Miao, X.: The technology for selective coordination of multilevel protection in intelligent power distribution system. Electr. Eng. (2016)
9. Fan, R.: On the implementation strategy of humanistic spirit education in ancient literature teaching in colleges and universities. Comparative Study Cultural Innov. (2019)
10. Liu, G.: The traning of reading and writing ability in ancient literature teaching. J. Hengshui Univ. (2018)
11. Xiu-Qin, W.U.: Application of role reversal teaching in ancient medical literature. Guiding J. Traditional Chin. Med. Pharmacy (2017)
12. Kun, H.E.: MOOCS and the teaching mode innovation for chinese ancient literature course. J. Hubei Correspondence Univ. (2017)
13. Yue, Z.G.: The study on teaching activity about ancient Chinese literature in universities for nationalities. Res. High. Educ. Nationalities (2016)
14. Dan, W.U., Library, University S: Study on library project teaching of the information retrieval course: enlightenment from the ancient literature exhibition campaign. J. Shaoguan Univ. (2016)
15. Wu, R., Xu, J., Qian, P.: Situational inquiry method in the research teaching mode for ideological and political courses. J. Intell. Fuzzy Syst. **40**(2), 1–12 (2020)
16. Liu, M.T., Liu, H.C.: Discussion on the teaching method of "Digital Image Processing" course based on "Internet +" multi-platform interaction. Educ. Teach. Forum (2019)
17. Zhong-Wei, L.I., Normal SO, Universty C: Design and implementation of interactive teaching model of ancient literature in colleges and universities. J. Chifeng Univ. (Philos. Soc. Sci. Chin. Edn.) (2019)
18. Lin, X.: On the value and implementation innovation of ancient literature in college Chinese teaching. Sci. Educ. Article Collects (2019)
19. Deng, X.Q.: A new exploration of Ancient Chinese literature teaching to improve interest stimulation and ability cultivation. J. Weinan Normal Univ. (2019)
20. Fan, X.: Research on the teaching strategies of ancient literature in colleges and universities in ethnic areas: taking the Chinese language and literature major of Tibet university as an example. Sci. Educ. Article Collects (2019)

College Students' Career Prediction Model Based on Association Rule Mining Algorithm

Lixin Nie[✉]

Jiangxi University of Applied Science, Nanchang, China
313726280@qq.com

Abstract. With the increasing employment pressure, college students' self-career planning is becoming more and more important. The student data in university campus is characterized by many types, large scale, fast updating speed and low density value. College students' career development behavior is just like data, and data mining technology can also be copied to college students' career development behavior. Career planning emphasizes setting career direction and goal, choosing career path, determining education plan and development plan, and determining action time and action plan to achieve career goal. Through the data mining of college students' career development behavior, this paper finds out which factors have important influence on college students' choice in the process of career planning development, and then analyzes and identifies the direct and indirect factors that affect students' choice, and obtains a lot of useful information on this basis, providing reference and decision support for the management of college students' career development behavior.

Keywords: Career planning · data mining · influence factor

1 Introduction

With the continuous acceleration of economic globalization, enterprises are facing fierce competition pressure, the uncertainty of organizational development increases sharply, the traditional sense of stability work is less and less, people's career uncertainty also increases, many people are no longer engaged in one kind of work or only work for one organization as before [1]. College Students' career planning has gradually become the top priority of school education, and also become the key to solve college students' career dilemma [2]. Career planning emphasizes the combination of their own situation, immediate opportunities and constraints, to establish career direction and career goals for themselves, choose career path, determine education plan and development plan, and determine action time and action plan to achieve career goals [3]. As far as the current situation is concerned, college students can not clearly recognize themselves, what are the influencing factors of their career planning, or how to do their career planning in order to make themselves effective [4]. Computer and network, initially as a special application of military, universities and scientific research institutes, has already become

© ICST Institute for Computer Sciences, Social Informatics and Telecommunications Engineering 2024
Published by Springer Nature Switzerland AG 2024. All Rights Reserved
Y. Zhang and N. Shah (Eds.): BigIoT-EDU 2023, LNICST 584, pp. 378–384, 2024.
https://doi.org/10.1007/978-3-031-63142-9_38

a social public service, deep into all aspects of life [5]. In order to overcome the lack of objectivity, this paper uses data mining technology to analyze the influencing factors of career planning.

The student data in university campus has the characteristics of many types, large scale, fast update speed, low density value and so on. Today, almost all colleges and universities have established their own management information system to collect and manage the information of students [6]. In order to effectively promote college students' employment and entrepreneurship, many colleges and universities begin to pay attention to college students' career planning education, set up employment guidance courses, provide career planning services, and carry out employment and entrepreneurship education activities [7]. In the job interview, the unclear understanding of self positioning ability, the inability to make correct judgment on the ability requirements of being competent for the post, the ignorance of the development prospect and employment requirements of the industry, the blind obedience to others, the lack of relevant professional qualification certificates and corresponding interview skills are all the reasons leading to the failure of job search [8]. From the increasingly severe employment situation of college students in China, it is urgent and important to carry out career planning education for college students [9]. College Students' career development behavior is just like data, and data mining technology can also be copied into college students' career development behavior [10]. Based on the data mining of College Students' career development behavior, this paper finds out which factors have an important impact on College Students' choice in the process of their career planning and development, so as to analyze and identify the direct and indirect factors that affect students' choice, and on this basis, obtain a lot of useful information to provide reference and decision support for the management of College Students' career development behavior.

2   The Connotation of College Students' Career Planning

Everyone has their own strengths and advantages, and is unique in personality characteristics. Everyone has development potential different from others. Whether these strengths, strengths, personality and potential can be well recognized, that is, whether they can know themselves correctly, affects or determines a person's development plan to a great extent, and then affects the future of personal development. Career planning for college students is not only the design and choice of their own career development goals and roads, but also how to apply various information and methods, constantly adjust the planning, seek a realistic path and seek greater development during their career [11]. Only through objective self-awareness, can we objectively evaluate and correctly treat our own strengths and weaknesses, thus making full use of our strengths and avoiding weaknesses in career planning. Knowing yourself can sum up lessons from failures, keep growing, and make your career more exciting.

College students' career planning means that college students carefully analyze their professional expertise and knowledge structure on the premise of fully understanding themselves and combining with the current environmental situation, and make directional plans and arrangements for future work, so as to realize the correspondence between people and posts and lay the foundation for their career development. Every college student's career planning and development should have self-knowledge. The composition of employment competitiveness of college students is shown in Fig. 1.

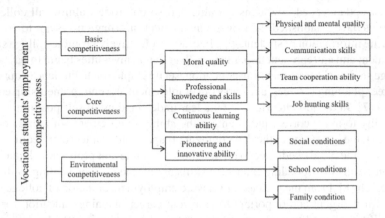

Fig. 1. The composition of the employment competitiveness of college students

Successful career planning requires proper understanding of one's own abilities, being the master of one's own life, and showing one's best self on the basis of truly understanding one's own. Providing Decision Support for Career Planners According to the data of a large number of historical successful people, various successful career models can be mined, and corresponding planning strategies can be put forward for different career models. Standardized management of classified information of successful people through data mining can provide subdivision standards for the analysis of relevant planners, classify planners according to certain standards, and identify the basic career characteristics of each kind of planners [12]. The evaluation index system in the stage of basic education emphasizes the imparting and accumulation of knowledge, but neglects the cultivation of students' ability and skills, and shows insufficient respect for students' subjective function. Both home schools and society pay insufficient attention to the cultivation of students' interest in learning. By mining and analyzing the basic attributes of planners, we can identify planners, build a decision tree model of planners, and draw the conclusion of career planning.

College students' ability of innovation and entrepreneurship is closely related to their psychological quality. Only when they have good psychological quality can they better cope with the difficulties in the process of innovation and entrepreneurship. The effect of active entrepreneurship education on college students' entrepreneurial psychological quality is shown in Fig. 2.

When many college students graduate, they are generally at a loss when facing their career choices, and they can't form effective plans for their work and personal development and growth in the future. The fundamental reason is that they don't know much about society. To accomplish the task of "knowing each other", it is necessary to fully understand the practical application goals of the major you have learned, the social needs of your major, and the specific situation of your personal professional and

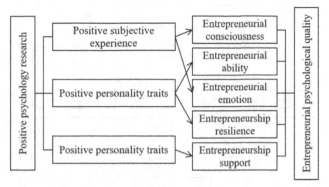

Fig. 2. The effect of active entrepreneurial psychological education on the improvement of college students' entrepreneurial psychological quality

personal career development goals and positions. The increasingly serious employment situation makes college students gradually realize that the arrival of graduation also means the beginning of unemployment, which increases students' psychological burden to a certain extent and causes heavy pressure on students. This phenomenon has aroused widespread concern in colleges and universities, and at the same time, it has brought some confusion to the psychological counseling work in schools. Through the analysis of college students' career planning and related influencing factors, it is helpful to find out the crux of college students' low employability, so as to take targeted measures to improve their job-seeking competitiveness and promote employment.

3 Analysis of Career Planning and Influencing Factors of College Students

With the rapid development of market economy, economic factors begin to occupy the first place in college students' career planning. When evaluating the employment situation of college students, it is often based on the economic income of college students engaged in occupation, the well-known degree and status of employment units. Generally speaking, school career planning, college students' achievement motivation and general self-efficacy have strong predictive power for college students' self-career planning, that is, school career planning is an important external cause for college students to implement self-career management, while college students' achievement motivation and general self-efficacy are important internal causes for college students' self-career planning [13]. For freshmen entering university, students seldom consider future employment, or some students hold an ideal attitude towards future employment, and their hearts are full of expectations. Therefore, at this time, college students pay more attention to prestigious, prestigious and high-level jobs. For freshmen's psychological state, they should be given a certain sense of crisis, and at the same time, they should be instructed to know some contents of career planning consciously according to their own characteristics and hobbies, so as to lay a good foundation for future career planning. The data mining process in the analysis of influencing factors of college students' career planning is shown in Fig. 3.

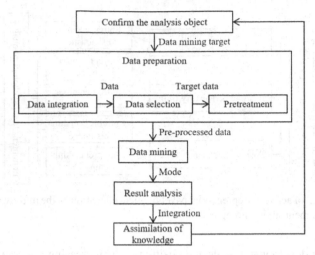

Fig. 3. Data mining process in the analysis of influencing factors of college students' career planning

Set the mixed sample set $X = \{x_1, x_2, x_3, \ldots, x_n\}$, based on a certain similarity measure, it is clustered into C separate subsets $X_1, X_2, X_3, \ldots X_c$, each of which is a type and contains $n_1, n_2, \ldots, n_c$ samples. In order to measure the quality of clustering, the error sum of squares criterion function is used, which is defined as:

$$J_c = \sum_{j=1}^{c} \sum_{k=1}^{n_j} \left\| x_k^{(j)} - m_j \right\|^2 \tag{1}$$

$$m_j = \frac{1}{n_j \left(\sum_{j=1}^{n_j} x_j \right)} \quad j = 1, 2, \ldots, c \tag{2}$$

In the formula, m_j represents the mean value of samples in the j-th category, and n_j represents the number of samples in the j-th category. The weighted average squared distance sum criterion is:

$$J_I = \sum_{j=1}^{c} p_j s_j^* \tag{3}$$

$$s_j^* = \frac{2}{n_j(n_j - 1)} \sum_{x \in x_i} \sum_{x' \in x_j} \left\| x - x' \right\|^2 \tag{4}$$

where s_j^* is the average squared distance between samples within a class. The distance between classes and the criteria are:

$$J_b = \sum_{j=1}^{c} (m_j - m)(m_j - m) \tag{5}$$

where m_j is the sample mean vector of type w_j, and m is the mean vector of all samples. The larger the distance between the clusters and the criterion function value, the better the separation of each type of the clustering results, so the clustering quality is high.

Specifically, professional support and consulting services in school career planning have a reverse effect on college students' self-career planning. The more professional support and consulting services provided by schools, the lower the self-career planning of college students. People with high self-efficacy are people with high self-confidence. They are more inclined to look for prestigious units and jobs that are conducive to giving full play to their strengths and realizing their own values, while considering less security factors, because people with strong self-confidence believe that they can do well everywhere. For people with low self-efficacy, they pay more attention to guarantee factors, which is in the lower stage of Maslow's hierarchy of needs theory. People with low self-efficacy always want to find a unit with good security and welfare to work for a long time. Relatively speaking, the chances of job-hopping are smaller, but they also lose many opportunities and dare not accept challenges [14]. Achievement motivation also has a positive impact on college students' self-career planning and management, which tells us that college students with strong achievement motivation always hope that they can make a difference, have lofty aspirations and achieve brilliant achievements in their future career. In order to achieve this goal, they often take the initiative to plan their college life, take their professional studies seriously, and try their best to achieve better results.

4 Conclusions

Every college student is a unique self, and there are some differences in temperament types and personality characteristics. Therefore, every college student should be able to scientifically analyze and evaluate his own advantages and disadvantages and career adaptability, so as to have a clear understanding of himself and his suitable career. Career planning is to set clear long-term career development goals, formulate corresponding development steps and specific activity plans on the basis of evaluating, analyzing and studying the internal characteristics and external environmental conditions of individuals. College students should have a sense of career planning, actively explore themselves, understand the external environment, clarify goals, optimize actions, break through themselves, develop their potential, and then realize their self-worth. From the perspective of self-efficacy, college students should constantly cultivate their self-efficacy and constantly improve their self-confidence in career planning. College students should make reasonable plans for their college life, and take more beneficial vocational training as far as possible. Only when college students enter the process of career planning as soon as possible, assess the situation, find the gap between themselves and social needs at any time, improve their comprehensive quality and improve themselves, can they get the first opportunity on the road to achieve their goals and meet their competent social responsibilities with the best attitude.

References

1. Fang, D.: Research on the career planning of university teachers based on big data. China Educ. Informatization **401**(14), 72–75 (2017)
2. Gao, B., Huang, P.: Investigation on the status quo of career planning of nurses at different levels in operating room and analysis of influencing factors. Chin. J. Mod. Nurs. **22**(9), 1193–1199 (2016)
3. Zhao, J., Zhang, R., Chen, X., et al.: Career planning and career satisfaction of hospital pharmacists, influencing factors and correlation analysis. China Pharmacy **626**(8), 11–15 (2018)
4. Ji, F.: The influencing factors and reasons of college students' career planning. Think Tank Times **215**(47), 120–121 (2019)
5. Zhang, L.: Innovative discussion on the construction of "Internet+" college students' career planning system. Inf. Rec. Mater. **19**(6), 242–243 (2018)
6. Xue, L., Fan, L., Sun, J., et al.: Investigation on the career planning of minority nursing interns and analysis of influencing factors. Electron. J. Pract. Clin. Nurs. **3**(28), 198–199 (2018)
7. Li, X., Sun, P.: Analysis of the career development path of accountants based on big data. China Manage. Inf. Technol. **23**(764), 33–34 (2017)
8. Zhu, D., Wang, L., Wang, Y., et al.: Investigation on the status quo of senior nursing students' career planning and research on influencing factors. Health Vocational Educ. **37**(24), 38–40 (2019)
9. Li, Y., Li, Y., Huang, W., et al.: Status quo of rural youth career planning and its influencing factors. Chin. Market **1032**(5), 180+198 (2020)
10. Yuan, H., Ruan, W., Zou, Y., et al.: Status quo and influencing factors of students' career planning in secondary vocational schools of health. Health Vocational Educ. **38**(9), 133–135 (2020)
11. Xiao, S., Yu, Y., Wang, T., et al.: The characteristics and influencing factors of rural youth life planning. J. Agricultural Forestry Econ. Manage. **15**(4), 482–488 (2016)
12. The correlation and influencing factors between career planning and job burnout of nurses in operating room. Chin. J. Nurs. **33**(1), 58–60 (2016)
13. Song, Q., Wang, L., Xiao, F., et al.: The current status of nurses' career management and planning and their influencing factors. J. Nurs. People's Liberation Army **35**(5), 45–48 (2018)
14. Liu, X., Liu, Z.: Analysis of influencing factors of college students' career planning in the new situation. Think Tank Times **152**(36), 67+69 (2018)

Design of an Intelligent College English Teaching Management Platform Based on Association Rules Mining

Dong Wu(✉)

School of Foreign Language, Sichuan Vocational and Technical College, Suining 629000, Sichuan, China
scwd1221@163.com

Abstract. The intelligent university English teaching management platform uses association rule mining algorithms to mine high-frequency vocabulary in English learning data, providing intelligent services for student learning and teaching resource management. This platform is divided into three modules: data collection, association rule mining, and resource recommendation. The data collection module collects student learning data, while the association rule mining module uses the Apriori algorithm and FP Growth algorithm to discover high-frequency vocabulary and related resources related to English learning. The resource recommendation module provides optimal learning resource recommendations based on student learning data and mined association rules. In addition, the platform also includes a score prediction module and a personalized learning path module to help students analyze and predict their final grades and learning paths, improving English learning efficiency. This platform fully utilizes artificial intelligence technology to integrate teaching resources, manage student learning, improve English learning efficiency, and cultivate students' autonomous learning ability, providing strong support for the intelligence and modernization.

Keywords: Association rules · intelligence

1 Introduction

Education is one of the important cornerstones of human development. With the rapid development of society and the continuous progress of technology, education is also constantly innovating and transforming. College English teaching is one of the important contents in modern education reform. In recent years, with the advancement of globalization and the increasingly close communication at home and abroad, college English education has also received more and more attention. As a globally recognized language, English is one of the skills that college students must master and is widely used in both the workplace and daily life [1]. Therefore, how to efficiently carry out college English teaching and improve students' English proficiency is one of the urgent problems that major universities need to solve, subject education has also begun to try to use

Y. Zhang and N. Shah (Eds.): BigIoT-EDU 2023, LNICST 584, pp. 385–393, 2024.
https://doi.org/10.1007/978-3-031-63142-9_39

artificial intelligence technologies such as machine learning to improve teaching quality and effectiveness [2, 3]. This platform uses association rule mining algorithms to mine and analyze English learning data, combining students' learning status and educational resources for association mining, providing personalized recommendations for learning resources, helping educators better meet students' learning needs, and improving the efficiency and effectiveness of education and teaching.

This article will provide a detailed introduction to the design of an intelligent college English teaching management platform based on association rule mining, and explore its application. Firstly, we will start with the characteristics and challenges of students' learning and analyze the problems and shortcomings in current English teaching [4]. Then, we will introduce the design principles and processes of an intelligent university English teaching management platform based on association rule mining, and deeply explore the association rule mining algorithms and key modules such as data collection and resource recommendation in the platform. Next, we will explore the practical effectiveness and application of the platform in college English teaching from the perspective of practical application. Finally, we will summarize the reflection and future prospects of platform design. Therefore, we must analyze the observed and collected data and identify unknown patterns contained in the data. For a large dataset, we cannot easily know the patterns in the data, even if they are obvious [5]. The rapid development, popularization, and convenient use of the internet, especially mobile internet, have made smart education the direction of future education development, greatly accelerating the speed of educational informatization.

This article will delve into the design of an intelligent university English teaching management platform based on association rule mining from both theoretical and practical perspectives. The purpose of this article is to provide reference for educators and students, promote the modernization and intelligence of college English education, and make contributions to cultivating students with global perspectives and cross-cultural communication abilities.

2   Concept Definition

2.1   Smart Classroom Teaching and Its Characteristics

Intelligent classroom teaching refers to the integration of advanced information technology into classroom teaching, and the monitoring, guidance, and evaluation of students' learning process through artificial intelligence technology, data mining, and other means, in order to achieve efficient teaching effects and personalized teaching experiences [6]. The main characteristics of intelligent classroom teaching include the following aspects.

Firstly, the teaching process is highly interactive. Intelligent classroom teaching can achieve interaction and communication between teachers and students through network connections and other means, promote student participation and feedback, and improve teaching effectiveness [7–9].

Secondly, the sharing of teaching resources is strong. In intelligent classroom teaching, teaching resources can be shared and integrated, including various forms such as online videos, teaching courseware, cloud notes, etc., making reasonable use of teaching resources and improving teaching efficiency and effectiveness.

Once again, the accuracy of teaching evaluation is high. Intelligent classroom teaching can monitor and analyze students' learning behavior and performance in real-time through methods such as data collection and mining, provide personalized learning suggestions and feedback, and accurately evaluate students' learning ability and subject level.

Finally, the diversity of teaching modes. Intelligent classroom teaching can adopt various teaching modes such as classroom teaching, online teaching, remote teaching, etc., to meet the different learning needs of students and the teaching objectives of teachers, enhancing the flexibility and sustainability of teaching.

Overall, intelligent classroom teaching is a teaching mode that integrates information technology, artificial intelligence technology, and teaching strategies. It has characteristics such as strong interactivity, resource sharing, high evaluation accuracy, and diverse modes, and is an important direction for educational modernization and intelligence [10]. Teaching objectives can be divided into three levels: educational training objectives, curriculum objectives and classroom teaching objectives. As shown in Fig. 1.

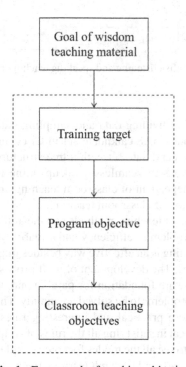

Fig. 1. Framework of teaching objectives

2.2 Evaluation Elements of College English Smart Classroom Teaching

The interdisciplinary TPACK framework, which integrates knowledge, technology and methods, provides theoretical guidance and action basis for college English educational technology. From the perspective of the combination of language learning theory and mobile new media technology, a set of visual, audible, cooperative and interactive intelligent teaching mode of college English is established, and teachers explain some error-prone knowledge points [11]. After class, the students submit their voice homework, the teachers evaluate it, push forward the tasks and exercises of English development learning, and carry out individual chemical learning and tutoring. As shown in Fig. 2.

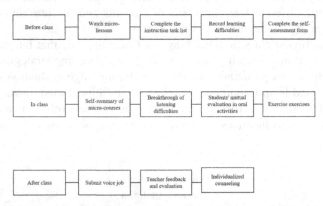

Fig. 2. Junior high school English listening and speaking teaching mode based on smart teaching system

Other variations involve dividing data and sampling data. Using some data structures, it is easier to find out which candidate set in Ci occurs in each row of the data set, such as organizing the candidate set with a tree structure with branching factor p. However, online teaching does not seamlessly link up online and offline teaching. Online teaching is completely independent of classroom teaching and can only be regarded as the extracurricular expansion of classroom teaching.

Appropriate knowledge of teaching methods and the ability to integrate information technology To solve the problem of efficiency and scalability of data mining algorithm, parallel and distributed mining is an effective way besides improving the performance of the algorithm itself [12–15]. The development of multiprocessor system and distributed system also provides hardware foundation for parallel and distributed mining. Among these algorithms, the key problems to be solved are mainly. Therefore, constraints should be set to order to find more practical and interesting rules. Although the frequency set algorithm is very practical in satisfying all the rules of simple frequency and accuracy standards, we do not want to see all the modes for some simple and important modes. The TPACK knowledge framework and in-depth learning theory cover both the perspectives of teachers' wisdom choice and students' wisdom learning.

3 Association Rule Mining Algorithm

3.1 Classical Association Rules Mining Algorithm

Association rule mining algorithm is a commonly used algorithm in data mining technology and also an important application algorithm in intelligent university English teaching management platform. The following is the application process of association rule mining algorithm in English teaching process:

1. Data collection: Collect students' English learning data, including information on their learning behavior, progress, and grades. These data will serve as the basic data for association rule mining.
2. Prepare data set: preprocess and clean the collected original data, remove duplicate data, fill in missing values, etc., and sort the data into a cleaned data set.
3. Develop a data analysis plan: Prepare an analysis plan based on teaching objectives and data analysis needs, such as determining thresholds for support and confidence.
4. Use association rule mining algorithms: Select association rule mining algorithms such as Apriori algorithm and FP Growth algorithm to process the dataset and discover the presence of high-frequency vocabulary and related resource association rules.
5. Data analysis and resource recommendation: Conduct data analysis and processing on the mined association rules, and recommend relevant English learning resources, such as learning materials, courses, and activities, to provide personalized learning suggestions for students and feedback to teaching administrators, providing corresponding inspiration and assistance for teaching.
6. After class analysis and evaluation: Based on the results of resource recommendations and student feedback, further analysis and corrections are made to the turnover of the entire link to improve the efficiency and effectiveness of the next round of teaching process.

With the help of the teacher, they can also effectively make up for their own shortcomings, and the teacher can also the students' learning ability. As shown in Fig. 3.

By creating a teaching environment suitable for students' intelligent learning, teachers make use of the intelligent classroom to prepare and implement teaching, so that students can prepare and activate their previous knowledge, thus acquiring new knowledge.

Candidate set distribution pattern in each round of calculation, each processor can calculate independently by dividing the data and candidate set into each processor. The algorithm uses the existing calculation results to update incrementally, and uses Poisson distribution to construct the upper and lower bounds of the probability that elements become frequent items to filter the data, which greatly reduces the query time. This algorithm has a big disadvantage, that is, it uses the way of generating candidate sets and testing them to get frequent sets. Therefore, the purpose of teaching evaluation is not to show the students' lack of learning, but to provide accurate data judgments for teachers' teaching decision-making.

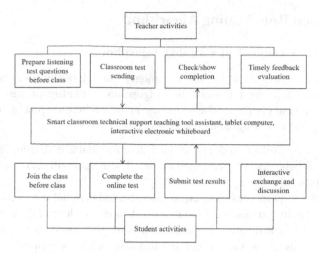

Fig. 3. Timely feedback process in the smart classroom

3.2 Association Rules Mining Based on Data Stream

Which is continuous, unbounded and disordered. According to the data dimension involved in the rule: if each item in the association rule only involves. If two or more dimensions are involved, they are called multidimensional association rules. The task of discovering association rules is to find out all the rules that meet the pre-specified support and credibility. Since the number of potential frequency sets is huge, the ideal algorithm is to read the data as few times as possible. Teacher comments not only fail to provide immediate feedback, but it is also difficult to perform statistical analysis on the results of students' homework, exams, etc. This paper conducts the first round of expert consultation. Whether online or offline, the evaluation system involves the evaluation subject, object, form and content. As shown in Fig. 4.

Data mining has a wide range of applications in college English teaching. Firstly, data mining can help educators better understand students' learning behaviors and needs. By mining and analyzing student learning data, educators can understand students' learning habits, progress, and needs, thereby better meeting their learning needs and improving the efficiency of education and teaching. Data mining can help educators develop better teaching strategies. By mining and analyzing student learning data, educators can understand the problems that students face during the learning process, develop corresponding teaching strategies based on the problems, and improve teaching effectiveness. Data mining can help educators better protect students' privacy. Before conducting data mining, educators need to protect data and privacy to ensure that students' privacy is protected. Data mining has extremely important applications in college English teaching. Through data mining, educators can better understand students' learning behaviors and needs, develop better teaching strategies, improve teaching effectiveness, and further promote the modernization process of college English teaching.

$$I(A, B) = \frac{P(A, B)}{P(A)P(B)} = \frac{f^N}{f_1 + f + 1} \tag{1}$$

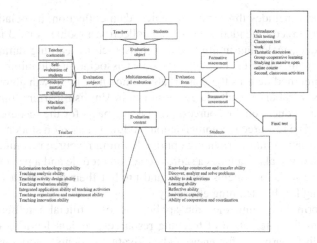

Fig. 4. Flow chart of multi-dimensional evaluation mode

The support threshold can be better used to cut down those negatively related and irrelevant association rules. Therefore, if the interest measure of the association rule includes the support degree, the interest degree of the rule can be more accurately defined. Don't give interesting indicators with support, program and association rules:

$$IS(A, B) = \sqrt{I(A, B) \times \frac{f_n}{N}} = \sqrt{\frac{P(A, B)P(A, B)}{P(A)P(B)}} \tag{2}$$

$$IS(A_1 A_2 \cdots \Rightarrow A_{k+1} \cdots A_n) = \frac{IS(A_1, A_2 \cdots A_k)}{IS(A_1, A_2 \cdots A_k)IS(A_{-1}, A_{-2} \cdots A_k)} \tag{3}$$

The above definition is based on the idea that calculating the interestingness of a rule only involves the calculation of the interestingness of related itemsets. In addition, the formula tells us that among the rules generated by a given itemset, the optimal rule should be one that can distinguish the product of $IS(A_1 A_2 \cdots A_n)$ and $IS(A_1 A_2 \cdots A_k)$ from $IS(A_{k+1} \cdots A_n)$ to the greatest extent.

4 Conclusions

The association rule mining is an innovative practice of applying intelligent algorithms, which can better serve college English teaching management. The goal of this platform is to achieve intelligent student learning and teaching resource management by mining high-frequency vocabulary in English learning data, combined with association rule mining algorithms. There is an urgent need to develop efficient mining tools. Many excellent mining tools have emerged one after another, and people have proposed many distortions to the Apriori algorithm in algorithm improvement. Introduces the ideas of association mining algorithms, including classic frequency set algorithms and their optimizations, and discusses other association rule mining algorithms. The English intelligent classroom teaching system aims to improve the intelligent teaching ability of college English teachers and develop students' intelligent learning.

This platform includes three main modules: data collection, association rule mining, and resource recommendation. The data collection module is used to collect student learning data, including multiple dimensions such as learning duration, learning frequency, listening, speaking, etc., for subsequent association rule mining. The association rule mining module uses the Apriori algorithm and FP Growth algorithm to mine high-frequency vocabulary and related resources in English learning through student learning data and educational resources, providing a basis for the resource recommendation module. The resource recommendation module is based on student learning data and mined association rules, providing optimal learning resource recommendations. In addition, the platform also includes a score prediction module and a personalized learning path module to help students analyze and predict their final grades and learning paths, improving English learning efficiency.

This platform fully embodies the application of artificial intelligence technology, strengthens the integration of teaching resources, student learning management, improves English learning efficiency, and cultivates students' autonomous learning ability. This platform will change the traditional English teaching mode, improve students' English learning efficiency, provide a better learning experience, and promote the intelligence and modernization of college English teaching.

References

1. Wei, H., Wang, L.: Design of a smart college English teaching management platform based on teaching evaluation. Crazy English: Theor. Edn. (4), 51–53 (2018)
2. Zhou, M., Zhou, X.: On the cultivation of college English teachers' informatization ability under the background of smart teaching. J. Jiamusi Vocation. Coll. (6), 157–158 (2018)
3. Li, Y.: Design and application of college English teaching model based on smart classroom. Campus English **530**(8), 31–32 (2020)
4. Qin, J., Ma, Z.: Research on wisdom teaching of college spoken English from the perspective of mobile internet. Sci. Educ. Wenhui (Mid-day Issue) **437**(10), 195–196 (2018)
5. Zhao, L.: Research on college English smart teaching model based on online learning space. J. Jiamusi Vocat. College **216**(11), 140–141 (2020)
6. Wang, M.: Research on ideological and political penetration in college English wisdom education—taking comprehensive English I as an example. J. Zhejiang Vocation. Tech. College Industry Trade **65**(02), 80–84 (2018)
7. Guo, Z., Li, Z.: Several questions about the second foreign language education of English majors in independent colleges——Taking H College of Northern Anhui as an example. J. Hubei Open Vocat. College **32**(05), 165–167 (2019)
8. Ma, Y.: The application and discussion of rain classroom in English teaching in secondary vocational schools. Mod. Educ. Forum **3**(9), 62–64 (2020)
9. Yang, Z.: From cultural literacy to cultural self-confidence: the integration of college English teaching and ideological and political elements. Educ. Res. **4**(4), 22–23 (2021)
10. Zhou, Q., Liu, J., Xin, L., et al.: Study on the changes of superoxide dismutase and association rule mining in 673 patients with osteoarthritis. World J. Integrat. Trad. Chin. Western Med. **12**(007), 958–961 (2017)
11. Zhao, Y., Xiang, M., Wang, X., et al.: Mining prescription rules for dry eye syndrome based on factor analysis and association rules. Chin. J. Trad. Chin. Med. **032**(010), 4708–4712 (2017)

12. Xie, S., Xiao, F., Ai, Q., et al.: Association rule mining for power quality disturbance event records in multi-domain distributed databases. Power Grid Clean Energy **250**(05), 39–45 (2020)
13. Zhu, X., Zhang, S., Wang, Z.: Mining method of association rules for aircraft fault maintenance records. J. Sichuan Armory Eng. **040**(007), 164–169 (2019)
14. Wang, C., Li, F.: Research on vehicle network intrusion detection technology based on association rules mining. Data Mining **007**(003), 65–69 (2017)
15. Bai, X.: Research on the application of association rule mining in teaching quality assurance. Mod. Comput. (Prof. Edn.) **33**, 24–26 (2016)

Educational Information Mining Model Based on Association Rule Algorithm

Mingjian Wang[1,2(✉)], Hailan Lu[1,2], and Jing Zhou[1,2]

[1] Wuyi University, Wuyishan 354300, Fujian, China
26452977@qq.com
[2] Beihai Campus of Guilin University of Electronic Technology, Beihai 536002, Guangxi, China

Abstract. Education informatization makes the education system accumulate a large amount of data related to education and teaching. Due to the lack of means to mine, it is impossible to discover valuable rules and knowledge contained in the teaching management and universities can provide scientific and reasonable data support for the teaching and management decisions. In this paper, association rules are used to deal with the mining of educational information. The correct, reliable and credible association rules mined from a large amount of educational information are very important to the educational system and have guiding significance to the educational and teaching reform. According to the research, the application of based on cloud clustering in the field of education can not only promote the progress, reform, perfection and development of the education system, but also provide the basis for various decision-making issues in the management of educational institutions, which is conducive to promoting the sustainable and healthy development of education.

Keywords: Association rule algorithm · Educational information · Mining model

1 Introduction

Effectively clustering Web users and web pages is of great significance to improve the quality of the website and improve the teaching effect [1]. The impact of basic courses on future professional courses, as well as other non-teaching factors that affect students' academic performance, all require further analysis for educational managers to study and make corresponding decisions [2]. The knowledge and internal laws that are hidden behind the data can best reflect the essence of the data, and have important reference value in the decision-making process. The purpose of data mining in educational informatization is to find useful information from the massive data in the educational system [3]. It is necessary for people to break the previous methods of student achievement analysis, find the real reasons that affect student achievement from the association rules of data mining, and formulate corresponding measures to improve the quality of education [4]. For education managers, educational information data mining can help

Y. Zhang and N. Shah (Eds.): BigIoT-EDU 2023, LNICST 584, pp. 394–401, 2024.
https://doi.org/10.1007/978-3-031-63142-9_40

them analyze students' learning situation and development trends, identify potential problems and needs of students, and formulate corresponding educational policies and improvement measures. At the same time, data mining can also help managers evaluate the teaching effectiveness of teachers and provide targeted training and guidance. For students, educational information data mining can help them understand their learning situation and level, identify potential subject hotspots and career directions. Students can also obtain learning resources and guidance recommendations through data mining to improve learning outcomes and outcomes [5]. Overall, the ultimate goal is to provide a basis for various participants in the education system, solve decision-making problems in the education field, and promote the development of educational informatization. By utilizing data mining technology, we can better understand and utilize educational data, optimize the allocation of educational resources and teaching processes, and improve the quality and effectiveness of education. [6]. Apply cloud-based data mining technology to the field of education, and discover a lot of useful information, which can not only promote the reform, improvement and development of the educational system, but also issues in the management of educational institutions. It is development of the education industry to a sustainable and healthy way [7].

2 Data Mining Overview

2.1 Data Mining

Although the history of development is short, since the 1990s, data mining has developed rapidly. Because it is the product of a variety of disciplines, there is still no unified definition. The definition of data mining is proposed by different scholars. Have different views [8]. Data mining is the most critical step in the KDD process. In practical applications, the terms data mining and KDD are often indistinguishable. After the birth of data mining, many factors have promoted the development and application of data mining technology. The mining is shown in Fig. 1.

The process of global economic integration is accelerating, and the pressure of market competition that enterprises are facing is becoming more and more serious. Enterprise managers hope to find problems in operation and management and countermeasures to solve them from a large amount of historical data accumulated by enterprises [9]. The information processing technology of data mining is mainly characterized by extracting, converting, a large amount of data in the database, and mining important information that is helpful for managers to make decisions. The classification of data mining technology is shown in Fig. 2.

With the popularization of information and the maturity of database technology, the amount of data accumulated by human beings is increasing exponentially. These large amounts of data information not only contain the great spiritual wealth of human beings, but also contain a large part of data garbage that has no value [10]. Previously that the information was not anticipated in advance. May be more valuable. Based on this situation of "data explosion" and "data excess", the main task of data mining now is how to extract the essence from these massive data and mine valuable knowledge.

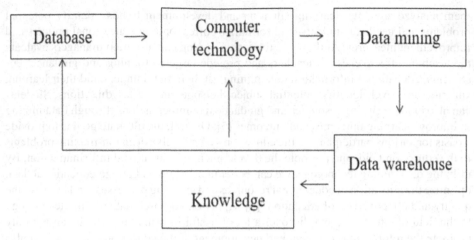

Fig. 1. The process of data mining

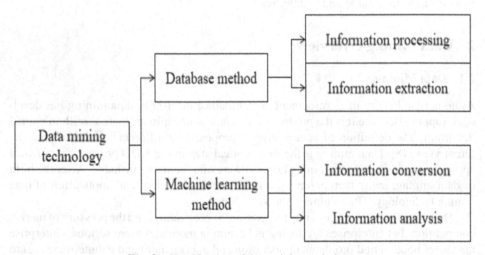

Fig. 2. Classification of data mining techniques

2.2 Application Status of Educational Information Data Mining

In the information age, education informatization has become an important educational policy for many countries. In foreign countries, developed countries also pay close attention to the development of education informatization and actively carry out information infrastructure construction. Many countries have built educational information networks. Data mining is widely used in business. In the field of marketing, it is used to discover the relationship between different commodity items in transaction data. These rules find out the customer's purchasing behavior patterns, such as the impact of purchasing a certain commodity on other commodities. It is found that such rules can be applied to product shelf design, inventory arrangement, and to classify users according to purchasing patterns. In the existing data mining, the and the mining of association rules directly on the data reflecting the academic situation of students is rarely seen [11]. The government and education departments are actively promoting the development strategy of education informatization and constantly reforming the means of education and teaching. In fact, data mining is guaranteed by the government's informatization policy, and the United States has begun to build a public through informatization, so that Internet information technology has been widely used in various fields of society [12].

Japan has taken multiple measures to implement educational informatization; the United Kingdom has legislated to promote the construction of educational informatization; Germany, Italy, the Czech Republic, Australia and other countries also attach great importance to the development of educational informatization., also achieved remarkable results. In general, the development of education informatization has shown the following trends: from attaching importance to management and education and teaching to improving students' ability to focus on learning; from relying on information technology to education-oriented; from attaching importance to master's construction to application construction; More the improvement of the intelligence of educational information, systems and teaching software. Online tests, etc., almost all information can be found through the computer.

3 Educational Information Mining Model Based on Association Rules Algorithm

3.1 Association Rules

To some extent, the data in the database have potential interrelationships. If there is some correlation between two or more sample data, then these sample data are called correlation. In a Web site, the server log file records information such as the user's access method, pages accessed, access time, and user IP address. By collecting the user browsing information recorded in the Web log, web pages and users can be clustered [13]. Recently, with the informatization, the content of the school database has greatly increased, and the school has almost achieved paperless management. Almost all information can be found on the computer, and the has been quite complete.

The membership of the association rule algorithm is counted according to the attribute with the smallest value, as shown in Tables 1 and 2.

Table 1. Membership of individual itemsets

Membership	A1	B2	B3
1	0.41	0.73	0.82
2	0.37	0.52	0.65

The association rules specifically refer to the smallest unit that cannot be divided in the transaction database, and its union is called an itemset. To preprocess the collected

Table 2. Binomial membership degree

Membership	{A1, B1}	{A2, B2}
1	0.44	0.23
2	0.56	0.47

data, obtain a sequence of web pages visited by each user. The sequence of web pages visited by a user during a continuous browsing of a particular website (from logging in to leaving the website) is called a user browsing transaction. The correct, reliable and credible association rules excavated from a large amount of educational information are very important to the educational system and have guiding significance for the reform of education and teaching. Correct, reliable, and trustworthy association rules can provide guidance for educational and teaching reform. By mining a large amount of educational information, we can understand which teaching methods, resources, environment and other factors are related to students' academic performance, interests, motivation, etc. These association rules can provide powerful references for the education system, guide the formulation and implementation of teaching reform measures, and improve the quality and effectiveness of education. If a user visits another website halfway, and then returns to this website, the sequence of web pages browsed after returning will constitute another user's browsing transaction. The database considerable which is directly related to teaching, and the other part of the data contains the basic data of students.

Assuming that T is the dataset, the category set is $\{C_1, C_2, C_3, \ldots, C_k\}$, and an attribute V is selected to divide T into multiple subsets.

Assuming that V has n non-overlapping values of $\{v_1, v_2, v_3, \ldots, v_k\}$, then T is divided into n subsets $T_1, T_2, T_3, \ldots, T_n$, where all instances in T_i have the value v_i.

Let: $|T|$ be the number of examples in dataset T, $|T_i|$ be the number of examples with $v = v_i$, $|C_j| = freq(C_j, T)$, be the number of examples with C_j classes, and $|C_j V|$ be the number of examples with C_j classes out of $V = v_i$ examples.

1 The probability of occurrence of category C_j:

$$P(C_j) = |C_j|/|T| = freq(C_j, T)/|T| \tag{1}$$

2 Occurrence probability of attribute $V = v_i$:

$$P(v_i) = |T_i|/|T| \tag{2}$$

3 Example of attribute $V = v_i$, with conditional probability of class C_j:

$$P(C_j|v_i) = |C_j v| /|T_i| \tag{3}$$

4 The information entropy of the category:

$$H(C) = -\Sigma_j P(C_j) \log_2(P(C_j))$$
$$= -\Sigma_j \frac{freq(C_j, T)}{|T|} \times \log_2(\frac{freq(C_j, T)}{|T|}) = \inf o(T) \tag{4}$$

In the whole process of association rules, the most basic and important thing is to identify the frequent items in the transaction database, and on this basis, the association rules are obtained. Online tests, etc., almost all information can be found through the computer. The association rules are mined on the preprocessed browsing transactions, and the association rules satisfying a certain degree of support are mined. Association rule algorithms compare words with discrete-valued dataset analysis. The data indicators in the original database of Tathagata are continuous. When using the association rule data mining algorithm, the relevant original data should be discretized. Whether the discretization process is reasonable will affect the mining results of association rules.

3.2 Mining Results and Analysis

The clustering results cluster the web pages with closely related content in the same category, for example, the web pages related to "selective structure programming" and "circular structure programming" are clustered in the same category, which shows that most students are online in the order of content connection. Study. The facts described by the first type of rules are consistent with the traditional pedagogy's understanding of related issues. The association rules obtained by data mining have confirmed the relevant discourses of educational theory with experimental data. Individual chapters, such as most of the web pages about "bit operation", do not appear in the clustering results, because "bit operation" is not the focus of assessment, and the number of people who study it seriously is relatively small. The second type of rules are the laws that people have not recognized or paid attention to in previous research and work., such rules reflect the laws of education and are new knowledge discovered through data mining. As shown in Fig. 3, we can find that the research on smart learning experience is increasing year by year.

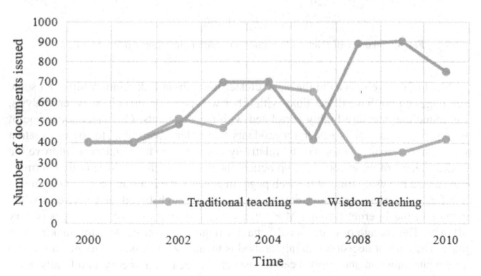

Fig. 3. Smarter classroom research trends

The clustering method considers the browsing time of web pages. If the browsing time is too short, and the visits to the web pages are not included in the browsing transaction during preprocessing, then these web pages cannot appear in the association rules and cannot appear in a certain in a cluster. The third type of rules are association rules that have not been discovered before and are not recognized by educational experts now, but are indeed association rules generated through data mining (it has a certain value of support and confidence), which at least reflect certain conditions under certain conditions. This is a representative phenomenon, and its connotation remains to be further studied. Figure 4 shows the number of relevant literature on smarter classrooms in core journals.

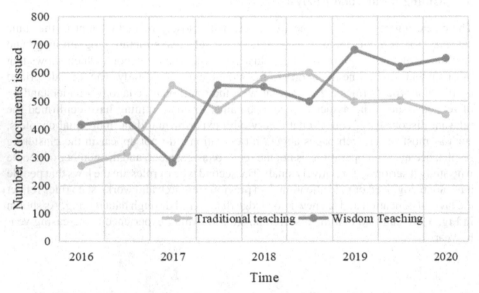

Fig. 4. Quantity of relevant literature on smarter classrooms in core journals

Most of the web pages in the same cluster have direct link relationships, but some web pages do not have direct links with other web pages in this class. After analysis, it is found that they are highly correlated with their contents. One can choose one of the three courses that is easier for students to master. According to the association rules, other related courses will be relatively easy to introduce and may improve the academic level of these courses. In practical the parameter that is difficult to determine is the actual browsing time of the web page. In general, the Internet access environment of different users is very different, some browse through broadband network, while others surf the Internet through Modem, the transmission time of web pages is very different. The change of educational behavior requires scientific decision-making as a guide. The current decision-making method is to analyze, reason and judge based on a certain phenomenon and apply a certain aspect of educational theory, and finally make a decision.

4   Conclusions

In teaching, the management of students is a science. However, the higher education is less, and the new field. These rules can be mined by different methods, and the rules can be mined according to different conditions. There are association rules in educational information. These rules hidden in the data. By mining the different rules hidden behind the data in the educational information, we can understand the significance of these rules in education and teaching work while understanding the data mining technology, which provides support for our future education. Utilize the allocate educational resources in a targeted manner, and reform teaching modes and curriculum settings, so that relevant courses can be strengthened and promoted, and educational reforms can be made more scientific.

References

1. Oyediran-Tidings, S.O., Nekhwevha, F.H., Ondari-Okemwa, E.M., et al.: Access to educational information enabled by ICT tools in the Fort Beaufort Education District (FBED), Eastern Cape, South Africa. Inf. Dev. 37(3), 402–416 (2021)
2. Yang, S., Lee, J.W., Kim, H.J., et al.: Can an online educational game contribute to developing information literate citizens? Comput. Educ. 161(4), 104057 (2021)
3. González García, C., Núñez-Valdez, E.R., Moreno-Ger, P., et al.: Agile development of multiplatform educational video games using a domain-specific language. Univ. Access Inf. Soc. 18, 599–614 (2019). https://doi.org/10.1007/s10209-019-00681-y
4. Razak, N.A., Jalil, H.A., Krauss, S.E., Ahmad, N.A., et al.: Successful implementation of information and communication technology integration in Malaysian public schools: an activity systems analysis approach. Stud. Educ. Eval. 58, 17–29 (2018)
5. Furze, M.Z., Phillips, J.P.: Integrating functional MRI information into the educational plan of a child with cerebral visual impairment: a Case Study. J. Vis. Impair. Blind. 112(5), 532–540 (2018)
6. Koç, H., van Kippersluis, H.: Thought for food: nutritional information and educational disparities in diet. J. Hum. Capital 11(4), 508–552 (2017). https://doi.org/10.1086/694571
7. Hare, S., Frye, J.M., Samuelson, B.L.: Open pedagogy as an approach to introducing doctoral students to open educational resources and information literacy concepts. Libr. Trends 69(2), 435–468 (2020)
8. Dockery, A.M., Bawa, S., Coffey, J., et al.: Secondary students' access to careers information: the role of socio-economic background. Aust. Educ. Res. 49, 1001–1023 (2022). https://doi.org/10.1007/s13384-021-00469-1
9. Madu, A., Musa, N.B., Makinta, Y., et al.: Information and communication technology (ICT) and library and information science (LIS) for sustainable development goals (SDGs). Br. J. Educ. Stud. 1(1), 149–164 (2018)
10. Lachner, A., Weinhuber, M., Nückles, M.: To teach or not to teach the conceptual structure of mathematics? Teachers undervalue the potential of Principle-Oriented explanations. Contemp. Educ. Psychol. 58, 175–185 (2019)
11. Menaha, R., Jayanthi, V.: Heuristics-based sequence labelling model for finding educational domain acronym expansions. Exp. Syst. Int. J. Knowl. Eng. 40(6), e13216 (2023)
12. Yang, J., Kinshuk, An, Y.: A survey of the literature: how scholars use text mining in educational studies? Educ. Inf. Technol. 28, 2071–2090 (2023). https://doi.org/10.1007/s10639-022-11193-3
13. Yilmaz, T., Ozcan, R., Altingovde, I.S., et al.: Improving educational web search for question-like queries through subject classification. Inf. Process. Manage. 56(1), 228–246 (2019)

Evaluation and Analysis of the Effect of College Students' Mental Health Education Based on Association Rules Mining Algorithm

Hong Leng[✉] and Junyong Gao

Hunan City University, Yiyang 413000, Hunan, China
13778765@qq.com

Abstract. This article aims to evaluate and analyze the effectiveness through association rule mining algorithms. Firstly, we collect and organize a certain amount of data on college students' mental health education, and then use the Apriori algorithm to mine association rules to obtain the key feature factors and corresponding educational effects. Education for college students include family, friendship, love, etc. These factors are closely related to the students' psychological state and mental health. Meanwhile, by mining data from educational practices, we have found that combining online and offline mental health education for students can effectively improve their mental health status. The conclusion of this article indicates that providing mental health education to college students and creating appropriate educational environments and methods can effectively improve their mental health level, enhance their awareness and attention to themselves and others, and facilitate better self-management and emotional communication. The above research results provide practical reference value for relevant education departments and educators, and can provide theoretical basis and practical guidance for the promotion and application of mental health education for college students.

Keywords: Association rule mining algorithm · Psychological health education · Effect analysis

1 Introduction

In recent years, with the rapid development of society and economy in China, the number of college students has been increasing year by year. However, due to the many problems faced by college students, such as job seeking pressure, academic pressure, and social pressure, many of them face serious challenges in their mental health. Psychological health issues not only harm the physical and mental health of college students, but also have serious negative impacts on their academic and interpersonal relationships, and may even lead to a series of behavioral problems and criminal behaviors [1]. Therefore, psychological health education for college students has become one of the hot topics of

Y. Zhang and N. Shah (Eds.): BigIoT-EDU 2023, LNICST 584, pp. 402–410, 2024.
https://doi.org/10.1007/978-3-031-63142-9_41

concern in today's society. Psychological health education for college students is an educational work to guide and help college students to reduce Psychological stress, improve psychological resilience, prevent and respond to psychological problems by carrying out psychological knowledge publicity, psychological counseling, mental health education activities and other forms. However, there are many problems in the current mental health education for college students, such as the lack of scientific educational methods and measures, and the failure to meet the personalized needs of students, resulting in unsatisfactory educational outcomes [2].

This article mainly introduces the research background, significance, survey methods for online and offline mental health education, the theoretical basis of association rule mining algorithms, and the research ideas of the article [3]. To explore the cognitive status of college students' mental health, this article mainly discusses the current situation of college students' mental health, reveals the factors related to college students' mental health, and provides data support for subsequent analysis.

To analyze the characteristics of college students' mental health education and its influencing factors, this paper mainly introduces the current situation and characteristics of college students' mental health education, excavates the influencing factors of college students' mental health education, and uses association rule mining algorithm to establish a Relational model between educational characteristics and educational factors. The effect analysis of college students' mental health education is mainly based on association rule mining algorithm to analyze the effect of college students' mental health education, and propose corresponding suggestions and measures to improve the effect and quality of mental health education.

This article aims to explore the key characteristic factors and educational effects of mental health education for college students, and provide the latest research results and ideas for mental health educators, teachers, and parents, combined with the theory and practice of mental health education [4]. Therefore, in order to solve the current problems and educate college students' mental health issues in a more scientific and effective way, this article uses association rule mining algorithms to evaluate and analyze the effectiveness of college students' mental health education. This article will collect and organize data on mental health education for college students, use association rule mining algorithms to analyze educational effects, explore the characteristics and key factors of mental health education, and provide effective theoretical basis and practical guidance for improving the effectiveness of mental health education.

2   Design of Association Rules Mining System for College Students' Psychological Problems

2.1   Data Preprocessing

The preprocessing of psychological data for college students is a prerequisite for analyzing their mental health status. Before data preprocessing, data collection work is required, usually including questionnaire surveys, psychological tests, face-to-face interviews, etc. Among them, questionnaire surveys are one of the most commonly used and effective data collection methods [5]. This article will take a questionnaire survey as an example to introduce the preprocessing process of psychological data for college students.

1. Data cleansing

    Data cleansing is the first step of data preprocessing, which aims to classify, filter and noise process the collected data. The specific operation steps are as follows:

    (1) Data classification: Classify all data by category, such as students' personal information, descriptions of psychological problems, lifestyle habits, etc.

    (2) Data filtering: Usually, there is a large amount of invalid and abnormal data in questionnaire surveys, which requires filtering, deduplication, and unified naming format.

    (3) Data noise processing: Based on psychological theories and experience, select data that may have symptoms of schizophrenia, mental disorders, delusions, and other diseases, and exclude them to ensure the authenticity and accuracy of the data.

2. Data standardization

    Data standardization is the process of converting data from different dimensions into a unified standard dimension, which makes the conclusions obtained from the studied problems more reliable [6]. The specific operation steps are as follows:

    (1) Attribute specification: Filter and delete unnecessary or redundant attribute information;

    (2) Attribute weighting: Based on psychological theory and experience, data attributes are weighted to ensure that different factors have different weights on the sample.

    (3) Data normalization: Perform a unified scale transformation on the data, so that different attribute data can be compared under a unified dimension. Usually, methods such as maximum minimum normalization or Z-Score normalization are used.

3. Data conversion

    Data conversion is the process of converting non numerical data into numerical data for subsequent mathematical operations and analysis. The specific operation steps are as follows:

    (1) Data encoding: Encode non numerical data, such as encoding gender as 0, 1, etc.;

    (2) Data Discretization: convert continuous data into discrete data. Common Discretization methods include equal frequency Discretization, equal distance discretization, etc.

4. Data normalization

    The main purpose of data normalization is to standardize the data to the same magnitude range, so that various indicators can be compared and weighted, and to avoid biased evaluation of results due to different numerical values. The specific operation steps are as follows:

    (1) Maximum-minimum normalization: linearly map data between $[0,1]$;

    (2) Z-Core normalization: convert data to standard Normal distribution.

    By preprocessing college students' psychological data, the original data can be converted into a dataset that can be used for further analysis, which lays the foundation for subsequent analysis of college students' mental health [7].

    That is, dealing with some relationships among multiple attributes. Data often implies a lot of unknown and meaningful information and knowledge, and these information and knowledge often have high or high value, and can provide a basis for decision-makers to make decisions. The raw data can be structured or semi-structured, or it can be heterogeneous data distributed on the network [8]. Data preprocessing is a very important link in the process of association rule mining, in order to improve the accuracy, effectiveness and scalability of association rule mining. Data mining techniques originate from multiple disciplines. As shown in Fig. 1.

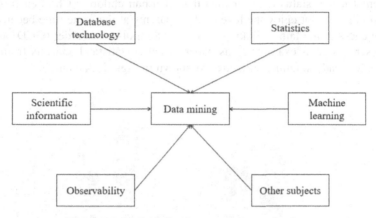

Fig. 1. Multi discipline impact mining technology

Moreover, there may be a lot of noise data, and there may be many reasons for it. It may be that students do not fill in standardly, resulting in wrong information when the machine reads the card, or it may be that students miss filling in when filling in, and so on.

2.2 Data Cleaning

Data cleaning can also be called data cleaning, including vacancy processing, noise processing and inconsistent data processing. However, the missing values of students' only child, student cadre, place of origin, family structure and other attributes have not been handled. The array structure and bit operation are adopted, which saves a lot of memory space, makes full use of the mining results of the original data set, scans the new data set only once, and does not need to scan the original data set [9]. The system has processed the missing values of some attributes of psychological problem data, and then generate the data into the data format required by the following mining modules, and help people build macro concepts. Because neural network is a distributed matrix structure, neural units have high parallelism and distribution. The ability of parallel computing and distributed storage of data makes the neural network self-adaptive, self-organizing and self-learning. As a student cadre, students have improved their coordination and communication ability with teachers and students in various trivial matters of daily life, and the proportion of interpersonal sensitivity is naturally lower than that of non-student cadres [10]. Data cleaning is mainly aimed at the problems of nonstandard, ambiguous, repeated and incomplete data in multiple data sources or data tables.

3 Application of Association Mining in Mental Health Assessment

3.1 Key Technology Realization

Data acquisition is the bottleneck of mass testing. Whether using ordinary manual statistics or traditional computer technology, it is quite inefficient when processing a large amount of data. Rural children are affected by economic pressure and employment pressure. Mental health status is lower than that of urban children; Children from single parent families cannot enjoy the love of their parents at the same time because of the incompleteness of the family. Taking obsessive-compulsive disorder (OCD) and interpersonal sensitivity as examples, this paper makes a statistical analysis from gender, origin, student cadres, family structure. As shown in Figs. 2, 3, 4 and 5.

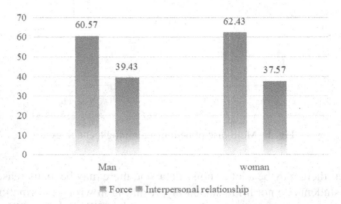

Fig. 2. Relationship between gender and psychological symptoms

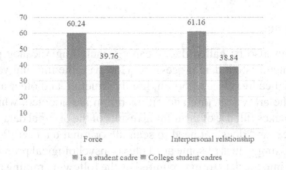

Fig. 3. The relationship between student cadres and their psychological status

There will be some extreme views on problems, and the mental health status can not be ignored. The scale of candidate itemsets that generate new data sets is huge. It takes a lot of time to process these candidate itemsets, and many of them are infrequent itemsets, which affects the efficiency of the algorithm.

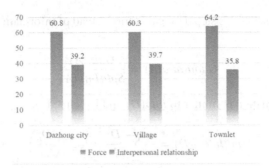

Fig. 4. The relationship between source and psychological symptoms

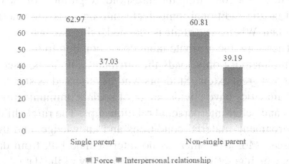

Fig. 5. The relationship between single parenting and psychological symptoms

3.2 Mining Implementation of Applied Algorithms

According to statistical knowledge, conclusions drawn from a smaller sample space may not be highly representative. Conclusions with general significance are often the result of statistical induction on a large number of samples. Adding a new constraint interest degree to the traditional algorithm, using interest degree to evaluate the effectiveness of rules and pruning boring rules can avoid generating "illusion" association rules.

Interest is defined as:

$$interesting(A \Rightarrow B) = \frac{P(A|B)}{P(A)P(B)} \tag{1}$$

Due to the influence of the social environment and the lack of quality education in schools, parents take care of their only children and cultivate their selfish psychology. In interpersonal communication, there are self-centeredness, self-isolation, social utility, suspicion, jealousy, friendship and so on. Compared with rural students, students living in large and medium-sized cities have greater pressure on their study and life, and their obsessive-compulsive symptoms are more obvious because of their parents' different educational concepts. The algorithm processes the data set in multiple steps, creates a candidate set of this step in each step of processing, and counts the support of each candidate item set. And compare with the predefined minimum support to determine the maximum itemset of this step. Use gain ratio instead of information gain as attribute selection metric.

$$GainRatio(A) = \frac{Gain(A)}{SplitInfo(A)} \tag{2}$$

The split information is similar to $Info(D)$ and is defined as:

$$SplitInfo_\Delta(D) = -\sum_{j=1}^{v} \frac{D_j}{D} \times \log 2\left(\frac{D_j}{D}\right) \tag{3}$$

The data of different attributes and different psychological symptoms are counted in advance as the reference for setting the threshold. Regardless of the common manual statistical method and the traditional computer technology, it is quite inefficient to process a large amount of data. When an attribute is scanned, other attributes do not participate in the calculation. Therefore, the attribute table corresponding to these attributes is saved to the disk, and the memory only loads the attribute table to be used. This saves the memory footprint to a great extent. Students who have served as student cadres or lived in large and medium cities have a wide range of social communication, relatively rich social experience, and better interpersonal relationships. The rural children are affected by the living environment, material conditions and knowledge, and the psychological pressure is too great. Moreover, there is no intermediate link from data collection to computer storage, which greatly improves the reliability of the data.

4 Experimental Results and Analysis

In order to study the effectiveness of mental health education for college students and explore the characteristics and key factors of mental health education for college students, this article uses association rule mining algorithm to evaluate and analyze. This article selects 150 college students for experiments, collects data through a questionnaire survey, and uses Apriori algorithm for association rule mining and analysis to identify the key characteristic factors and educational effects of mental health education for college students.

1. Experimental Results

   Through the analysis and evaluation of experimental results, we found that the characteristic factors of mental health education for college students include family, friendship, love, personal values, etc. These factors are closely related to students' psychological status and mental health. Meanwhile, through data mining on the practice of mental health education for college students, we found that combining online and offline mental health education for students can effectively improve their mental health status.

   Further use association rule mining algorithms to derive the following association rules:

   – If students have close family relationships, their mental health level is higher;
   – If students have good friendship, their mental health level is also high;

– If students can experience love, their mental health level is also higher;
– If students have self-affirmation and a positive outlook on life, their mental health level is also higher;
– If students actively participate in online and offline mental health education, their mental health level is also relatively high.

2. Experimental Process

The experiment used a questionnaire survey method to investigate the mental health status of college students, as well as their experiences and feelings related to mental health education. The questionnaire survey adopts a closed form questionnaire, which mainly includes four parts: personal basic information, mental health issues, personal evaluation, and educational suggestions.

We collected 150 valid questionnaires and preprocessed the questionnaire data, including Data cleansing, data standardization, data conversion, data normalization, etc. Using the Apriori algorithm for association rule mining and analysis, to identify key characteristic factors and educational effects of mental health education for college students.

3. Result Analysis

The experimental results indicate that the key characteristic factors of mental health education for college students mainly include family, friendship, love, personal values, etc., and combining online and offline mental health education for students can effectively improve their mental health status. At the same time, the association rules obtained through the association rule mining algorithm also verified this conclusion.

This article evaluates and analyzes using association rule mining algorithms, providing an effective data mining method for the field of mental health education. The experimental results show that analyzing the key characteristic factors and educational effects of mental health education for college students can effectively improve the quality and effectiveness of mental health education. This method can provide reference for effectiveness evaluation in other fields. This has certain practical application and promotion value.

5   Conclusions

This article evaluates and analyzes the effectiveness of mental health education for college students using association rule mining algorithms. The experimental results indicate that the key characteristic factors of mental health education for college students mainly include family, friendship, love, personal values, etc., and combining online and offline mental health education for students can effectively improve their mental health status. By deeply exploring the characteristic factors and association rules of mental health education for college students, important theoretical basis and practical guidance are provided for the work of mental health education. At the same time, the research method can provide reference for data mining and applications in other fields, and has great promotion and application value.

References

1. Zheng, X.: Mining of association rules based on apriori algorithm for psychology of high risk female prisoners. Inf. Technol. Inf. (2), 3 (2021)

2. Fan, M., Yang, G.: Association rule mining algorithm for privacy protection. Inf. Secur. Res. **7**(11), 10 (2021)
3. Wei, F.: An analysis system for college students' psychological control based on embedded data mining. Electron. Des. Eng. **29**(24), 5 (2021)
4. Chang, S.: Psychological big data evaluation method based on association rule feature extraction. J. Zhoukou Normal Univ. (2), 4 (2020)
5. Yao, X., Xiao, C., Yan, H., et al.: Analysis of association rules for neuropsychological delay in preschool children. China Health Stat. **37**(1), 3 (2020)
6. Liu, R.: Analysis of college students' mental health based on machine learning algorithms. China Educ. Technol. Equip. (22), 3 (2020)
7. Guo, Y.: Analysis and countermeasures of mental health problems of contemporary college students. Sci. Educ. J. Electron. Ed. (34), 2 (2020)
8. Zhang, Y.: Statistical analysis of mental health of college students in Jiangmen city. Sci. Educ. J. Electron. Ed. (9), 1 (2020)
9. Ruan, S., Zhao, L., Mo, H., et al.: A four-year longitudinal study on social rhythm and positive mental health of college students. Adv. Psychol. **2**(3), 7 (2022)
10. Zhong, Z., Yu, R.: Exploration and practice of group psychological counseling in mental health education of college students. Psychol. Mon. (9), 3 (2020)

Application of Improved Fuzzy Mathematics Comprehensive Evaluation Algorithm in Student Evaluation System

Zhang Chen[1(✉)], Xiangzhou Liu[2], and Zhang Li[2]

[1] School of Mathematices and Statistics, Longdong University, Qingyang 745000, Gansu, China
zch03120424@126.com
[2] Zhangjiagang Campus of Jiangsu University of Science and Technology, Suzhou City 215600, Jiangsu, China

Abstract. The direct purpose of student evaluation of teaching is to evaluate the teaching effect of the teachers of the course, but more importantly, it is to summarize the excellent teaching experience of teachers and find scientific norms for the stable improvement of undergraduate teaching quality. The defect of the traditional student evaluation system is that in the process of student evaluation, there are too many indicators and most of them belong to qualitative indicators, which makes comprehensive analysis difficult to master and operate. The application of the improved fuzzy mathematics comprehensive evaluation algorithm in the student evaluation system is a method to evaluate students' academic achievements. This method is based on the concept that every student has different learning styles, and every student has some difficulties in learning new things. Therefore, if we can use this idea to establish an effective evaluation system for students, it will be better. The main purpose of this paper is to introduce the application of the improved fuzzy mathematics comprehensive evaluation algorithm in the student evaluation system, and discuss its advantages and disadvantages.

Keywords: Fuzzy mathematics · Student evaluation system · Evaluation algorithm

1 Introduction

In recent years, many colleges and universities have changed the traditional practice of implementing teacher evaluation from top to bottom by school leaders alone, and established a teacher evaluation system involving multiple subjects including students. This has become an important development trend of the current teacher evaluation reform. The object of this paper is to improve and optimize the online teaching evaluation system of college students, and take Southwest University of science and technology as an example to analyze the effectiveness of the implementation [1].

Teaching quality is the lifeline of a school's survival and development. The student evaluation system is an important measure of the school's teaching quality monitoring

Y. Zhang and N. Shah (Eds.): BigIoT-EDU 2023, LNICST 584, pp. 411–421, 2024.
https://doi.org/10.1007/978-3-031-63142-9_42

system and an effective way to improve teaching quality. With the help of pedagogy, statistics, psychology and other discipline theories, the student evaluation system evaluates teachers' teaching quality according to the pre-set evaluation index The assessment and evaluation have played a positive role in monitoring the quality of classroom teaching, helping teachers improve teaching and improving teaching level [2]. The student evaluation system has a strong theoretical basis, which can provide the most direct basis for the school's education and teaching strategies, and facilitate the decision-makers to make decisions.

Student evaluation of teaching plays an important role in college evaluation because it has multiple functions and can serve a variety of purposes. Generally speaking, its functions and functions mainly include: increasing the opportunities of teachers' self-evaluation, encouraging teachers to improve teaching, improving the communication between teachers and students in teaching, enhancing students' learning motivation, providing democratic training opportunities for teachers and students, reflecting teachers' teaching performance, serving as a reference for teachers' personnel decision-making, and providing evidence for academic research [3].

The traditional way of teaching evaluation in Colleges and universities is mainly to feed back the teaching situation of teachers to the academic affairs office through the informants in the majors and classes, or to issue questionnaires to students to evaluate teachers' teaching. This has promoted the monitoring of teaching quality to a certain extent, but its shortcomings and disadvantages are also obvious. Therefore, it is of great theoretical significance and practical value to deeply analyze the shortcomings of traditional students' teaching evaluation methods, combine modern education theory, and use network information technology on the basis of university management informatization to form an effective students' online teaching evaluation system.

Teaching quality is the lifeline of colleges and universities, and is an important indicator of the teaching effect and comprehensive influence of colleges and universities, which is related to the quality of talent training and reputation of colleges and universities. At present, limited to the conditions of incomplete data and outdated evaluation methods, the evaluation of teaching quality in colleges and universities is not deep enough, and it is impossible to use the accumulated teaching evaluation information to carry out a reasonable evaluation of the teaching quality in colleges and universities and explore the key factors affecting the teaching quality in colleges and universities.

Therefore, this paper will use the attribute reduction idea of fuzzy teaching to complete the task of finding the key factors of college teaching quality evaluation, and mining the hidden rules from the surface of college teaching quality data, and extracting the corresponding decision rules to assist managers to make decisions.

The research of this paper will have the following research significance:

(1) Standardize the teaching quality evaluation process. Through the construction of index system, data processing, attribute reduction and other work, this project will form a relatively complete teaching quality evaluation process, which is of great research significance to ensure the teaching quality of colleges and universities and continuously improve the teaching level.

(2) Effective data processing. In order to better deal with the teaching quality data, this project will reasonably conduct quantitative analysis on the teaching quality data of

colleges and universities, simplify the constructed index system through the attribute reduction idea of rough set, and then find the key factors affecting the teaching quality of colleges and universities, and finally complete the evaluation of teaching quality of colleges and universities, which will provide necessary theoretical support for the reform of the teaching system of colleges and universities.

(3) Improve the efficiency of teaching quality evaluation. Developing technology to design and complete the teaching quality evaluation system related to the project will be of great help to improve the efficiency of data management, simplify the evaluation process, and dynamically monitor the teaching quality of colleges and universities.

2   Related Work

2.1   Mathematical Model of Students' Fuzzy Comprehensive Evaluation

Establish factor set and evaluation set. The comprehensive evaluation of students is a multi-level fuzzy comprehensive evaluation problem. The factor set is:

$$U = \{u_1, u_2, \cdots, u_n\} \tag{1}$$

Each subset is:

$$U = \{u_{i1}, u_{i2}, \cdots, u_{is_i}\}, (i = 1, 2, \cdots, n) \tag{2}$$

The formula indicates that there are s factors in U_i and there are si factors in U, and the evaluation set is:

$$V = (v_1, v_2, \cdots, v_m) \tag{3}$$

Determining the score of intellectual education in the indicator system of the membership function is related to the question of whether students can get scholarships and the scholarship grade. It is a prominent item in the comprehensive evaluation. The fuzzy set teaching evaluation framework is shown in Fig. 1 below.

2.2   Research Status of Student Evaluation of Teaching

The significance and function of students' evaluation of teaching. Most literatures think that students' evaluation of teaching is of great significance. For example, Chen Lin and others believe that students' evaluation of teaching reflects the educational concept of focusing on students; It is beneficial to the optimization and perfection of teaching plan, course structure and teaching system; It is conducive to the communication between students and teachers, and promotes the mutual growth of teaching and learning; It provides an important decision-making basis and basis for the leadership management and decision-making of colleges and universities [4].

Problems in students' evaluation of teaching. Most documents point out the problems in teaching evaluation from the perspective of students. Chen Lin and others believe that the main problems are the subjectivity of students' evaluation of teaching and the distortion of information. Gao Suzhen believes that from the perspective of the reliability of

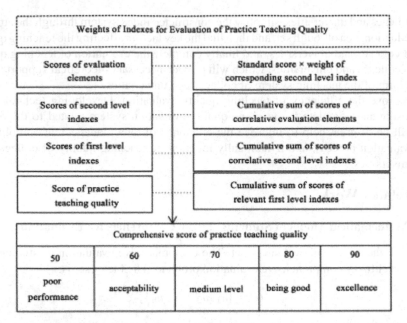

Fig. 1. Fuzzy set teaching evaluation framework

teaching evaluation, the subjective and objective factors in the evaluation process affect the fairness and accuracy of the evaluation results; Judging from the validity of teaching evaluation, the evaluation index system is not scientific and reasonable; From the perspective of evaluation purpose, the function of developmental evaluation is ignored, and the analysis and effective use of evaluation results are relatively lacking [5]. Deng Hongmei analyzed the misconceptions in college students' teaching evaluation: ignoring the limitations of students' teaching evaluation results, exaggerating the reliability and validity of students' teaching evaluation results, and treating students' teaching evaluation results as the only basis for recognizing teachers' teaching quality or directly equivalent to teachers' teaching quality evaluation [6]; Abusing students' teaching evaluation results to implement "last elimination" and "one vote veto"; One sided emphasis on the authority and effectiveness of the results of students' evaluation of teaching and their application suppresses and deprives teachers of their right to speak on the issue of students' evaluation of teaching [7]. In addition to pointing out that the index system in student evaluation of teaching is not perfect and the results of student evaluation of teaching are not reasonably used, Liu Shuping and others also believe that the current organizational procedure in student evaluation of teaching is not reasonable; The early publicity of students' evaluation of teaching is also insufficient, which greatly affects the role of students' evaluation of teaching.

Li Danqing and others believe that effective student evaluation of teaching needs to be guaranteed by a perfect system. Among them, in order to improve the recognition of students' evaluation of teaching, we must establish the concept of developmental teaching evaluation, so that the diagnostic and incentive role of evaluation can be highlighted;

Let the evaluation index system be scientific and reasonable and fully reflect the characteristics of the curriculum and teaching personality; Let the organizers, evaluators and evaluated strengthen communication and understand the significance of evaluation; Let the form of teaching evaluation be standardized and the operation process be standardized; Make the results and feedback of teaching evaluation scientific and establish an efficiency tracking mechanism of "promoting teaching through evaluation" [8]. Wang Hong believes that it is possible to consider establishing a student teaching evaluation committee, electing Committee representatives through democratic election by students, and regularly evaluating teachers' teaching performance. The evaluation results should be included in Teachers' year-end assessment as one of the important standards for teachers' teaching evaluation.

2.3 Acquisition of Student Evaluation Indicators (Metrics)

(1) Connotation of student evaluation index system

Student evaluation of teaching is a process in which the relevant departments of the school organize students to evaluate and feedback the teaching work of teachers according to certain evaluation indicators and standards. In a narrow sense, student evaluation of teaching is limited to specific teaching work, but because undergraduate teaching activities also involve many teaching contents, methods and means, the object of student evaluation of teaching will be expanded to all elements of the teacher's teaching process [9].

The index system of students' evaluation of teaching is the embodiment of a standard in students' evaluation of teaching. The index system of teaching evaluation is actually a standard that teachers should achieve in the teaching process and daily teaching process. This standard plays a guiding role in the teaching work of schools. In other words, what kind of index system there is will be what kind of teaching work level and teaching quality.

(2) Framework of student evaluation index system

The indicator framework of students' evaluation of teaching is generally given by the relevant departments of the school. According to certain principles, the indicators of the whole evaluation of teaching are listed from large to small, from broad to subdivision. The index framework should give the participants a simple and clear feeling, which is conducive to the participants' understanding and operation of teaching evaluation, and at the same time, it should include the content of teaching evaluation as comprehensively as possible [10]. The management framework set is shown in Fig. 2 below.

The judgment matrix is constructed. According to the principle of the analytic hierarchy process, the analytic hierarchy process model is used to judge and contrast the importance of two pairs to form a matrix. The scale of 1–9 is used to identify the expert's judgment ability.

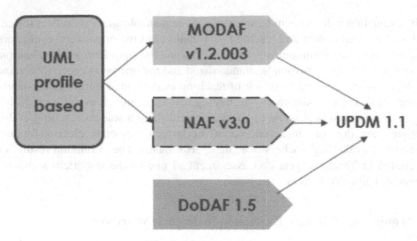

Fig. 2. Manage framesets

Set a_{ij} refers to the The relative importance of u_j indicators, then the judgment matrix A is:

$$A = \begin{pmatrix} a_{11} & \cdots & a_{1n} \\ \vdots & \ddots & \vdots \\ a_{n1} & \cdots & a_{nn} \end{pmatrix} \tag{4}$$

where, $a_{ij} = 1 (i = j), a_{ij} = 1/a_{ji}$.

$$\mathbf{w}_i^- = \sum_{j=1}^n \bar{a}_{ij}(i = 1, 2, \cdots, n) \tag{5}$$

Find the sum of elements in each row of judgment matrix A w_i:

$$w_i = w_i^- / \sum_{j=1}^n w_i^- (i = 1, 2, \cdots, n) \tag{6}$$

The evaluation system of informatization teaching includes six first-level indicators, namely, informatization strategy, informatization environment construction, management and service, informatization application, informatization talents and teaching effect [11]. The judgment matrix is formed by consulting experts on their relative importance (Table 1).

A good teaching evaluation index framework should have different descriptions of indicators for different courses. Of course, the teaching effects or teaching methods corresponding to the indicators are basically the same. In this way, it can provide more comprehensive and specific services for students of different majors and students who choose different courses, and better serve teaching evaluation work, so as to obtain more in-depth and detailed teaching evaluation data, Give full play to the role of students' evaluation of teaching in teaching guidance. The teaching evaluation standard is a specific requirement for evaluating the actual degree of teaching reaching the indicators[12]. There are different levels of achievement. In the student evaluation index system, each

Table 1. Comprehensive Evaluation Form of Student Moral Education

subject	weight coefficient	Rating
sanitary	0.12	good
Code of conduct	0.16	excellent
Practice and labor	0.16	excellent

group of indicators must clearly specify the standards of evaluation and quantify the data of evaluation.

Knowledge acquisition, knowledge representation and knowledge processing are the three pillars of constructing human and industrial intelligence systems. It is generally believed that knowledge is at the center, and knowledge representation is not only the basis of knowledge acquisition, but also the premise of knowledge application. As a part of the application of AI technology, knowledge representation is very important in ICAI. Teaching is the process of knowledge dissemination, and the knowledge of teaching field is the core of all kinds of knowledge in teaching activities. When establishing an ICAI system, it is necessary to provide standardized, adaptive, open and operable service facilities for knowledge input, organization and maintenance of all disciplines based on educational theory and in close cooperation with educational experts, so as to achieve reasonable classification, effective access and management of knowledge[13]. A good knowledge representation method can not only organize domain knowledge reasonably and effectively, provide information for the system, but also help students establish clear conceptual relationships, which is what learners should focus on.

3   Improved Fuzzy Mathematics Comprehensive Evaluation Algorithm

The comprehensive evaluation algorithm in this paper is based on the fuzzy comprehensive evaluation algorithm, which corrects the score of the evaluated person, and tries to make the score of the evaluated person more fair and objective. The algorithm is divided into three steps: the evaluator's credibility calculation, the improved fuzzy comprehensive evaluation method, and the score correction [14].

Generally, the score of each evaluation factor of the evaluated person is the sum of the scores of all evaluators and then averaged. This method is simple and intuitive, and can reflect the actual situation of the evaluated person well when there are a large number of evaluators. The disadvantage of this method is that it can't effectively remove abnormal data, that is, it can't objectively evaluate the data of the evaluated. For example, in the satisfaction survey, "satisfied" is selected for all evaluation factors or a certain score is randomly selected, which is considered as "abnormal data". Especially when the number of evaluators is small, the abnormal data has a significant impact on the scores of the evaluated, resulting in the deviation of the results [15]. The evaluation of teachers by "abnormal data" is not objective enough, that is, "credibility" is low.

In order to overcome the credibility problem of evaluators and better exclude the impact of non objective evaluation on the score, this algorithm calculates the "credibility" of each evaluator based on cosine similarity as a parameter for statistics of the score of the evaluated [16]. Cosine similarity uses the angle between two vectors in vector space to measure the similarity between vectors. Unlike distance measurement, cosine similarity pays more attention to the difference in direction. Assuming that a and B are vectors in the same problem space, their similarity is calculated as follows:

$$similarity = \cos(\theta) = \frac{A \cdot B}{\|A\| \|B\|} \tag{7}$$

The fuzzy comprehensive evaluation algorithm is a comprehensive evaluation method based on fuzzy mathematics. This method transforms qualitative evaluation into quantitative evaluation based on the membership theory of fuzzy mathematics, that is, converts the evaluation set with multiple evaluation factors into comprehensive evaluation. The results are clear, suitable for dealing with difficult to quantify and fuzzy problems, and have good effects on uncertain problems, which are widely used in industrial and agricultural production. After many years of research and development, fuzzy comprehensive evaluation algorithm has achieved remarkable results, such as operator adjustment and category overview.

The fuzzy evaluation algorithm is based on the principle of fuzzy transformation and the theory of membership degree, and comprehensively evaluates the relevant evaluation factors of the evaluated person [17]. Fuzzy comprehensive evaluation algorithm can be divided into single-level fuzzy comprehensive evaluation and multi-level fuzzy comprehensive evaluation.

4   Application of Improved Fuzzy Mathematics Comprehensive Evaluation Algorithm in Student Evaluation System

4.1   Conception of Student Evaluation System Design

Design objectives of system software. This system takes the campus network as the background, applies the Internet technology, the database technology, and the comprehensive man-machine technology combined with the characteristics of student evaluation and management. This system adopts the B/S/D (Browser/server/database) architecture, advanced Dreamweaver dynamic web page development technology, combines the actual situation of the school, and utilizes the existing achievements in student management, teacher management and teaching management to realize the online evaluation of students on teachers.

Online teaching evaluation overcomes the difficulties of a large number of manual statistical data, and makes all data on the evaluation form automatically generated; Paperless evaluation of teaching, saving a lot of costs of printing evaluation forms; Because of the convenience of data statistics, all students can directly participate in the evaluation of teaching, eliminating the worries of some students when evaluating teaching, thus making the evaluation of teaching more objective and fair; It promotes the scientific and informatization of the school's educational administration and provides strong support for improving the teaching quality [18].

Functions realized by the system. The system is mainly based on the function of teaching evaluation. The main functions include: the function of students logging in and evaluating a certain teacher; University leaders, academic affairs office leaders, college leaders, relevant system administrators and teachers can view the evaluation results and maintain the database function; Teachers can and can only modify their login passwords.

The data of students' evaluation of teaching (course information, teacher information, password account, etc.) are directly obtained from the student course selection system of the self-learning scoring system, and students must evaluate all the courses they have learned in the current semester at least once, otherwise, they will lose the qualification of course selection in the next semester [19]. This not only ensures the accuracy of course selection data and the simplicity of operation, but also ensures the participation rate of students in teaching evaluation.

The system adopts the humanized design concept. The intermediate data of students' evaluation of teaching (data before the end of the semester) can only be consulted by teachers and individual leaders, and only the statistical results can be consulted, and the personal information of students can not be seen. In this way, it not only reflects the respect for teachers, leaves enough time and psychological space for teachers to improve teaching, but also ensures the objectivity of students' evaluation of teaching, as shown in Fig. 3.

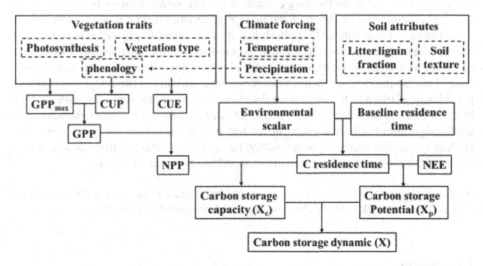

Fig. 3. Structure of student evaluation system

4.2 Determination of Evaluation Index Weight

Generally, arithmetic mean is used as the method to determine the weight of evaluation indicators. In this method, multiple experts give the weight of each evaluation element in the large element set, and then take the arithmetic mean of the ownership value of one factor. However, due to the preference of management experts for the rights of various elements, Cheng mengke The calculation results of this method are largely affected by personal subjective factors, and the influence of extreme weight values on the determination of weight values cannot be avoided.

In view of the shortcomings of the arithmetic mean method, this paper proposes the following methods to determine the weight of evaluation factors on the basis of practice[20]. The steps are as follows:

Remove the maximum and minimum weights;

The remaining weights are divided into the same K intervals, where k = 5;

Find the interval with the most weight; The average value of the ownership value in the interval is obtained, and the ownership value is normalized.

5 Conclusion

By designing an improved fuzzy mathematics comprehensive evaluation algorithm, combining with the actual situation of the school where the author works, using computer program design, using PHP built-in functions and other means to achieve function optimization, modifying the reviewer's score based on cosine similarity and fuzzy comprehensive evaluation, and referring to the historical data of the reviewers, the score is more objective and fair. The improved fuzzy mathematics comprehensive evaluation algorithm is applied in the teaching evaluation system, which is different from the traditional evaluation system. Based on the fuzzy mathematics theory, it is a comprehensive evaluation algorithm with wide applicability. It uses a scientific algorithm to statistically analyze the evaluation data, which can make a more scientific and reasonable evaluation of things with multiple attributes and comprehensive attributes or factors, and can well control human interference factors to improve the credibility of the evaluation results, It provides objective and fair evaluation data for the work of teacher evaluation, and has higher reference significance. The improved fuzzy mathematics comprehensive evaluation algorithm has been used in the student evaluation system for many years. The student evaluation system operates stably, has excellent safety performance and high reliability. It provides decision-making support data for school leaders.

Acknowledgements. Project supported by the Natural Science Foundation of Gansu Province, China (Grant NO. 21JR1RM330), N-complexes and Gorenstein Homology theory.

References

1. Liu, J., Cai, J., Dawei, H.U., et al.: Application of fuzzy mathematics comprehensive evaluation method in registration supervision for the export-food manufactures. J. Inspect. Quarant. (2017)
2. Yang, Z., Liu, Y., Zhao, G.D., et al.: Application of comprehensive evaluation model based on the fuzzy mathematics method in certain decommissioned uranium tailing pond's environmental quality evaluation. J. Univ. South China (Sci. Technol.) (2016)
3. Zheng, L., Ouyang, W.: A model of teacher evaluation system based improved fuzzy clustering algorithm. Rev. Facult. Ingenieria **32**(7), 461–466 (2017)

4. Ji, S, Tsai, S.B.: A study on the quality evaluation of English teaching based on the fuzzy comprehensive evaluation of bat algorithm and big data analysis. Math. Prob. Eng. (2021)
5. Dou, Y, Fei, X., Zhu, R., et al.: Application of improved eclat algorithm in students' evaluation of teaching (2018)
6. Mao, L.: Analysis of entrepreneurship education in colleges and based on improved decision tree algorithm and fuzzy mathematics. J. Intell. Fuzzy Syst.: Appl. Eng. Technol. **40**(2) (2021)
7. Meng, Z.Y., Liu, T., Xia, M.X., et al.: Application of fuzzy mathematics in the evaluation of the effectiveness of HACCP certification. J. Food Safety Qual. (2016)
8. Li, X., Zhang, Y.: Application of fuzzy comprehensive evaluation algorithm in doctor evaluation system. Electric Eng. (2019)
9. Zhan, .X, Zhang, R., Niu, X., et al.: Comprehensive evaluations of a prototype full field-of-view photon counting CT system through phantom studies. arXiv eprints (2022)
10. Liu, D.: Fuzzy comprehensive evaluation method of ecological environment damage compensation system and management based on improved association rule algorithm. Mob. Inf. Syst. (2021)
11. Wang, Z., Lima, S., Rocha, Á.: Fuzzy comprehensive evaluation of physical education based on high dimensional data mining. J. Intell. Fuzzy Syst. **35**(3), 1–12 (2018)
12. Gao, T.: Application of improved random forest algorithm and fuzzy mathematics in physical fitness of athletes. J. Intell. Fuzzy Syst. Appl. Eng. Technol. **40**(2) (2021)
13. Wang, L.: Research on human resource performance and decision-making evaluation based on fuzzy mathematics and clustering model. J. Intell. Fuzzy Syst. 1–14 (2019)
14. Wu, D.: The application of fuzzy mathematics in the post practice performance evaluation. J. Jilin Inst. Chem. Technol. (2016)
15. Zhang, B.X., Liang, X.L., Xue, L.: The application study of F comprehensive evaluation method in the teaching evaluation system of application-oriented undergraduate education. Sci. Technol. Vision (2019)
16. Shi, D., Bao, B.Z.: Potential evaluation of ecotourism development in Chongming Island based on AHP-fuzzy mathematics methods. J. Guilin Univ. Technol. (2019)
17. Zhang, H.D., Shi, X.S.: An improved fuzzy comprehensive evaluation model in the product assessment. J. Huaiyin Inst. Technol. (2016)
18. Jiao, J., Ren, H., Sun, S.: Assessment of surface ship environment adaptability in seaways: a fuzzy comprehensive evaluation method. Int. J. Naval Architect. Ocean Eng. **8**(4), 344–359 (2016)
19. Deng, M., Zhang, YJ., Li, Y.-Y., et al.: Fuzzy mathematics-based comprehensive evaluation of atmospheric environmental quality in take ecological protection zones. J. Southwest China Norm. Univ. (Nat. Sci. Edn.) (2017)
20. Kong, H., Fan, H., Yan, Z., et al.: Design of teaching quality evaluation model based on fuzzy mathematics and SVM algorithm. J. Intell. Fuzzy Syst. **35**, 1–9 (2018)

Implementation of Early Warning Algorithm for the Achievements of Foreign Students in Colleges and Universities Based on Grey Theory Model

Yanyu Chen[✉] and Shan Wang

International School, Jinan University, Guangzhou 510632, Guangdong, China
cyy1201@jnu.edu.cn

Abstract. With the increase in the number of college graduates employed, employment data and course performance data are also increasing exponentially. Under certain circumstances, there are certain rules between these data, which have certain guiding significance for the study, graduation and employment of school students and future students. Academic early warning is an important means to strengthen school academic management, improve students' ability of self-management and self-discipline, and form a joint management mode between schools and parents. The grey prediction model shows strong adaptability in the information mining of the laws contained in complex systems. In order to further enhance the prediction performance of the model, this paper focuses on the improvement of modeling ideas and methods, and the construction method of grey system prediction model. The results show that among the calculation students, those who have put forward early warning account for 60.33% of the students who cannot graduate normally. By collecting a variety of behavior data generated by college students in campus activities, including consumption data, access control data, Internet data, etc., a student behavior data set is constructed. It proves that the proposed method can effectively improve the accuracy of College Students' performance early warning.

Keywords: Grey theory model · College students · Achievement early warning algorithm

1 Introduction

The position and role of colleges and universities in practicing the important thought of scientific development concept is very important and special [1]. It is the historical mission of colleges and universities to implement the scientific concept of development, contribute to the development of advanced productive forces, advanced culture and the realization of the fundamental interests of the overwhelming majority of the people. Building a good style of study is the prerequisite for colleges and universities to implement the important thought of the scientific concept of development, the inevitable

Y. Zhang and N. Shah (Eds.): BigIoT-EDU 2023, LNICST 584, pp. 422–432, 2024.
https://doi.org/10.1007/978-3-031-63142-9_43

requirement for building a harmonious university campus, and one of the effective means and ways to prevent the group crisis of college students [2]. Academic early warning mechanism is a kind of teaching management mode gradually explored and established in colleges and universities in recent years. By early warning and intervention of possible or existing learning problems in the course of students' study at school, specific academic guidance can be provided in time to help students return to normal academic track [3]. The development of information technology has brought brand-new ideas and convenient methods to higher education management. Constructing an information-based academic early warning mechanism will help improve the efficiency and level of teaching management [4]. With the increase of the number of international students, it is more difficult to manage international students. At the same time, international students' safety accidents happen from time to time, which not only threaten the individual international students, but also may endanger the national security. Therefore, the safety of international students has become a key issue. At present, most colleges and universities in China have no safety warning measures for international students [5]. Therefore, an early warning system for international students' safety is developed and designed [6].

The current situation of the style of study in Colleges and universities is not optimistic. The main problems are: lack of learning motivation, lack of a good learning atmosphere, lack of effective evaluation and incentive mechanism [7]. To analyze, predict and evaluate the style of study in Colleges and universities, both qualitative and quantitative issues should be correctly handled in terms of evaluation criteria and evaluation methods [8]. Theoretically, many behaviors of students, such as ideology, morality, cultivation and other fuzzy factors, should not be analyzed completely quantitatively. Based on this consideration, it is necessary to introduce fuzzy mathematics and grey system theory [9]. Grey system theory is a theory that studies and solves the analysis, modeling, prediction, decision-making and control of grey system. Grey prediction is quantitative with grey model. It requires little modeling information, convenient operation and high modeling accuracy. At the same time, macroeconomic prediction is a typical nonlinear problem, because macroeconomic operation is affected by many factors, such as policy changes, economic development level, etc., so these factors must be considered in the process of prediction [10].

2 Methods

2.1 Grey Prediction Model

Grey prediction model is the core content and classic part of grey system theory. Since the birth of the grey system theory, the grey prediction theory has aroused great interest of scholars and experts. Grey prediction model can achieve better accuracy in the case of modeling with little data and poor information, and it overcomes the shortcoming of traditional statistical methods that modeling needs a large sample database. Grey system theory is a theory that studies and deals with complex systems from the incompleteness of information. It doesn't study systems from the special laws inside the system, but through mathematical processing of the observation data at a certain level of the system, it can achieve a higher level of understanding of the internal changing trends and interrelations of the system [11]. Its mathematical method is a non-statistical method, and it is more practical when the system data is less and the conditions do not meet the statistical requirements. There are many combination methods of grey neural network prediction, such as the combination grey artificial neural network model for seasonal prediction. This method mainly considers the dual trends of seasonal time series with growth and volatility, and combines the complex seasonal prediction problems of the two trends with the combination model to improve the prediction accuracy. In addition, there is a method of forecasting with grey model first, and then correcting the prediction residual error with neural network model [12].

2.2 Basic Process of Grey Prediction Model

The basic process of the grey prediction model is as follows: the grey prediction model generates the exponential law contained in the grey system through the accumulation of the original sequence, and establishes a discrete grey prediction model with parameters through the discrete approximation of the first-order differential equation; The parameters are estimated by the least square method; Then, the newly generated prediction sequence is reduced to obtain the approximate sequence of the original sequence; Finally, the prediction sequence can be obtained by testing the accuracy of the results and extending the fitting formula that meets the accuracy requirements.

The dominance measure sequences under different classification standards may be consistent or partially similar. Visualization of dominance measures provides a method to visually compare different sequences, but it can also be combined with the grey theory to analyze the grey absolute correlation between the feature sequences of dominance measures, and quantitatively measure the similarity between the sequences from the perspective of geometric proximity. The adopted method is that a series of predicted values of the original series can be obtained after GM models are established for a plurality of economic index series respectively, and there must be some deviation between these predicted values and the original values, and there is also a certain correlation among these macroeconomic indexes. Therefore, the deviation relationship between these predicted values and the actual values and the relationship between the series can be integrated into the neural network model for consideration, and the predicted values can be used as the input samples of the neural network. The actual values are taken as output samples, and then the weights and thresholds of the corresponding nodes can be obtained by training the network. The next or more predicted values of GM models are input into the neural network, and the output obtained is the final predicted value. As shown in Table 1:

The method of forecasting the main macroeconomic indicators by using the neural network is mainly based on the situation of multiple correlation series forecasting, considering both the relationship between data columns and the relationship between data columns. It can improve the forecasting accuracy while avoiding the accuracy test of GM and model, and provides a new method for multi-series forecasting. In the face of complex systems and a large number of seemingly irregular and messy data, it is difficult for traditional data processing methods to discover the rules, let alone realize the prediction of the system. However, based on a certain range of data, for a specific time series, when the structure, level and relationship of the information contained in the system show fuzzy features in the dynamic process, we express this feature as the gray of the system, that is to say, the data in the system can't fully express the state of

Table 1. Predicted value of Grey Theory

Index	Actual value	GM Estimate	GM Relative error	Combined forecast value	Combined prediction error
Total output value	1569874	1756892	2.7%	1526988	1.3%
Total sales	265874	366247	3.6%	746358	1.5%
Property investment	11886654	116085	7.6%	116069	2.4%
Local budget	56016	658947	3.2%	83126	3.2%
Disposable	2509	3069	6.3%	8089	3.9%
Average net income	5693	3568	5.0%	5350	2.1%

the system. Therefore, the system with this state is also called a grey system, and we can build a grey model for these data, so as to achieve the prediction effect. The model is the systematic and structured establishment of key information in a system, in which the extraction of key information in the system is the extraction of corresponding factors in the model, which can be called variables. The construction of the model is also based on the basic variables in the system and their mathematical relationships. Grey theoretical model is based on the extraction of key information of systems in many fields and the study of the mathematical relationship between variables. By using this relatively stable mathematical relationship, it can realize the reflection of the changing trend of system state by some data through various transformation operations. This model is called grey model.

Grey prediction is based on grey model. In order to better understand the basic principle of grey theoretical model prediction, we first introduce the GM grey theoretical model, which is the most widely used and the most theoretical basis. As a prediction model with the highest frequency in the application of grey model, GM model is widely used in mining, agriculture, finance and other fields because of its accurate prediction accuracy, and the expression of GM formula is also similar to grey model. The data expression of GM model is a first-order differential equation, which includes a variable factor. The grey model searches for the hidden rules between the existing sample data sequence data, so as to construct the corresponding grey prediction model. Then, the predicted data values are directly applied to the data prediction of the constructed grey model, so as to obtain the prediction results of the grey model and test the effect. The prediction principle and derivation process of the grey model are as follows:

The mathematics that defines GM model is a first-order differential equation, and its expression is:

$$\frac{dx}{dt} + ax = u \tag{1}$$

There are two unknown parameters in formula (1), which are a and u respectively. a is the development coefficient in the model expression, u is the gray input in the model expression, and x represents the data sequence in the system.

$$x(k) = \sum_{i-1}^{k} x(i), k = 1, 2, n \tag{2}$$

Next, we need to further generate the mean sequence for the generated sequence. The specific method is: average the adjacent elements in the generated sequence x to get the mean sequence $M(k)$ in turn. The purpose of this is to observe the dynamic characteristics of the sequence. The formula for generating the mean sequence is as follows:

$$M(k) = \frac{1}{2}x(k) + x(k-1) \tag{3}$$

$$M(k) = \frac{(k+1)}{(k+1)} - k = x \tag{4}$$

When the grey model performs prediction processing, the first thing we get is the original initialization data sequence x. We make an accumulative change to this sequence. If the conditions are met, that is, an accumulative change is generated to get a new sequence; Can be converted through one-time accumulation generation.

The advantage of grey prediction model is that it needs fewer samples, its model structure is simple, and its application range is wide. However, its main disadvantage is that the accuracy of prediction results is generally not accurate enough compared with other prediction algorithms, and there is a big error. Moreover, the prediction result is greatly influenced by the input data of the sample. If the input sample data has a high degree of dispersion, the error of the prediction result data generated by the sample will be correspondingly increased, so the stability of the convergence of the prediction result of the grey prediction model is poor. As shown in Fig. 1:

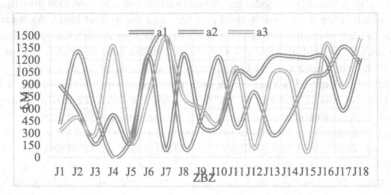

Fig. 1. Data stability prediction

The advantage of the grey model is that it can make a good overall judgment on the changing trend of sample data, but it can't have the constant adjustment learning process like the neural network, and its limited academic ability leads to its inability to reflect the fluctuation of the overall data performance. When the original input data type is of high index, the grey prediction model will not get satisfactory training results, so the model is deficient in adapting to various system scenarios.

In addition, the performance and efficiency of the network are also closely related to the size of the data sequence group. When building BP neural network, it is necessary to statistically analyze each group of training sample data, so as to adjust the weight and threshold. Therefore, when the training sample is large, the modeling time of the direct consequence is long, so the training efficiency is low, and finally the prediction result takes too long.

3 Predict the Achievement Trend of International Students in Colleges and Universities

With the increasing popularity of college students, college students are no longer the place to cultivate elite talents, but have become the cultural level that people should naturally achieve in their ideas, which we usually call popular education. This kind of education mode makes colleges and universities constantly expand their enrollment and recruit more and more college students, which not only leads to the change of education mode, training mode and management mode, but also poses new challenges to college students' own concepts such as career development direction, comprehensive quality and employment.

Students hope that they can successfully complete their college studies, and whether they can successfully graduate, the academic performance often plays a decisive role. However, most teaching managers do not understand the method of predicting the future trend of students' course scores. This paper studies the related technology of early warning of College Students' grades, mines college students' course scores, finds out the correlation between disciplines, analyzes the mining results in combination with actual data, modifies the related technology, and finally finds a mining algorithm with good performance to help college students predict the future trend of subject scores. Analyze the prediction results, formulate scientific methods, and provide support for teaching managers to improve teaching methods. The expansion of data mining algorithms is divided into: rough set, fuzzy set, clustering analysis, neural network, genetic algorithm, etc. these algorithms promote the development of student achievement early warning technology. In the idea of these algorithms, researchers continue to put forward new improved methods to improve the algorithm. The execution efficiency of the improved algorithm has been improved, and the space expenditure of the algorithm has also been reduced, With the help of the new algorithm, the function range of student achievement early warning technology is gradually expanded, and the accuracy of early warning results has also been improved. As shown in Fig. 2:

Learning atmosphere is the spiritual outlook that students show in the process of studying and living in school. It is the behavior trend that students gradually form after long-term education and influence on campus. The evaluation of academic atmosphere in Colleges and universities is a process of value judgment, evaluation of its value advantages and disadvantages, and improvement. To establish a scientific evaluation

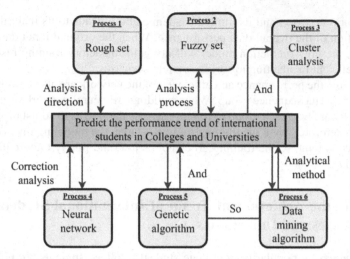

Fig. 2. The performance trend of international students in colleges and universities.

index system of academic atmosphere in Colleges and universities, we must follow certain principles. The historical achievements of students' learning in school are not only the basis for the construction of students' curriculum relationship network in this paper, but also one of the important features of prediction later. The historical achievements of students' learning in school are not only the basis for the construction of students' curriculum relationship network in this paper, but also one of the important features of prediction later.

4   Machine Learning Model

In the field of machine learning, there are a lot of unbalanced data, and general machine learning models train models with overall accuracy, and treat different types of samples equally. For unbalanced data, some machine learning models seem to have high accuracy, but they don't actually solve the classification problem, because when the classification models classify unbalanced data, the results often show that the classification accuracy of most classes is high, while that of a few classes is low. The overall high accuracy is all contributed by the accuracy of most classes, so it is necessary to process the unbalanced data before the experiment to make the data more balanced. There are two ways to solve the problem of unbalanced data: one is to process the data. To solve, the other is to use algorithms to solve. Now, the first method is used to solve the problem of unbalanced data, which is mainly to increase or decrease the samples by some algorithm, so that unbalanced data can be converted into relatively balanced data. Feature selection is a very important part of data preprocessing. Generally, feature selection is used for two purposes: one is to reduce the dimension of features, which can improve the training speed of models; The other is to remove irrelevant or redundant features and get the optimal feature subset to improve the performance of the trained model. As shown in Fig. 3:

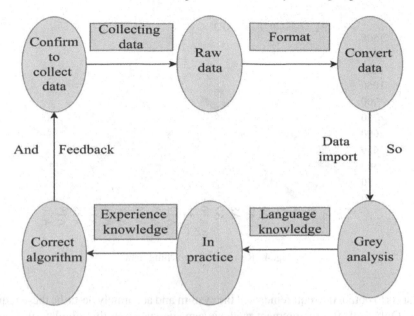

Fig. 3. Machine learning model process

After training a machine learning model, it is necessary to evaluate the performance of the model to verify whether the model can be used for the problem under study. Different learning tasks use different evaluation indicators. This paper studies the classification of students' achievement prediction, and the evaluation indexes used include accuracy, precision and recall. In the same place and different time periods, the functions are not exactly the same, and the action size, action time and action range of the factors add a strong gray to the system.

4.1 Experimental Analysis

4.1.1 Experimental Process and Result Analysis

Based on the existing historical grades design database, we use machine learning technology to mine the correlation between course data, predict the future probability of failing course grades, and give an early warning in time before the failure event, so that the early warning is accurate to a certain course of a student, so that the early warning of grades is more targeted, and also for managers to help and intervene the early-warning students It provides a basis for students to formulate a more scientific and reasonable learning plan, and has strong application value. As shown in Fig. 4:

4.1.2 For the Development of Any System, Requirement Analysis is the First Step and a Very Important Link

Through the demand analysis, we can determine what functions the system needs to achieve and what work to complete. Only by determining the system construction objectives, can we better complete the system design work. The main work of requirement

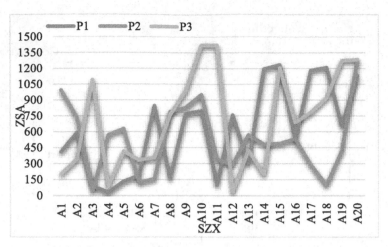

Fig. 4. Results early warning data

analysis is to obtain the requirements of the system and accurately describe these require-ments. Only with the requirement analysis can we successfully complete the system design and development.

The most important function of the achievement early warning system is to help the school improve the level of education and teaching and help students finish their studies smoothly. The system not only serves the students, but also the counselors who manage them. For students, the performance early warning system can give an early warning of the students' final exam results when there is a period of time before the end of the term, so as to remind the warned students to study hard in the next few weeks and get excellent results in the final exam. For counselors, the achievement early warning system can help them know the students' learning situation in time, intervene in time, and help them learn better. The achievement early warning module is a module for early warning students. For different roles, the functional requirements of the performance early warning module are also different. As shown in Fig. 5:

The security of the system is very important. Part of teachers' information and most of students' data are stored in the achievement early warning system. Most of these data involve personal privacy, so it is necessary to ensure the security of the data when saving it. The reliability of the score early warning system requires that the system can run for a long time without any problems, and some functions of the system can be fused in case of errors, so as to ensure the normal operation of other functions. Query the number of students who can't actually graduate normally, analyze these students, and calculate that they belong to those who have given early warning. These students who have given early warning account for 60.33% of the number of students who can't graduate normally. If the proportion reaches the minimum confidence requirement, it can be judged that the early warning result of students' achievement is accurate, and early warning has certain practical significance. Analyze which courses of these students who can't graduate normally don't get corresponding credits, analyze the main courses that affect students' normal graduation, compare these courses with the related courses

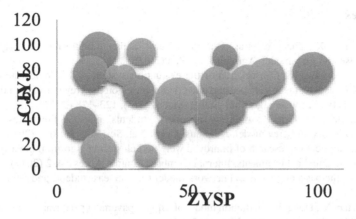

Fig. 5. Performance warning module

obtained by mining algorithm, and verify the guiding significance of the related algorithm for students' early warning.

5 Conclusion

With the continuous progress of science and technology, computer technology has made rapid development and achievements, especially the development of artificial intelligence and data mining technology, which plays a more and more important role in the processing of large amounts of data. The emergence of a variety of intelligent algorithms brings new hope for the modeling and prediction of complex systems. Through continuous research, intelligent algorithms can reasonably use these data, so they have great advantages in dealing with large-scale data. Grey theory model and neural network model have their own advantages and disadvantages and applicable scenarios, in order to better construct the optimal prediction model. An early warning model of grades is established in order to give early warning of students' grades in the semester and truly achieve the effect of early warning. Finally, the grade early warning system is designed and implemented according to the constructed grade classification prediction model. In this system, the administrator needs to upload the student's characteristic information. After uploading the student's characteristic information, the system will automatically predict the student's final grade according to the grade prediction model saved in the background. Through this system, counselors can view students' early warning information and historical grades. When students are warned, counselors can send emails to students through this system to remind students. Through this system, students can view their early warning situation and historical score information, and can also modify their personal information. From the analysis of employment dimensions and course categories to the analysis of course categories and course categories, and then to the analysis of courses and courses, it can not only provide certain reference suggestions for students' learning, graduation and employment, but also have certain reference significance for the setting of courses and the arrangement of course sequence.

References

1. Shen, Y., Dai, X., Zhan, Y., et al.: Design of water quality monitoring and early warning system based on grey model. Agricult. Eng. 8, 4 (2019)
2. Liu, Z., Xu, J., Jia, X.: Construction of the evaluation system of ideological and political education of new media in colleges and universities-based on the grey correlation theory and BP neural network model algorithm. Statist. Manag. 7(5), 123–128 (2019)
3. Zhao, G., Hao, S., Tian, Z.: Analysis of college students' physical fitness test based on correlation theory and grey model. J. Jiamusi Univ.: Nat. Sci. Edn. 36(5), 4 (2018)
4. Chen, H.: Application research of improved weighted clustering algorithm in early warning of college students' achievements. Internal Combust. Engine Access. 4, 2 (2017)
5. Wei, Y.: On the basis of grey neural network model for overseas students and returnees. (69), 4–6 (2021)
6. Wu, D., Tian, X., Dong, F.: Prediction model of asphalt pavement performance based on grey theory. China-Foreign Highway 37(5), 4 (2017)
7. Cosine, Z.Y.: Research on college students' achievement early warning based on random forest algorithm under the background of big data. Jiangsu Sci. Technol. Inf. 37(20), 4 (2020)
8. Li, Z., Hao, Z.: Simulation analysis of book recommendation model based on grey theory. Comput. Simulat. 34(3), 4 (2017)
9. Wang, M., Wang, Z., Gao, Y., et al.: Analysis of settlement deformation of mountain high-speed railway subgrade based on improved grey theory model. Railw. Stand. Des. 61(12), 5 (2017)
10. Wang, C., Gong, W., Fang, Z., et al.: Grey prediction model based on system impact and its application research. Oper. Res. Manag. 26(3), 172–177 (2017)
11. Zhang, X., Fan, D.: Optimization model of pile arrangement scheme of foundation pit based on grey fuzzy theory. Bullet. Sci. Technol. 45(85), 6 (2020)
12. Shen, Z., Wang, N., Zhou, X., et al.: Research on power planning based on grey model theory. 65(87), 2 (2021)

Author Index

Printed in the United States
by Baker & Taylor Publisher Services